The Rorschach: A Comprehensive System, in two volumes
by John E. Exner, Jr.

Theory and Practice in Behavior Therapy
by Aubrey J. Yates

Principles of Psychotherapy
by Irving B. Weiner

Psychoactive Drugs and Social Judgment: Theory and Research
edited by Kenneth Hammond and C. R. B. Joyce

Clinical Methods in Psychology
edited by Irving B. Weiner

Human Resources for Troubled Children
by Werner I. Halpern and Stanley Kissel

Hyperactivity
by Dorothea M. Ross and Sheila A. Ross

Heroin Addiction: Theory, Research and Treatment
by Jerome J. Platt and Christina Labate

Children's Rights and the Mental Health Profession
edited by Gerald P. Koocher

The Role of the Father in Child Development
edited by Michael E. Lamb

Handbook of Behavioral Assessment
edited by Anthony R. Ciminero, Karen S. Calhoun, and Henry E. Adams

Counseling and Psychotherapy: A Behavioral Approach
by E. Lakin Phillips

Dimensions of Personality
edited by Harvey London and John E. Exner, Jr.

The Mental Health Industry: A Cultural Phenomenon
by Peter A. Magaro, Robert Gripp, David McDowell, and Ivan W. Miller III

Nonverbal Communication: The State of the Art
by Robert G. Harper, Arthur N. Wiens, and Joseph D. Matarazzo

Alcoholism and Treatment
by David J. Armor, J. Michael Polich, and Harriet B. Stambul

A Biodevelopmental Approach to Clinical Child Psychology: Cognitive Controls and
Cognitive Control Theory
by Sebastiano Santostefano

Handbook of Infant Development
edited by Joy D. Osofsky

Understanding the Rape Victim: A Synthesis of Research Findings
by Sedelle Katz and Mary Ann Mazur

Childhood Pathology and Later Adjustment: The Question of Prediction
by Loretta K. Cass and Carolyn B. Thomas

Intelligent Testing with the WISC-R
by Alan S. Kaufman

Adaptation in Schizophrenia: The Theory of Segmental Set
by David Shakow

Psychotherapy: An Eclectic Approach
by Sol L. Garfield

Handbook of Minimal Brain Dysfunctions
edited by Herbert E. Rie and Ellen D. Rie

Handbook of Behavioral Interventions: A Clir
edited by Alan Goldstein and Edna B. Foa

Art Psychotherapy
by Harriet Wadeson

Handbook of Adolescent Psychology
edited by Joseph Adelson

Psychotherapy Supervision: Theory, Research and Practice
edited by Allen K. Hess

Continued on back

WOMEN IN
THE MIDDLE YEARS

WOMEN IN THE MIDDLE YEARS

Current Knowledge and Directions for Research and Policy

Sponsored by the Social Science Research Council

Edited by

JANET ZOLLINGER GIELE

Brandeis University

175 YEARS OF PUBLISHING

1807 1982

A WILEY-INTERSCIENCE PUBLICATION

JOHN WILEY & SONS

New York · Chichester · Brisbane · Toronto · Singapore

This publication is designed to provide accurate and
authoritative information in regard to the subject
matter covered. It is sold with the understanding that
the publisher is not engaged in rendering legal, accounting,
or other professional service. If legal advice or other
expert assistance is required, the services of a competent
professional person should be sought. *From a Declaration
of Principles jointly adapted by a Committee of the
American Bar Association and a Committee of Publishers.*

Library of Congress Cataloging in Publication Data:
Main entry under title:

Women in the middle years.

(Wiley series on personality processes,
ISSN 0195-4008 ; 1341)
"A Wiley-Interscience publication."
Includes index.
1. Middle aged women—Addresses, essays,
lectures, I. Giele, Janet Zollinger. II. Series.
HQ1154.W8837   305.2'44   82-1885
ISBN 0-471-09611-3   AACR2

Printed in the United States of America

10 9 8 7 6 5 4 3 2 1

Series Preface

This series of books is addressed to behavioral scientists interested in the nature of human personality. Its scope should prove pertinent to personality theorists and researchers as well as to clinicians concerned with applying an understanding of personality processes to the amelioration of emotional difficulties in living. To this end, the series provides a scholarly integration of theoretical formulations, empirical data, and practical recommendations.

Six major aspects of studying and learning about human personality can be designated: personality theory, personality structure and dynamics, personality development, personality assessment, personality change, and personality adjustment. In exploring these aspects of personality, the books in the series discuss a number of distinct but related subject areas: the nature and implications of various theories of personality; personality characteristics that account for consistencies and variations in human behavior; the emergence of personality processes in children and adolescents; the use of interviewing and testing procedures to evaluate individual differences in personality; efforts to modify personality styles through psychotherapy, counseling, behavior therapy, and other methods of influence; and patterns of abnormal personality functioning that impair individual competence.

IRVING B. WEINER

University of Denver
Denver, Colorado

Foreword

Since 1972 when the Social Science Research Council established its Committee on Work and Personality in the Middle Years, the study of the life course has changed remarkably. At that time the "middle years" were a largely unexplored phase of the human life-span and had received relatively little attention. Students of human development tended to concentrate on childhood, adolescence, or old age. Contrary to the common view that the middle years were a stable period of life, the new committee set out to discover the major life challenges and important personality changes of adulthood.

As Ronald P. Abeles and I wrote in 1975, new social patterns and policy issues were emerging that made the committee's research and development efforts especially pertinent to the 1970s.[1] Increasing numbers of people were retiring early, changing to second careers, or obtaining education in midlife. More women were entering or reentering the labor market during their middle years. There was a new mix of education, work, and leisure throughout the life span.

The committee recognized that in the development of its work it must draw on many areas of social science and deal with fundamental questions about work productivity and career trajectories: the use of human resources, personality change through the life-span, and changes in age norms and role expectations. The committee meetings were organized around specific themes, and over the course of several years they examined the epidemiology of stress, theories and facts about the "midlife crisis," the concept of social time, the age norms for behavior in middle age, and such concepts as being "on time" and "off time."

To one of those committee meetings on the interaction between work and personality, Dr. Janet Z. Giele brought several critical questions. After hearing reports on personality change in six developing countries, on the middle years in modern Japan, and on the evolution of male and female personalities during the ages 30 to 50, she asked why the experience of women was so frequently underrepresented in studies of work and adult-

[1]*Items*, Vol. 29, No. 3, New York: Social Science Research Council.

hood. She also asked why work was given so much more emphasis than leisure or family life. To some extent these biases reflected the social structure of the past rather than the future. They focused attention on the dual sex-typed occupational and family structures of industrial society rather than on the new work and family patterns now being devised by men and women. Current research also focused mainly on such psychological characteristics as sense of personal efficacy and cognition to the neglect of affective and affiliative concerns and the family and social responsibilities that traditionally have absorbed a great deal of women's energies.

Subsequently, Dr. Giele joined the committee as a continuing member. As one of her principal activities, she proposed to organize a year-long seminar series to study the relationships among work, personality, and the quality of life as experienced by adult women in their middle years. In establishing this special study group, the committee noted that, although a fair amount of work had been done on the origins of life satisfaction for men, the results of these studies were not always applicable to women. For example, psychological stages leading from concern with achievement to generativity did not fit women particularly well. The concept of career trajectory was virtually meaningless to the housewife who reentered the work force in midlife or the woman professional who had no steady job because of family moves. What was needed was, first, a search for the central events in women's adult lives, then an examination of variations that depend on individual differences, and then on women's social and cultural circumstances.

Establishment of the seminar brought together persons with a major research interest in one of three aspects of adulthood. The first was research on careers, work, and achievement. The second was family responsibility and friendship—the more affective side of life. The third was the biographical or clinical description and understanding of adult personality, including the biomedical aspects of aging. Funds from the National Institute of Mental Health and the National Institute on Aging supported various study group activities.

This fine volume of essays stimulated by the seminar shows what is distinctive in the life events and development of women in their middle years. It also opens a window on the evolving research and theory of life-span development. Through the work of the Study Group on Women, its convener, Dr. Giele, and the contributors to this volume, I believe that the Committee on Work and Personality in the Middle Years has achieved a significant part of the mission with which it was charged. For their accomplishment I wish to express the thanks of the committee and of its parent organization, the Social Science Research Council.

ORVILLE G. BRIM, JR.

Foundation for Child Development
New York City

Preface

Women in their middle years are a contemporary topic. Yet if the truth were known, the roots of this book could probably be found as far back as the 1930s. Two important developments occurred in that period that provided the foundations for contemporary studies of women in adulthood. One was a trend to interdisciplinary cooperation in the academic world that resulted in an effort to understand the links between personality and social structure. The other was the economic and demographic climate that would eventually change the whole shape of women's life course.

Perhaps no contemporary scientific enterprise more neatly joined these two themes than the Social Science Research Council's Committee on Work and Personality in the Middle Years. Established in 1972, the very title of the committee reflected its underlying conceptual schema. By linking work and personality, the committee suggested the reciprocal influences between social roles and psychological makeup and thereby expressed what had become an implicit tenet of contemporary social science. The first meeting of the committee that I attended in February 1975 provided a stunning array of evidence on the interconnections between individual work history and intellectual and emotional functioning. At the same time the committee's title also expressed an interest in complex questions associated with aging. In that same meeting I heard how the life course varied in different cultures, how difficult it was to unravel the temporal order of life events (which came first, the social role or the personality structure?), and how, finally, all these issues came together during a special stage of life called the middle years. Especially intriguing was the likelihood that patterns of life course were themselves changing as the people who experienced them lived through different social and historical conditions.

Here was an ideal intellectual matrix for examining the ferment in women's work and the impact on the middle years of their life course. Yet with only one or two exceptions, all the research reported at the February meeting was about *men*. In his foreword to this book Orville Brim outlines how this gap in the research early became evident and eventually led to the formation of the Study Group on Women under the sponsorship of the SSRC parent committee.

Planning for the study group began in the fall of 1976. I invited three other persons to help me: anthropologist Beatrice B. Whiting, economist Hilda Kahne, and psychologist Grace K. Baruch. This small group, an interdisciplinary team in microcosm, discussed topics, membership, and format. We early agreed on several points. The group shall be kept small and be drawn from the Boston area so that we could meet regularly. It should include representatives from the sciences, social sciences, and humanities. We should try to meet every month in pleasant and relaxed circumstances where we could begin a topic before dinner and continue through the evening. In addition to hearing from our own members, we should invite outside experts to share with us the results of their research. Finally, we should leave some written record of what we learned.

The resulting study group that met during the next year was fortunate in the quality, diversity, and loyalty of its members. Representing the medical and psychiatric dimension were Malkah Notman, M.D. (Beth Israel Hospital and Harvard Medical School), and later Jean Baker Miller, M.D. (Boston University Medical School). Psychologists included Lotte Bailyn (Massachusetts Institute of Technology), Grace K. Baruch (Brandeis University), Rosalind C. Barnett (Brandeis University), Carol Gilligan (Harvard Graduate School of Education), Joseph H. Pleck (Wellesley College), and Samuel D. Osherson (Massachusetts Mental Health Center). There were two socioligists, Kristine Rosenthal and I (Brandeis University); and two economists, Anne Carter (Brandeis University) and Hilda Kahne (Wheaton College). Among those concerned with the historical and cultural dimensions of women's experience the group could count two historians, John Demos (Brandeis University) and Barbara Sicherman (Radcliffe College); an anthropologist, Beatrice B. Whiting (Harvard Graduate School of Education); and an author and literary critic, Carolyn G. Heilbrun (Columbia University and Radcliffe Institute).

Regular monthly meetings of the study group began in January 1977 and continued more than a year, through the early spring of 1978. Not only did members form friendships and engage in scholarly discussion outside their ordinary pattern of professional and academic activity; the meetings also brought distinguished guests from the Boston area and outside the region. Lillian Rubin (Scientific Analysis Corporation, San Francisco) shared with us preliminary results from her survey of middle-aged women in California. Johanna F. Perlmutter, M.D. (Beth Israel Hospital), and Sonja M. McKinlay (Boston University) reviewed physical changes accompanying midlife, especially the menopause. Robert A. LeVine (Harvard Graduate School of Education) provided a cross-cultural reference with descriptions of the midlife period in Kenyan society. Angus Campbell (University of Michigan), George Goethals (Harvard University), and Roger L. Gould, M.D. (Santa Monica, California), discussed the possible alternative methodologies and interpretations available for study of the middle years. Work roles and their relation to personality were the topics of Paul Andrisani (Temple University) and Joanne R. Miller (National Institute of Mental Health). Finally, Nancy F. Cott (Yale University) placed women's work and adulthood in historical perspective by giving examples and drawing contrasts with patterns that existed during the first half of the nineteenth century.

Given the pleasure that these meetings engendered, and the sense that something important was being discussed, it was natural enough for us all to feel that what we discovered should not be lost, but should be recorded and used as a basis for others' future work. Part of the recording function was satisfied by concise and accurate minutes written by our research assistant, Lise Vogel. But another part, concerning the implicit understandings about interconnections among different dimensions of life experience, was not easily captured by a description of what went on in the meetings. Instead, this aspect of our nascent group culture could be made manifest only in future work that our discoveries could shape. Near the end of the year of meetings, we began to discuss what form our generative contribution might take. A book with chapters devoted to the major dimensions of women's midlife experience seemed to be the answer. Work roles and work histories were one obvious topic. Psychological issues were another. Health, sexuality, and the physical aspect of midlife change seemed to be a third. The theme of needed research and practical programs and policies ran throughout. Then there was a surprising dramatic suggestion—that we should invite a chapter on women in another country, preferably one of the socialist nations where all the utopian social policies that American feminists desired had already been instituted.

First so tentatively proposed, that framework tells the story of this book. My introductory chapter sets the intellectual stage. Then four specialized chapters follow—one touching health and the physiological dimension, another focusing on a particular aspect of psychological development, a third on social roles, a fourth on a comparison from another country, the German Democratic Republic. My concluding chapter summarizes and integrates the many suggestions for needed research and policy reforms that surface not only in these chapters but in the wider literature and discussion of women in the middle years. The appendix by Toni Antonucci provides a compendium listing primary source materials for future study.

The whole study group enterprise and this book in particular owe thanks for encouragement and support to many people. Without the stimulation and sponsorship of the Social Science Research Council, the project never would have been launched. Orville G. Brim, as chairman of the Committee on Work and Personality in the Middle Years, and Ronald P. Abeles and Lonnie R. Sherrod, as staff associates of the Social Science Research Council, kept resources and encouragement steady throughout. Undergirding SSRC sponsorship as well as providing funds for the study group itself were generous grants from the National Institute of Mental Health and the National Institute on Aging.

At Brandeis several persons facilitated our monthly meetings and helped to make the whole enterprise pleasurable as well as instructive, especially Nita Goldstein, then Assistant Dean of the Heller School, and Lise Vogel and Joyce Medverd, research assistants to the project. Ruth Daniels ably typed a large part of the manuscript.

In the end the accomplishments of the study group stemmed from the loyalty and contributions of its members. Several were ready to venture outside their specialties to explore this new field. The few men among us kindly bore their minority status. Two members in particular, Beatrice B. Whiting and Hilda Kahne, gave special encouragement and helped me as chairman to maintain a steady vision of the interdisciplinary cooperation, scholarly benefits, and lasting friendships that could arise from such a group. In addition, Grace K. Baruch and Rosalind C. Barnett taught me a great deal about the psychology of women in adulthood during a course that we later taught together at the Heller School.

Finally, the chapter authors deserve special thanks. Constance Nathanson, Gerda Lorenz, and Toni Antonucci lived outside the Boston area and had not been associated with the study group. They were willing, however, to take on their assignments and lend them their own definition. Joan Ecklein, likewise not a study group member, came to our attention at the close of our sessions but succeeded in converting her research on German women to a form that addressed a number of comparative questions that the study group had raised. Carol Gilligan, during the meetings of the study group, began with a brilliant glimmer of an original idea and in the process of developing her chapter for this volume made it grow into an exciting alternative theory of moral development in women. Last, in my own chapters, I have benefitted from the obligation to produce an integrative framework for the book. Such responsibility pulled my own work forward and encouraged a fledgling interest in the life cycle to become a full-blown commitment to research on the aging process and adult development. My thanks to the SSRC Committee and the Study Group on Women for the rare opportunity and stimulation that they provided.

JANET ZOLLINGER GIELE

Waltham, Massachusetts
February 1982

Contents

Foreword *Orville G. Brim, Jr.*

1 WOMEN IN ADULTHOOD: UNANSWERED
QUESTIONS   1

Janet Zollinger Giele

2 WOMEN AND HEALTH: THE SOCIAL DIMENSIONS
OF BIOMEDICAL DATA   37

Constance A. Nathanson and Gerda Lorenz

3 ADULT DEVELOPMENT AND WOMEN'S
DEVELOPMENT: ARRANGEMENTS FOR A
MARRIAGE   89

Carol Gilligan

4 WOMEN'S WORK AND FAMILY ROLES   115

Janet Zollinger Giele

5 WOMEN IN THE GERMAN DEMOCRATIC REPUBLIC:
IMPACT OF CULTURE AND SOCIAL POLICY   151

Joan Ecklein

6 FUTURE RESEARCH AND POLICY QUESTIONS   199

Janet Zollinger Giele

Appendix: LONGITUDINAL AND CROSS-SECTIONAL
DATA SOURCES ON WOMEN IN THE
MIDDLE YEARS   241

Toni C. Antonucci

Index   275

CHAPTER 1

Women in Adulthood: Unanswered Questions

JANET ZOLLINGER GIELE
Heller School
Brandeis University

During the 1970s the new topic of adulthood appeared in popular magazines and bestsellers. It concerned what happened to people after the formative years of childhood, the storm and stress of adolescence, and the uncertainties of getting launched. Did men reach a career plateau, then stagnate and decline into old age? Did women after going through "the change of life" somehow wither and withdraw as they slid into their later years? Or were these changes on the whole more positive, or perhaps even less important, than commonly believed? The surprising success of Gail Sheehy's *Passages* (1976) was testimony to the interest in these new questions. It not only reflected an emerging new psychology of adulthood; it also spoke to people whose actual lives were changing and who were encountering issues that had not been confronted by earlier generations in quite the same way.

Historians and sociologists have speculated on why so many people are currently interested in adulthood. Is one of the reasons demographic? Demos (1977, 1978) suggests that because more people live longer now, they have to face up to developmental changes after youth that are much more commonly experienced than in the past. Another part of the explanation may be social and economic. From an examination of adulthood in Anglo-American society Neil J. Smelser (1980) infers that adult tasks of integrating love and work are more problematic in complex and highly differentiated economies.

In recent years expert scholars and social scientists have also devoted more research time to adults. Along with their findings they have expanded their theories of human development well beyond childhood and adolescence and speculated on changes during midlife and old age. As early as 1950 Erik Erikson made one of the most important contributions to the new

1

psychology of adulthood. In his famous "Eight Stages of Man," the eighth chapter of *Childhood and Society,* he suggested some of the universal adult dilemmas: in midlife between generativity and stagnation; and in old age between integrity and despair. During the 1960s Bernice Neugarten (1968) and her colleagues at the University of Chicago documented midlife experience and aging in samples of men and women in the United States. By the mid-1970s a number of scholarly efforts were under way to interpret the stages of adulthood. Levinson (1978) at Yale intensively examined a small group of men in their middle years. Vaillant (1977) analyzed changes in a group of Harvard alumni who attended college in the 1940s. At UCLA, Roger Gould (1978) observed the typical dilemmas and transformations that occurred in young and middle-aged adults, women and men, who came for psychiatric help and counseling at an outpatient clinic. He also found the same issues in a large sample of nonpatients who answered a questionnaire.

For the authors and sponsors of this book on *Women in the Middle Years* perhaps the most important aspect of earlier work was that it was largely written by and about men. As my foregoing preface proclaims, mere intellectual thoroughness demands that attention be given to the distinct adult dilemmas and issues experienced by women. Until this is done, one cannot be sure that the categories of analysis and theories of development are not somehow flawed by attention to only half the human race. Of course, it should be mentioned right at the outset that there are two points of view about whether any sex differences will be found in the adult development of women and men. Some hold that any valid theory already encompasses the experience of both sexes. Others are more skeptical.

BASIC ASSUMPTIONS

In the end, the actual adult experience of women and men reveals both similarities and differences between the sexes. Four themes in the emerging scholarship of adulthood nicely demonstrate the shared as well as the differentiated experiences of each gender. The first two trends—(1) growth of life-span development theory, and (2) increase in cross-disciplinary research—necessitate common underlying concepts and measures to observe and compare the adult experience of women and men. On the other hand, two other trends—(3) a willingness to seek out and recognize different themes in women's lives, and (4) a growing sense of historical change in women's roles—have had the effect of heightening perception and acceptance of sex differences in the adult years of the life cycle. These four themes permeate the chapters of this book and provide a context for each author's treatment of a particular dimension of women's midlife experience.

Life-Span Perspectives on the Middle Years

When psychologists and sociologists realized that not all development stopped with childhood and adolescence, they turned their attention to the middle years. Keniston (1965) probed changes in the life of young adults. Brim (1966) listed the many types of socialization that occur on the job and in many other roles of adult life. In a few years the Social Science Research Council capitalized on this growing scholarly interest by establishing its Committee on Work and Personality in the Middle Years, whose work eventually led to this volume.

Even among those working on the middle years, however, it soon became evident that the midlife period was merely one arbitrary demarcation, a temporary conceptual stepping stone on the way to a more comprehensive and continuous theory of the life course. Rather than picture the life cycle as a series of discrete stages, social scientists were discovering a new paradigm for understanding adult development. Instead of metamorphosis in the individual, much as one might expect in a butterfly at each stage of its life cycle, proponents of the new life-course perspective have a variety of new images for visualizing constancy and change during the aging process. Their metaphors are complex and differentiated, more difficult to summarize in a neat issue or dilemma than one might have hoped after initial exposure to Erikson or Sheehy.

The dominant theme of the life-course perspective is the interweaving of many different dimensions of development and experience over the entire life-span of the individual. As Glen Elder (1975) put it in an early formulation, "The life span perspective views human development, socialization, and adaptations as lifelong processes within an interage framework [p. 167]." It recognizes development beyond youth. It allows many types of life pattern to be accounted for. It monitors social change through the shifting life patterns of different generations or cohorts. In the end it implies a many-faceted explanatory model that accounts for multiple links between antecedent and consequent events over the entire life-span. Brim and Kagan (1980) visualize a grid with chronological age on the side and many types of human characteristics along the top: "Bodily changes, the course of achievement, the nature of social relationships, conformity and independence, or understanding of death could be studied in a way that describes the lifetime passage of each characteristic. . . . The challenge is to relate knowledge of what goes on before and after the age period under study, so that research can contribute to the understanding of constancy and change as well as of a particular age [p. 15]."

These images pose no mean challenge to those who would study the middle years and the adult period of the life-cycle. Where do the middle years begin and where do they end? If the drama of midlife inheres in the "lack of solidity or fixedness in the adult role," as Mortimer and Simmons (1978) suggest, how can one study that period anyway? The life-span perspective nevertheless turns out to be convenient for the study of adulthood precisely because it analyzes stages of development by multiple dimensions and overlapping criteria.

Take the problem of defining the middle years: It is not a new one. There has long been a lack of consensus. Economists and the U.S. Department of Labor can alone take credit for five alternative definitions. In their publications middle age at different times refers to ages 25−54, 30−44, 45 years and over, 35 years and over, or age 30 to the end of one's work life (Kahne, 1978). Psychologists and sociologists have also variously set the boundaries at 35−55, 40−60, or to correspond more roughly with adulthood—after youth and before old age—a period between 30 and 60. In the face of this confusion the life-span perspective offers some comfort; it theoretically accounts for the fact that definition of the middle years is so difficult. Moreover, it shifts the research focus away from neat and orderly transitions to a quest for an explanation of why changes occur when they do.

The life-span perspective also deepens understanding of developmental stages when they exist. As Alice S. Rossi (1980) has so perceptively reported, life course theories comprise at least two major types, one that emphasizes stages and transitions, the other that focuses on timing of events and is much less likely to observe or document clearly demarcated developmental steps. Rather than proceed to suggest that one of these perspectives is more "true" than the other (as I fear Brim and Kagan and Rossi may have done), I think there is a chance that each theory is correct but limited in explanatory power to somewhat different types of people and circumstance. Rather than trying to prove or disprove stage theories or timing models, I prefer to look for insights in each and then construct an overarching framework that combines the two positions. This larger framework gives a context for the chapters in this book. An acquaintance with stage theories gives a background for understanding Gilligan's chapter on some aspects of women's psychological development. Familiarity with the nonstage alternatives gives one an orientation to the more sociological chapters by Nathanson and Lorenz on women's health behaviors, by Giele on work and family roles, and by Ecklein on women's adulthood in a society quite different from our own. Finally, Antonucci's compendium on data sources opens up the possibility of testing and combining both theories to look for those individuals and situations to which stages do or do not apply.

Stage Theories. Classic stage theories in many ways parallel biological images of growth and development. Like Erik Erikson's (1950) epigenetic model in which the child's personality gradually unfolds from the psychologically undifferentiated newborn infant, stage theories of midlife show adults continuously tending toward a more individuated and complex self. At times development is slowed—people sometimes remain too enthralled by idealized parent figures, mentors, or unrealistic hopes to take charge of themselves. But when they let go these bonds, they are able to reconstitute themselves adaptively and achieve the integrity and satisfaction that wait as rewards.

In *The Seasons of a Man's Life* Daniel Levinson (1978) pictures the developmental steps graphically as shown in Figure 1.1. The staircase model

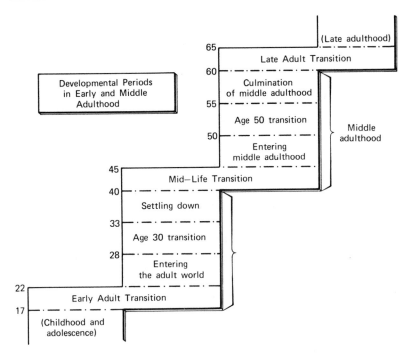

Figure 1.1. Levinson's model of the life course. [From *The Seasons of a Man's Life,* by Daniel J. Levinson, et al. Copyright © 1978 by Daniel Levinson. Reprinted by permission of Alfred A. Knopf, Inc.]

suggests successively more distinct and complex resolutions the higher one goes; each step rests on those preceding. Two chapters of Levinson's book concern midlife individuation, which is one of the chief developmental tasks of adulthood. Only when the person has become his own man, given up the unrealistic parts of his dream, and developed occupationally and affectionally, can he enjoy both the external and internal freedom to develop polarities within his own personality (the Old and Young, the Masculine and Feminine, etc.). As the person proceeds up the developmental staircase through middle adulthood, he develops a "stronger sense of self while maintaining his ties and responsibilities in the world [p. 336]." This theme of individuation also figures prominently in Osherson's (1980) analysis of men who changed career in midlife. Similarly, Gould (1978) sums up the accomplishment of the midlife transition with this theme: "I own myself."

As Carol Gilligan remarks later in Chapter 3 of this book, the individuation theme is derived from male experience and perhaps is more appropriate to men than it is to women. Yet, although there may be a difference in *theme,* there may be similarity in the phase-like *form* of development. Just recently Maggie Scarf (1980) sketched a stage schema for women. Her periodization of the life course roughly corresponds with those of other stage theorists. Only the themes and content differ somewhat. Rather than individuation, women's theme is the satisfaction of relationships and the pain of loss. Accordingly, Scarf says, the typical life passages for women focus on somewhat different dilemmas:

...the replies I was getting varied—in relatively systematic ways—with the various stages of the life cycle. ...Women in the same phase of life were, by and large, depressed about similar sorts of things.

In adolescence...with such matters as the wrench of separation from one's parents, and with changing body-image—the frightening journey of transformation from child to sexual woman.

In the years of the twenties...with the search for intimacy and commitment: the career costs that might be incurred, should one put the "loving" tasks ahead of the work ones—, or indeed, should one do things the opposite way around!

Issues of the thirties were, frequently, the mistakes that had already been made and the payment that had been exacted: an "I've been cheated" sense that the fantasies and dreams of girlhood had not been and might never *be* satisfied.

At mid-life, major preoccupations were with the loss of certain identity-conferring roles or ways of being—roles which, in many an instance, had been perceived as a person's sole source of interpersonal power or meaning. It might be the fading of a woman's attractiveness. ...Or it might be that a woman's depressive symptoms had emerged around the departure of a child, perhaps the youngest child—and the subsequent loss of the nurturing mothering role which she'd conceived of as her identity, her reason for being [pp. 6–7].

With such relatively clear boundaries between phases of development, one might ask whether stage theorists really share a life-span perspective. The answer seems to be yes. Despite their tendency to find themes typical of a particular period, they recognize the many-faceted and interconnected nature of development on many dimensions. The eras of the life-cycle are overlapping. There are biological and social as well as psychological changes, and not all may be perfectly coordinated. In Levinson's (1978) words, "We are never ageless. As we gain a greater sense of our own biographies, however, we can begin to exist at multiple ages [321]." In certain ways this view is compatible with the emphasis of the nonstage theorists who focus on the sometimes incompatible or asynchronous timing of events during the life cycle.

Timing Models.   In contrast with the search for stages, a number of psychologists and sociologists have been skeptical that any such clear and orderly pattern exists. A recent book of essays on adulthood (Smelser & Erikson, 1980) provides ample evidence of this strong countertrend among the observers of midlife. Along with chapters by Erikson, Gould, and Levinson showing the evidence for stages, there are chapters by sociologists like Kohn, Pearlin, and Fiske that raise an alternative theme. The latter say that the case for stages is tenuous at best and that it is more likely that change occurs on one or several dimensions of the life course triggered by specific personal or environmental events. The person either copes and adapts or fails to do so, and development occurs in the affected area. Transformations of a more general sort that are associated with a particular age are, however, relatively rare.

To visualize development using the timing-of-events model is difficult. Graphic representations usually take the form of statistical regression models. That of Kohn and Schooler (1978), for example, shows the impact of an individual's work complexity on his intellectual flexibility. A more general image, however, comes from Perun and Bielby (1980) who picture changes throughout the life course as analogous to the operation of a disk pack in a computer. As shown in Figure 1.2 they conceptualize human development in terms of many dimensions, each internally regulated by a multiplicity of timetables. With their structure "each of the constituent dimensions is in simultaneous operation, moving in time at a rate specific to itself [p. 103]." Each has its own developmental progression with its own antecedents, transitions, and sequelae. Using their model, one way to summarize differences between individuals' life course structures is in terms of synchrony or

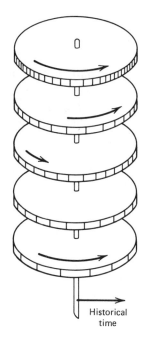

Figure 1.2. Perun and Bielby's model of the life course. [P.J. Perun and D.D.V. Bielby. 1980. "Structure and Dynamics of the Individual Life Course." In K.W. Back (Ed.), *Life Course: Integrative Theories and Exemplary Populations*. Boulder, CO: Westview Press. Reprinted by permission of Westview Press. Copyright © 1980, the American Association for the Advancement of Science.]

asynchrony among the many timetables. In this idea is a bridge to the larger theoretical framework that can embrace both stage and nonstage theories.

Synthesis: Varieties of Adult Development. It is probably not accidental that most stage theorists are trained in psychology or psychoanalysis and that most nonstage theorists are trained in sociology and other social sciences. The former look for change triggered primarily by the internal timetable of individual learning and growth, whereas those especially interested in environmental influences take note of the often random and arbitrary timing of events. The timing theorists thus accord considerable importance to what Bronfenbrenner (1979) has called the "ecology of development." In that ecology there may be such coherence of custom and synchrony of developmental events that clearly defined stages are not only expected but experienced. In other chaotic or rapidly changing environments, however, no such order may emerge. It is in the classification of such different types of experience that I have discovered one possible synthesis between the stage theories and the timing models.

Evidently some people experience distinct stages of adult development while others do not. It is the degree of social complexity on the job or in other aspects of everyday life that appears critical. Those who must learn a great deal and adapt to many different roles seem to be the most concerned with trying to evolve an abstract self, conscience, or life structure that can integrate all these discrete events. By contrast, those with a simple job, limited by meager education and narrow contacts, are less apt to experience aging as a process that enhances autonomy or elaborates one's mental powers. In this connection it is perhaps significant that the stages of adult development have been worked out by psychiatrists such as Erikson and Levinson whose observations are heavily influenced by contacts with a privileged upper-middle class and professional elite. Investigators like Marjorie Fiske (1980) or Leonard Pearlin (1978), who have observed a wider range of lower-middle class or blue-collar people, simply do not see the same clear patterns emerging among them. Identifiable developmental stages thus appear more likely to occur in some persons and in some social settings than in others. Absence of stages is the norm among their opposites (Giele, 1980).

Ultimately, this complicated life-span perspective gives useful insights into the lives of women. It pictures development as multifaceted and complex. It also provides for the wide variety of life patterns that women actually experience.

Major Dimensions of the Life Course

Using a life-span perspective, what are the key dimensions for charting women's experience through the middle years? Interestingly enough, among researchers in the field there are opposite perceptions of where more work needs to be done. A number of investigators—Neugarten (1968), Notman and Nadelson (1978), and others—suggest that there may have been too much emphasis on physical change, such as menopause, or that the significance of menopause may have been wrongly understood because it was divorced from important correlated changes in occupation and social role. Rossi (1977, 1980), on the other hand, contends that social scientists have underrated the importance of sex differences in physical and bodily change; her concern is to lift this neglected dimension to a more important place.

These claims point to the topics that should be on any comprehensive checklist for monitoring development and change during the middle years. A quick perusal of the recent writing on the subject immediately indicates that physical and psychological changes in the individual, social roles in family and work place, and characteristics of the larger economic and cultural context should be included. It is precisely around these themes that the succeeding chapters have been organized: Nathanson and Lorenz on the physical aspect of women's experience, Gilligan on the psychological, Giele on work and family roles, and Ecklein on the impact of a specific economic and cultural context.

These categories of analysis reflect a larger consensus among social and behavioral scientists on the important dimensions of human experience. Implicit in most modern theories is a strong belief in the interaction of bodily change, personality, social roles, and cultural beliefs. The challenge is to describe each major level of experience in as much depth as possible, yet leave room for seeing the interconnections.

Discussions in the SSRC Study Group on Women gave ample proof of implicit agreement on these major issues. Physicians and psychiatrists noted several important types of physical change during the middle years. The psychologically oriented spoke of basic needs for affection, competence, a sense of control, and physical gratification. Economists and sociologists charted work histories and career ladders, and asked how demands of work and family life were timed either to fit or conflict with one another.

A number of such questions were cast in a self-contained mode, but others crossed disciplinary boundaries and pointed toward the interconnections. One strategy for integration was to ask what combination of circumstances led to the greatest sense of well-being and satisfaction among women (Barnett & Baruch, 1978; Campbell, Converse & Rodgers, 1976; Whiting, 1978). Another was to ask what outcomes social planning and social change might accomplish. What if the whole cultural and institutional context were different, with entirely different social policies toward women's work and family roles? Would entirely different patterns of experience emerge in midlife?

Findings on these interconnections are in many respects still fragmentary and impressionistic. Several chapters of this book nevertheless present suggestive data that point future directions for research on women's well-being and the policies that will enhance it. Ecklein's chapter sketches some tentative connections between social policies and women's situation in the German Democratic Republic. My concluding chapter on emerging policy themes in the United States summarizes what have been main strategies for improving women's position and satisfaction in this country. Antonucci's compendium on data sources spreads before the reader some of the research materials already available that could be used to test hypotheses on inter-connections between physical, psychological, and social dimensions of women's experience for the future.

Differences between Women and Men

As presented so far, the categories and theoretical models of the life course perspective are universal enough to encompass the experience of both women and men. These common dimensions are reassuring not only because they point to a more general theory of human behavior, but also because they make comparison possible between the sexes.

It would be foolish, however, to ignore a counter theme that, although timid at first, has recently grown in importance. Betty Friedan (1979), the famous author of *The Feminine Mystique,* now urges goals and values more oriented to the family and the quality of human relationships. Her move is significant for it is in keeping with a larger trend among social scientists who are now willing to identify and analyze differences in goals and values between the sexes, without attributing inferiority to one or superiority to the other.

The newest and clearest contrast between the sexes appears in Maggie Scarf's *Unfinished Business* (1980), an account of women's reactions to depression and loss. At the outset Scarf, who is primarily a journalist and scientific writer, tells how she discovered depression to be two to six times more common in women than in men, and then set out to find the reason why. She recounts a fascinating conversation with the late Marcia Guttentag, a psychologist studying depression in women. Guttentag had been conducting a content analysis of major themes in men's and women's popular magazines. The stories for men primarily concerned adventure, achievement, and triumph over difficult odds. The women's stories were strikingly different; their central theme was coping with loss. Scarf puts these facts together and weaves a picture of women's development through the life course that is based on the centrality of relationships and the critical losses that occur at each age.

Others have also noted distinctive traits in women that involve relationship to others. Psychiatrist Jean Baker Miller (1976) was one of the first authorities to recognize women's peculiar sensitivity to others and vulnerability to loss. Where others, however, had deemed these characteristics weakness, Miller called them strengths. In my book *Women and the Future*

(Giele, 1978), I also challenge "male" value systems that put mastery and achievement ahead of "female" concerns for interdependence and relationship; I call for a better balance of both emphases in individuals as well as society. Now in this book we have Gilligan's original contribution that notes the themes of responsibility and care in statements of young women and that contrasts them with the success and achievement themes that are more common among men of the same age.

In the present ideological climate the possibility of important psychological differences between women and men is in some ways so explosive that it is always put forward tentatively and cautiously. Despite the dangers of having their motives regarded as traitorous to women, a number of analysts have persisted, believing not only that women have nothing to be ashamed of (their distinctive qualities are strengths), but also that there are logical reasons to expect that women should be psychologically different in certain respects. First, since women alone have the biological capacity for pregnancy and lactation, it is likely that their hormonal responses and instinctive reactions to the newborn and very young child have through 40,000 years of human evolution been peculiarly adapted to care for the human infant (Rossi, 1977). Second, the socialization process is symmetrical between mothers and daughters but asymmetrical between mothers and sons. This simple formal difference of a child's being the same or opposite sex as the major caretaker has a major impact on his or her capacity for empathy or independence (Chodorow, 1978). Third, women's and men's social roles are quite different with respect to family and employment responsibility. Where a man may expect greater continuity, women are likely to experience an immense variety of timing patterns—starting a family, finishing school, going back to work, stopping briefly, and so on (McGuigan, 1980).

It may not be the dimensions of development that are so different between males and females as the form of the life course by which these strands are intertwined. Instead of an orderly stepwise progression of the kind that Levinson pictures in *The Seasons of a Man's Life,* McGuigan (1980) envisions women's development as "a braid of threads in which colors appear, disappear, and reappear [p. xii]."

It is always possible, of course, that sex differences increase or diminish over time. If fathers take a greater role in child care, patterns of empathy and independence might become more similar between daughters and sons. If more women enter the labor force and remain in it continuously, while more men retire early or change careers, the form of men's and women's lives may become more similar. Yet in no society are such dramatic changes so widespread that these hypotheses can easily be tested. Ecklein's account of 30 years of very rapid change in the German Democratic Republic, however, supplies some tantalizing evidence on the degree to which sex differences in life patterns can be attenuated. Yet it is also noteworthy that important contrasts still persist in that society.

Impact of History on the Life Course

These complex questions involving changes in life pattern over time inevitably bring us to the question of how much change over the life course is due to growth and development (aging), how much to the times in which one was born and grew up (cohort effects), and how much to the historical conditions under which one lives at the moment (period effects). This is a classic conundrum in the field of aging and the social sciences. The three types of explanation are perfectly correlated in time, and it is difficult if not impossible to disentangle the effects of each (Elder, 1975; Riley, 1978).

In the lives of women the question is no more clearly illustrated than in Judith Bardwick's graphic representation of women's emotional concerns at different ages as shown in Figure 1.3. As the footnote to Bardwick's graph reminds us, the figure does not represent longitudinal changes in a group of individuals over their own life course. Instead, the bar graph showing proportions of emphasis on self, interdependence, or dependence are used to describe different *age groups*. Thus, the graph is not meant to be a history of a person but rather a cross-sectional view of a multiaged population. Yet notice how easy it is to read into the graph something not intended—namely, a picture of stages in women's development. The very fact that the two perspectives are so easily confused nicely demonstrates the intercorrelation of aging with historical changes and the hazards of trying to infer universal developmental patterns. It may be, as both Riley (1978) and Rossi (1980) have warned, that characteristics attributed to a particular stage in life (e.g., the midlife crisis) may actually be caused by historical accident. That is, the life experience of a particular birth cohort who face a given set of social or economic circumstances may result in a distinctive developmental pattern. But for other cohorts, brought up differently and encountering a quite different environment, these patterns may not recur.

Such questions regarding historical change and developmental patterns are especially important in the case of contemporary women. In less than a century the length of women's lives has doubled between the time they bear their last child and their own death. Since 1940 the proportion of adult women in the labor force has grown from one-quarter to one-half. These demographic and economic changes have had enormous impact on the life patterns of women.

Each of the following chapters indirectly touches these questions. In their discussion of health and illness behaviors Nathanson and Lorenz refer to the changing patterns of fertility control in different age groups. Because employed women also report less illness, there is a possibility that women's health behaviors will change as more women participate continuously in the labor force.

Gilligan, by the very fact of interviewing young women, poses the classic methodological problem of aging research: Are the moral concerns she

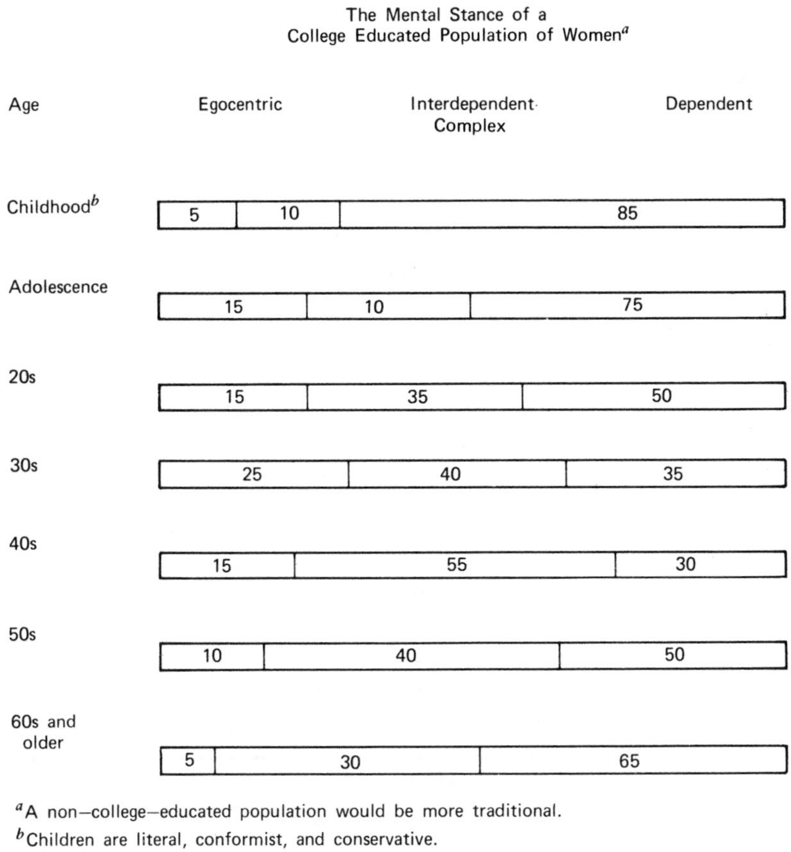

The Mental Stance of a
College Educated Population of Women[a]

Age	Egocentric	Interdependent Complex	Dependent

Childhood[b]	5	10	85

| Adolescence | 15 | 10 | 75 |

| 20s | 15 | 35 | 50 |

| 30s | 25 | 40 | 35 |

| 40s | 15 | 55 | 30 |

| 50s | 10 | 40 | 50 |

| 60s and older | 5 | 30 | 65 |

[a]A non—college—educated population would be more traditional.

[b]Children are literal, conformist, and conservative.

Figure 1.3.   Bardwick's graph of women's concerns. This figure is a static not a developmental model. It is an estimate of what the generations are like *now* and is *not* a statement of the psychological changes that would be experienced over anyone's lifetime. "The latter is implied but cannot be stated with certainty, because sociocultural values are a major influence and it is difficult to predict such values for the future [p. 42]." [J.M. Bardwick. 1980. "The Seasons of a Woman's Life." In D.G. McGuigan (Ed.), *Women's Lives: New Theory, Research and Policy.* Ann Arbor, MI: University of Michigan, Center for Continuing Education of Women.]

finds in young women truly a result of different developmental sequences in females, or do her findings apply only to a particular birth cohort who were raised during the Viet Nam war and came of age in the early 1970s? Although Gilligan does not state this question directly, it is an important one for the reader to bear in mind.

My chapter on women's changing work and family roles addresses the historical issue more directly. It is quite evident that over the past 40 years social scientists have changed their theories about the life course and about sex differences as social circumstances have invalidated their earlier predictions. The question for the future is whether current increasing interpenetration of work and family life will continue, or whether cyclical ups and downs in the economy and the birth rate will make us revise our theories once again in the 1980s.

Ecklein's chapter on women in the German Democratic Republic provides some insight into the effects of catastrophe and planned social change on different age groups of women. The younger women adapted more easily to policy changes and to official encouragement to participate in the labor force. They provide a clear contrast with older women who were more set in their ways when the new policies were instituted.

MAJOR RESEARCH DOMAINS

The life-span perspective shapes all current work on women in the middle years, but specialized research efforts concentrate on the traditional dimensions of experience—physical, psychological, social, and cultural. Each of the remaining chapters in this book addresses one of these dimensions, but none attempts to be comprehensive. Companion pieces still wait to be written on aspects of women's lives not covered here. Along with Nathanson's review of sex differences in physical health, a parallel review of mental health is needed. Accompanying Gilligan's summary of themes in women's moral development, it would be desirable to have a preliminary sketch of stages in intellectual and emotional development. In addition to my description of women's work and family roles, women's civic and volunteer activities need further attention, as well as their experiences in the educational and cultural world. Finally, with Ecklein's account of women in East Germany, it would be instructive to have comparable material from a developing nation or another industrial society.

Rather than wait for such comprehensive treatment to appear, this volume makes initial forays into the growing literature on adult women. Each chapter organizes a mass of relevant material and thereby more clearly reveals the work that has yet to be done. The remainder of this chapter places each of these efforts in the context of a specialized research domain and thus points the reader to other possible issues and future research topics.

The Physical Dimension

Out of all the possible physical aspects of women's lives that change in the adult years, the menopause has received the most, and some would say undue, emphasis. Estelle Fuchs' (1978) popular book on women in midlife and Marilyn Block's (1978) review of useful facts on middle aged and older women each devote several chapters to the menopause and medical problems associated with the reproductive system. Of special interest are annoying symptoms of the menopause (hot flashes, headaches, irritability, dizzy spells) and new medical procedures such as estrogen replacement therapy. Breast cancer, surgical menopause (caused by removal of the uterus and/or the ovaries), and the hazard of unnecessary surgery are also discussed. Such a list of topics raises the question: What *should* be the research issues and the principal questions regarding physical changes in adulthood?

In their chapter on women's health and illness behavior Nathanson and Lorenz have focused on what is presently the most active and controversial topic in the field. Researchers are faced with a paradox of more reported illness and hospitalization among women, yet lower mortality than among men. There are several possible explanations. Women may be more likely to report illness but really are no sicker than men. Or their reproductive functions—pregnancies, cancer of the breast, and other malfunctions—may account for the difference. Finally, it may be that women's social roles—marriage, employment, parenthood—make their illnesses different from men's.

After considering all these possibilities, various researchers have concluded that social rather than biological factors are probably the most important explanation for differences in men's and women's physical health. Experts disagree, however, on which social factors are most important. Nathanson and Lorenz in their chapter note that employed women report far fewer health problems than do housewives. The difference may result from social contacts and satisfactions (or requirements) of the job; or it may be a reporting difference; or both. On the other hand, Gove and Hughes (1979) argue that housewives and other women facing heavy demands as nurturers may be *really* more ill because of fatigue and accumulated stress. Their work has, however, been the object of extensive criticism on conceptual and methodological grounds because they do not clearly distinguish between response differences caused by role demands and those caused by differences in self-reports (Marcus & Seeman, 1981; Mechanic, 1980; Verbrugge, 1980).

In many ways Nathanson and Lorenz's chapter is an excellent illustration of ways to organize research findings in a fashion compatible with the new life course perspective. They have shown how data can be interpreted by demonstrating an interaction between internal physical and external social factors. In addition, they point to the potential contribution of psychological sex differences such as women's greater willingness to seek help or their greater awareness of health problems. Finally, they refer to cross-cultural differences, such as those between France and the United States, where there are striking differences in rates of women's hospitalization and surgery.

Clearly, however, Nathanson and Lorenz, and others working on sex differences in illness behavior have addressed only a portion of the relevant questions connecting physical aspects of adulthood to women's satisfaction and emotional well-being. Other possible topics include the varieties of physical experience associated with menstruation and menopause, sexuality and sexual activity, the impact of childbearing and lactation, and the effects of a sedentary life-style on women as compared with a more rigorous physical regimen. In connection with all these variables it could be asked how different types of women fare, and what physical antecedents and correlates are apparently connected with health and emotional well-being.

Several important beginnings on these topics have been made by others. Parlee (1973), for example, has critically examined the medical literature on the premenstrual syndrome and found that it is difficult to find clear and independent agreement on its principal characteristics. Weideger (1977), however, points to the ancient importance of taboos surrounding menstruation that work to distort and suppress reports of what it is really like. In a questionnaire study Weideger found that two-thirds of her respondents would just as soon do without menstruation whereas 31 percent thought of it in a positive light. Given these attitudes and current trends in the women's movement that seek to minimize male and female differences, Weideger warns that real and valuable information about actual experience of menstruation may be denied or suppressed. A painful condition such as dysmenorrhea (menstrual cramps) may be treated as a merely psychological problem rather than a real physical difficulty that deserves treatment. Weideger's own bent is to recognize and celebrate rather than minimize or deny male–female differences. She advocates a sharing of "new wives' tales," women's personal experiences in both coping with pain and finding enjoyment. Her own book reports such useful remedies as how to deal with menstrual cramps and postcoital pain. In response to her questionnaire, women reported personal observations that regular exercise and proper diet reduced menstrual distress.

Similar themes are emerging in contemporary work on menopause. Notman (1979) notes that a gradual shift is under way from thinking of menopause as a deficiency disease to thinking of it as one of life's normal transitions. In the earlier view all sorts of issues at midlife that might be social in origin—women's role changes, husbands' career crises—were inappropriately attributed to a woman's menopause. To shatter these myths, critical studies such as that by McKinlay and McKinlay (1973) have been necessary to show the dubious methodology and inferential processes by which many claims about the menopause have been derived. Clearly, proper scientific studies are needed in the place of stereotypes.

Yet, as with menstruation, there are some real symptoms associated with menopause for which good descriptive data are needed. Paula Weideger notes that virtually no good longitudinal studies are available. She would like to see women from the ages of 45 to 55 keep logs on their own physical changes and accompanying moods and behavior. She also suggests that shared knowledge may help women to experience the menopause more positively (as did one member of a California sharing group who found after discussion of hot flashes that to her surprise she found them pleasurable). At present it is generally agreed that most women in the United States experience the menopause around age 50. (But it may have occurred somewhat earlier a generation ago when Parker [1960] reported the typical age as 45 to 48.) Roughly three-fourths of all women experience hot flashes. Other accompanying symptoms that are frequently mentioned are headaches, palpitation, dizzy spells, and weight gain (Perlmutter, 1978).

Perhaps the most important sign of a changing attitude toward menopause is medical and popular opinion on the value of estrogen replacement therapy. If menopause is no longer viewed as a deficiency disease resulting from the drop in estrogen, then the use of estrogen against hot flashes, headaches, and depression seems questionable, especially given its risks of stimulating cancer. Such a critical assessment is now evident in both scientific and popular works (Bart & Grossman, 1978; Block, Davidson, Grambs & Serock, 1978; Notman, 1979; Seaman, 1972; Weideger, 1977).

Much as with menstruation and menopause, good descriptive accounts are needed of the childbearing process: pregnancy, delivery, and lactation. Ten years ago Grimm (1969) reported that she knew of no research that reported on the motivations and feelings behind women's experiences of motherhood. A few years later Seymour Fisher (1973) collected accounts from young women of their first delivery. It is Alice Rossi's (1977) review of literature on hormonal changes accompanying ovulation, pregnancy, childbirth, and lactation that is the best available integration of biomedical, psychological, and social factors in a woman's experience as a mother. She makes several fascinating suggestions based on available data: that a mother is bonded to her child ("hooked" on it) partly as a result of the biological experience of gestation and lactation, and that a woman's later enjoyment of sexual intercourse is probably enhanced by her experience of pregnancy. Such statements obviously raise many fascinating questions concerning women who have not experienced motherhood, and concerning women for whom it was not a positive experience. More recent research on some of these questions is reported by Parsons (1980).

And what about sexuality apart from motherhood? Rossi suggests that the full range of women's sexual behavior be considered—that nursing a child may be as gratifying sexually as intercourse. Nevertheless, sexual gratification between adults (whether homosexual or heterosexual) is the more usual way in which sexual behavior is understood. Reports by Kinsey (1953), Masters and Johnson (1966), and Hite (1976) all show, despite popular myth to the contrary, that sexual interest and capacity for gratification continue in older women well beyond menopause (Block et al. 1978). Another interesting issue is how women fare who are without sexual partners. Does physical exercise or nonsexual contact—touching, hugging, sitting close, holding a child on the lap—partly gratify these needs? And how does frustration, satisfaction, or sublimation of sexual needs affect the rest of a woman's development, role performance, and sense of well-being? Very little can be said definitively on the subject.

Finally, the mechanical dimension of physical exercise and activity has been sorely neglected. From the time they are little girls, females in our society not only are less physically active but have been less encouraged to take part in athletics than boys. Fewer physical demands are made on them. And for many, after a brief period when their children are young, life becomes sedentary (just as it does for most men in the United States.) It is intriguing to consider how women's lives would be different, how their self-image would change, if they were more physically active, more confident of their own strength and endurance, and more socialized to participate on a regular basis in competitive or individual sports (Scott, 1974). Weideger's observations suggest that regular exercise may ease the discomforts of menstruation and menopause. Women's chances for exercise have diminished as their work in the home has been mechanized. Jogging, hiking, and biking are probably useful correctives. More needs to be learned about the impact of opportunities for physical exertion not only on women's health but on their emotional and social outlook as well.

Implicit in all these topics for further research are potential policy suggestions as well. Two prominent themes relate to the educational system and health delivery. In education, the open treatment of physical facts of menstruation, childbearing, and menopause is long overdue. Fortunately, changes are already in progress to encourage women's greater participation in sports and athletics. Title IX of the Higher Education Act has brought concern for investment in women's sports at the college and university level. And the Women's Educational Equity Act has encouraged less sex-differentiated physical education programs at the elementary and secondary level.

In health delivery, more needs to be done to change the hierarchical doctor–patient relationship (Heide, 1978; Notman & Nadelson, 1978; Ruzek, 1978). Many women still unquestioningly accept unnecessary surgery (Seaman, 1972). At the same time, the type of preventive care at which some women have long been expert—being sensitive to symptoms, taking action quickly—should receive greater legitimation in the health care system.

Psychological Issues

In the recent flowering of psychological research on the midlife period, a number of authors have put forward developmental schemes that give a time sequence and sometimes even a chronological age by which a certain stage of development should be attained. In her chapter for this volume Carol Gilligan questions whether this work is truly applicable to women. She has pinpointed a key theoretical problem of the moment. In their studies of all male populations, Levinson (1978) and Vaillant (1977) have built their theories on a "staircase" model of development first introduced by Erik Erikson (1950). The question is whether women face the same issues or pass through the same stages.

Gould (1978) and Sheehy (1976) both include women in their descriptions, yet they also subsume the female case under the stage pattern that applies to men. Gould finds that a central issue for women is to give themselves permission to try new roles. He emphasizes that separation and autonomy are key issues for women just as they are for men. Sheehy, while using the stage model, also shows how women devise various other means for realizing both achievement and nurturance.

Gilligan more directly addresses the issue of sex difference in development. She subjects stage and sequence notions to critical scrutiny. She also questions whether women ever deal separately with the issues of autonomy and intimacy. Although Gilligan does not yet propose a grand theoretical formulation for women that is comparable with Erikson's eight stages of man, she has accomplished the theoretical groundwork by posing the central development issues for women in an entirely fresh and promising way. She suggests that women's concern for others—their sensitivity to caring and not hurting—should not be considered a simple failure of ego development but a different pattern to be understood and valued in its own right.

In addition to this question concerning developmental differences between the sexes, another important issue is whether any developmental pattern exists at all in persons of either sex. Gutmann (1977) perceives a crossover in sex roles at middle age when, because of a combination of organic and social forces, males seek more opportunity for affiliation and females for assertion and power. Other authors, however, emphasize the impact of social circumstance and life events on the aging process. Fiske (1980), using longitudinal studies of individuals in their middle years, finds no evidence for an internal developmental clock associated with chronological age. Instead, she notes the impact of income, education, and occupation on a person's central concerns. On the basis of large surveys conducted in Chicago on stressful life events, Pearlin (1978) also concludes that such events as major illness, being fired, or losing a child by death are not necessarily associated with one's age but are heavily influenced by one's status and role in the larger social and economic structure. It is these life events and the roles and statuses associated with them that present adults with different developmental tasks.

Attention to such environmental factors has been important to unraveling the causes of high rates of depression among women. Possibly the housewife role or the empty nest explains why twice as many middle-aged women are depressed as middle-aged men. There may be an imbalance in women's lives between demands to care for others and opportunity to care for themselves. Or it may be that opportunities for expression of dependency and competence are insufficient or out of proportion to each other.

Pauline Bart and Jessie Bernard were among the first to suggest that the housewife role was dangerous to women's health. In a study of middle-aged women admitted to mental hospitals Bart (1971) noted that their depression seemed to arise because their children were leaving home and their opportunities to play an active mother role were therefore diminishing. After reviewing survey findings on psychiatric symptoms in the general population, Jessie Bernard (1972) contended that the housewife role literally made some women sick. But Campbell et al. (1976), in a national survey on satisfaction and the quality of life, did not find evidence to support Bernard's interpretation.

Other studies that have tried to explain women's high rates of depression have reported a bewildering array of results. Several studies propose a "learned helplessness" theory to explain women's greater vulnerability to depression (Guttentag & Salasin, 1977; Radloff, 1975). This explanation suggests that women have learned so well the dependency expected of the feminine role that they are unable to respond actively to stressful situations in ways that will fend off threats to their well-being. Then there is another possibility: Depression bears some resemblance to boredom, and it may be that the traditional woman's role simply is not stimulating or demanding enough (Pearlin, 1975).

Employment is a possible buffer against depression. Birnbaum (1975) found higher self-esteem and sense of competence in employed married college graduate women than among the full-time housewives. Having a job can also speed recovery from depression (Brown, Bhrolchain & Harris, 1975; Mostow & Newberry, 1975). However, the conditions of employment are crucial and include such factors as the prestige of a woman's occupation and the conditions under which she enters it. Women in occupations of high prestige have fewer symptoms (Barnett, 1975; Ilfeld, 1977). In addition, women who have chosen employment rather than been forced to take it as a result of economic necessity also appear happier (Segrè, 1978).

As in the case of employment, so also in marriage it appears that it is the conditions of the marriage and the nature of the role obligations that determine a woman's chances for depression. The most persuasive explanation for impact of these variables on psychological distress is given by Gove and Hughes (1979). They demonstrate that physical illness is more prevalent among women in single-parent families and similar situations where demands are greatest on a woman and where she is less able to attend to her own needs. Because it is likely that such illnesses arise from psychological stress generated by role demands, it is but a short step to extend this argument to the etiology of depression. One would expect to find higher rates of depression and lower satisfaction where the role demands are particularly heavy, as in the case of a mother with numerous young children. Indeed, greater vulnerability to depression was found in a London survey made among those women with several children under 14 (Brown et al., 1975). In the Quality of American Life Survey, parents of young children in the United States also showed lower satisfaction (Campbell et al., 1976).

By the same logic it is possible to picture marriages that in some instances act as a positive force to help women cope with stress and satisfy needs. This argument is consistent with results of the London study by Brown et al. (1975) and other findings by Pearlin and Johnson (1977) that marriage in some cases acts as a buffer against stressful life events that cause depression. One can also thereby explain the Quality of American Life Survey finding that young married women before they have children and middle-aged married women with children over 18 are among the happiest members of the sample. Clearly, these women have more time for themselves relative to the demands made on them.

In the most recent studies of depression and well-being, two themes stand out. One is the contribution made by a sense of competence and effectance to women's sense of well-being. If women's traditional roles only allow them to be dependent or meet others' demands and not their own, their self-esteem suffers and they may experience depression (Birnbaum, 1975; Miller, 1976). The second theme is that there is no one single role—such as being employed or being a full-time homemaker—that guarantees women a high sense of competence and self-esteem. Instead, much depends both on the structure of the role in which a woman finds herself (e.g., whether it permits the exercise of competence) and on the value attached to that role (as revealed in a husband's attitude or in the role a woman's mother would have preferred for her). It is possible for women in the home to feel a sense of competence and satisfaction. The same is true for married women who are employed (Barnett & Baruch, 1978; Fidell, 1978).

Finally, one other significant stream of research on women's psychological functioning deserves special mention. This is the work of Melvin Kohn and associates on the impact of work on intellectual style and capacity. Kohn at first studied men only and reported that jobs with a greater variety of tasks and an opportunity for self-direction made their occupants more intellectually flexible, over and above prior differences in mental functioning that existed before they entered the job (Kohn & Schooler, 1978). The interesting question in the case of women was whether the general shape of these findings would hold for them as well. Recent publications by Kohn's research group now indicate that women's intellectual flexibility and functional intelligence are also improved under conditions where they occupy complex jobs that permit considerable self-direction (Miller, Schooler, Kohn & Miller, 1979).

What do these findings suggest about the effects of the housewife role on intellectual performance? There is no simple answer. It may be that some women structure the housewife role to be a complex package of responsibilities with myriad managerial, social, and productive activities while others do not. Similarly, a woman's job in the paid labor force may also be complex and demanding or simple and repetitive. Although Miller et al. (1979) report results from employed women only, it is likely that in the future a meticulous examination of the structural imperatives of the housewife role will yield findings that also show an impact on intellectual functioning.

Social Roles

Apart from a woman's satisfaction in a particular role, there is another level of discourse that deals directly with the role itself. What do women's jobs require? What is the history of women's employment, childbearing, or marital status? How are women's separate roles in the educational, work, or family spheres related to one another?

Later in this volume my chapter on work and family roles deals with a number of these questions but particularly with the integrative mechanisms that help women to mesh their potentially conflicting roles in the family and the paid labor force. One major integrative mechanism is timing, and it may be observed in the changing shape of women's life cycles. They live longer, bear fewer children, are more vulnerable to separation and divorce, and have more time after their children are launched to engage in other pursuits. The result is a new kind of "role package" in women's middle years that enables them to meet many competing obligations.

Another major integrative mechanism is society's changing response to women's new roles. A great many new social norms have emerged that reveal more tolerant and supportive public attitudes toward women's work. Special programs and policies for equal employment opportunity, flexible working hours, child care, and pension coverage for the woman worker have either been instituted or are the objective of reformers and feminists.

Women also receive support in the private realm from family, friends, and neighbors. These social networks constitute what Kahn and Antonucci (1980) have called a "convoy of social support." Although not examined in detail here, the impact of women's social networks on their life course is a topic ripe for further research.

In addition to outside social influences on women's social roles, another factor central to change in women's life patterns is not treated in my chapter. This factor is a woman's own choice of career. An increasing number of women are following a nontraditional path of combining family and paid employment; yet an important minority still opt solely for the housewife role. Over the past two decades an important question among researchers has been what background characteristics make it likely that a girl will choose one option or another. Answers have included such factors as achievement motivation, ideal role, and whether a woman's own mother was in the labor force. Gradually, over time, as more women have gone into the work place, there has been growing recognition that employed women, merely by virtue of being employed, do not display any common identifiable personality pattern (Hoffman, 1974). Instead, there is a variety of patterns shaped both by background factors and by present circumstance.

Early work on personal factors in women's employment did point to certain family experiences as possible influences on a girl's aspirations. For example, in their review of the effects of maternal employment, Nye and Hoffman (1963) found daughters of employed middle-class mothers to have higher educational and occupational aspirations. Douvan and Adelson (1966) discovered that adolescent girls aiming for a traditional role took their mothers and female relatives as role models whereas the adolescents geared to occupational achievement took nonfamily members as objects for emulation. Lipman–Blumen (1972) identified direct achievement modes as more frequent in women graduate students pursuing an advanced degree and vicarious achievement more common in the wives of graduate students not so engaged. Birnbaum (1975) studied women honors graduates of the University of Michigan who had finished college 10 to 15 years earlier. Comparing the married employed women, the married nonemployed, and the single, she was able to describe characteristic patterns in the backgrounds of each. The single women more often came from somewhat lower socioeconomic circumstances, were less confident of the ability of males to be providers, were very task-oriented, and saw that social mobility depended on their own occupational distinction. The homemakers came from a successful middle-class background with a traditional nonassertive mother in the home: social activity and motherhood were of prime importance to them. The married employed women also came from successful middle-class backgrounds; however, they had mothers who themselves had followed a nontraditional pattern that combined interest in warm relationships with independent and assertive behavior.

The importance of background factors in shaping a woman's career orientation also appears in Glen Elder's (1974) study of children of the Great Depression. His findings are somewhat different from Birnbaum's, perhaps because of an age difference in the groups studied. He discovered that women who were girls during the Depression and had experienced relatively deprived circumstances were more likely to be full-time homemakers as adults. In many instances their own mothers had been employed by necessity during the Depression, and many household chores had fallen to the girls. They early were inducted into the homemaker role, and their education was foreshortened. By contrast, the girls who later combined marriage and employment were more likely to have come from a less deprived background, to have had more freedom from home responsibilities while they were growing up, and greater opportunity to continue their education.

Studies of mature women interviewed by the National Longitudinal Surveys demonstrate not only the importance of such background factors in women's employment but also the contribution of present circumstance. It is true that nontraditional attitudes toward the woman's role are positively associated with a woman's employment (except in the case of blacks, where there is no difference). And these attitudes are associated with small-town and rural origins and also with having an employed mother as a teenager (Macke, Hudis & Larrick, 1977; Stephan and Schroeder, 1976). However, in addition, women who exhibit some career attachment are more likely also to have a husband with health problems, longer spacing between births of their children, and a husband with a positive attitude toward his wife's employment (Parnes, Jusenius, Blau, Nestel, Shortlidge & Sandell, 1975).

As the rise in women's employment continues, the search for factors in women's decision to work will move to a new level. Rather than explaining life patterns based on static cross-sectional differences (married, employed, etc.), it will be necessary to think of additional factors and a more complex array of patterns. One dimension to add, for example, is the timing and sequence of employment, education, and family commitments. To some extent Sheehy (1976) developed one possible typology with her six categories for women: caregiver, nurturer with delayed achievement, achiever who delays nurturance, never-married, integrator, transient. Another important variable to incorporate in future typologies of women's life patterns is the type and status of employment.

In the end, any comprehensible description of women's social roles must also confront the fact of social change. An increasingly important factor in explanation of traditional or contemporary orientation to the feminine role is the age cohort of the women involved. Changing patterns of women's roles are filtering into the socialization process and altering the very nature of the antecedents and correlates of women's roles (Hoffman, 1977). It is still too soon to say just what is the nature of change, partly because it is still in process, partly because the research has not been done. Yet it soon should be possible to piece together a picture of the relationships between background characteristics and current social role as found cross-sectionally in different groups. Or it may be possible longitudinally to construct a picture of change over time in the lives of a few small groups that have been intensively studied, as did Elder using the Oakland Growth Study (persons born 1922–1923). Or in the future it might be done using Bennett and Elder's (1979) Berkeley sample (born in 1928–1929) or the Birnbaum study (women born in the 1930s).

Taken together, these topics demonstrate the growing complexity of the life course perspective. Psychological issues such as depression and a sense of well-being are significant outcomes to be explained. To understand them one must chart connections over time between earlier and later events in the life-span. Many factors are involved, ranging from internal forces such as physical state, motives, and attitudes to external factors such as stressful life events or economic climate.

In addition some larger institutional and cultural forces and specific types of social policy can intentionally be used to shape the lives of women. These forces are now being mobilized in the United States and abroad as described in the following pages.

Institutional and Cultural Context

Aside from any individual woman's decision to marry, have children, or enter the labor market, there are also institutional forces that affect women's life patterns. Since 1950 the aggregate change in women's employment has been dramatic, reflecting not only the accumulation of many private decisions but also the changing social environment in which such choices were made. Between 1940 and 1968 the proportion of women aged 45 to 54 in the labor force more than doubled, from 25 percent to 53 percent (Women's Bureau, 1969). The labor force participation of mothers with children under 18 multiplied from 9 percent in 1940 to 46 percent in 1974 (Women's Bureau, 1975). The birth rate fell, the divorce rate rose, and the proportion of all single-parent families with children headed by a female now stands around 15 percent, up from 8 percent in 1950 (Ross & Sawhill, 1975). The result today appears to be a greater variety of life options for women: Their family behavior is more varied; their work life may follow any one of several patterns of continuity or interruption; the meshing of family and career is a salient issue for many of them.

These changes in private lives both reflect and require changes in public expectation and practice. Ecklein's chapter in this volume makes clear that changes in women's employment and family behavior are not confined to the United States. Women in the German Democratic Republic have also experienced a marked rise in employment, divorce, obstacles to combining parenting with paid work, and efforts by government to alleviate the problem. Although these developments are more accentuated in the German Democratic Republic than in the U.S., they clearly touch many of the same women's issues. Because women's greater participation in the labor force has occurred throughout the industrial world, the typical modes of response appear to be structurally intertwined with the nature of modern society. Individuals have had to make a variety of adaptations in their social roles and personal lives; the accumulation of their individual actions can be summarized in the issue of *timing,* an issue already briefly reviewed above in connection with changes in social roles and life cycle. In addition, however, governments, employers, and other major institutions of society also have to respond with adjustments and programs aimed at making it somewhat easier for women to follow a flexible life course that intermingles work, education, and family commitments. Such corporate response can be addressed under the rubric of *social policy,* and developments on this front are summarized briefly here. Further consideration of these policy questions appears in my chapter on women's work and family roles, in Ecklein's account of social policies in the German Democratic Republic, and in my concluding chapter.

Ecklein shows how the postwar demography of eastern Germany after World War II, heavy war losses, loss of emigres to the West, in company with its socialist ideology, resulted in a policy of aggressive recruitment of women into the labor force. Women were offered training opportunities with generous stipends and support services. Practical programs instituted maternity leaves, facilities for child care, and paid leaves to pursue further education and technical training. East German programs are very advanced by Western standards, and they constitute a demonstration of the kind of support systems desired by many feminists in both the United States and Europe. Ecklein's account raises two major questions for cross-national study of women in the middle years. First, what programs and policies among advanced industrial societies facilitate women's changing roles? Second, do these programs, when adopted, really "work"? Do they relieve the conflict between family and work responsibility? Are women more satisfied? And what are the difficulties that persist?

Reviews of women's employment and family policies in several countries now make it possible to summarize what appear to be some common themes. Most practical programs fall into three major categories: (1) efforts to promote women's equal employment opportunity; (2) training and compensation to help women reenter the labor market; and (3) support systems and pension rights for the mother and homemaker. In the United States at the present time, the principal legislative and feminist efforts appear to be devoted to the first two types of program, although the third is fast gaining attention. Among European nations, however, particularly in the Eastern bloc, Hilary Land (1979) notes that there is a clear tension between employing women to ease the labor shortage and encouraging them to stay at home to avoid a population crisis. In those countries most concerned with a falling birthrate, family policy encourages women's presence in the home rather than the workplace by instituting such devices as long parental work leaves.

For midlife women in the United States, all three types of policy are relevant because they shape women's life options and ultimate well-being. This is the message of two major U.S. government publications on women in midlife that were recently prepared for the U.S. Congress Joint Economic Committee (1977) and the U.S. House of Representatives Select Committee on Aging (1978). Both publications treat the major types of policy needed to improve women's lives. Significantly, each one gives attention to the three types of policy outlined in the foregoing paragraph related to employment, job reentry, and credit or support for work in the home.

Work-oriented policies would improve women's employment opportunties by innovative work scheduling, provision of child care, and enforcement of affirmative action guidelines. (Giele & Kahne, 1978; Sandell, 1977; Strober, 1977).

Reentry policies consider women's prior experience, paid or unpaid, as worthy of credential. If such experience is given credit, it provides an otherwise "inexperienced" woman with a record of activity that constitutes legitimate background for further education or paid employment (Hybels & Mueller, 1978). Educational opportunities are expanding to foster more continuing education, counseling, apprenticeship, and vocational training (Briggs, 1977; Entine, 1978; Roby, 1977; Schlossberg & Waters, 1978). The displaced homemaker, a woman with homemaking experience who seeks to reenter the labor market after the loss of a breadwinner, is increasingly receiving psychological support, benefit from advocacy of her cause, and instruction on self-help (Sommers & Shields, 1978).

Family-oriented policies would give credit to the woman who has devoted a significant portion of her life to homemaking and child care. She would receive special Social Security retirement benefits through an earnings-splitting device that would establish her work record in conjunction with her husband's and lessen the effect of work discontinuities on retirement income (Blumberg, 1977; Giele & Kahne, 1978). New proposals by the Social Security Administration (U.S. Department of Health, Education, and Welfare, 1979) and various economists (Holden, 1980) promise further developments along these lines to give explicit recognition to women's unpaid work in the home. Already existing European programs for family allowances and benefits covering children suggest that the future will probably bring more public programs in support of the family—such as preschool programs and health screening—even where the mother is not employed.

The appearance of these common policy themes in several countries suggests that there are some predictable public responses to the changing life patterns of women. What evidence do we have, however, that these policies are serving the purposes intended? It is, frankly, too soon to tell. The German Democratic Republic is one of the few places where a widespread policy of sex equality and encouragement of women's participation in the labor force has been accompanied by a wide array of educational, family, and employment policies that many other contemporary working women desire. Yet it is difficult to gauge what part of women's happiness in East Germany may be directly attributed to these programs.

Ecklein's chapter suggests some of the satisfactions and frustrations that are experienced where such programs are adopted. On the happiness side of the ledger, East German women register satisfaction with employment, promotion, and pay opportunities. They use the maternity leaves, public child care facilities, and family allowances with evident enthusiasm. Nonetheless, certain frustrations and disappointments remain: personal ties appear to be fragile, as reflected in the high divorce rate; women still do more than their fair share of housework and show signs of overburdening. The family's and society's interest in proper care for the next generation also competes with socialist and feminist goals for women's equal rights and occupational achievement. Ultimately, Ecklein's chapter thus raises questions about whether the same pattern of gains and frustrations will accompany adoption of advanced social programs for women's equalty in other countries as well.

NEW DATA SOURCES AND FUTURE QUESTIONS

Because interest in the middle years is relatively recent, there is still some question as to how they should be studied. This chapter suggests that an implicit schema has already emerged in the life course perspective. In addition, there is rough agreement on the dimensions of experience that should be examined. The chapters presented here, however, leave many questions open for future appraisal. Fortunately, this volume includes a valuable appendix by Toni Antonucci that gives a number of available data sources for future research. Antonucci identifies the major sources of *primary* data on women's changing life patterns. Her list includes extensive longitudinal studies that have systematically followed the lives of selected individuals, sometimes over several decades. It also includes large data sets with background variables, present social characteristics, and career patterns that permit comparisons across several age groups at different historical periods.

Antonucci's work provides the raw material for testing connections between the major dimensions of women's lives. In addition, it suggests a range of possible methods—longitudinal and cross-sectional, quantitative and qualitative—for deriving patterns of midlife in different eras. Ideally, one might use these data to reconstruct the life histories of one age group in depth and then compare them with those of another generation. Such a contrast would help to identify both what is common to the middle years in every period and every class and what is peculiar to the women of one background or another.

Such questions are already discernible in present research and policy discussion and should receive further elaboration. One major set of questions has to do with the *universals* of the middle years. What are the patterns of psychological development in adulthood? Are there any predictable and recurring sequences that we see in the lives of women? Are some human needs universal? For women, do those needs result in some recurrent role structures, scheduling patterns, or other solutions that should be identified and safeguarded? Or alternatively, where change is pervasive, are there new social programs and tested solutions that promote the well-being of adult women?

Within these broad outlines, *particular variations* in life pattern among midlife women are still bound to occur. To what extent do they depend on historical circumstance, background, or present social condition? What different family origins lead to each of the major options in the adult female role? What determines such patterns as early marriage, high fertility, or low education and unemployment? And what consequences do all these alternative roles have for health and happiness?

This introductory chapter appropriately ends on such a questioning note. The codification of research on women in the middle years has begun. Ultimately, however, the test of such conceptual frameworks as presented in this volume will be made on new research. Some future work can profitably be based on data that are already available but still untapped. In other instances, new facts must be collected. Both types of effort will move forward with benefit from insights contributed by the authors of this volume.

REFERENCES

Bardwick, J.M. 1980. "The Seasons of a Woman's Life." In D.G. McGuigan, (Ed.), *Women's Lives: New Theory, Research & Policy*. Ann Arbor, MI: University of Michigan, Center for Continuing Education of Women.

Barnett, R.C. 1975. "Sex Differences and Age Trends in Occupational Preference and Occupational Prestige." *Journal of Counseling Psychology* **22**(1):35–38.

Barnett, R.C., and G.K. Baruch. 1978. "Women in the Middle Years: A Critique of Research and Theory." *Psychology of Women Quarterly* **3** (2):187–197.

Bart, P. B. 1971. "Depression in Middle-Aged Women." In V. Gornick and B.K. Moran (Eds.), *Woman in Sexist Society*. New York: Basic Books.

Bart, P.B., and M. Grossman. 1978. "Menopause." In M.T. Notman and C.C. Nadelson (Eds.), *The Woman Patient: Medical and Psychological Interfaces*. New York: Plenum Press.

Bennett, S.K., and G.H. Elder, Jr. 1979. "Women's Work in the Family Economy: A Study of Depression Hardship in Women's Lives." *Journal of Family History* **4** (2):153–176.

Bernard, J. 1972. *The Future of Marriage*. New York: World Publishing.

Birnbaum, J.A. 1975. "Life Patterns and Self-Esteen in Gifted Family-oriented and Career-oriented Women." In M. Mednick, S. Tangri, and L.W. Hoffman (Eds.), *Women and Achievement: Social and Motivational Analysis*. New York: Hemisphere–Halsted.

Block, M.R., J.L. Davidson, J.D. Grambs, and K.E. Serock. 1978. *Uncharted Territory: Issues and Concerns of Women Over 40*. University of Maryland, Center on Aging. Silver Spring, MD: Lifespan Research Associates.

Blumberg, G.G. 1977. "Federal Income Tax and Social Security Law." In U.S. Congress, Joint Economic Committee. *American Women Workers in a Full Employment Economy*. Washington, DC: Government Printing Office.

Briggs, N. 1977. "Apprenticeship." In U.S. Congress, Joint Economic Committee. *American Women Workers in a Full Employment Economy*. Washington, DC: Government Printing Office.

Brim, O.G., Jr. 1966. "Socialization through the Life Cycle." In O.G. Brim, Jr. and S. Wheeler (Eds.), *Socialization after Childhood: Two Essays*. New York: Wiley.

Brim, O.G., Jr., and J. Kagan. 1980. "Constancy and Change: A View of the Issues." In O.G. Brim, Jr. and J. Kagan (Eds.), *Constancy and Change in Human Development.* Cambridge, MA: Harvard University Press.

Bronfenbrenner, U. 1979. *The Ecology of Human Development: Experiments by Nature and Design.* Cambridge, MA: Harvard University Press.

Brown, G.W., M.N. Bhrolchain, and T. Harris. 1975. "Social Class and Psychiatric Disturbance Among Women in an Urban Population." *Sociology* 9:225–254.

Campbell, A., P.E. Converse, and W.L. Rodgers. 1976. *The Quality of American Life: Perceptions, Evaluations, and Satisfactions.* New York: Russell Sage Foundation.

Chodorow, N. 1978. *The Reproduction of Mothering.* Berkeley: University of California Press.

Demos, J. 1977. "Changing Life Cycles in American History." Paper presented at the Smithsonian Institution's Sixth International Symposium. June 14–17.

———. 1978. "Old Age in Early New England." In J. Demos and S.S. Boocock (Eds.), *Turning Points: Historical and Sociological Essays on the Family.* Chicago: University of Chicago Press.

Douvan, E., and J. Adelson. 1966. *The Adolescent Experience.* New York: Wiley.

Elder, G.H., Jr. 1974. *Children of the Great Depression: Social Change in Life Experience.* Chicago: University of Chicago Press.

———. 1975. "Age Differentiation and the Life Course." *Annual Review of Sociology* 1:165–190.

Entine, A.D. 1978. "The Role of Continuing Education." In U.S. House of Representatives. Select Committee on Aging. *Women in Midlife—Security and Fulfillment* (I). Washington, DC: Government Printing Office.

Erikson, E.H. 1950. *Childhood and Society.* New York: W.W. Norton & Co., Inc.

Fidell, L. 1978. "Employment Status, Role Dissatisfaction, and the Housewife Syndrome." Unpublished manuscript. Psychology Department, California State University at Northridge.

Fisher, S. 1973. *Understanding the Female Orgasm.* New York: Basic Books.

Fiske, M. 1980. "Changing Hierarchies of Commitment in Adulthood." In N.J. Smelser and E.H. Erikson (Eds.), *Themes of Work and Love in Adulthood.* Cambridge, MA: Harvard University Press.

Friedan, B. 1979. "Feminism Takes a New Turn." *The New York Times Magazine.* November 18, pp. 40ff.

Fuchs, E. 1978. *The Second Season: Life, Love and Sex for Women in the Middle Years.* New York: Doubleday.

Giele, J.Z. 1978. *Women and the Future: Changing Sex Roles in Modern America.* New York: The Free Press.

———. 1980. "Adulthood as Transcendence of Age and Sex." In N.J. Smelser and E.H. Erikson (Eds.), *Themes of Work and Love in Adulthood.* Cambridge, MA: Harvard University Press.

Giele, J. and H. Kahne. 1978. "Meeting Work and Family Responsibilities: Proposals for Flexibility." In U.S. House of Representatives. Select Committee on Aging. *Women in Midlife—Security and Fulfillment* (I). Washington, DC: Government Printing Office.

Gould, R.L. 1978. *Transformations: Growth and Change in Adult Life*. New York: Simon and Schuster.

Gove, W.R., and M. Hughes. 1979. "Possible Causes of the Apparent Sex Differences in Physical Health: An Empirical Investigation." *American Sociological Review* **44** (1):126–146.

———. 1981. "Beliefs vs. Data: More on the Illness Behavior of Men and Women." *American Sociological Review* **46** (1):123–128.

Grimm, E.E. 1969. "Women's Attitudes and Reactions to Childbearing." In G.D. Goldman and D.S. Milman (Eds.), *Modern Woman, Her Psychology and Sexuality*. Springfield, IL: Charles C. Thomas.

Gutmann, D. 1977. "The Cross-Cultural Perspective: Notes Toward a Comparative Psychology of Aging." In J.E. Birren and K.W. Schaie (Eds.), *Handbook of the Psychology of Aging*. New York: D. Van Nostrand.

Guttentag, M., and Susan Salasin. 1977. "Women, Men, and Mental Health." In L.A. Cater, A.F. Scott, and W. Martyna (Eds.), *Women and Men: Changing Roles, Relationships, and Perceptions*. New York: Praeger.

Heide, W.S. 1978. "Feminism: Making a Difference in Our Health." In M.T. Notman and C.T. Nadelson (Eds.), *The Woman Patient: Medical and Psychological Interfaces*. New York: Plenum Press.

Hite, S. 1976. *The Hite Report: A Nationwide Study of Female Sexuality*. New York: Macmillan.

Hoffman, L.W. 1977. "Changes in Family Roles, Socialization, and Sex Differences." *American Psychologist,* **32** (8):644–657.

Holden, K.C. 1980. "Supplemental OASI Benefits to Homemakers, through Current Spouse Benefits, a Homemaker's Credit, and Child-care Drop-out Years." Conference on Social Security and the Changing Roles of Women. Madison, WI: University of Wisconsin, Institute for Research on Poverty and the Women's Studies Research Center, April 11, 12.

Hybels, J.H., and M.W. Mueller. 1978. "Volunteer Work: Recognition and Accreditation." U.S. House of Representatives. Select Committee on Aging. *Women in Midlife—Security and Fulfillment* (I). Washington, DC: Government Printing Office.

Ilfeld, F., Jr. 1977. "Sex Differences in Psychiatric Symptomatology." Paper presented at the annual meeting of the American Psychological Association, San Francisco.

Kahn, R.L., and T.C. Antonucci. 1980. "Convoys over the Life Course: Attachment, Roles and Social Support." In P.B. Baltes and O.G. Brim, Jr. (Eds.), *Life Span Development and Behavior,* Vol. 3. New York: Academic Press.

Kahne, H. 1978. "Memo on Economics-Related Research on Women and Work in the Middle Years." Paper presented to the SSRC Study Group on Women: Work and Personality in the Middle Years. Waltham, MA., Brandeis University, January 28.

Keniston, K. 1965. *The Uncommitted: Alienated Youth in American Society*. New York: Dell.

Kinsey, A.C., W.B. Pomeroy, C.J. Martin, and O.H. Gebhard. 1953. *Sexual Behavior in the Human Female.* Philadelphia: W.B. Saunders.

Kohn, M.L., and C. Schooler. 1978. "The Reciprocal Effects of the Substantive Complexity of Work and Intellectual Flexibility: A Longitudinal Assessment." *American Journal of Sociology* **84** (1):24–52.

Land, H. 1979. "The Changing Place of Women in Europe." *Daedalus* **108** (2): 73–94.

Levinson, D.J. 1978. *The Seasons of a Man's Life.* New York: Knopf.

Lipman–Blumen, J. 1972. "How Ideology Shapes Women's Lives." *Scientific American,* March, 34–42.

McGuigan, D.G. 1980. "Exploring Women's Lives: An Introduction." In D.G. McGuigan (Ed.), *Women's Lives: New Theory, Research & Policy.* Ann Arbor, MI: University of Michigan, Center for Continuing Education of Women.

McKinlay, S.M., and J.B. McKinlay. 1973. "Selected Studies of the Menopause: An Annotated Bibliography." *Journal of Biosocial Science* **5**:533–555.

Macke, A.S., P.M. Hudis, and D. Larrick. 1977. "Sex Role Attitudes and Employment among Women: A Dynamic Model of Change and Continuity." Paper prepared for the Secretary of Labor's Invitational Conference on the National Longitudinal Surveys of Mature Women. Washington, DC. January 26.

Marcus, A.C., and T.E. Seeman. 1981. "Sex Differences in Health: A Reexamination of the Nurturant Role Hypothesis." *American Sociological Review* **46** (1):119–123.

Masters, W.H., and V. Johnson. 1966. "Geriatric Sexual Response." In *Human Sexual Response.* Boston: Little, Brown.

Mechanic, D. 1980. "Comment on Gove and Hughes." *American Sociological Review* **45** (3):513–514.

Miller, J.B. 1976. *Toward a New Psychoiogy of Women.* Boston: Beacon Press.

Miller, J., C. Schooler, M.L. Kohn, and K.A. Miller. 1979. "Women and Work: The Psychological Effects of Occupational Conditions." *American Journal of Sociology* **85** (1):66–94.

Mortimer, J.T., and R.G. Simmons. 1978. "Adult Socialization." *Annual Review of Sociology* **4**:421–454.

Mostow, E., and P. Newberry. 1975. "Work Role and Depression in Women: A Comparison of Workers and Housewives in Treatment." *American Journal of Orthopsychiatry* **45** (4):538–548.

Neugarten, B.L., V. Wood, R.J. Kraines, and B. Loomis. 1968. "Women's Attitudes Toward Menopause." In B.L. Neugarten (Ed.), *Middle Age and Aging.* Chicago: University of Chicago Press.

Notman, Malkah T. 1979. "Midlife Concerns of Women: Implications of the Menopause." *American Journal of Psychiatry* **136** (10):1270–1274.

Notman, M.T., and C.C. Nadelson. 1978. "The Woman Patient." In M.T. Notman and C.C. Nadelson (Eds.), *The Woman Patient: Medical and Psychological Interfaces.* New York: Plenum.

Nye, F.I., and L.W. Hoffman. 1963. *The Employed Mother in America.* Skokie, IL: Rand McNally.

Osherson, S.D. 1980. *Holding On or Letting Go: Men and Career Change at Midlife.* New York: Free Press.

Parker, E. 1960. *The Seven Ages of Woman.* Baltimore: The Johns Hopkins Press.

Parlee, M.B. 1973. "The Premenstrual Syndrome." *Psychology Bulletin* **80** (6): 454–465.

Parnes, H.S., C.L. Jusenius, F. Blau, G. Nestel, R. Shortlidge, Jr., S. Sandell. 1975. *Dual Careers: A Longitudinal Analysis of the Labor Market Experience of Women,* Vol. 4. Columbus, OH: Center for Human Resources Research, Ohio State University.

Parsons, J.E. (Ed.) 1980. *The Psychobiology of Sex Differences and Sex Roles.* New York: McGraw-Hill.

Pearlin, L.I. 1975. "Sex Roles and Depression." In N. Datan and L.H. Ginsberg (Eds.), *Life-Span Developmental Psychology: Normative Life Crises,* New York: Academic Press.

———. 1978. "Social Differences in the Problematic Experiences of Adulthood." Paper delivered at the Annual Meeting of the American Sociological Association, San Francisco, September 4–8.

Pearlin, L.I., and J.C. Johnson. 1977. "Marital Status, Life Strains, and Depression." *American Sociological Review* **42** (5):704–715.

Perlmutter, J.F. 1978. "A Gynecological Approach to Menopause." In M.T. Notman and C.C. Nadelson (Eds.), *The Woman Patient: Medical and Psychological Interfaces.* New York: Plenum.

Perun, P.J., and D. D.V. Bielby. 1980. "Structure and Dynamics of the Individual Life Course." In K.W. Back (Ed.), *Life Course: Integrative Theories and Exemplary Populations.* AAAS Selected Symposium 41. Boulder, CO: Westview Press.

Radloff, L. 1975. "Sex Differences in Depression: The Effects of Occupation and Marital Status." *Sex Roles* **1** (3):249–265.

Riley, M.W. 1978. "Aging, Social Change, and the Power of Ideas." *Daedalus* **107** (4):39–52.

Roby, P.A. 1977. "Vocational Education." In U.S. Congress, Joint Economic Committee. *American Women Workers in a Full Employment Economy.* Washington, DC: Government Printing Office.

Ross, H.L., and I.V. Sawhill. 1975. *Time of Transition: The Growth of Families Headed by Women.* Washington, DC: Urban Institute.

Rossi, A.S. 1977. "A Biosocial Perspective on Parenting." *Daedalus* **106** (2):1–31.

———. 1980. "Life Span Theories and Women's Lives." *Signs* **6** (1, Part 2): 4–32.

Ruzek, S.B. 1978. *The Women's Health Movement: Feminist Alternatives to Medical Control.* New York: Praeger.

Sandell, S.H. 1977. "Life-time Participation in the Labor Force and Unemployment among Mature Women." In U.S. Congress, Joint Economic Committee. *Amer-*

ican Women Workers in a Full Employment Economy. Washington, DC: Government Printing Office.

Scarf, M. 1980. *Unfinished Business: Pressure Points in the Lives of Women.* New York: Doubleday.

Schlossberg. N.K., and E.E. Waters. 1978. "Counseling: Shifting the Balance from Problem to Possibility." In U.S. House of Representatives. Select Committee on Aging. *Women in Midlife—Security and Fulfillment* (I). Washington, DC: Government Printing Office.

Scott, A.C. 1974. "Closing the Muscle Gap." *Ms. Magazine,* September, 49ff.

Seaman, B. 1972. *Free and Female; The New Sexual Role of Women.* New York: Fawcett Books Group—CBS Publications.

Segrè, J. 1978. "Self-Concept and Depression: Mothers Returning to Work or Remaining at Home." Paper presented at the annual meeting of the Eastern Psychological Association. Washington, DC. March 30.

Sheehy, G. 1976. *Passages: Predictable Crises of Adult Life.* New York: Dutton.

Smelser, N.J. 1980. "Vicissitudes of Work and Love in Anglo-American Society." In N.J. Smelser and E.H. Erikson (Eds.), *Themes of Work and Love in Adulthood.* Cambridge, MA: Harvard University Press.

Smelser, N.J., and E.H. Erikson (Eds.) 1980. *Themes of Work and Love in Adulthood.* Cambridge, MA: Harvard University Press.

Sommers, T. and L. Shields. 1978. "Problems of the Displaced Homemaker." In U.S. House of Representatives. Select Committee on Aging. *Women in Midlife—Security and Fulfillment* (I). Washington, DC: Government Printing Office.

Spilerman, S. 1977. "Work During the Middle and Late Years." In Russell Sage Foundation (Ed.), *The Future and the Past: Essays on Programs.* New York: Russell Sage Foundation.

Stephan, P., and L.D. Schroeder. 1976. "Career Commitment and Labor Force Participation of Married Women." Revised version of paper presented at 1976 meeting of the Western Economic Association.

Strober, M.H. 1977. "Economic Aspects of Child Care." In U.S. Congress, Joint Economic Committee. *American Women Workers in a Full Employment Economy.* Washington, DC: Government Printing Office.

U.S. Congress. Joint Economic Committee. 1977. *American Women Workers in a Full Employment Economy.* Washington, DC: Government Printing Office.

U.S. Department of Health, Education, and Welfare. 1979. *Social Security and the Changing Roles of Men and Women.* Washington, DC: Department of Health, Education, and Welfare.

U.S. House of Representatives. Select Committee on Aging. 1978. *Women in Midlife—Security and Fulfillment* (I). Washington, DC: Government Printing Office.

Vaillant, G.E. 1977. *Adaptation to Life.* Boston: Little, Brown.

Verbrugge, L.M. 1980. "Comment on Walter R. Gove and Michael Hughes, 'Possible Causes of the Apparent Sex Differences in Physical Health.'" *American Sociological Review* **45** (3):507–513.

Weideger, P. 1977. *Menstruation and Menopause.* New York: Dell.

Whiting, B.B. 1978. "Problems of American Middle Class Women in Their Middle Years—A Comparative Approach." Paper prepared for the SSRC Study Group on Women: Work and Personality in the Middle Years. Waltham, MA: Brandeis University.

Women's Bureau. U.S. Department of Labor. 1969. *1969 Handbook of Women Workers.* Bulletin 294. Washington, DC: Government Printing Office.

——. U.S. Department of Labor. 1975. *1975 Handbook of Women Workers.* Bulletin 297. Washington, DC: Government Printing Office.

CHAPTER 2

Women and Health: The Social Dimensions of Biomedical Data

CONSTANCE A. NATHANSON
School of Hygiene and Public Health
Johns Hopkins University

GERDA LORENZ
Department of Social Relations
Johns Hopkins University

It is in great part . . . the anxiety of being a woman that devastates the feminine body.

SIMONE DE BEAUVOIR (1971)

The role played by women's physical selves in the shaping of their adult lives is, in the current climate of feminist opinion, a question as much political as social or biological. And, as Janet Giele notes in her introductory chapter to this volume, it is a question on which experienced researchers disagree. In this chapter, we have attempted to present and evaluate the most recent evidence regarding women's health and physical status with an even hand, and to eschew polemics. As sociologists, we adopt the point of view that women's biological functions and capacities represent a set of unique possibilities. How these possibilities are employed and interpreted is, to a large but not unlimited extent, socially determined.

Any study of the place of women in society must inevitably deal with questions of health and disease. The social position of women has direct consequences both for their health, as Preston's (1976) studies of sex differences in mortality have shown, and for the quality of their medical care. In an address to the American Gynecological Society in 1941, the medical historian, Henry Sigerist (1960) remarked that the progress of gynecology owed as much to changes in society's attitudes toward women and in their position in the social structure as to advances in medical science.

The significance of illness to the sociological study of women, however, goes beyond the fact of observed correlations between social status and health levels. Illness among women is not simply an outcome of their relative position in the social structure; it is a defining characteristic of that position. From time immemorial, feminine biology has been regarded as a source of physical incapacity. Aristotle is quoted by Simone de Beauvoir (1971) as saying that, "We should regard the female nature as afflicted with a natural defectiveness" [xvi]. Vulnerability to disease has been used both as a reason for limiting the participation of women in roles outside of the domestic sphere and as a sanction against those women who have not accepted their customary fate. How the twin threats of illness and sterility were used by nineteenth century physicians to bolster traditional gender role norms has been extensively documented by recent historical research (Burstyn, 1973; Ehrenreich & English, 1979; Smith-Rosenberg & Rosenberg, 1973). And in contemporary American society, health and disease have become major symbols in the struggle for social equality between men and women. Women's traditional roles are described as postively harmful to their health (Bernard, 1972; Gove & Tudor, 1973), and health care is seen as a vehicle for the emancipation of women from male-dominated institutions. Indeed, the women's health movement is at the forefront among challengers of the traditional norms (Boston Women's Health Book Collective, 1979; Marieskind, 1975).

Women themselves are hardly immune to the elaborate framework that society has constructed around their biological functions. Bodily sensations are perceived, labeled, and responded to within the context of meanings and behavioral expectations supplied by that framework. In this report, data are presented on the status of the physical health of American women in their middle years as reflected in statistics on mortality, illness, and use of health services. These data are very largely the outcome of social rather than biological processes.

The body of the report is divided into three sections. The first section is a descriptive summary of data currently available on the health of adult women in the United States. Although the central focus is on the status of women's health, considerable use is made of data on sex differences in health indexes, both in this section and throughout the report. These data draw attention to the social determinants of variation in health and disease, since relatively few of the myriad sex differences observed can be explained on a direct biological basis.

The second major section of the report attempts to answer the question of how mortality and illness among women are related to their biological makeup and to their various social roles. The final section identifies the major research issues suggested by this review and indicates how these issues might be addressed in empirical investigation.

MORTALITY, ILLNESS, ILLNESS BEHAVIOR, AND THE USE OF HEALTH SERVICES

Mortality

In the United States, as in other developed countries, death rates among females are substantially below male death rates (Spiegelman & Erhardt, 1974; Wunsch, 1980). This difference is present in all age groups and has been observed since at least the beginning of the twentieth century (Retherford, 1975). During this period, sex mortality differentials have increased owing both to greater improvement in female relative to male death rates and to increases in male death rates relative to those of females for leading causes of death (Preston & Weed, 1976; Shryock & Siegel, 1975; Wunsch, 1980). Furthermore, it is in the age group over 50 that death rates for men and women have most sharply diverged. Between the ages 5 and 50 the pattern of sex mortality differentials has remained relatively stable (Retherford, 1975). There are major variations in the size of the male excess of mortality during adult life, however. It is between the ages of 15−24 and 45−64 that men have the highest death rates relative to women (Enterline, 1961; National Center for Health Statistics, 1973, Series 20, No.15).

A series of mortality studies carried out over the last few years have clearly demonstrated that the cause of death primarily responsible for increasing sex mortality differentials is cardiovascular disease (National Center for Health Statistics, 1971, Series 20, No.11; Preston & Weed, 1976; Retherford, 1975). Death rates from cardiovascular disease have declined over the past 25 years, and they have declined more rapidly for women than for men (National Center for Health Statistics, 1974, Series 20, No.16). Other causes of death that contribute substantially to sex mortality differentials are cancer of the lung and bronchitis (Preston, 1970; Preston & Weed, 1976; Retherford, 1975).

With these data as background, we can begin to look more closely at the mortality experience of adult women. In the United States in 1977, the expectation of life at birth was 70.0 years for white males and 77.7 years for white females. The corresponding figures for nonwhites (95 percent or more black) were 64.6 years and 73.1 years respectively (National Center for Health Statistics, 1980c). The average 25-year-old woman in the United States has two-thirds of her total life span before her; at age 54 approximately one-third still remains (National Center for Health Statistics, 1980c). Her probability of dying at age 25 is less than one in 1000 if she is white, and slightly larger than one in 1000 if she is black. By age 54 these probabilities have increased about ten-fold, but they are still about half the comparable probabilities for men.

Among women aged 25−39, the leading causes of death are cancer (primarily breast cancer), cardiovascular disease, accidents, and suicide. In the 40−54 age group, cirrhosis of the liver displaces suicide among these four principal causes. However, the highest rates of suicide among women are observed in the 40−54 age group in contrast to a much later age peak among men (National Center for Health Statistics, 1980b).

There is widespread consensus that current sex mortality differentials are due primarily to environmental rather than to biological factors (Kitagawa, 1977). Differences in life-style are postulated to create different mortality risks for men and women (Gove, 1973; Nathanson, 1977a, 1977b; Ortmeyer, 1979). Consequently, there has been considerable speculation concerning the possible effects on women's mortality rates of changes in life-style that bring women's roles into closer correspondence with those of men (House, 1974; Ibrahim, 1980; Lewis & Lewis, 1977; Nathanson, 1977b; Reeder, 1976; Waldron, 1976). This speculation has focused on three causes of death: cardiovascular disease, suicide, and lung cancer. However, although there is unequivocal evidence to support the contention that lung cancer death rates are increasing among women (Beamis, Stein, & Andrews, 1975; Gentlemen & Forbes, 1974; Johnson, 1977; Stolley, 1977), the evidence for increases in cardiovascular disease and suicide rates is conflicting at best (Johnson, 1977). Examination of the death rates among adult women for these three causes over the period 1968−1978 shows uniform declines in mortality rates from cardiovascular disease, no consistent trends in suicide rates, and uniform increases in lung cancer rates (National Center for Health Statistics: Annual). The latter finding is directly attributable to increases in the proportion of women smokers in each successive age cohort (Gentleman & Forbes, 1974; National Center for Health Statistics, 1970, Series 10, No.59).

On the basis of his analysis of recent changes in sex mortality differentials in the United States, Johnson (1977) concludes that increases in stress-related mortality among women, resulting from their "entry into statuses once occupied overwhelmingly by men . . . will not be reflected in mortality rates for some time to come. The most that can be said now is that it is too soon to tell [24]."

Illness and Illness Behavior

The high rates of reported illness and associated limitation of activity among adult women relative to the frequency of illness reported by men in the same age groups have been documented in several recently published papers (Nathanson, 1975, 1977a; Verbrugge, 1976a, 1976b), and the problems of interpretation presented by these data have been given extensive consideration (Gove & Hughes, 1979; Mechanic, 1976; Nathanson, 1978; Verbrugge, 1979). Data to describe the health status of the United States population are derived primarily from population-based health surveys, in which the presence of illness is determined from self-reports rather than from physical examinations or laboratory tests. Furthermore, the criteria by which illness is defined are behavioral; the individual must have taken some action, either to limit his or her "usual" activities or to obtain medical attention, for his condition to be counted as an illness. In evaluating the illness data that we present, it is essential that these aspects of survey methodology be kept in mind.

Total acute and chronic condition rates and days of restricted activity and bed disability (days confined to bed) associated with these conditions are presented in Table 2.1 by age and sex. These rates are based on data collected by the U.S. National Health Survey during 1977–1978.[1] Pregnancy is omitted from the calculation of the rates shown (it is defined as an acute condition by the National Center for Health Statistics) not because it is unimportant in its impact on women's health status, but because it is a conceptually distinct condition, and its impact should and will be considered

Table 2.1. Selected Indexes of Illness by Sex and Age: United States, 1978

Indexes of Illness	Age			
	<17	17–44	45–64	65+
Number of acute conditions per 100 persons per year[a]				
Male	306.1	202.7	123.5	96.3
Female	311.4	235.1	160.7	119.2
Ratio (female/male)	1.02	1.16	1.30	1.24
Number of chronic conditions per 100 persons per year				
Male	4.2	9.1	24.3	48.2
Female	3.6	7.9	23.0	42.7
Ratio (female/male)	0.86	0.87	0.95	0.89
Days of restricted activity per person per year[a,b]				
Male	10.7	12.7	23.2	35.1
Female	11.8	15.7	28.1	43.9
Ratio (female/male)	1.10	1.24	1.21	1.25
Days of bed disability per person per year[a,b]				
Male	4.9	4.3	7.3	14.2
Female	5.6	6.5	10.1	14.8
Ratio (female/male)	1.14	1.51	1.38	1.05

[a] Deliveries and disorders of pregnancy and the puerperium excluded from these rates.

[b] Includes days of restricted activity and bed disability associated with acute and chronic conditions combined.

Sources: National Center for Health Statistics, 1979. Current Estimates from the Health Interview Survey, United States, 1978. *Vital and Health Statistics,* Series 10, Number 130. DHEW Publication No. (PHS) 80–1551. Hyattsville, MD. National Center for Health Statistics, 1979. Acute Conditions: Incidence and Associated Disability, United States, July 1977–June, 1978. *Vital and Health Statistics.* Series 10, Number 132. DHEW Publication No. (PHS) 79-1560. Hyattsville, MD.

[1] Unless otherwise indicated, morbidity data are either taken directly or calculated from National Health Survey statistics published by the National Center for Health Statistics. All National Health Survey publications used in this report are listed in the bibliography.

separately. Deliveries and disorders of pregnancey and the puerperium comprise 4 percent of acute conditions reported by women 17−44 and account for 10 percent of the restricted activity days and 11 percent of the bed disability days attributed to acute conditions.

In agreement with repeated observations, acute conditions are more frequently reported by adult women than by adult men; the largest sex difference is in the age group 45−64. Women in this age group are, furthermore, substantially more likely than their male age peers to report that they limited their usual activities or took to bed in response to a perceived illness. Although chronic conditions are more often reported by men than by women, women consistently have more restricted activity or bed disability days per condition. The data presented in Table 2.1 are for the years 1977−1978, as noted earlier. Rates and sex ratios for both acute and chronic conditions fluctuate from year to year. However, examination of these data over a 13-year period (1963−1976) does not indicate any underlying trends, either upward or downward, in these rates.

Respiratory illness is the acute condition most frequently reported by both men and women. The principal chronic conditions reported by women in the two age groups, 17−44 and 45−64, are shown in Table 2.2, together with the sex ratio for each condition. Among younger women, the leading chronic conditions are back problems (impairments, back or spine), asthma, with or without hay fever, and mental or nervous conditions, whereas arthritis and rheumatism, heart conditions, and hypertension are more often reported by women in the older age group. Both older and younger women are much more likely than men of the same age to report arthritis, rheumatism or hypertension. The difficulties in interpretation of these data are suggested by the results of a study in which diagnoses of heart disease and hypertension made on the basis of a health examination were compared with diagnoses based on a self-administered medical history (National Center for Health Statistics, 1967, Series 2, No. 22). The medical history led to substantially more diagnoses of both conditions among women; health examination results indicated about the same number of conditions in both sexes. As Mechanic (1976) notes, "These and other data make measures of chronic disease by sex based on self-reported medical history appear highly suspect [35]."

Health survey data do not allow the investigator to conclude that adult women are sicker than adult men. Thoughtful analyses of these data (cited earlier) have led to a number of explanatory hypotheses, many of which will be considered in the course of this report. Although it has been suggested that women indeed *are* more frequently ill than men (Bernard, 1972; Gove & Hughes, 1979; Thompson & Brown, 1980), it is more often assumed that sex differences found in health surveys are an artifact caused either by differences in reporting tendencies (women are more likely than men to reveal illness to a health interviewer) or in illness behavior (women are both

Table 2.2.   Major Chronic Conditions Causing Limitation of Activity Among Women 17–44 and 45–64, and Sex Ratio for these Conditions: United States, 1974

Condition	Age	
	17–44	45–64
Impairments, back or spine		
Rate per 1000 women	7.427	16.441
Ratio (female/male)	1.18	0.87
Asthma, with or without hay fever		
Rate per 1000 women	6.217	6.817
Ratio (female/male)	0.93	0.90
Mental or nervous conditions		
Rate per 1000 women	4.085	14.614
Ratio (female/male)	1.01	1.11
Impairments, lower body		
Rate per 1000 women	3.824	10.03
Ratio (female/male)	0.60	0.57
Other musculoskeletal		
Rate per 1000 women	3.769	18.134
Ratio (female/male)	0.82	0.92
Arthritis and rheumatism		
Rate per 1000 women	3.466	51.46
Ratio (female/male)	1.78	1.63
Heart conditions		
Rate per 1000 women	2.875	36.00
Ratio (female/male)	0.83	0.59
Hypertension without heart involvement		
Rate per 1000 women	2.146	27.09
Ratio (female/male)	1.93	1.81

Source: National Center for Health Statistics. 1977. Limitation of Activity Due to Chronic Conditions. *Vital and Health Statistics* Series 10, No. 111. DHEW Publication No. (HRA) 77-1537. Rockville, MD.

more aware of illness symptoms and more likely to take action in response to perceived symptoms).

Data from a large number of studies suggest that there are sex differences in illness behavior. Women are more likely than men to express their fears and worries (Knupfer, Clark, & Room, 1966; Warheit, Holzer, Arey, 1973), to be sensitive to symptoms of illness (Hetherington & Hopkins, 1969), and to believe themselves susceptible to disease (Kirscht, Haefner, Kegeles, et al., 1966). At the same time, their levels of health knowledge are higher than those of men, and they have a more "scientific" approach to medical care (Feldman, 1966; Suchman, 1965). The contrasting illness behavior of men and women is further highlighted in data reported by Andersen, Lion, and Anderson (1976). When asked to give a reason for their last physical examination, the overwhelming majority of women in all age groups (18–64) stated that it was voluntary (in response to a symptom or for preventive purposes), whereas over half of men aged 18−34, and one-third of older men, stated that it was involuntary (required for a job, insurance, or something else). These studies do not, of course, explain the differences in illness behavior between men and women. They do, however, strongly suggest that these differences exist and must be reckoned with in any evaluation of women's health status.

Use of Health Services

Like their more frequent reporting of symptoms and disability, women's higher use of physician and hospital services relative to the use of these services by men has been thoroughly documented (Nathanson, 1977a). In this report, we call attention to some specific dimensions of use that are relevant to evaluation of the health status of adult women.

As shown in Table 2.3, rates for both physician visits and hospital episodes increase progressively with age. However, the largest sex differences in use of these services occur between the ages of 15 and 64. Data collected by the National Center for Health Statistics make it possible to partially account for these differences.

Pregnancy is, of course, a major cause of increased use of health services among United States women in the 15−44 age group. Fifteen percent of the physician visits made by these women are for a pregnancy examination and 31 percent of hospitalizations are for delivery. These events have been

Table 2.3. Use of Physician and Hospital Services by Sex and Age, United States, 1975 (Physician Visits) and 1977 (Hospital Discharges)

Utilization Index	Age				
	Under 15	15−24	25−44	45−64	65 and over
Office visits to a physician per person per year					
Male	2.0	1.5	1.9	2.8	4.0
Female[a]	1.8	2.8	3.7	4.0	4.5
Ratio (female/male)	.90	1.9	1.9	1.4	1.1
Hospital discharges per 1000 persons per year					
Male	81.4	— 98.5 —		195.2	393.9
Female[b]	64.4	— 149.8 —		201.2	358.6
Ratio (female/male)	0.79	— 1.52 —		1.03	0.90

[a] Excludes visits for prenatal care.
[b] Excludes deliveries.

Sources: National Center for Health Statistics, 1978. The National Ambulatory Medical Care Survey 1975 Summary, United States, January−December, 1975. *Vital and Health Statistics.* Series 13, Number 33. DHEW Publication No. (PHS) 78-1784. Hyattsville, MD.

National Center for Health Statistics, 1979. Utilization of Short-Stay Hospitals, United States, 1977. *Vital and Health Statistics,* Series 13, Number 41. DHEW Publication No. (PHS) 79-11551. Hyattsville, MD.

excluded from the rates shown in Table 2.3. An additional 10 percent of physician visits by adult women under 65 are for "obstetrical/gynecological" reasons; this proportion reaches a maximum of 13 percent among women aged 25−44. However, even when the entire category of visits to obstetrician−gynecologists is excluded from consideration, women aged 15−64 continue to have higher rates of office visits to physicians than do men in the same age group.[2]

A dimension of women's use of physician services that has received widespread attention is their consumption of medically prescribed psychotropic drugs (Cooperstock, 1971, 1978; Linn & Davis, 1971). A brief review of the literature in this area would suggest that psychotropic drug use is largely a problem of "middle-aged" women (Borgman, 1973; Linn, 1971; Linn & Davis, 1971). Cooperstock (1978) cites recent United States studies identifying "nonworking housewives aged 35 and over as the largest single group of tranquilizer users [8]." However, this image is not supported by national survey data. Mellinger, Balter, Parry, et al., (1974) report that 29 percent of women 18 and over, as compared with 13 percent of men, had used a medically prescribed psychotropic drug (predominantly tranquilizers and sedatives) within the past year. The percentage of users among women in each age group varied from 23 percent among the 18−29 year olds to 32 percent among women aged 30−44, and the rate remained stable at 31 percent in older age groups.[3] Although the fact of women's relatively greater consumption of medically prescribed psychotropic drugs is well established (there are no sex differences in use of "over-the-counter drugs", the significance of the use of these drugs as an index of women's physical and/or emotional health status is unclear (Pflanz, Basler, & Schwoon, 1977; Walcott, 1979), a statement equally applicable to other indexes of the use of health services.

Although women's relatively high rate of office visits to physicians cannot be wholly explained by reproduction and conditions of the reproductive organs, these conditions do account for women's high rate of hospital discharges. Women have over twice the number of surgical operations that are reported for men, and these operations account for 47 percent of hospital discharges among women in the 15−64 age group. As shown in Table 2.4, although surgery increases with age among men, it is actually less

---

[2] It is possible that these data underestimate the proportion of women's visits to physicians that are essentially obstetrical/gynecological; some visits for this purpose to general and family practitioners may have been omitted (and could not be included because of the way in which the NAMCS data are presented).

[3] Although "out-of-pocket" expenditures for all medically prescribed drugs increase with age for both men and women, the largest sex difference in expenditure is in the 17−24 age group, when women's expenditure is more than double that for men. The sex difference gradually declines after that, although expenditures for medically prescribed drugs by women aged 25−44 are nearly twice those of men (NCHS, 1977, Series 10-No. 108).

Table 2.4.   Rates and Sex Ratios, by Age, for Surgical Operations in Short-Stay Hospitals, United States, 1975

Age	Rate per 100,000 Population		Sex Ratio (female/male)
	Male	Female	
Under 15	3,500	2,800	0.80
15–44	4,200	10,010	2.38
45–64	7,140	9,360	1.31
65 and over	12,730	9,940	0.78

Source: National Center for Health Statistics. 1978. Surgical Operations in Short-Stay Hospitals, United States, 1975. *Vital and Health Statistics*, Series 13, Number 34. DHEW Publication No. (PHS) 78-1785, Hyattsville, MD.

frequent in women over 45 than among younger women. The reason for this difference becomes apparent on examination of data on the specific operations performed. Thirty-six percent of surgical operations on women aged 15–64 are gynecological or obstetrical procedures; the two largest categories are diagnostic dilation and curettage of the uterus and hysterectomy. When these sex-specific procedures are substracted from the total number of operations, the female surgical excess is reduced by about two-thirds.

Earlier calculations by Nathanson (1977a, 1978) have provided additional documentation for the point that women's excess hospital use, an excess that principally affects women in their middle years, is largely explained by hospitalization for conditions of the reproductive organs. Furthermore, a comparative analysis of hospital discharge data from six Western countries has shown that the size of the sex differential in hospital discharge rates (excluding deliveries, but including other sex-specific conditions) varies quite markedly from one country to another (Nathanson, 1978). It is virtually absent in France, and it is most marked in the United States and Canada. Disorders of menstruation and prolapsed uterus are the principal conditions (apart from delivery) for which North American women are hospitalized (National Center for Health Statistics, 1973, Series 13, No. 12; Statistics Canada, 1971).

In addition to their higher use of curative health services, women also exceed men in the use of preventive health measures that require entry into the health care system. A major component of use is generated by fertility and its control. In addition, two (Pap smear and breast examination) of seven major preventive procedures in use today are directed solely at women. Eighty-six percent of women aged 25–64 have had both examinations, the majority within the past year. However, even when preventive behavior is not obviously sex-specific, women take action more frequently than men (Nathanson, 1977b).

Summary

As a way of briefly summarizing some of the data that have been presented, sex ratios by age based on mortality rates, rates of acute and chronic illness, and hospital discharge rates, averaged for the three years, 1972—1974, are presented graphically in Figure 2.1. All points below the horizontal line represent an excess of males over females; above the line, the direction is reversed, and females are in excess. This figure rather strikingly demonstrates the contrast between higher rates of mortality among males and higher rates of reported illness and use of health services among females. These differences are most pronounced during the middle years of life and tend to converge in the younger and the older age groups.

On the basis of the data presented in this section, what inferences is it possible to draw about the health of United States women between the ages of approximately 25 and 54?

1.   Their current mortality rates indicate that women in this age group are relatively healthy and can look forward to many additional years of life. How this picture may be affected by changes in women's roles that reduce sex differences in life-styles cannot be readily predicted on the basis of present evidence.

2.   Examination of hospital discharge data presents a somewhat contradictory picture that is difficult to interpret. Women in this age group unquestionably experience frequent hospitalization and surgery associated with disorders of the reproductive system. However, it is not clear from these data what proportion of this hospitalization is "necessary"; what proportion is generated by the fact that women in this age group so frequently come to the attention of physicians (partly as a consequence of their reproductive capacities); and what proportion is generated by a more complex set of attitudes about women, their bodies, and the meaning and value of medical intervention, a point to be taken up again in the next section of this chapter. A large proportion of the conditions for which women are hospitalized may not be "serious." (Recent data from the National Ambulatory Medical Care Survey [National Center for Health Statistics: March 13, 1978] show that 77 percent of the problems women bring to an obstetrician-gynecologist are defined by the physician as "not serious.")

Regardless of reasons or "seriousness," hospitalization and surgery, particularly surgery that requires anesthesia, are not trivial matters and may have substantial morbidity associated with them. If only for this reason, a more complete understanding of factors that underlie the high hospital discharge rates experienced by United States women would be of substantial importance.

3.   Patterns of illness and health behavior among adult women differ profoundly from those of adult men. As noted earlier, women appear more sensitive to symptoms of illness and more active in their orientation toward the detection and cure of disease. Explanation of these differences requires the consideration of many complex issues both theoretical and methodological (cf. Mechanic, 1976). However, entirely apart from the question of explanation, it is important to consider what impact the behavior in question

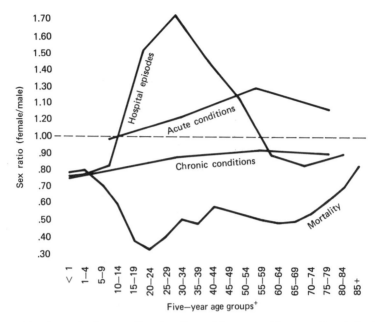

Figure 2.1. Sex ratios for mortality, chronic conditions, acute illness, and hospital episodes, United States, 1972–1974. Sources:

Mortality: National Center for Health Statistics. 1974. "Advance Report, Final Mortality Statistics, 1972." In *Monthly Vital Statistics Report,* Vol. 23, No. 7 (Supplement). Rockville, MD: Health Resources Administration. 1975. "Advance Report, Final Mortality Statistics, 1972." In *Monthly Vital Statistics Report.* Vol. 23, No. 11 (Supplement). Rockville, MD: Health Resources Administration. 1976. "Advance Report, Final Mortality Statistics, 1974." In *Monthly Vital Statistics Report,* Vol. 24, No. 11 (Supplement). Rockville, MD: Health Resources Administration.

Chronic Conditions: National Center for Health Statistics. 1973. "Current Estimates from the Health Interview Survey, United States—1972." In *Vital and Health Statistics,* Series 10, No. 85. DHEW Publication No. (HRA) 74-1512. Rockville, MD: 1974. "Current Estimates from the Health Interview Survey, United States—1973." *Vital Health Statistics,* Series 10, No. 95. DHEW Publication No. (HRA) 75-1522. Rockville, MD: 1977. "Current Estimates from the Health Interview Survey, United States—1974." *Vital and Health Statistics,* Series 10, No. 100. DHEW Publication No. (HRA) 76-1527. Rockville, MD.

Acute Conditions[a]: National Center for Health Statistics. 1976. "Health Characteristics of Persons with Chronic Activity Limitation, United States—1974." *Vital and Health Statistics.* Series 10, No. 112. DHEW Publication No. (HRA) 77-1539. Rockville, MD.

Hospital Episodes: National Center for Health Statistics. 1975. "Utilization of Short-Stay Hospitals: Summary of Nonmedical Statistics, United States, 1972." *Vital and Health Statistics,* Series 13, No. 19. DHEW Publication No. (HRA) 75-1770. Rockville, MD: 1976 "Utilization of Short-Stay Hospitals: Summary of Nonmedical Statistics, United States—1973." *Vital and Health Statistics,* Series 13, No. 23. DHEW Publication No. (HRA) 76-1774. Rockville, MD: 1976. "Utilization of Short-Stay Hospitals: Annual Summary for the United States, 1974." *Vital and Health Statistics,* Series 13, No. 26. DHEW Publication No. (HRA) 76-1777. Rockville, MD.

[a]Acute condition ratios are based on 1974 data only.

may have on health status. Are women, in fact, protected against health hazards by their greater health consciousness and more positive orientation toward use of health services, and do these orientations account in part for women's favorable mortality? Evidence to answer these questions is scanty indeed. However, highly intriguing follow-up studies from the 1965 Alameda County, California, health interview survey (Belloc, 1973; Berkman, 1975) have found that desirable health practices (in relation to smoking, weight, regularity of meals, and physical activity) and "a modicum of indulgence in the sick role" (some vs. no activity restriction due to illness) are associated with lower subsequent mortality. Interestingly enough, the positive effect of health practices was greater for men than for women. Clearly, the relationship between health behavior and health status is an area in which much more work needs to be done.

BIOLOGICAL AND SOCIAL ROLES

In earlier papers Nathanson (1977a, 1977b) has suggested that the values, attitudes, and social roles characteristic of particular statuses and groups in a society vary in the degree to which they are protective or destructive of the individual's physiological integrity. At one end of the spectrum are attitudes and expectations that, consciously or unconsciously, expose the individual to health risks, whereas at the other end fall normatively expected behaviors that are highly protective of the individual. Sex roles in American society vary along this dimension, as do other social roles (marital, parental, and occupational roles, for example). In order to further understanding, not only of women's health status and health behavior, but of the protective or hazardous dimension of social roles generally, we believe it is necessary to go beyond the descriptive level employed in the second section of this report and to determine how both the biologically defined, relatively invariant component of women's roles and the variant component (the cultural and social conditions in which women live and the changes in these conditions over time and over the individual life-cycle) influence indexes of health, illness, and death.

INVARIANT ROLE DIMENSIONS

What we designate as the *relatively* invariant dimensions of women's roles are those dimensions that are given by genetic makeup and by the hormonal cycle. We also include under this heading woman's capacity to bear children, not because she invariably will bear children, but because her biological capacity to do so means that even a negative decision about childbearing may have consequences for her health and well-being.

The question that we try to answer in this section of the report is what, if any, are the consequences of women's unique biological makeup for their health status as adult women. These consequences are further divisible into those that have a clearly physical dimension—mortality is the least ambiguous example—and those in which physical and social dimensions are inextricably linked (self-reported symptoms and use of health services, for example). We also distinguish between health outcomes that are directly attributable to physiological processes and outcomes that result from attempts to interfere with these processes for the purpose of controlling them—for example, the use of oral contraceptives.

Genetic Factors

The essential biological differences between human males and females are genetic in origin. The female possesses two large X chromosomes, the male one X and a very much smaller Y. The X chromosome carries many genes in addition to those responsible for sex determination, and the possession of an additional X chromosome is thought to have beneficial consequences for the female sex. These genetic differences have been held at least partially responsible for lower infant mortality rates among females (Naeye, Burt, Wright, et al., 1971), for women's greater longevity (Childs, 1965), and possibly for the male's greater susceptibility to many cancers of nongenital organs (Lingeman, 1979). However, variation in patterns of morbidity and mortality among adult women cannot be explained on a genetic basis, and differences in the size of the adult sex mortality differential among countries (Preston, 1976) and over time (Retherford, 1975) are also difficult to account for genetically. Thus, although women may have an underlying genetic advantage in resistance to disease, explanations for the bulk of observed differences in adult health status both among women and between the two sexes must be sought for elsewhere.

Menstruation and the Menopause

Menstruation and the menopause are universal and invariant physiological dimensions of women's lives. However, the meaning of these events and their consequences for physical and mental health vary widely in relation to cultural, social, and individual characteristics. The sources of these variations are poorly understood. Critical reviews of research on menstruation have been published by Sommer (1973), Koeske (1976), and Parlee (1978); a current review of work on the relationships between behavior and the menstrual cycle is presented in Friedman, Hurt, Aronoff, et al. (1980). Literature on the menopause, covering the three decades up to 1973, is comprehensively reviewed and sharply criticized in an excellent article by McKinlay and McKinlay (1973); a more recent methodological evaluation appears in Goodman (1980). The purpose of this review is to examine the evidence for effects of menstruation and the menopause on women's health status both directly and indirectly as a consequence of medical treatment generated by these conditions. In contrast to the approach frequently employed in the literature, these two physiological events are considered together. From a sociological perspective, the issues raised by this literature are very similar, irrespective of the specific focus on menstruation or the menopause. These issues concern, first, the nature of relationships among physiological processes, physical morbidity, and health and illness behavior and, second, the ways in which individuals' experience of physiological events is molded by the social and cultural expectations that surround these events.

Both the menstrual cycle and the menopause can be described in purely physiological terms, and perhaps it would be well to begin with these. The menstrual cycle is initiated by a series of hormonal changes that culminate in the production of sufficiently high levels of estrogen to induce ovulation. Following ovulation, further changes stimulate the production of progesterone, which will maintain pregnancy should it occur. Just prior to menstruation, both estrogen and progesterone drop sharply, and both are at their lowest levels when menstruation starts. Menopause is brought about through the gradual decline in estrogen production by the ovaries that is associated with aging. As the complex series of hormonal changes necessary to bring about menstruation is interrupted, menstruation becomes irregular, the time between periods increases, and the amount of blood loss gradually diminishes, until the menses cease altogether.[4]

A direct relationship between hormonal changes associated with the menopause and increased risk of cardiovascular disease among post menopausal women has been postulated. However, currently available evidence pertaining to this question is conflicting and inconclusive. In most Western societies, the male to female ratio of myocardial infarction before age 50 is 3:1; it becomes less than 2:1 after age 50 (Stolley, 1980). This shift in women's cardiovascular disease risk coincident with the average age of menopause has led to the hypothesis that estrogens provide some protection against cardiovascular disease, although the precise mechanism by which protection might be afforded remains unclear (Gordon, Kannel, Hjortland, et al., 1978). The lack of consensus on the basic issue of protection itself is reflected in recent research reviews concluding that (1) menopausal changes have no influence on risk of cardiovascular disease (Shoemaker, Forney, MacDonald, 1977), and (2) only premature menopause is a risk factor (Schiff & Ryan, 1980). Adding to the uncertainty surrounding this question are the facts that sex differences in coronary heart disease, although marked in the United States, are marginal or absent in other countries, notably

---

[4] This summary of hormonal changes is based on very clear and detailed descriptions by Bardwick (1971) and Flint (1975).

Japan (Shoemaker, Forney & MacDonald, 1977; Schiff & Ryan, 1980; Waldron, 1978) and that estrogen treatment provides no protection from coronary heart disease to either sex (Shoemaker, et al., 1977; Schiff & Ryan, 1980).

In contrast to the confusion surrounding the relationship between the menopause and cardiovascular disease, there is substantial consensus among physicians that loss of ovarian function after menopause is a contributing factor to osteoporosis (loss of calcium from the bones) in older women (Furuhjelm & Zador, 1979; Lindsay & Hart, 1978; Prill, 1978; Sarto, 1977; Schiff & Ryan, 1980). Decline in estrogen levels impairs the absorption of calcium by the body; the resulting loss of bone mass is associated with substantial morbidity caused by spine and hip fractures (Lindsay & Hart, 1978; Lindsay, Hart, Altken, et al., 1978; Schiff & Ryan, 1980; Shoemaker, et al., 1977). These injuries have been estimated to be six to 10 times more frequent in women than in men over age 50 (Prill, 1978).

The influence of naturally occurring hormonal changes on a third condition of major importance to women, breast cancer, has been extensively investigated. Epidemiologic studies have clearly demonstrated variations in breast cancer risk associated with women's reproductive histories. These findings are briefly reviewed in a later section. Although the risk of breast cancer increases with advancing age, this change is thought to be age-rather than endocrine-related (Vorherr & Messer, 1978). Increased risks have also been associated with menarche prior to age 16 and with menopause at age 55 or older (Vorherr & Messer, 1978; Paffenbarger, Kampert & Chang, 1980); the mechanism of these relationships is unclear.

In arriving at any conclusions concerning specific disease risks directly associated with the menopause, it is important to keep three points in mind: (1) virtually all the studies in which these risks are investigated are retrospective case-control studies, subject to the selection and other biases inherent in this research design (cf. Feinstein & Horwitz, 1978); (2) adequate age controls are seldom employed, so that it is difficult to separate the effects of menopause from the effects of aging as such (Goodman, 1980); (3) there is considerable disagreement among physicians and epidemiologists about both the existence of specific risks and their causal mechanisms. The only disease risk that has been shown with any persuasiveness to be *causally* associated with the cessation of menstruation is the risk of osteoporosis. The consequences of osteoporosis are potentially severe, however, and have been estimated to affect as many as 25 percent of postmenopausal women (Lindsay & Hart, 1978). Although the risk of cardiovascular disease does increase *coincidentally* with the menopause, a clear causal connection remains to be demonstrated. Breast cancer incidence increases with age, but no direct connection with the menopause has been shown. Although the diminished estrogen secretion associated with the menopause has relatively few agreed-on direct pathogenic effects, there are well-documented risks of estrogen *therapy* for menopausal and other aging symptoms. These risks are indirect consequences of the menopause and are reviewed and evaluated subsequently.

Even a cursory review of the literature shows that the number of somatic, psychological, and behavioral symptoms that have been associated with the menstrual cycle and/or the menopause is legion (Bardwick, 1971; Dalton, 1964; McKinlay & Jeffreys, 1974; McKinlay & McKinlay, 1973; Moos, 1969; Neugarten & Kraines, 1965; Parlee, 1973), and that there is substantial disagreement concerning both the universality of particular symptoms and their relationship to underlying biological processes (Bart & Grossman, 1976; Flint, 1975; Koeske, 1976; Koeske & Koeske, 1975; Osofsky & Seidenberg, 1970; Paige, 1973; Parlee, 1974, 1978, 1980; Tucker, 1977). Furthermore, the methodological limitations of much of this work (Goodman, 1980; McKinlay & McKinlay, 1973; Parlee, 1974, 1978; Sommer, 1973) are such that the results would be inconclusive even if the investigators agreed. The following brief account focuses on those few points on which there is reasonable consensus.

Currently, the average age of menarche in the United States is just under 13 (Romney, Gray, Little, et al., 1975), the average age of menopause about 50 (MacMahon & Worchester, 1966). Overt symptoms for which a physiological basis is generally conceded are pain and water retention associated with menstruation (Lenanne & Lenanne, 1973; Wilcoxon, Schrader & Sherif, 1976) "hot flashes," vaginal atrophy and related atrophic changes, and osteoporosis (as described above) associated with the menopause (Connell, 1979; Perlmutter, 1978). However, even these symptoms are not universally reported. Estimates of the frequency of dysmenorrhea ("cramps") vary from 50 (Lenanne & Lenanne, 1973) to 80 percent of women (Romney et al., 1975); estimates of the prevalence of "hot flashes" range from 30 to 80 percent (Shoemaker et al., 1977). In a population survey of women aged 45−54, McKinlay and Jeffreys (1974) inquired about a series of physiological and psychosomatic symptoms said to constitute the menopausal syndrome. Of these symptoms, they reported, "only hot flashes and night sweats appear to reach any clear peak in frequency in the menopausal group [110]." (Other symptoms that may be associated with the menopause, such as vaginal atrophy and the problem of bone loss discussed earlier, were not included among the symptoms specified by these researchers. In any case, they would rarely be mentioned among self-reported symptoms because they develop quite gradually, and women do not usually connect them with the hormonal changes of menopause.) Although negative mood changes are regularly attributed to the menstrual cycle phase ("premenstrual tension," irritability, depression, fatigue), and to the menopause (depression, crying spells, feelings of "inadequacy"), there is little evidence concerning the frequency with which these changes are experienced by unselected populations of "well" women or their uniqueness to any particular stage of women's lives (Goodman, 1980; Koeske, 1976; McKinlay & Jeffreys, 1974; Neugarten & Kraines, 1965).

Estimates of symptom prevalence are, of course, based on women's self-reports. The volume of reporting depends not only on women's own perceptions and expectations about a particular physiological process but also on the expectations that are conveyed to her within her family, by friends, and by physicians. The importance of social expectations in accounting for some portion of reported effects of the menstrual cycle (principally mood and behavioral changes) has been suggested by Sommer (1973), on the basis of her review of the literature in this area. This hypothesis is further reinforced in recent work reported by Parlee (1974, 1978, 1980) and Koeske and Koeske (1975). In carefully designed studies, these investigators document, respectively, the existence of stereotypic beliefs about menstruation common to both men and women and the use of information about the menstrual cycle phase to account for emotional states, again by both sexes. Finally, in an ingeniously designed study in which the potential for "social expectation" effects on symptom reporting was controlled by disguising the study's focus on the menstrual cycle, Wilcoxon, Schrader, and Sherif (1976) found that measures of negative affect were unrelated to the menstrual cycle phase but were related to stressful events in the environment. Unfortunately, no comparable studies of menopausal symptoms have been carried out, although cross-cultural data suggest that the experience and/or reporting of these symptoms is also strongly affected by social norms (Bart and Grossman, 1976; Flint, 1975).

On the basis of this brief review, it must be concluded that scientifically validated evidence for *direct* physiological effects of menstruation or the menopause exists for only a limited range of physical symptoms. The evidence reviewed suggests that much of women's experience of these events is mediated by the social and psychological expectations that surround the events themselves and perhaps by other dimensions of their social roles that we have yet to consider. It is important to emphasize, however, that the quality of this experience may have profound consequences for women's health behavior and use of health services. In a study of five ethnic groups in Miami, Scott (1975) found that regular menstrual periods were very important for women's feelings of health and well-being; these data are confirmed by recent evidence from a cross-cultural study of menstruation carried out in ten countries (WHO Task Force on Psychosocial Research in Family Planning, 1980). Women's sensitivity to and low tolerance for alterations in their patterns of menstrual bleeding may partially account for the high proportion of "disorders of menstruation" among hospital admissions. Similarly, socially shared negative attitudes toward the menopause and toward "menopausal" women (Maoz, Dowty, Antonovsky, et al., 1970; Neugarten, Wood, Kraines, et al., 1963; Rossi, 1980) may be potentially damaging to the sense of well-being and the self-esteem of women undergoing these physiological changes in their reproductive system. As Rossi points out, research showing that menopause itself may not be as traumatic as has sometimes been painted does not mean that women have no difficulty adjusting to visible signs of aging, to which endocrine changes contribute. However, most signs and symptoms related to aging do not coincide with menopause, but occur somewhat later. An excellent analysis of the dilemma created for women by the gap between social aging (a woman socially defined as old after menopause) and biological aging (actual physical deterioration) has recently been published by Stearns (1980). Stearns' focus is on France in the nineteenth century, but his analysis is pertinent to other Western societies and to the present as well as the past.

Indirect effects of physiological processes on health, illness behavior, and use of health services may come about as a consequence of the ways in which these processes are defined and treated. There is a substantial historical and contemporary literature attributing much of women's illness experience to the social control of physiological processes exercised by medical practitioners (Ehrenreich & English, 1979; Nathanson, 1977a, 1977b; Notman and Nadelson, 1978; Scully, 1980). Although not all of these relationships are equally well documented, two frequent medical prescriptions with potentially iatrogenic effects have received substantial attention in both the medical and the lay literature and are briefly reviewed here: estrogen replacement therapy and oral contraception.

Estrogen Replacement Therapy. A recent article in the *New England Journal of Medicine* comments that "few medical interventions have had as widespread application as exogenous estrogen treatment in postmenopausal women" (Weinstein, 1980). A careful survey carried out in a metropolitan area of the state of Washington in 1973–1974 indicated that 51 percent of menopausal women had used estrogen for over three months, with a median use of 10 years (Stadel & Weiss, 1975). Given this level of use, the question of health risks that may be associated with estrogen becomes of appreciable public health importance. There is strong evidence that significant risks do exist (Hulka, 1980); of these risks, cancer of the endometrium (i.e., lining of the uterus) has received the greatest attention. The relative risk of endometrial cancer has been estimated to be between three and 12 times as high among women taking estrogen as among controls; this risk has been found to increase with duration of treatment and with the size of the dosage (Antunes, Stolley, Rosenshein, et al., 1979; Hammond, Jelovsek, Lee, et al., 1979; Hulka, 1980). Following publication in 1975 of the initial case-control studies demonstrating a relationship between estrogen use and endometrial cancer, there was a substantial reduction in estrogen prescriptions; recent evidence indicates an accompanying drop in incidence of endometrial cancer (Jick, Watkins, Hunter, et al., 1979).

Estrogens are prescribed for the treatment of a variety of symptoms that are associated with or that develop subsequent to the menopause, including hot flashes, vaginal atrophy, and osteoporosis (Perlmutter, 1978). In view of the documented health hazards associated with estrogen replacement therapy, the question of whether and under what circumstances risks outweigh benefits has received a great amount of attention (Hulka, 1980; Weinstein, 1980). At present there is no definitive *medical* answer to this question. Estrogen therapy does appear to afford symptomatic relief to many women (Connell, 1979; Perlmutter, 1978; Schiff & Ryan, 1980), but the time when it was routinely prescribed for no indication but menopause itself in the belief that it prevented aging and kept women "feminine forever" (Wilson, 1966) is past.

Given the major medical questions that currently surround estrogen replacement therapy, carefully designed, sociologically oriented studies of the circumstances under which it is prescribed could have considerable value in testing hypotheses about the influence of social norms on physicians' diagnostic and treatment behavior. Suggestive information on physicians' expectations about "menopausal" women—that they are "grieving" for their lost reproductive powers, that they feel "inadequate," that menopause is a developmental crisis similar to adolescence—is presented in the medical literature (Kerr & Vaughan, 1975; Klaus, 1974; Romney, et al., 1975), but it is not clear how widely these expectations are held, and how or under what conditions they influence physicians' actual responses to women in the age groups in which menopause is most likely to occur.

Fertility and Its Control

In investigations of sex differences in health and illness (but not in mortality studies), pregnancy and delivery are frequently excluded in order to eliminate "obvious" reasons for women's higher rates of illness behavior and use of health sevices. This exclusion has led to the neglect of a set of events, including childbirth, birth control, abortion, and sterilization, that loom very large in the experience of adult women and may contribute, in subtle as well as in obvious ways, to observed sex differences in health status.

As we suggested in the introduction to this section of the chapter, the impact of women's childbearing capacities on their health and well-being comes both from the experience of childbirth itself and from the means that are used to prevent unwanted births. In 1976 about 44 percent of the then currently married women aged 25–44 reported using some form of contraception; another 35 percent were protected against conception by surgical sterilization (of which about one-third was due to male sterilization)(Ford, 1978). In this same year, 5.2 percent of women in this age group gave birth. Together, problems of fertility and its control affect all but a small minority of women under 45.

Delivery itself is an increasingly infrequent event in women's lives. In 1976 the average woman aged 45–49 had three children (U.S. Bureau of the Census,1976). If fertility rates continue at their present levels and if currently reported birth expectations are translated into actual behavior, completed fertility in the United States will drop still lower.

In Table 2.5 data are presented in an attempt to give a more detailed picture of how the lives of women in their middle years are affected by their reproductive capacities. The percentage of these women with a birth in 1977 was highest in the youngest age group, and it dropped rapidly to less than one-half of 1 percent among women aged 40–44. In the older age groups, over four times as many women have abortions as give birth. Thirty-four percent of the younger women are using medical methods of contraception—23 percent are on the pill, but in the older age group sterilization is more frequent than pill use. The popularity of female sterilization as a method of fertility control has increased markedly in recent years (Ford, 1978).

Our essential concern in this report is with the impact of reproductive behavior on the health of women in their middle years and on their use of physician and hospital services. Included in this evaluation are both direct effects of pregnancy and childbirth and indirect effects from methods of fertility control. Maternal mortality rates in the United States are very low, ranging from around 20 deaths per 100,000 live births for younger women to

Table 2.5. Selected Indexes of Reproductive Behavior Among United States Women Aged 25–44

Indexes of Reproductive Behavior	Age			
	25–29	30–34	35–39	40–44
Percentage of women giving birth (1976)	10.9	5.4	1.9	0.4
Percentage of women having an abortion (1976)	2.5	1.5	0.9	0.3
Percentage of currently married women using various medical methods of contraception (1976)				
Pill	—	23.3	—	—	7.9	—
IUD	—	7.2	—	—	4.6	—
Diaphragm	—	3.1	—	—	2.9	—
Percentage of women sterilized[a] (1976)	—	10.6	—	—	13.0	—

[a] These figures exclude female sterilization for medical reasons, male sterilization, and the use of nonmedical methods of contraception (condom, douche, rhythm, etc.) Inclusion of these data would, of course, substantially increase the total proportion of married women protected from conception.

Sources: Bureau of the Census. 1979. Estimates of the Population of the United States, by Age, Sex, and Race: 1976 to 1978. *Current Population Reports.* Series P-25, No. 800, Washington, DC.

Ford, K. 1978. "Contraceptive Use in the United States, 1973–76." *Family Planning Perspectives* **10**, (September/October): 264–269.

Forrest, J.D., C. Tietze, and E. Sullivan. 1978. "Abortion in the United States, 1976–77." *Family Planning Perspectives* **10** (September/October): 271–279.

National Center for Health Statistics. 1980. *Vital Statistics of the United States, 1976.* Volume I—Natality. (PHS) 81-1100. Hyattsville, MD.

close to 70 deaths per 100,000 live births in the age group 40−44 (Tietze & Lewit, 1979). Variations in patterns of sexual and reproductive behavior have been associated with differential risks for breast cancer (Lyle, 1980; Paffenbarger, et al., 1980) and cancer of the cervix (Terris, 1966), but the mechanism of these relationships is unclear (Terris, Wilson & Nelson, 1980).

As pointed out by Beral (1979), an accurate measure of mortality and morbidity associated with reproduction must take into account illness and death associated with fertility control as well as with pregnancy and childbirth. Increased risks of circulatory system disease have been shown to be associated with use of oral contraceptives. These risks are marked for women who smoke and for women over 35. Their significance among younger women is less well established (Krueger, Ellenberg, Bloom, et al., 1980; Population Information Program, 1979b; Rosenfield, 1978; Shapiro, Rosenberg, Slone, et al., 1979; Stolley, Shapiro, Slone, et al., 1978; Vessey and Mann, 1978). The intrauterine device is relatively safer than the pill from the standpoint of mortality (Population Information Program, 1979a) but is associated with increased incidence of gynecological complications (Mishell, 1979). Perhaps in part because of the publicity given to risks of oral contraceptives in this age group, sterilization has become an increasingly important method of fertility control among women 35 and over; as with any operative procedure, medical complications occasionally ensue, although these are hardly ever fatal (Rioux, 1979).

Few women chose to avoid the hazards of reproduction and its control altogether. On the basis of a careful evaluation of these hazards, Tietze and Lewit (1979) conclude, first, that for women up to age 30 all major methods of contraception, and abortion, are safer in terms of risk to life than are pregnancy and childbirth; second, that after age 30 the risk to life rapidly increases among users of oral contraceptives. By age 35, mortality risk from use of oral contraceptives exceeds that from pregnancy and childbirth even among nonsmokers, and this risk continues to increase with advancing age. Mortality risk is lowest at all ages for women who use barrier methods (diaphragm, condom) backed up by abortion (Tietze & Lewit, 1979).

Despite low rates of fertility and maternal mortality and relatively low mortality risks associated with methods of fertility control, reproductive system conditions add substantially to the overall volume of illness behavior (restricted activity and bed disability days) and use of physician and hospital services documented earlier in this chapter. Part of this volume may be explained by ill health that is a direct consequence of childbirth or by conditions attributable to the control of fertility (contraceptive use, sterilization, abortion). However, an additional contributing factor, we believe, is the set of attitudes and expectations that defines pregnancy, childbirth, and the control of fertility as specifically medical problems. Once that definition has been made, then the probability is overwhelming that women in the reproductive years will come frequently to the attention of physicians, and that diagnosis and treatment of reproductive (and other) complaints will correspondingly increase. Among specific consequences of the pronounced "medicalization" of women's reproductive capacities in the United States are unusually high rates of cesarian section (Francome & Huntingford, 1980) and of hysterectomy (Sloan, 1978).

Summary

The question with which we began this section of the chapter was: What are the consequences of women's unique biological makeup for their health status as adults? To answer this question, it is necessary to distinguish, as we have done earlier, between consequences at different levels.

There are, first, direct physical consequences that can be described in terms of clinically diagnosed organic disease or death. Women may have some genetic protection against these outcomes that men do not have, although the role of this protection in accounting for sex mortality differentials among adults is probably small relative to other factors. Nor is there any clear evidence for direct positive or negative effects of the female hormones on disease risks for the major causes of death among women.

Indirect physical risks may result from the measures that are taken to control physiological processes. Increased risks of endometrial cancer associated with the use of estrogens to treat menopausal symptoms and of cardiovascular disease among users of oral contraceptive pills are reasonably well established, although the relative risk of oral contraceptive use compared with childbirth is small among women under 35. As noted earlier, this risk increases rapidly with advancing age.

Beyond these few statements, which can be made with comparative certainty, the contribution of women's biological makeup to their illness experience is extremely difficult to evaluate. The significance of women's physiological processes for their "health" is possibly less a function of these processes themselves than of their definition and management within the context of American society and American values. It may be that the monthly anticipation and experience of menstruation and the constant possibility of pregnancy, as well as the experience of pregnancy itself, create a relatively high level of bodily awareness among women. Men have no comparable barometers. On the other hand, it seems clear that the way in which these signals are interpreted and the actions they evoke are a social product, not "given" by the signals themselves. In American society, bodily processes are defined as requiring medical management. Women's biology, therefore, may indeed play a role, even if an indirect one, in their relatively greater reported illness and health services use.

VARIANT ROLE DIMENSIONS

Although women share a common biology, they vary in their marital, parental, occupational, and other social roles. The differences in health status among women in different social positions are significant in their own right for what they show about the variety of women's experience. However, examination of these differences is also of strategic importance theoretically, both for the development of a framework to account for sex differences in health indexes and for identification of the specific dimensions of social roles that underlie variations in mortality and morbidity, in illness behavior, and in use of health services. One example serves to illustrate this point. If sex differences in cardiovascular disease are caused in part by males' greater occupational stress (House, 1974), then women employed in predominantly masculine occupations might be expected to exhibit higher rates of cardiovascular disease than women in traditionally female occupations or than housewives. Furthermore, sex differences in rates for disease would be expected to decline as the numbers of women in "masculine" occupations increased. Should these latter outcomes be observed, current sex differences in cardiovascular disease would be partially explained, and the case for occupational stress as a causal factor in cardiovascular disease would be strengthened.

The purpose of this section is both to document existing variation in health status among women in different social roles and to lay the groundwork for a research approach that focuses on theoretically strategic variations in these roles.

Marital Status

Studies of differential mortality by marital status have uniformly demonstrated that married women have lower age-adjusted mortality rates than women who are single or formerly married (National Center for Health Statistics, 1970, Series 20, No. 8a). However, marital status differentials in mortality are substantially less for women than for men (Berkman & Syme, 1979; Gove, 1973; NCHS 1970, Series 20, No. 8a; Verbrugge, 1979a), and they decline with age (Kobrin & Hendershot, 1977). The combined effects of sex and age on mortality rates are shown in Table 2.6, taken from Kobrin and Hendershot's recent paper. The difference in death rates by marital status is highest for both sexes during the middle years, from 35–54.

The interpretation of sex-age-marital status differentials in mortality presents major problems, clearly recognized by investigators in this field (Carter & Glick, 1976; Gove, 1973; Kobrin & Hendershot, 1977). The major alternatives are the *selection* hypothesis (i.e., healthy people are more likely to marry in the first place) versus the *protection* hypothesis (marriage itself is the causal factor, creating an environment that increases the individual's chances of survival). These two hypotheses are not, of course, mutually

Table 2.6.   Deaths per 100,000 of Population by Age, According to Sex and Marital Status: United States, 1966–1968

Marital Status and Sex	Age			
	35–44	45–54	55–64	65–74
Male				
Married	323	814	2,042	4,456
Nonmarried	1,008	2,125	4,276	5,944
Ratio, nonmarried to married	3.12	2.61	2.09	1.33
Female				
Married	212	464	910	2,379
Nonmarried	408	757	1,278	2,595
Ratio, nonmarried to married	1.92	1.63	1.40	· 1.09

Source: Computed by Kobrin and Hendershot (1977) from data provided by the U.S. Public Health Service (n.d.) and the U.S. Bureau of the Census (1969). Copyrighted 1977 by the National Council on Family Relations. Reprinted by permission.

exclusive and may even be mutually reinforcing. This latter perspective leads to the further question (not addressed by the investigators cited) of the conditions under which each hypothesis has the greater predictive value. Gove (1973) and Kobrin and Hendershot (1977) both argue that the protection hypothesis fits the overall pattern of sex-age-marital status differentials better than does the selection hypothesis. Marriage, following Durkheim (1952), is taken to be an indicator of social integration, and social integration, or the presence of many social ties, both deters self-destructive, risk-taking behavior and encourages positive self-protection. Significant empirical support for the influence of social ties in reducing mortality is presented in a recent paper by Berkman and Syme (1979). The social integration argument does not, however, account for sex *differences* in the beneficial effects of marriage, and here two additional hypotheses have been advanced: first, that women have more informal social ties than men outside of marriage (Gove, 1973), and, second, that women's ties inside of marriage are of relatively low status and thus not so advantageous to them as they are to men (Kobrin & Hendershot, 1977).

Recent work (Bernard, 1972; Gove & Tudor, 1973) has gone so far as to suggest that marriage is positively disadvantageous to women's health, but it is important to note that these investigators have focused on mental rather than on physical illness. Careful examination of data on reported physical illness and health services use categorized by marital status offers no consistent support for this hypothesis when tested using these latter health indexes (Nathanson, 1977a).[5] Among women, as among men, the formerly married exceed both currently married and single persons on virtually all measures of ill health, and there are no consistent differences in health indicators *among*

---

[5] Several recent papers have disputed the application of this thesis to mental illness as well (Glenn, 1975; Meile, Johnson & St. Peter, 1976)

marital status categories by sex (NCHS, 1976, Series 10, No.104).[6] Single women, although they report as much as or more disability (activity limitation or restricted activity days) than currently married women, make less use of physician or hospital services (excluding delivery). The difference in use of medical care between married and single women is greater (although in the same direction) than the difference between married and single men.

The inconsistency of relationships between marital status and various "health" indexes reemphasizes the point that these indexes refer to very different underlying concepts and may, consequently, be linked in different ways to the presence or absence of the social ties created by marriage. For example, although strong social ties, particularly ties that are associated with responsibility for the welfare of other persons, may make it difficult for individuals to restrict their daily activities, these same ties may support the use of health services (Rivkin, 1972; Nathanson, 1975). Early recourse to medical care may, in turn, protect the individual against mortality.

Parenthood

The argument that social integration protects against mortality leads to the prediction that parenthood will have an effect on death rates similar to that of marriage. Data presented by Kobrin and Hendershot (1977) demonstrate that the presence of children in the household is associated with lower death rates among both women and men, and that this effect is strongest in the 35−44 age group. However, the possibility of selection in accounting for these results cannot be ruled out.

Several studies (Cole & Lejeune, 1972; Geertsen & Gray, 1970; Nathanson, 1980; Rivkin, 1972;) have investigated how the presence or absence of young children influences women's illness behavior. Although the indexes of illness behavior that they employ are somewhat different, these studies are generally consistent in showing that the presence of preschool children in the home disinclines women to define themselves as sick or to take health action. Pushing this analysis further, Rivkin (1972) demonstrated that, when they were sick, women with young children who had additional role responsibilities as well (unmarried household head, employed) were likely to use health services rather than take care of themselves at home. Parallel findings are reported by Nathanson (1980).

There is some slight evidence that the presence of children in the home is also associated with fewer, or less severe, menopausal symptoms. Van Keep and Kellerhals (1974) present data showing that the highest percentage of "menopausal" symptoms are reported by women with regular menstrual

---

[6] Marital status categories differ markedly in their age distributions. All comparisons discussed in this section are based on age-adjusted rates (published by the NCHS) or data for defined age groups. The age groups used in the National Health Survey publication on which much of this discussion is based are 25−34, 35−44, and 45−64.

periods but with no children living at home. Similarly, Crawford and Hooper (1973) found higher menopausal symptom levels among women anticipating the marriage of a daughter (but not a son). These data are generally consistent with the social integration hypothesis; they particularly call attention to the need for studies of how role shifts over the life course are related to a variety of health indexes.

Employment

The relationship of paid employment outside the home to women's health status is extremely important and extremely difficult to unravel, both as a consequence of data limitations and as a consequence of limitations in our understanding of the *meaning* of employment in relation to health status and health behavior. Women's participation in the labor force has increased dramatically over the past 15 years, so that women in 1979 constituted 42 percent of the labor force. In the age group, 25–54, over 59 percent were employed (U.S. Bureau of the Census, 1980). Increased participation in the labor force has been most marked among married women and among women with preschool children (Oppenheimer, 1973; U.S.Bureau of the Census, 1980). However, the long-standing pattern of sex segregation in *occupations* has been largely unaffected by these changes (Oppenheimer, 1972; Williams, 1979), although there is recent evidence of decreased occupational segregation among younger cohorts of women (Freemen, 1976). Thus, although the *roles* occupied by women have markedly altered, there is relatively little evidence for comparable changes in their relative *status* (cf. Ridley, 1969; *The Lancet*, 1980).

The implications of increased participation by women in the labor force for their mortality, illness patterns, and use of health services have only begun to be considered, and the data on which to base an evaluation of these implications either do not exist or exist only in relatively crude form (cf. Muller, 1979). A serious limitation is that most available data are cross-sectional, making it extremely difficult to resolve questions of cause and effect between employment and health status. Employment is treated as an all-or-none category in most statistics; almost no consideration is given to full versus part-time employment, to "transitional" employment categories (cf. Welch & Booth, 1977), or to timing of employment in relation to the life course. Breakdowns by occupation are very limited; health indexes are seldom presented by the variables of employment and family status simultaneously. As noted in a recent review, women workers are frequently omitted from study populations in the United States, even when they are part of the work population (Hunt, 1977).

Employment is a variable dimension of women's roles, and the question we address in this section is what variations in mortality, in reported illness, and in use of health services are associated with the presence or absence of this dimension. The significance of employment for women's health and well-being has been alternatively construed as positive when the focus is on employment as a source of social ties and increased feelings of self-esteem (Brown & Harris, 1978; Gore, 1978; Gove & Geerken, 1977; Nathanson, 1980) and negative when the focus is on increased role demands and the psychic strains believed to be associated with occupational competition (House, 1974; Johnson, 1977; Reeder, 1976; Waldron, 1976). Within the limits of available data, we propose to explore these alternative (but not, of course, mutually exclusive) formulations, giving particular attention to the *circumstances* under which employment is or is not associated with particular health outcomes.[7]

In the majority of health surveys that include employment as a variable, employed women have reported less illness than housewives (Baetjer, 1946; Feld, 1963; Nathanson, 1980; Rivkin, 1972; Welch & Booth, 1977). A detailed comparison of employed women and housewives based on data from the 1974 Health Interview Survey demonstrates that among midlife women (aged 45−64) the employed are substantially more likely to report themselves in "excellent" health (38.7 percent as compared with 27.6 percent among housewives), that they report fewer days of restricted activity due to illness, and that they make fewer physician visits (Nathanson, 1980). In fact, the *only* difference in these health indexes between employed women and employed *men* is in the larger number of physician visits reported by women.

The data on which to base a comprehensive evaluation of the apparent positive relationship between women's employment and their health status are not currently available. However, some limited steps have been taken toward specifying this relationship further, and these latter data are reported here. Nathanson (1980) hypothesized that if the positive effects of employment are caused by the increased access to social ties and greater feelings of self-esteem that employment affords, then these effects could be expected to vary among women having differential access to *alternative* sources of social support and esteem, as indicated by their marital and parental roles and their educational achievement. This hypothesis received some support in an analysis of data from the United States Health Interview Survey. Employment contributed independently to positive reported health status *only* among divorced or separated women and among women with less than a high school education. For these women, it is argued, employment outside the home provides the social ties and feelings of self-esteem that other women are able to obtain from their marital relationships or through the increased opportunities education makes available to them. By

---

[7] This limited focus omits reference to at least two very important health issues: first, the management of pregnancy, childbirth, and its immediate aftermath within the context of employment and, second (and related, in part) the existence of health hazards within the workplace that are of particular concern to women. These issues are reviewed in recent papers by Hunt (1975) and Muller (1979).

the same token, the *absence* of employment is particularly devastating when alternative roles and statuses are lacking as well. It is of interest to note that parallel structural interpretations have recently been advanced to account for the greater vulnerability of working class women and unmarried women to depression (Brown & Harris, 1978; Pearlin & Johnson, 1977).

The work so far reviewed in this section uses women's self-reports to indicate their health status. The few studies comparing employed women and housewives in which health status was measured clinically give much more equivocal results (Bengtsson, Hallstrom & Tibblin, 1973; Hauenstein, Kasl & Harburg, 1977; Haynes & Feinleib, 1980). The question of a possible association between occupational stress and heart disease among women has been of some interest to researchers in light of women's increased entry into the labor force. However, in the three studies cited *no* overall relationship was found between employment status and blood pressure levels (Hauenstein, et al., 1977), ischemic heart disease (Bengtsson, et al., 1973), or coronary heart disease (Haynes & Feinleib, 1980). The latter study, however, did find significantly *higher* rates of coronary heart disease among clerical workers than among housewives.

Employment has been hypothesized to have consequences for women's *response* to illness as well as for their vulnerability to illness (Nathanson, 1975; Nathanson, 1980). Employment adds to women's role obligations, and it is suggested that women with heavier role obligations (greater role density) will be less likely to take action in response to perceived symptoms. Furthermore, if they do take action, they will be more likely to visit a physician and less likely to engage in self-treatment at home. Several tests of the latter hypotheses have been reported in the literature with contradictory results, perhaps owing in part to their considerable differences in methodology (Nathanson, 1980; Thompson & Brown, 1980; Woods & Hulka, 1979). As noted earlier, Health Interview Survey data show markedly higher restricted activity days and physician visit rates among housewives as compared to women employed outside the home. Furthermore, the ratio of physician visits to days at home is about 40 percent higher among employed women, suggesting that the latter are relatively more likely than housewives to visit a physician when illness strikes rather than to restrict their activities at home. More detailed analyses in Nathanson's (1980) article are generally consistent with the role density hypotheses; however, role configurations add relatively little to the total explained variance in illness behavior.

Earlier it was suggested that social roles vary in the degree to which the behaviors and relationships they entail are protective of physical health. Adoption of this perspective casts a somewhat different light on the relationships between employment and illness behavior described in the foregoing paragraphs. If the effect of employment is, as suggested by the Health Interview Survey data, to decrease women's responsiveness to symptoms of illness, then the long-run consequences of employment for health status may not necessarily be beneficial. That "a modicum of indulgence in the sick role" has positive consequences for survival is suggested in an intriguing paper by Berkman (1975). The ambiguous character of employment as a conferer of health benefits is further indicated by the consistent portrayal of occupational stress as a factor in mortality from coronary heart disease (Haynes, Feinleib & Levine, 1978; House, 1974; Mettlin, 1976; Russek & Russek, 1976). It has been suggested that women's lesser occupational involvement protects them against coronary heart disease (as well as other stress-related conditions) and that increasing rates of these conditions can be anticipated as their commitment to occupational roles becomes stronger (Garbus & Garbus, 1980; House, 1974; Johnson, 1977; Lewis & Lewis, 1977).

As noted earlier, there is no current evidence of convergence between male and female death rates from any of the major causes of death, with the exception of lung cancer. Women's mortality rates from heart disease have, in fact, continued to decline, and the mortality ratios between the sexes from this condition have continued to increase up to the present time. However, current rates are clearly an inadequate reflection of the occupational experience of more recent cohorts of women.

Alternative approaches to the examination of employment effects on mortality are to compare the mortality experience of employed women with that of housewives or with that of men of comparable occupational status. Mortality statistics are not routinely published by occupation, and there have been very few studies specifically focused on differential mortality among women by employment or occupational status. Furthermore, the data that are available, although intriguing, have methodological weaknesses that limit their interpretation.

Two studies have been reported comparing mortality rates among housewives and employed women (Cumming, Lazar & Chisholm, 1975; Morton & Ungs, 1979). Cumming, Lazar and Chisholm examined suicide rates among women in British Columbia in 1961 and again in 1971. Morton and Ungs present data on cancer mortality rates in Lane County, Oregon, for the years 1958 through 1972. Both investigations have found substantially higher mortality rates among housewives than among women in the labor force. These results are difficult to evaluate, however. Women with emotional or physical health problems may be more likely to quit their jobs, or not to take jobs in the first place, thereby inflating the mortality of the housewife category. Controls over potential differences between employed women and housewives other than labor force participation are limited to age and in the Cumming, Lazar, and Chisholm study, marital status. Other differences in socio-economic characteristics may be of equal importance.

The few studies of mortality *among* employed women have been remarkably consistent in reporting *higher* than expected total mortality (Goodman, 1975; Ladbrook, 1977) and suicide rates (Mausner & Steppacher, 1973;

Steppacher and Mausner, 1974) among younger professionals. The studies cited are based on quite different populations and vary in the groups with which women's mortality rates are compared. Goodman's study of American physicians examines age-specific mortality rates of male and female physicians and compares these with mortality data from the total U.S. population. The two investigations of suicide rates present data on psychologists and physicians respectively and compare observed rates with those expected on the basis of total population data. Finally, Ladbrook compares the sex- and occupation-specific mortality rates of members of the Wisconsin labor force. These studies all refer to approximately the same time period, centering around 1970.

Sex mortality ratios calculated from Goodman's data are presented in Figure 2.2. Data for the total United States population are shown as a solid line; the dotted line represents the same set of ratios for physicians. The pattern described by the solid line is a familiar one. Excess male mortality in the total population is reflected in ratios that consistently fall well below equality (a ratio of 100). The pattern of sex mortality differentials among physicians, however, departs markedly from that for the United States

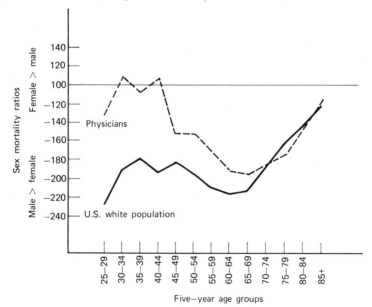

Figure 2.2.   Sex mortality ratios of death rates for physicians (1969–1973) and for the U.S. white population (1971).[a]

[a]To calculate ratios above the horizontal line (female > male), female rates are divided by male rates. To calculate ratios below the horizontal line (male > female), male rates are divided by female rates and subtracted from 100. This ensures that equivalent departure from equality in rates are reflected in equivalent distances above and below the horizontal line. [Goodman (1975), Table 2, p. 359. Ratios calculated by the authors from data presented by Goodman.]

population as a whole. In the age groups between 30 and 44, death rates for women physicians equal or surpass male rates. Furthermore, whereas death rates among younger male physicians are approximately 50 percent below comparable rates in the population as a whole, mortality among women physicians in the 30—44 age group is almost 90 percent of mortality among U.S. women of comparable age.

Although the unexpected pattern of sex mortality ratios among physicians might possibly be dismissed (as it is by Goodman) as an artifact caused by the small number of females, this explanation becomes less plausible when the pattern is repeated in a larger and more representative population. In his study of mortality rates among members of the Wisconsin labor force, Ladbrook (1977) observed that in professional and technical occupations, women have higher mortality rates than men in every age group between 16 and 64. Death rates for women professionals and for managers and administrators were higher than comparable age-specific rates for the Wisconsin female work force as a whole, but only among professionals did women's mortality rates exceed those for men.

On the basis of his careful study, Ladbrook (1977) concludes that: "the major contribution to the reversal in the sex differential in mortality among professionals is due to the reduction of male mortality [p. 352]." Males in professional occupations are substantially less likely than other males to die of conditions (lung cancer and cirrhosis of the liver) associated with overt risk-taking behavior. Ladbrook also suggests that the life-styles of professional women expose them to mortality risks that are greater than average although the evidence for this possibility is less compelling. However, Ladbrook presents data that are consistent with findings from the two studies of suicide (Mausner & Steppacher, 1973; Steppacher & Mausner, 1974) in demonstrating suicide rates higher than expected among women with professional occupations.

The material that has been presented on the relation of employment outside the home to women's health status can be briefly summarized. Employed women experience higher levels of subjective health status than housewives and engage in less illness *behavior*, although the former benefit is confined primarily to women who are less well educated and/or unmarried. Certain mortality rates have also been shown to be lower among employed women. Although neither set of results suggests that employment is *harmful* to women's health, far more detailed analyses employing prospective data would be required to arrive at a definitive interpretation. It is particularly important to ascertain the causal direction of these relationships as well as the specific mechanisms by which they are produced.

In contrast to the generally positive relationship between employment and health status among women, occupation-specific mortality data indicate mortality rates *higher* than expected among certain groups of professional women. However, before accepting these findings as evidence for the potentially negative effects on women of high occupational achievement, it is important to keep two points in mind. First, careful analysis suggests that convergence of sex–mortality ratios at higher occupational levels (if convergence were demonstrated definitively) is caused less by women's adoption of masculine role behavior than to the reverse: adoption by male professionals of the more self-protective life-styles characteristic of adult women. Women's mortality rates are already extremely low, and it is perhaps not surprising that variations in life-style associated with occupational status should have the greatest influence on *male* mortality, where there is the most room for mortality reduction.

Finally, although there is some evidence of higher mortality risks among professional and managerial women as compared to other employed women, this evidence is not sufficiently clear or consistent to indicate how future changes in women's occupational status will affect their mortality. It may be, for example, that it is the marginal status of women in certain male-dominated occupations that increases their mortality risks (this is a plausible hypothesis to explain suicide rates that are higher than expected), and that these risks will decrease rather than increase as a consequence of women's greater representation in nontraditional occupations.

Summary

Levels of mortality, reported illness, and use of health services are not uniform across women's principal social roles but vary in ways that are still only partially known and even less well understood. The direction of relationships, furthermore, is different depending on whether "health" is defined in terms of mortality, in terms of illness as reported in health surveys, in terms of reported disability, or in terms of physician or hospital care. There is some evidence of social role variation in the frequency of particular causes of death among women.

Because of these variations that depend on the definition of "health" and because any single investigator is likely to focus on only one health index (e.g., mortality, "physical conditions," psychiatric symptoms, work days lost), the conclusions drawn about the effects of any particular role or role-set on "health" and "well-being" are frequently contradictory. Marital status, parenthood, and employment, without further specification, are ambiguous conceptual categories, taking on a variety of colorations to fit the problem at hand. Although mortality is generally conceded to be a negative event, whether illness behavior and seeking medical care are defined as desirable health practices or as responses to frustration and a lack of alternative roles appears to depend on the orientation of the investigator. These conceptual problems can be solved only within the context of research designed specifically to test alternative hypotheses about the effects of theoretically relevant variables on women's health status and health behavior. Some interesting leads (for example, the influence of variations in number and quality of interpersonal ties on health-relevant behavior) are suggested by the foregoing review.

WOMEN AND HEALTH: PERSPECTIVES AND ISSUES FOR RESEARCH

In the course of the preceding pages, we have raised a number of methodological, conceptual, and substantive issues that need to be addressed if research on sex differences in health status generally, and on the health of adult women in particular, is to progress beyond its current relatively primitive state. In this section, we review what are, we believe, the major research issues in this area and suggest some directions that future research might take.

Issues of Method and Meaning

In the area of sociomedical research on health, questions of method and questions of substance are almost inextricably intertwined. The criteria that are used to define disease states and the methods by which data on health and illness are collected largely determine what these data will mean. And whether data on health status are taken to reflect organic conditions or behavioral manifestations determines, in turn, what research questions are posed and what explanatory models are employed.

The myriad problems involved in interpretation of morbidity data from health surveys have been reviewed in detail by Nathanson (1977a, 1978) and Mechanic (1976). Briefly, the volume of illness reported by women relative to men is liable to be affected both by the illness criteria that are employed and by the research methods. In addition to differential effects of research methodology on reported illness, women also differ from men and from each other in the probability that they will perceive symptoms and take action in response to these symptoms. Because behavior in response to symptoms *is* the illness criterion in most surveys, these behavioral tendencies clearly will affect the level of reported morbidity. Further progress in research on sex differences in health status and in the understanding of health and illness behavior among women requires that these difficult methodological and conceptual issues be confronted directly (see, for instance, Verbrugge, 1979b).

To add yet another level of complexity, evaluation of the meaning of reported illness among women demands attention not only to their own attitudes and social roles but also to social and cultural arrangements that bring women into the sphere of medical attention and cause them to define a variety of problems in medical terms. Women's use of medical care services is likely to be initiated as often by physicians as by women themselves, and use, in turn, may cause illness to be more readily remembered and reported to a health interviewer. One of the major gaps both in conceptualization and data collection related to women's health is the failure to link behavior associated with the management of reproduction to other dimensions of health and illness behavior. (This point is also made in a recent paper by Muller [1979]).

As the foregoing comments suggest, "health status" or "illness" as reflected in data that are currently available to describe them are not simple or unidimensional concepts. Although organic disease, illness behavior, and the use of health services are equally legitimate topics for sociological inquiry, it is important to be clear which of these topics is at issue in any particular case. Maintaining necessary conceptual distinctions does not, however, preclude combining a variety of health indexes in the same research design. Data presented earlier suggest that the direction of effects may be different depending on which index is used. Hypotheses, therefore, should be constructed to allow for this complexity.

Mortality as an index of health status is relatively immune to many of the conceptual and methodological problems that plague the softer health indexes. However, the relationship of mortality to health and illness behavior is a question of substantial interest that remains relatively unexplored. Examination of data on sex differences in a range of health relevant behaviors, including risk taking (smoking, alcohol consumption, illegal drug use, automobile driving) as well as risk avoiding (preventive examinations, dental care, immunizations) suggests that these behaviors form an underlying spectrum in terms of their relationship to mortality (Nathanson, 1977b). At one end of the spectrum are those actions by which an individual directly exposes himself or herself to the risk of disease, injury, or death; at the other end are actions that protect against these outcomes. This analysis suggests that sex differences in mortality are to some extent a consequence of sex differences in health and illness behavior.

Research Issues and Research Designs

Approaches to research on sex roles, illness, and health vary depending on how the phenomenon requiring explanation is defined and what mechanisms are postulated to produce variation in this phenomenon. Sex differences in mortality, for example, may result from biological factors, from differential exposure to stress, from differences in risk-taking and risk-avoiding behavior, from differences in use of health services, or from other factors as yet undefined (or from any combination of these factors). The mechanisms that are selected (either explicitly or implicitly) largely determine the choice of an explanatory model.

Comprehensive reviews of the literature as well as analyses of existing data have led to the conclusion that sex differences in health indexes are largely a consequence of socially determined, sex-linked attitudes and behavior rather than of biological sex differences (Mechanic, 1976; Nathanson, 1977a; Verbrugge, 1976b). However, although biological makeup probably determines relatively few of these differences, variations in the social construction of biological processes seem likely to play a major role in health and illness behavior among women (and probably among men as well).

Within this broad perspective, a wide variety of research approaches are possible and appropriate. Our purpose here is to identify those issues that are of greatest potential interest and importance and to consider how research might be designed to approach these issues. A basic assumption underlying this presentation is that if observed differences in health indexes among men and women are caused largely by the social norms that define sex-appropriate behavior, then a research strategy that focuses on variations in these norms, both in time and in place, is likely to prove most productive. (A case for the interaction of biological and sociocultural factors in determining gender role differences is made by Rossi [1977, 1980] although her focus is not specifically on health.)

The degree of social integration and the quality of social ties have been advanced to account for variations in mortality, in reported symptoms, in illness behavior, and in the use of health services, although the mechanisms that underlie these relationships are often unspecified and even contradictory. The precise nature of these effects might usefully be investigated in two types of studies. First, studies should be conducted of women who vary both in the nature and quality of their social relationships and in their perception of the rewards and costs of these relationships, since we would hypothesize that objective ties and the way in which these ties are subjectively perceived are both important in determining the effects of social integration on health and illness behavior. Second, prospective studies of the correlation between changes in social ties over the life cycle and changes in health indexes would be extremely valuable in pinpointing the effects of social integration on health status. It is very important that the types of research described include a wide variety of health indexes, not excluding clinical evaluations, because it is quite clear that effects on one index cannot be generalized to others.

A second major research issue concerns the effects of changing sex role norms on mortality and on the various behavioral health indexes. If socialization processes and situational pressures specific to males are partly responsible for their higher mortality and lesser responsiveness to symptoms of illness, will women's adoption of "masculine" behavior patterns effect corresponding changes in their health status? The hypothesis that this question implies is supported by the rise in death rates from lung cancer among recent age cohorts of women, but there is no conclusive evidence of changes in rates for other causes of death in females. Furthermore, the hypothesis itself may require modification to take into account the social changes in the management of reproduction that bring women earlier and more frequently into the medical care system and the possibility that changing sex role norms will be associated with the adoption by both sexes of entirely new life-styles. These latter changes may counteract or reinforce the postulated effects of changes in other sex role dimensions.

In the short run, the consequences for health status of converging or changing life styles could usefully be addressed by investigators in critical areas such as occupation and health or cardiovascular disease. Carefully designed comparative studies of health indexes and patterns of medical care among women in occupational categories selected on a theoretically relevant basis would be particularly valuable.

There is evidence to suggest that sex differences in health attitudes and health and illness behavior begin to emerge in childhood (Campbell, 1978; Lewis, Lewis, Lorimer, et al., 1977; Mechanic, 1964), yet there are relatively few studies of the socialization processes that shape these dimensions of behavior. A critical research area from the perspective of this chapter is the process by which adolescent girls and young women learn to label and respond to internal bodily signals. Cross-cultural studies of women's illness behavior that are focused on the effects of variation in socialization patterns and in the meaning attributed to biological events would help to answer questions about the role of early learning in symptom responsiveness and health actions among adults.

Finally, we believe that the structural arrangements developed in American society for the management and control of women's reproductive cycle encourage women to define their life problems, whether of biological, psychological, or social origin, in medical terms and to seek professional help for them (cf. Cloward & Piven, 1979). Historically, women have been regarded by the American medical profession as peculiarly vulnerable to disease (Smith−Rosenberg & Rosenberg, 1973; Wood, 1973). A standard early nineteenth century text on female diseases proclaimed that "woman was subject to twice the sicknesses that affected men just because she has a womb" (Smith−Rosenberg & Rosenberg, 1973). Today, the control of fertility, the management of the menopause, and the wide spectrum of "female complaints" in between continue to be the focus of professional medical attention. The significance for women's health and illness behavior of the social system within which their physiological processes are defined and treated has yet to be systematically examined. Such an examination would be particularly valuable at the present time. Traditional models of health care for women are currently under pressure for change from the feminist health movement (Span, 1980) and may come under additional pressure as increasing numbers of women physicians enter obstetrics and gynecology (Weisman, Levine, Steinwachs, et al., 1980).

Research on this question would need to consider the attitudes and behavior of providers of health care as well as of women themselves.

Comparative cross-national studies in countries with different patterns of fertility control and different patterns of health services use by women (for example, the United States or Canada compared to France) would contribute immeasurably to understanding in this area. Comparative studies of health care and health outcomes in countries with different political systems (such as China and the United States), or in capitalist countries with different health care systems, e.g., the United States and West Germany would be of particular interest. Studies of different structural arrangements within the United States (comparing, e.g., health care patterns and outcomes among women enrolled in feminist health centers versus women receiving traditional medical care) would be very valuable and timely as well.

The research program that we have proposed centers on variations in the social conditions and social roles of women: (1) over the individual life course, (2) between generations, (3) contemporaneously, between subsystems within the same society, and (4) cross-culturally and cross-nationally. Understanding of the social dimensions of health status both as a generic issue and among women specifically will be advanced by carefully designed studies of the health indexes and outcomes associated with these variations.

Women's biological uniqueness has profound consequences for their adult lives. How they experience that uniqueness and what it means to them are as much the products of social as of biological processes. The question as to which of these two processes is the more important has no single or simple answer. The most that can be said is that the relative influence of nature, nurture, and social structure on the health outcomes that are the focus of this chapter varies depending on the particular mortality, illness, or medical care rates that are under investigation; frequently, all three sets of influences are inextricably intertwined. This is an area only recently opened up to research by social as well as biological scientists, and a large part of the evidence is not in or is in dispute. We have attempted, therefore, to avoid taking dogmatic positions. At best, we have provided a set of guideposts to the physical dimension of women's lives, a dimension that cannot be safely ignored by any serious student of women in the middle years.

REFERENCES

Andersen, R., J. Lion, and O.W. Anderson. 1976. *Two Decades of Health Services: Social Survey Trends in Use and Expenditure.* Cambridge, MA: Ballinger.

Antunes, C.M.F., P.D. Stolley, P.D. Rosenshein, et al., 1979. "Endometrial Cancer and Estrogen Use—Report of a Large Case-Control Study." *New England Journal of Medicine* **300** (January 4): 9–13.

Baetjer, A.M. 1946. *Women in Industry: Their Health and Efficiency.* Philadelphia: Saunders.

Bardwick, J.M. 1971. *Psychology of Women: A Study of Bio-Cultural Conflicts.* New York: Harper & Row, Pub.

Bart, P.M., and M. Grossman. 1976. "Menopause." *Women and Health* **3** (May-June): 3−11.

Beamis, J.F., A Stein, and J.L. Andrews, Jr. 1975. "Changing Epidemiology of Lung Cancer: Increasing Incidence in Women." *Medical Clinics of North America* **59** (March): 315−325.

Belloc, N.B. 1973. "Relationship of Health Practices and Mortality." *Preventive Medicine* **2** (March): 67−81.

Bengtsson, C., T. Hallstrom, and G. Tibblin. 1973. "Social Factors, Stress Experience, and Personality Traits in Women with Ischaemic Heart Disease, Compared to a Population Sample of Women." *Acta Medica Scandinavia* **549** (Supplement): 82−92.

Beral, V. 1979. "Reproductive Mortality." *British Medical Journal* **2** (September 15): 632−634.

Berkman, L.F., and S.L. Syme. 1979. "Social Networks, Host Resistance, and Mortality: A Nine-Year Follow-Up Study of Alameda County Residents." *American Journal of Epidemiology* **109** (February): 186−204.

Berkman, P.L. 1975. "Survival, and a Modicum of Indulgence in the Sick Role." *Medical Care* **13** (January): 85−94.

Bernard, J. 1972. *The Future of Marriage.* New York: Bantam.

Borgman, R.D. 1973. "Medication Abuse by Middle-Aged Women." *Social Casework* **54** (November): 526−532.

Boston Women's Health Book Collective. 1979. *Our Bodies, Our Selves—A book by and for Women.* 2nd ed., revised and expanded. New York: Simon & Schuster. Touchstone Book.

Brown, G., and T. Harris. 1978. *Social Origins of Depression.* London: Tavistock.

Burstyn, J.N. 1973. "Education and Sex: The Medical Case Against Higher Education for Women in England, 1890−1900." *Proceedings of the American Philosophical Society* **117** (April): 79−89.

Campbell, J.D. 1978. "The Child in the Sick Role: Contributions of Age, Sex, Parental Status, and Parental Values." *Journal of Health and Social Behavior* **19** (March): 35−51.

Carter, H., and P.C.Glick. 1976. *Marriage and Divorce: A Social and Economic Study.* Cambridge, MA: Harvard University Press.

Childs, B. 1965. "Genetic Origin of Some Sex Differences Among Human Beings." *Pediatrics* **35** (May): 798−812.

Cloward, R.A., and F.F. Piven. 1979. "Hidden Protest: The Channeling of Female Innovation and Resistance." *Signs: Journal of Women in Culture and Society* **4** (Summer): 651−669.

Cole, S., and R. Lejeune. 1972. "Illness and the Legitimation of Failure." *American Sociological Review* **37** (June): 347−356.

Connell, E.B. 1979. "When are Estrogens Safe for your Patient?" *Modern Medicine* **47** (7, April): 89−98.

Cooperstock, R. 1971. "Sex Differences in the Use of Mood-Modifying Drugs: An Exploratory Model." *Journal of Health and Social Behavior* **12** (September): 238−244.

_____. 1978. "Sex Differences in Psychotropic Drug Use." *Social Science and Medicine* **12B** (July): 176–186.

Crawford, M.P., and D. Hooper. 1973. "Menopause, Ageing and Family." *Social Science and Medicine* **7** (June): 469–482.

Cumming, E., C. Lazar, and L. Chisholm. 1975. "Suicide as an Index of Role Strain Among Employed and Not Employed Married Women in British Columbia," *Canadian Review of Sociology and Anthropology* **12** (November): 462–470.

Dalton, K. 1964. *The Premenstrual Syndrome.* Springfield, IL: Charles C Thomas.

De Beauvoir, S. 1971. *The Second Sex.* New York: Knopf.

Durkheim, E. 1952. *Suicide: A Study in Sociology.* New York: Free Press.

Ehrenreich, B., and D. English. 1979. *For Her Own Good: 150 Years of Expert Advice to Women.* Garden City, NY: Anchor Press/Doubleday, 1978. Anchor Book Edition.

Enterline, P.E. 1961. "Causes of Death Responsible for Recent Increases in Sex Mortality Differentials in the United States." *Milbank Memorial Fund Quarterly* **38** (April): 312–328.

Feinstein, A.R., and R.I. Horwitz. 1978. "A Critique of the Statistical Evidence Associating Estrogens with Endometrial Cancer." *Cancer Research* **38** (November): 4001–4005.

Feld, S. 1963. "Feelings of Adjustment." In F.I. Nye and L.W. Hoffman (Eds.), *The Employed Mother in America.* Chicago: Rand McNally.

Feldman, J.J. 1966. *The Dissemination of Health Information.* Chicago: Aldine.

Flint, M. 1975. "The Menopause: Reward or Punishment?" *Psychosomatics* **16** (4) (October–December): 161–163.

Ford, K. 1978. "Contraceptive Use in the United States, 1973–1976." *Family Planning Perspectives* **10** (September/October): 264–269.

Forrest, J.D., C. Tietze, and E. Sullivan. 1978. "Abortion in the United States, 1976–77." *Family Planning Perspectives* **10** (September/October): 271–279.

Francome, C., and P.J. Huntingford. 1980. "Births by Cesarian Section in the United States of America and in Britain." *Journal of Biosocial Science* **12** (3, July): 353–362.

Freeman, Richard B. 1976. *The Overeducated American.* New York: Academic Press.

Friedman, R.C., S.W. Hurt, M.S. Aronoff, et al., 1980. "Behavior and the Menstrual Cycle." *Signs: Journal of Women in Culture and Society* **5** (Summer): 719–738.

Furuhjelm, M., and G. Zador. 1979. "Present Status of Estrogen Treatment for Prevention of Postmenopausal Osteoporosis," *Acta Obstetrica et Gynecologica Scandinavica* **88** (Supplement November): 97–101.

Garbus, S.B., and S.B. Garbus. 1980. "Will Improvement in the Socioeconomic Status of Women Increase Their Cardiovascular Morbidity and Mortality?" *Journal of the American Medical Women's Association* **35** (November): 257–261.

Geertsen, H.R., and R.M. Gray. 1970. "Familistic Orientation and Inclination Toward Adopting the Sick Role." *Journal of Marriage and the Family* **32** (November): 638–646.

Gentleman, J.F., and W.F. Forbes. 1974. "Cancer Mortality for Males and Females and Its Relation to Cigarette Smoking." *Journal of Gerontology* **29** (September): 518–533.

Glenn, N.D. 1975. "The Contribution of Marriage to the Psychological Well-Being of Males and Females." *Journal of Marriage and the Family* **37** (August): 594–600.

Goodman, L.J. 1975. "The Longevity and Mortality of American Physicians, 1969–1973." *Milbank Memorial Fund Quarterly* **53** (Summer): 353–375.

Goodman, M. 1980. "Toward a Biology of Menopause." *Signs: Journal of Women in Culture and Society* **5** (Summer): 739–753.

Gordon, T., W.B. Kannel, M.C. Hjortland et al., 1978 "Menopause and Coronary Heart Disease—The Framingham Study." *Annals of Internal Medicine* **89** (2, August): 157–161.

Gore, W. 1978. "The Effect of Social Support in Moderating the Health Consequences of Unemployment." *Journal of Health and Social Behavior* **19** (June): 157–165.

Gove, W.R. 1973. "Sex, Marital Status, and Mortality." *American Journal of Sociology* **79** (July): 45–67.

Gove, W.R., and M.R. Geerken. 1977. "The Effect of Children and Employment on the Mental Health of Married Men and Women." *Social Forces* **56** (September): 66–76.

Gove, W.R., and M. Hughes. 1979. "Possible Causes of the Apparent Sex Differences in Physical Health: An Empirical Investigation." *American Sociological Review* **44** (February): 126–146.

Gove, W.R., and J. Tudor. 1973. "Adult Sex Roles and Mental Illness." *American Journal of Sociology* **78** (January): 812–835.

Hammond, C.G., F.R. Jelovsek, K.L. Lee, et al. 1979. "Effects of Long-term Estrogen Replacement Therapy—II. Neoplasia." *American Journal of Obstetrics and Gynecology* **133** (5, March 1): 537–547.

Hauenstein, L.S., S.V. Kasl, and E. Harburg. 1977. "Work Status, Work Satisfaction, and Blood Pressure Among Married Black and White Women." *Psychology of Women Quarterly* **1** (Summer): 334–349.

Haynes, S.G. and M. Feinleib. 1980. "Women, Work and Coronary Heart Disease: Prospective Findings from the Framingham Heart Study" *American Journal of Public Health* **70** (February): 133–141.

Haynes, S.G., M. Feinleib, and S. Levine. 1978. "The Relationship of Psychosocial Factors to Coronary Heart Disease in the Framingham Study. II. Prevalence of Coronary Heart Disease." *American Journal of Epidemiology* **107** (May): 384–402.

House, J.S. 1974. "Occupational Stress and Coronary Heart Disease: A Review and

Theoretical Integration." *Journal of Health and Social Behavior* **15** (March): 12–27.

Hetherington, R.W., and C.E. Hopkins. 1969. "Symptom Sensitivity: Its Social and Cultural Correlates." *Health Survey Research* **4** (Spring): 63–75.

Hulka, B.S. 1980. "Effect of Exogenous Estrogen on Postmenopausal Women: The Epidemiologic Evidence." *Obstetrical and Gynecological Survey* **35**, Supplement (June): 389–399.

Hunt, V.R. 1975. "Reproduction and Work." *Signs: Journal of Women in Culture and Society* **1** (Winter): 543–552.

Hunt, V.R. 1977. *The Health of Women at Work*. Occasional Papers No. 2. Program on Women, Northwestern University, Evanston, IL.

Ibrahim, M.A. 1980. "The Changing Health State of Women." *American Journal of Public Health* **70** (February): 120–121.

Jick, H., R.N. Watkins, J.R. Hunter et al. 1979. "Replacement Estrogens and Endometrial Cancer." *The New England Journal of Medicine* **300** (February 1): 218–222.

Johnson, A. 1977. "Recent Trends in Sex Mortality Differentials in the United States." *Journal of Human Stress* **3** (March): 22–32.

Kerr, M.D. and C. Vaughan. 1975. "Psychohormonal Treatment During the Menopause." *American Family Physician* **11** (February): 99–103.

Kirscht, J.P., D.P. Haefner, S.S. Kegeles, et al. 1966. "A National Study of Health Beliefs." *Journal of Health and Human Behavior* **7** (Winter): 248–254.

Kitagawa, E.M. 1977. "On Mortality." *Demography* **14** (November): 381–389.

Klaus, H. 1974. "The Menopause in Gynecology: A Focus for Teaching the Comprehensive Care of Women." *Journal of Medical Education* **49** (December): 1186–1189.

Knupfer, G., W. Clark, and R. Room. 1966. "The Mental Health of the Unmarried." *American Journal of Psychiatry* **122** (February): 841–851.

Kobrin, F.E., and G.E. Hendershot. 1977. "Do Family Ties Reduce Mortality? Evidence from the United States, 1966–1968." *Journal of Marriage and the Family* **39** (November):737–745.

Koeske, R.D. 1976. "Premenstrual Emotionality: Is Biology Destiny?" *Women and Health* **1** (May-June): 11–14.

Koeske, R.D., and G.F. Koeske, 1975. "An Attributional Approach to Moods and the Menstrual Cycle." *Journal of Personality and Social Psychology* **31** (March): 473–478.

Krueger, D.E., S.S. Ellenberg, S. Bloom, et al. 1980. "Fatal Myocardial Infarction and the Role of Oral Contraceptives." *American Journal of Epidemiology* **111** (June): 655–674.

Ladbrook, D.A. 1977. "Social Contexts of Premature Death in Contemporary America." Unpublished Ph.D. dissertation, University of Wisconsin-Madison, Madison, WI.

The Lancet. 1980. "Women, Work, and Coronary Heart Disease." (Editorial) **2** (8185, July 12): 76–77.

Lenanne, K.J., and R.J. Lenanne. 1973. "Alleged Psychogenic Disorders in Women—A Possible Manifestation of Sexual Prejudice." *New England Journal of Medicine* **288** (February 8): 288–292.

Lewis, C.E., M.A. Lewis, A. Lorimer, et al. 1977. "Child-Initiated Care: The Use of School Nursing Services by Children in an 'Adult-Free' System." *Pediatrics* **60** (October): 499–507.

Lewis, C.E., and R.N. Lewis. 1977. "The Potential Impact of Sexual Equality on Health." *New England Journal of Medicine* **297** (October 20): 863–869.

Lindsay, R., and D.M. Hart. 1978. "Oestrogens and Post-Menopausal Bone Loss." *Scottish Medical Journal* **23** (January): 13–18.

Lindsay, R., D.M. Hart, J.M. Aitken, et al. 1978. "Bone Response to Termination of Oestrogen Treatment." *Lancet* **1** (June 24): 1325–1327.

Lingeman, C.H. 1979. "Hormones and Hormonomimetic Compounds in the Etiology of Cancer." *Recent Results in Cancer Research* **66** (Annual): 1–48.

Linn, L.S. 1971. "Physician Characteristics and Attitudes Toward Legitimate Use of Psychotherapeutic Drugs." *Journal of Health and Social Behavior* **12** (June): 132–140.

Linn, L.S. and M.S. Davis. 1971. "The Use of Psychotherapeutic Drugs by Middle-Aged Women." *Journal of Health and Social Behavior* **12** (December): 331–340.

Lyle, K.C. 1980. "Female Breast Cancer: Distribution, Risk Factors, and Effect of Steroid Contraception." *Obstetrical and Gynecological Survey* **35**, Supplement (July): 413–427.

MacMahon, B., and J. Worcester. 1966. "Age at Menopause, United States, 1960–1962." *Vital and Health Statistics*. Public Health Service Publication No. 1000– Series 11, No. 19, Washington, DC: U.S. Government Printing Office.

Maoz, B., N. Dowty, A. Antonovsky, and H. Wijsenbeek. 1970. "Female Attitudes to Menopause." *Social Psychiatry* **5** (January) 35–41.

Marieskind, H. 1975. "The Women's Health Movement." *International Journal of Health Services* **5** (January):217–223.

Mausner, J.S., and R.C. Steppacher. 1973. "Suicide in Professionals: A Study of Male and Female Psychologists." *American Journal of Epidemiology* **98** (December): 436–445.

McKinlay, S.M., and M. Jeffreys. 1974. "The Menopausal Syndrome." *British Journal of Preventive and Social Medicine* **28** (May): 108–115.

McKinlay, S.M., and J.B. McKinlay. 1973. "Selected Studies of the Menopause: A Methodological Critique." *Journal of Biosocial Science* **5** (October): 533–535.

Mechanic, D. 1964. "The Influence of Mothers on their Children's Health Attitudes and Behavior." *Pediatrics* **33** (March): 444–453.

———. 1976. "Sex, Illness, Illness Behavior, and the Use of Health Services." *Journal of Human Stress* **2** (December): 29–40.

Meile, R.L., D.R. Johnson, and L. St. Peter. 1976. "Marital Role, Education, and Mental Disorder Among Women: Test of an Interaction Hypothesis." *Journal of Health and Social Behavior* **17** (September): 295–301.

Mellinger, G.D., M.B. Balter, H.J. Parry, et al. 1974. "An Overview of Psychotherapeutic Drug Use in the United States." In E. Josephson and E.E. Carroll (Eds.), *Drug Use, Epidemiological and Sociological Approaches.* New York: Wiley.

Mettlin, C. 1976. "Occupational Careers and the Prevention of the Coronary Prone Behavior Pattern." *Social Science and Medicine* **10** (July/August): 367−372.

Mishell, D.R. 1979. "Intrauterine Devices: Medicated and Nonmedicated." *International Journal of Gynaecology and Obstetrics* **16** (May-June): 482−487.

Moos, R.H. 1969. "Typology of Menstrual Cycle Symptoms." *American Journal of Obstetrics and Gynecology* **103** (3, February): 390−402.

Morton, W.E., and T.J. Ungs. 1979. "Cancer Mortality in the Major Cottage Industry." *Women and Health* **4** (Winter): 345−354.

Muller, C. 1979. "Women and Health Statistics: Areas of Deficient Data Collection and Integration." *Women and Health* **4** (Spring): 37−59.

Naeye, R.H., L.S. Burt, D.L. Wright, et al. 1971. "Neonatal Mortality, The Male Disadvantage." *Pediatrics* **48** (December): 902−906.

Nathanson, C.A. 1975. "Illness and the Feminine Role: A Theoretical Review." *Social Science and Medicine* **9** (February): 57−62.

———. 1977a. "Sex, Illness, and Medical Care: A Review of Data, Theory, and Method." *Social Science and Medicine* **11** (January): 13−25.

———. 1977b. "Sex Roles as Variables in Preventive Health Behavior." *Journal of Community Health* **3** (Winter): 142−155.

———. 1978. "Sex Roles as Variables in the Interpretation of Morbidity Data: A Methodological Critique." *International Journal of Epidemiology* **7** (April): 253−262.

———. 1980. "Social Roles and Health Status Among Women: The Significance of Employment." *Social Science and Medicine* **14A** (December): 463−471.

National Center for Health Statistics. 1967. "Three Views of Hypertension and Heart Disease." *Vital and Health Statistics,* Series 2, No. 22, DHEW, Rockville, MD.

———. 1970. "Changes in Cigarette Smoking Habits Between 1955 and 1966." *Vital and Health Statistics,* Series 10, No. 59, DHEW, Rockville, MD.

———. 1973. "Current Estimates from the Health Interview Survey, United States—1972." *Vital and Health Statistics,* Series 10, No. 85, DHEW Publication No. (HRA) 74-1512, Rockville, MD.

———. 1974. "Current Estimates from the Health Interview Survey, United States—1973." *Vital and Health Statistics,* Series 10, No. 95, DHEW Publication No. (HRA) 75-1522, Rockville, MD.

———. 1975. "Current Estimates from the Health Interview Survey, United States—1974." *Vital and Health Statistics,* Series 10, No. 100. DHEW Publication No. (HRA) 76-1527, Rockville, MD.

———. 1976. "Differentials in Health Characteristics by Marital Status, United States—1971−1972." *Vital and Health Statistics,* Series 10, No. 104. DHEW Publication No. (HRA) 76-1531, Rockville, MD.

———. 1977. "Out of Pocket Cost and Acquisition of Prescribed Medicines, United States, 1973." *Vital and Health Statistics,* Series 10, No. 108, DHEW Publication No. (HRA) 77-1542. Rockville, MD.

———. 1977. "Use of Selected Medical Procedures Associated with Preventive Care, United States, 1973." *Vital and Health Statistics,* Series 10, No. 110. DHEW Publication No. (HRA) 77-1538. Rockville, MD.

———. 1977. "Limitation of Activity Due to Chronic Conditions, United States, 1974." *Vital and Health Statistics,* Series 10, No. 111, DHEW Publication No. (HRA) 77-1537. Rockville, MD.

———. 1976. "Health Characteristics of Persons with Chronic Activity Limitations, United States—1974." *Vital and Health Statistics,* Series 10, No. 112. DHEW Publication No. (HRA) 77-1539. Rockville, MD.

———. 1979. "Current Estimates from the Health Interview Survey, United States, 1978." *Vital and Health Statistics,* Series 10, No. 130. DHEW Publication No. (PHS) 80-1551. Hyattsville, MD.

———. 1979. "Acute Conditions: Incidence and Associated Disability, United States, July, 1977—June, 1978." *Vital and Health Statistics,* Series 10, No. 132. DHEW Publication No. (PHS) 79-1560. Hyattsville, MD.

———. 1973. "Inpatient Utilization of Short-Stay Hospitals by Diagnosis, United States, 1968." *Vital and Health Statistics,* Series 13, No. 12. DHEW Publication No. (HSM) 73-1763. Rockville, MD.

———. 1975. "Utilization of Short-Stay Hospitals: Summary of Nonmedical Statistics, United States, 1972." *Vital and Health Statistics,* Series 13, No. 19, DHEW Publication No. (HRA) 75-1770. Rockville, MD.

———. 1976. "Utilization of Short-Stay Hospitals: Summary of Nonmedical Statistics, United States—1973." *Vital and Health Statistics,* Series 13 (No. 23. DHEW Publication No. (HRA) 76-1774. Rockville, MD.

———. 1976. "Utilization of Short-Stay Hospitals: Annual Summary for the United States, 1974." *Vital and Health Statistics,* Series 13, No. 26. DHEW Publication No. (HRA) 76-1777. Rockville, MD.

———. 1978. "The National Ambulatory Medical Care Survey, 1975 Summary. United States, January—December, 1975." *Vital and Health Statistics,* Series 13, No. 33. DHEW Publication No. (PHS) 78-1784. Hyattsville, MD.

———. 1978. "Surgical Operations in Short-Stay Hospitals, United States, 1975." *Vital and Health Statistics,* Series 13, No. 34. DHEW Publication No. (PHS) 78-1785. Hyattsville, MD.

———. 1979. "Utilization of Short-Stay Hospitals: Annual Summary for the United States, 1977." *Vital and Health Statistics,* Series 13, No. 41. DHEW Publication No. (PHS) 79-1557. Hyattsville, MD.

———. 1970. "Mortality from Selected Causes by Marital Status, United States—Part A." *Vital and Health Statistics,* Series 20, No. 8a. DHEW, Rockville, MD.

———. 1971. "Leading Components of Upturn in Mortality for Men, United States—1952-67." *Vital and Health Statistics,* Series 20, No. 11. DHEW Publication No. (HSM) 72—1008, Rockville, MD.

————. 1973. "Mortality Trends: Age, Color, and Sex, United States—1950−69." *Vital and Health Statistics,* Series 20, No. 15. DHEW Publication No. (HRA) 74-1852. Rockville, MD.

————. 1974. "Mortality Trends for Leading Causes of Death, United States—1950-69." *Vital and Health Statistics,* Series 20, No. 16. DHEW Publication No. (HRA)74-1853. Rockville, MD.

————. 1980a. *Vital Statistics of the United States,* 1976. Volume I—Natality. (PHS) 81-1100, Hyattsville, MD.

————. 1980b. *Vital Statistics of the United States,* Volume II—Mortality, Part A. DHHS Publication No. (PHS) 80-1101. Washington, D.C.

————. 1980c. *Vital Statistics of the United States,* 1977, Life Tables. Volume II, Section 5. DHEW Publication No. (PHS) 80−1104 Hyattsville, MD.

————. 1974. "Advance Report, Final Mortality Statistics, 1972." *Monthly Vital Statistics Report.* Vol. 23, No. 7 (Supplement). Health Resources Administration, Rockville, MD.

————. 1975. "Advance Report, Final Mortality Statistics, 1972." *Monthly Vital Statistics Report.* Vol. 23, No. 11 (Supplement). Health Resources Administration, Rockville, MD.

————. 1976. "Advance Report, Final Mortality Statistics, 1974." *Monthly Vital Statistics Report.* Vol. 24, No. 11 (Supplement). Health Resources Administration, Rockville, MD.

————. 1980. "Advance Report, Final Mortality Statistics, 1978." *Monthly Vital Statistics Report.* Vol. 29, No. 1 (Supplement). DHHS Publication No. 80-1120. Hyattsville, MD.

————. 1978. "Office Visits to Obstetrician-Gynecologists: National Ambulatory Medical Care Survey, United States, 1975." *Advance Data From Vital and Health Statistics.* DHEW Publication No. (PHS) 78−1250. March 13, Hyattsville, MD.

Neugarten, B.L., V. Wood, R.J. Kraines, et al. 1963. "Women's Attitudes Toward the Menopause." *Vita Humana* 6 (Annual): 140−151.

Neugarten, B.L., and R.J. Kraines. 1965. "Menopausal Symptoms in Women of Various Ages." *Psychosomatic Medicine* 27 (May−June): 266−273.

Notman, M.T., and Nadelson, C.C. (Eds.) 1978. *The Woman Patient: Medical and Psychological Interfaces,* Vol. 1. New York: Plenum.

Oppenheimer, V.K. 1972. "Rising Educational Attainment, Declining Fertility and the Inadequacies of the Female Labor Market." In Commission on Population Growth and the American Future, Research Reports, Vol. I. *Demographic and Social Aspects of Population Growth,* Westoff, C.F. and Parke, Jr., R. (Eds.). Washington, DC Government Printing Office.

Oppenheimer, V.K. 1973. "Demographic Influence on Female Employment and the Status of Women." In Joan Huber (Ed.), *Changing Women in a Changing Society.* Chicago: University of Chicago Press.

Ortmeyer, L.E. 1979. "Females' Natural Advantage? Or, the Unhealthy Environment of Males? The Status of Sex Mortality Differentials." *Women and Health* 4 (Summer): 121−133.

Osofsky, H., and R. Seidenberg. 1970. "Is Female Menopausal Depression Inevitable?" *Obstetrics and Gynecology* **36** (October): 611–615.

Paffenbarger, R.S., J.B. Kampert, and H.G. Chang. 1980. "Characteristics That Predict Risk of Breast Cancer Before and After the Menopause." *American Journal of Epidemiology* **112** (2): 258–268.

Paige, K.E. 1973. "Women Learn to Sing the Menstrual Blues." *Psychology Today* **7** (4): 41–46.

Parlee, M.B. 1973. "The Premenstrual Syndrome." *Psychological Bulletin* **80** (December): 454–465.

———. 1974. "Stereotypic Beliefs About Menstruation: A Methodological Note on the Moos Menstrual Distress Questionnaire and Some New Data." *Psychosomatic Medicine* **36** (May–June): 229–240.

———. 1978. "Psychological Aspects of Menstruation, Childbirth, and Menopause." In J.A. Sherman and F.L. Denmark (Eds.), *The Psychology of Women: Future Directions of Research.* New York: Psychological Dimensions, Inc.

———. 1980. "Social and Emotional Aspects of Menstruation, Birth, and Menopause." In D.D. Youngs and A.A. Ehrhardt (Eds.), *Psychosomatic Obstetrics and Gynecology.* New York: Appleton-Century-Crofts.

Pearlin, L., and J.S. Johnson. 1977. "Marital Status, Life Strains, and Depression." *American Sociological Review* **42** (October): 704–715.

Perlmutter, J.F. 1978. "A Gynecological Approach to Menopause." in M.T. Notman and C.C. Nadelson (Eds.), *The Woman Patient: Medical and Psychological Interfaces,* Vol. 1. New York: Plenum.

Pflanz, M., H.D. Basler, and D. Schwoon. 1977. "Use of Tranquilizing Drugs by a Middle-Aged Population in a West German City." *Journal of Health and Social Behavior* **18** (June): 194–205.

Population Information Program. 1979a. "Oral Contraceptives—Update on Usage, Safety, and Side Effects." *Population Reports*, Series A (January): 133–187.

———. 1979b. "Intrauterine Devices—Update on Safety, Effectiveness, and Research." *Population Reports*, Series B (May): 49–99.

Preston, S.H. 1970. "An International Comparison of Excessive Adult Mortality." *Population Studies* **24** (March): 5–20.

———. 1976. *Mortality Patterns in National Populations.* New York: Academic Press.

Preston, S.H., and J.A. Weed. 1976. "Causes of Death Responsible for International and Intertemporal Variation in Sex Mortality Differentials." *World Health Statistics Report* **29** (3, March): 144–214.

Prill, H.J. 1978. "Ueber das Klimakterium zur Physiologie und Pathologie der Altersvorgaenge bei der Frau." *Zeitschrift fuer Gerontologie* **11** (January/February): 39–53.

Reeder, L. 1976. "Future Research in Coronary Disease." Paper read at the Annual Meeting of the American Sociological Association, New York City, August.

Retherford, R.D. 1975. *The Changing Sex Differential in Mortality.* Westport, CT: Greenwood Press.

Ridley, J.C. 1969. "Changing Position of Women." In *The Family in Transition*. A Round Table Conference sponsored by the Fogarty International Center, National Institutes of Health, Bethesda, MD.

Rioux, J.E. 1979. "Sterilization of Women: Benefits vs. Risks." *International Journal of Gynaecology and Obstetrics* 16 (May–June): 488–492.

Rivkin, M.O. 1972. "Contextual Effects of Families on Female Responses to Illness." Unpublished Ph.D. dissertation. Johns Hopkins University, Baltimore, MD.

Romney, S.L., M.J. Gray, A.B. Little, et al. 1975. *Gynecology and Obstetrics*. New York: McGraw-Hill.

Rosenfield, A. 1978. "Oral and Intrauterine Contraception: A 1978 Risk Assessment." *American Journal of Obstetrics and Gynecology* 132 (September 1): 92–106.

Rossi, A.S. 1977. "A Biosocial Perspective on Parenting." *Daedalus* 106 (Spring): 1–31.

———. 1980. "Life-Span Theories and Women's Lives." *Signs: Journal of Women in Culture and Society* 6 (Autumn): 4–32.

Russek, H.I., and L.G. Russek. 1976. "Is Emotional Stress an Etiologic Factor in Coronary Heart Disease?" *Psychosomatics* 17 (2, April–June): 63–67.

Sarto, G.E. 1977. "Risks and Benefits of Postmenopausal Exogenous Estrogen." *International Journal of Gynaecology and Obstetrics* 15 (2): 189–192.

Schiff, I., and K.J. Ryan. 1980. "Benefits of Estrogen Replacement." *Obstetrical and Gynecological Survey*. (Supplement) 35 (6): 400–411.

Scott, C.S. 1975. "The Relationship Between Beliefs About the Menstrual Cycle and Choice of Fertility Regulating Methods within Five Ethnic Groups." *International Journal of Gynecology and Obstetrics* 13 (3, May–June): 105–109.

Scully, D. 1980. *Men Who Control Women's Health: The Miseducation of Obstetrician-Gynecologists*. Boston: Houghton Mifflin.

Shapiro, S., L. Rosenberg, D. Slone, et al. 1979. "Oral-Contraceptive Use in Relation to Myocardial Infarction." *The Lancet* 1 (April 7): 743–747.

Shoemaker, E.S., J.P. Forney, and P.C. MacDonald. 1977. "Estrogen Treatment of Postmenopausal Women: Benefits and Risks." *Journal of the American Medical Association* 238 (October 3): 1524–1530.

Shryock, H.S., and J.S. Siegel. 1975. *The Methods and Materials of Demography*, Vol. 2. Rev. ed. Washington, DC: U.S. Department of Commerce, Bureau of the Census.

Sigerist, H. 1960. "Developments and Trends in Gynecology." In F. Marti-Ibañez (Ed.), *Henry E. Sigerist on the History of Medicine*. New York: MD Publications.

Sloan, D. 1978. "The Emotional and Psychosocial Aspects of Hysterectomy." *American Journal of Obstetrics and Gynecology* 131 (July 15): 598–605.

Smith-Rosenberg, C., and C. Rosenberg. 1973. "The Female Animal: Medical and Biological Views of Women and Her Role in Nineteenth Century America." *Journal of American History* 60 (2) 332–356.

Sommer, B. 1973. "The Effect of Menstruation on Cognitive and Perceptual Motor Behavior: A Review." *Psychosomatic Medicine* **35** (November–December): 515–533.

Span, P. 1980. "A New Era for Feminist Health Clinics." *The New York Times Magazine* (November 23).

Spiegelman, M., and C. Erhardt. 1974. "International Comparisons of Mortality and Longevity." In C.L. Erhardt and J.E. Berlin (Eds.), *Mortality and Morbidity in the United States.* Cambridge, MA: Harvard University Press.

Stadel, B.V., and N.S.Weiss. 1975. "Characteristics of Menopausal Women: A Survey of King and Pierce Counties in Washington, 1973–1974." *American Journal of Epidemiology* **102** (September): 209–216.

Statistics Canada. 1971. Hospital Morbidity. Ottawa.

Stearns, P.N. 1980. "Old Women: Some Historical Observations." *Journal of Family History* **5** (Spring): 44–57.

Steppacher, R.C., and J.S. Mausner. 1974. "Suicide in Male and Female Physicians." *Journal of the American Medical Association* **228** (April 15): 323–328.

Stolley, P.D. 1977. "Lung Cancer: Unwanted Equality for Women." *New England Journal of Medicine* **297** (October 20): 886–887.

———. 1980. "Epidemiologic Studies of Coronary Heart Disease: Two Approaches." *American Journal of Epidemiology* **112** (No. 2, August) 217–224.

Stolley, P.D., S. Shapiro, D. Slone et al. 1978. "Cardiovascular Effects of Oral Contraceptives." *Southern Medical Journal* **71** (July): 821–824.

Suchman, E.A. 1965. "Social Patterns of Illness and Medical Care." *Journal of Health and Human Behavior* **6** (Spring): 2–16.

Terris, M. 1966. "Epidemiology of Cancer of the Cervix." In G.C. Lewis, Jr., W.B. Sentz, and R.M. Jaffe (Eds.), *New Concepts in Gynecological Oncology,* Philadelphia: F.A. Davis.

Terris, M., F. Wilson, and J.H. Nelson. 1980. "Comparative Epidemiology of Invasive Carcinoma of the Cervix, Carcinoma in situ, and Cervical Dysplasia." *American Journal of Epidemiology* **112** (August): 253–257.

Thompson, M.K., and J.S. Brown. 1980. "Feminine Roles and Variations in Women's Illness Behaviors." *Pacific Sociological Review* **23** (October): 405–422.

Tietze, C., and S. Lewit. 1979. "Life Risks Associated with Reversible Methods of Fertility Regulation." *International Journal of Gynecology and Obstetrics* **16** (May–June): 456–459.

Tucker, S.J. 1977. "The Menopause: How Much Soma and How Much Psyche." *Journal of Obstetrical, Gynecological, and Neonatal Nursing* **6** (September–October): 40–47.

U.S. Bureau of the Census. 1976. Prospects for American Fertility: June 1976 (Advance Report). *Current Population Reports.* Series P-20, No. 300 (November). Washington, DC: Government Printing Office.

———. 1979. "Estimates of the Population of the United States by Age, Sex, and Race: 1976–1978." *Current Population Reports,* Series P-25, No. 800. Washington, DC: Government Printing Office.

————. 1979. *Statistical Abstract of the United States: 1979* (100th Edition) Washington, DC: Government Printing Office.

————. 1980. "Population Profile of the United States: 1979." *Current Population Reports*, Series P-20, No. 350. Washington, DC: Government Printing Office.

Van Keep, P.A., and J.M. Kellerhals. 1974. "The Impact of Socio-Cultural Factors on Symptom Formation: Some Results of a Study of Ageing Women in Switzerland." *Psychotherapy and Psychosomatics* **23** (Annual): 251–263.

Verbrugge, L.M. 1976a. "Sex Differentials in Morbidity and Mortality in the United States." *Social Biology* **23** (Winter): 275–296.

————. 1976b. "Females and Illness: Recent Trends in Sex Differences in the United States." *Journal of Health and Social Behavior* **17** (December): 387–403.

————. 1979a. "Marital Status and Health." *Journal of Marriage and the Family* **41** (May): 267–285.

————. 1979b. "Female Illness Rates and Illness Behavior: Testing Hypotheses about Sex Differences in Health." *Women and Health* **4** (Spring): 61–79.

Vessey, M.P., and J.I. Mann. 1978. "Female Sex Hormones and Thrombosis." *British Medical Bulletin* **34** (May): 157–162.

Vorherr, H., and Robert H. Messer. 1978. "Breast Cancer: Potentially Predisposing and Protecting Factors: Role of Pregnancy, Lactation, and Endocrine Status." *American Journal of Obstetrics and Gynecology* **130** (April 15): 335–358.

Walcott, I. 1979. "Women and Psychoactive Drug Use." *Women and Health* **4** (Summer): 199–202.

Waldron, I. 1976. "Why Do Women Live Longer Than Men?" *Social Science and Medicine* **10** (July–August): 349–362.

————. 1978. "Type of Behavior Pattern and Coronary Heart Disease in Men and Women." *Social Science and Medicine* **12B** (July): 167–170.

Warheit, G.J., C.E. Holzer, and S.A. Arey. 1973. "An Analysis of Social Class and Racial Differences in Depressive Symptomatology: A Community Study." *Journal of Health and Social Behavior* **14** (December): 291–299.

Weinstein, M.C. 1980. "Estrogen Use in Postmenopausal Women—Costs, Risks, and Benefits." *The New England Journal of Medicine* **303** (August 7): 308–316.

Weisman, C.S., D.M. Levine, D. Steinwachs, et al. 1980. "Male and Female Physician Career Patterns: Specialty Choices and Graduate Training." *Journal of Medical Education* **55** (October): 813–825.

Welch, S., and Booth, A. 1977. "Employment and Health Among Married Women." *Sex Roles* **3** (August): 385–396.

WHO Task Force on Psychosocial Research in Family Planning, 1980. "A Cross-Cultural Study of Menstruation: Implications for Contraceptive Development and Use." *Studies in Family Planning* **12** (January): 3–16.

Wilcoxon, L.A., S.L., Schrader, and C.W. Sherif. 1976. "Daily Self Reports on Activities, Life Events, Moods, and Somatic Changes During the Menstrual Cycle." *Psychosomatic Medicine* **38** (November–December): 399–417.

Williams, G. 1979. "The Changing U.S. Labor Force and Occupational Differentiation by Sex." *Demography* **16** (February): 73–87.

Wilson, R.A. 1966. *Feminine Forever.* New York: M. Evans and Co.

Wood, A. 1973. "The Fashionable Diseases: Women's Complaints and Their Treatment in Nineteenth Century America." *Journal of Interdisciplinary History* **4** (Summer): 25–52.

Woods, N.F., and B.S. Hulka. 1979. "Symptom Reports and Illness Behavior Among Employed Women and Homemakers." *Journal of Community Health* **5** (Fall): 36–45.

Wunsch, G. 1980. "Sex Differentials and Cause of Death in some European Countries." In R.W. Hiorns (Ed.), *Demographic Patterns in Developed Societies,* Symposia of the Society for the Study of Human Biology, Vol. 19. London: Taylor and Francis.

CHAPTER 3

Adult Development and Women's Development: Arrangements for a Marriage

CAROL GILLIGAN
Graduate School of Education
Harvard University

In considering women's life-cycle and the stages and sequence of their development, a critical question is one of judgment, how that development is to be assessed. Because in its recent expansion, the field of adult development has been explored largely on the territory of the masculine domain (*Daedalus*, 1976; Levinson, 1978; Osherson, 1980; Vaillant, 1977), it is easy to interpret the lives of women through constructs derived from studies of men.

Do women have mentors, we begin to ask? Are their lives steered by pursuit of a dream? Through such questions, the pattern of male experience that has shaped theories of child and adolescent development begins to impose its dimensions as well on the emergent psychology of adult development. To expand the conception of adulthood that retrospectively shapes a developmental account (hanging, always, as Piaget saw, from its vertex of maturity), the study of women must begin with a descriptive or ethnographic approach in order to admit new constructs to the understanding of what constitutes maturity.

To illustrate the problem, I begin with the central concepts of attachment and separation that inform the psychology of human development and describe the cycle of human life. These concepts, which arise from the study of infancy, resurface in adolescence as identity and intimacy and then in adulthood as love and work. When, however, development is charted, following the initial attachment of mother and child, through a series of progressive separations that extend through childhood and adolescence, continuing relationships appear as impediments to growth, smothering the possibilities for development that lie in autonomy and independence. Although the apogee of separation in adolescence is presumed to be followed by the return of attachment and care in the intimacy and generativity of adult love and work, the line of their development remains unclear. Current studies of men's lives in their insistent focus on self and work provide scanty illumination of an adulthood spent in activities of relationship and care. It is not clear from Erikson's studies that identity is followed by intimacy; Levinson reports that his men lack friendships and Vaillant's have trouble describing their wives.

Thus there seems to be a line of development missing from current psychological accounts, a failure to describe the progression of relationships toward a maturity of interdependence or to trace the evolution of the capacity for responsible care. The truth of separation is recognized in most developmental texts, but the reality of continuing connection is lost or relegated to the shadowy background where the figures of women appear.

My work at present is directed toward tracing the development of relationships of care by delineating a progression in the understanding of responsibility and in the experience of connection. In this chapter, I discuss two aspects of that work: (1) a study of men and women's development in the time between adolescence and adulthood, and (2) a view of women's personality and work in the middle years. In doing so, I show how the addition of a second line of developmental interpretation attuned to the history of attachment and care expands the understanding of life-cycle development and changes the view of both of the sexes.

In this chapter, I do not set out to cover all aspects of women's development, nor do I attempt to review the existing literature in a systematic way. Instead, I address the question of theory, focusing on the problem of interpretation and showing how the lives of women—the group left out in the construction of current theory—provide the discrepant data on which to generate a more comprehensive view. To this end, I undertake four tasks: (1) to review and assess current theories that are derived primarily from a male perspective and to illuminate the adulthood they portray; (2) to present some findings from research that suggest a different framework of interpretation; (3) to relate the findings of my research to the work of others in the field; and (4) to point to some implications of this work for the interpretation of women's lives in the middle years and to indicate the directions for future research that arise out of these observations.

"THE SEASONS OF A MAN'S LIFE . . . A VIEW OF ADULT DEVELOPMENT"

Of arms and of the man, I sing.
   VIRGIL. *THE AENEID.*

McClelland (1975) reports that "psychologists have found sex differences in their studies from the moment they started doing empirical research [p.

81]." But because it is difficult to say "different" without saying "better" or "worse," and because there has been a tendency to construct a single scale of measurement, and because that scale has been derived and standardized on the basis of men's observations and interpretations of research data predominantly or exclusively drawn from studies of males, psychologists have tended, in McClelland's words, "to regard male behavior as the 'norm' and female behavior as some kind of deviation from that norm [p. 81]." Thus, when women do not conform to the standards of psychological expectation, the conclusion has been that something is wrong with the women.

To address this conclusion as it pertains to the assessment of women's development in the adult years, it is necessary first to consider the expectations themselves and the studies from which they derive. In doing so, it readily becomes apparent how easily psychologists have moved from studies of men's lives to theories of adult development. Levinson (1978), despite his evident distress about the exclusion of women from his necessarily small sample, sets out on the basis of his all-male study "to create an overarching conception of development that could encompass the diverse biological, psychological and social changes occurring in adult life [p. 8]."

This conception is informed by the idea of "the Dream" that orders the seasons of a man's life in the same way that Jupiter's prophecy of a glorious destiny steered the course of Aeneas' journey. The dream about which Levinson writes is also a vision of glorious achievement whose realization or modification will shape the character and life of the man. In the salient relationships in Levinson's analysis, the "mentor" facilitates the realization of the Dream and the "special woman" is the helpmate who encourages its hero to shape and live out its vision. In Levinson's description:

> As the novice adult tries to separate from his family and pre-adult world, and to enter an adult world, he must form significant relationships with other adults who will facilitate his work on the Dream. Two of the most important figures in this drama are the "mentor" and the "special woman" [p. 93].

The significant relationships of early adulthood are thus construed as the means to an end of individual achievement, and the "transitional figures" must be cast off or reconstructed following the realization of success. If in the process, however, they become, like Dido, an impediment to the fulfillment of the Dream, then the relationship must be renounced to allow the developmental process to continue. This process is defined by Levinson explicitly as one of individuation: "Throughout the life cycle, but especially in the key transition periods . . . the developmental process of *individuation* is going on." The process refers "to the changes in a person's relationships to himself and to the external world"—the relationships that constitute his "Life Structure [p. 195]."

If in the course of "Becoming One's Own Man," this structure is discovered to be flawed and threatens the great expectations of the Dream, then to avert "serious Failure or Decline," the man must "break out" to salvage his

Dream. This act of breaking out is consummated by a "marker event" of separation, such as "leaving his wife, quitting his job, or moving to another city [p. 206]." Thus the road to midlife salvation either lies in achievement or runs through separation.

From the array of human experience, Levinson's choice is the same as Virgil's, charting the progress of adult development as an arduous struggle toward a glorious destiny. Like pious Aeneas on his way to found Rome, the men in Levinson's study direct their lives by their steadfast devotion to realizing their dream, measuring their progress in terms of their distance from the shores of its promised success. Thus, in the stories that Levinson recounts, relationships, whatever their particular intensity, play a relatively subordinate role in the individual drama of adult development.

The focus on work is also apparent in Vaillant's account of *Adaptation to Life* (1977). The variables that correlate with adult adjustment, like the interview that generated the data, bear predominantly on occupation and call for an expansion of Erikson's stages. Filling in what he sees as "an uncharted period of development" that Erikson left "between the decades of the twenties and forties," Vaillant describes the years of the thirties as the era of "Career Consolidation," the time when the men in his sample sought, "like Shakespeare's soldier, the bauble Reputation [p. 202]." With this analogy to Shakespeare's Rome, the continuity of intimacy and generativity is interrupted to make room for a stage of further individuation and achievement, realized by work and consummated by a success that brings societal recognition.

Erikson's notion of generativity, however, is changed in the process of this recasting. Conceiving generativity as "the concern in establishing and guiding the next generation," Erikson (1950) took the "*productivity* and *creativity*" of parenthood in its literal or symbolic realization to be a metaphor for an adulthood centered on relationships and devoted to the activity of taking care. To Erikson (1950) generativity was *the* stage of adult development encompassing "man's relationship to his production as well as to his progeny [pp. 266, 268]." For Vaillant (1977) this relationship instead is relegated to midlife, confirming a pattern that he finds reported "for both men and women by the major American studies of adult development [p. 202]."

Asserting that generativity is "not just a stage for making little things grow," Vaillant argues against Erikson's metaphor of parenthood by cautioning that "the world is filled with irresponsible mothers who are marvellous at bearing and loving children up to the age of two and then despair of taking the process further [p. 202]." Generativity, in order to exclude such women, is uprooted from its earthy redolence and redefined as "responsibility for the growth, leadership, and well-being of one's fellow creatures, not just raising crops or children [p. 202]." Thus, the expanse of Erikson's conception is narrowed to development in mid-adulthood and in the process made more restrictive in its definition of care.

Vaillant's interview, reproduced at the end of his book, corroborates the predominance of his concern with work, emphasizing the relation of self to society and minimizing, like Levinson, the attachment of self to others. In an interview that inquires about work, health, stress, deaths, and a variety of family relationships, Vaillant (1977) says to the men in his study that "the hardest question I shall ask (is): Can you describe your wife?" [p. 387]. This prefatory caution presumably arose from his experience with this particular sample of men but points to the limits of their adaptation, or, perhaps to its psychological expense.

Thus, the models for a healthy life cycle are men who seem distant in their relationships, finding it difficult to describe their wives, though acknowledging their importance in their lives. The same sense of distance between self and others is evident as well in Levinson's (1978) conclusion that, "In our interviews, friendship was largely noticeable by its absence. As a tentative generalization we would say that close friendship with a man or a woman is rarely experienced by American men [p. 335]." Obviously caught by this impression, Levinson pauses in his discussion of the three "tasks" of adulthood (building and modifying the life structure, working on single components of the life structure, and adult individuation) to offer the following elaboration:

A man may have a wide social network in which he has amicable, "friendly" relationships with many men and perhaps a few women. In general, however, most men do not have an intimate male friend of any kind that they recall fondly from boyhood or youth. Many men have had casual dating relationships with women, and perhaps a few complex love–sex relationships, but most men have not had an intimate non-sexual friendship with a woman. We need to understand why friendship is so rare, and what consequences this deprivation has for adult life [335].

Thus, we have on the one hand studies that convey a view of adulthood in which relationships are subordinated to the ongoing process of individuation and achievement whose progress is predicated on prior attachments and thought to enhance the capacity for intimacy. On the other hand, there is the observation that among these men whose lives have served as the model for adult development, the capacity for relationships was in some sense diminished and the men constricted in their emotional expression. Descriptions of relationships (Vaillant, 1977) often were cast in the language of achievement, characterized by their success or failure, and impoverished in their affective range:

At forty-five Lucky enjoyed one of the best marriages in the Study, but probably not as perfect as he implied when he wrote, "You may not believe me when I say we've never had a disagreement, large or small [p. 129]."

The biography of Adam Carson illustrates his halting passage from identity to intimacy, through career consolidation, and finally, into the capacity to *care* in its fullest sense. . . . . he had gone through divorce, remarriage, and a shift from research to private practice. His personal metamorphosis had continued. The mousy researcher had become a charming clinician . . . suave, untroubled, kindly, and in control. . . . The vibrant energy that had characterized his adolescence had returned . . . now his depression was clearly an *affect*; and he was anything but fatigued. In the next breath he confessed, "I'm very highly sexed, and that's a problem, too." He then provided me with an exciting narrative as he told me not only of recent romantic entanglements, but also of his warm, fatherly concern for patients [pp. 203, 205, 206].

The notion that separation leads to attachment and that individuation eventuates in mutuality, although reiterated throughout by both Vaillant and Levinson, is belied by the lives they put forth in support. Similarly, in Erikson's studies of Luther and Gandhi, although the relationship between self and society is achieved in magnificent articulation, both men are compromised in their capacity for intimacy and live at great personal distance from others. Thus, Luther in his devotion to Faith, like Gandhi in his devotion to Truth, ignore the people most closely around them while working instead toward the glory of God. These men, then, resemble in remarkable detail, pious Aeneas in Virgil's account, who also overcame the bonds of attachment that impeded the progress of his journey to Rome.

In all these accounts the women are silent, except for the sorrowful voice of Dido who, imploring and threatening Aeneas in vain, in the end silences herself on his sword.

RESTORING THE MISSING TEXT OF WOMEN'S DEVELOPMENT

I felt caught in a dilemma that was new to me then but which since has become horribly familiar: the trap of adult life, in which you are held, wriggling, powerless to act because you can see both sides. On that occasion, as generally in the future, I compromised.

Mary McCarthy, *Memories of a Catholic Girlhood*

I will not serve that in which I no longer believe, whether it calls itself my home, my fatherland or my church: and I will try to express myself in some mode of life or art as freely as I can and as wholly as I can, using for my defense the only arms I allow myself to use—silence, exile and cunning.

James Joyce, *A Portrait of the Artist as a Young Man.*

In young adulthood, when identity and intimacy converge in dilemmas of conflicting commitment, the relationship of self and other is exposed, revealing the lines of its articulation. That the understanding of this relationship differs in the experience of men and women is a steady theme in the literature on adolescent development and is a finding of my research. From the different dynamics of separation and attachment in their gender identity formation through the divergence of identity and intimacy that marks their experience in the adolescent years, males and females typically have spoken of the importance of different truths: males of the role of separation in development as it comes to define and empower the self; females of the ongoing process of attachment that creates and sustains the human community.

Because this dialogue contains the dialectic that creates the tension of human development, the silence of women in "adult development" distorts the conception of its stages and sequence. In this section I restore in part the missing text of women's development, as they describe their conceptions of self and morality in the time of transition from adolescence to adulthood. In focusing primarily on evidence of differences between the accounts of women and men, my aim is to enlarge developmental understanding by including the perspectives of both sexes. Although the judgments considered in the following discussion come from a small and highly educated sample, they inform an understanding of adult development that makes it possible to recognize in women's development not only what is missing but also what is there.

This problem of recognition was illustrated in a literature class at a women's college in which the students were discussing the moral dilemma that appeared in the novels of Mary McCarthy and James Joyce. In comparing the clarity of Joyce's character Stephen's *non serviam* with Mary McCarthy's "zigzag course," the women were unanimous in their decision that Stephen's was the better choice. Stephen was powerful in his certainty of belief and armed with strategies to avoid confrontation; the shape of his identity was clear and tied to a compelling justification. He had, in any case, taken a stand.

Wishing that they could be more like Stephen, in his clarity of decision and certainty of desire, the women in the class saw themselves instead like Mary McCarthy, helpless, powerless, and constantly compromised. The contrasting images of power and helplessness in their explicit tie to separation and attachment caught the dilemma of the women's development, the conflict between integrity and care. In Stephen's simpler construction, however, separation seemed the empowering condition of free and full self-expression while attachment appeared a paralyzing entrapment and caring an inevitable prelude to compromise.

The novels showed a different dynamic in their contrasting developmental accounts. For Stephen, leaving childhood meant renouncing relationships in order to guarantee freedom of self-expression, while for Mary growing up meant relinquishing freedom of expression in order to sustain relationships. (McCarthy, 1946):

A sense of power and Caesarlike magnanimity filled me. I was going to equivocate, not for selfish reasons but in the interests of the community, like a grown-up, responsible person [p. 162].

These divergent constructions of identity in self-expression and in self-sacrifice leave different problems of further development—the former a problem of human connection and the latter a problem of truth. These seemingly disparate problems, however, are subsequently discovered to be intimately related since shrinking from truth impedes relationship, and separation removes parts of the truth. In the study to which I now turn, the men's return from exile and silence parallels the women's return from equivocation, until intimacy and truth converge in the discovery of the connection between integrity and care. Then only a difference in tone reveals what it was that men and women knew from the beginning and what they only later discovered through experience.

The instant choice of self-deprecation in the women's preference for Stephen was matched in another group of college women by a childlike readiness for apology. These women were participants in a study of moral and ego development designed to describe and trace over time the related conceptions of self and morality and the changes in understanding that accrue from life experience. The participants in the study were an unequal number of men and women selected on the basis of their decision as sophomores in college to take a course on moral and political choice. When interviewed at age 27, the five women in the study all were actively pursuing careers, two in medicine, one in law, one in graduate study, and one as an organizer of labor unions. In the five years following their graduation from college, three had married and one had a child.

When they were asked at age 27, "How would you describe yourself to yourself?" one of the women refused to reply but the other four gave the following descriptions as their first response to the interviewer's question:

This sounds sort of strange, but I think maternal, with all its connotations. I see myself in a nurturing role, maybe not right now, but whenever that might be, as a physician, as a mother. . . . it's hard for me to think of myself without thinking about other people around me that I'm giving to.

I am fairly hard-working and fairly thorough and fairly responsible, and in terms of weaknesses, I am sometimes hesitant about making decisions and unsure about myself and afraid of doing things and taking responsibility, and I think maybe that is one of the biggest conflicts I have had. . . . the other very important aspect of my life is my husband and trying to make his life easier and trying to help him out.

I am a hysteric, I am intense, I am warm, I am very smart about people. . . . I have a lot more soft feelings than hard feelings, I am a lot easier to get to be kind than to get mad. . . . if I had to say one word, and to me it incorporates a lot, "adopted."

I have sort of changed a lot. As I told you before, at the point of the last interview [at age 22] I felt like I was the kind of person who was interested in growth and trying hard, and it seems to me that the last couple of years, the not trying is someone who is not growing, and I think that is the thing that bothers me the most, the thing that I keep thinking about, that I am not growing. It's not true, I am, but what seems to be a failure partially is the way that T. and I broke up. The thing with T. feels to me like I am not growing . . . the thing I am running into lately is that the way I describe myself, my behavior doesn't sometimes come out that way. Like, I hurt T. a lot and that bothers me. So I am thinking of myself as somebody who tried not to hurt people, but I ended up hurting him a lot, and so that's something that weighs on me, that I am somebody who unintentionally hurts people. Or a feeling, lately, that it is simple to sit down and say what your principles are, what your values are, and what I think about myself but the way it sort of works out in actuality is sometimes very different. You can say you try not to hurt people, but you might because of things about yourself, or you can say this is my principle, but when the situation comes up, you don't really behave the way you would like . . . so I consider myself contradictory and confused.

The request for self-description came at the end of an interview in which the women described personal experiences of moral conflict and choice and discussed their resolution of hypothetical moral dilemmas. Throughout the interviews qualification punctuated their moral judgments and self-descriptions, indicating not only doubt and confusion but also an attentiveness to others, an overriding concern with seeing both sides, and an awareness of the context and consequences of choice. The fusion of identity and intimacy, however, which has been repeatedly described in women's development (Bettelheim, 1965; Douvan & Adelson, 1966; Erikson, 1968), is perhaps most clearly articulated in the text of these self-descriptions. In response to the request to describe themselves, all the women describe a relationship, depicting their identity *in* the connection of future mother, present wife, adopted child, or past lover. Similarly, the standard of moral judgment that informs their assessment of self is a standard of relationship, an ethic of nurturance, responsibility, and care. Measuring their strength in the activity of attachment ("giving to," "helping out," "being kind," and "not hurting"), these highly successful and achieving women do not mention their academic and professional distinction in the context of describing themselves. If anything, they regard their professional activities as jeopardizing their own sense of themselves, and the conflict they encounter between achievement and care leaves them either divided in judgment or feeling betrayed:

When I first applied to medical school, my feeling was that I was a person who was concerned with other people and being able to care for them in some way or another, and I was running into problems the last few years as far as my being able to give of myself, my time and what I am doing to other people. And medicine, even though it seems that profession is set up to do exactly that, seems to more or less interfere with your doing it. . . . To me it felt like I wasn't really growing, that I was just treading water, trying to cope with what I was doing that made me very angry in some ways because it wasn't the way that I wanted things to go.

The woman who refused to describe herself said it was "too tough" and "I can't get it together" at the end of what "really had been a rough week." During the week, she had as a lawyer faced the dilemma of whether to tell the opposing counsel in a trial of the existence of a document providing critical support for his client's "meritorious claim." Deciding that in her own tenuous position, she could not take on the adversary system of justice or make an exception to its rules, she nevertheless felt the adversarial system had interfered not only with the search for truth but also with the expression of her concern for the client on the other side. When asked to describe someone important to her, she described her mother as "a very caring person," although with the qualification that she cared only about family and close friends. The person whom she said she admired was Albert Schweitzer because he was "selfless" and "a great man . . . going to Africa and living in conditions that I would consider difficult to live in and treating, helping those who need help with very little reward for it really."

Thus is all of the women's descriptions, identity is defined in a context of relationship and judged by a standard of responsibility and care. Morality is seen by these women as arising from the experience of connection and conceived of as a problem of inclusion rather than one of balancing claims. This underlying assumption that morality stems from attachment was explicitly stated by one of the women in her response to the question of whether a man should steal an overpriced drug in order to save the life of his wife. Her reason for saying the husband should steal stemmed not from a priority of rights but rather from the need to sustain human connection. In her view, the moral problem in the dilemma lay in the druggist's failure to see the connection between himself and the wife rather than in the violation of law constituted by the husband's theft. Explaining her judgment, she elaborated the assumption on which her understanding of social reality is based:

> By yourself, there is little sense to things. It is like the sound of one hand clapping, the sound of one man or one woman, there is something lacking. It is the collective that is important to me and that collective is based on certain guiding principles, one of which is that everybody belongs to it and that you all come from it . . . (and) you have to love someone else because while you may not like them, you are inseparable from them. In a way, it is like loving your right hand, *they are part of you*, that other person is part of that giant collection of people that you are connected to.

To this aspiring maternal physician, the sound of one hand clapping does not seem a miraculous transcendence but rather a human absurdity, the illusion of a person standing alone in a reality of interconnection. For the women in this sample and others, the principles of morality are principles of relationships—an ethic of nonviolence and love that engenders responsibility for taking care.

For the men, the tone of identity is different, clearer, more direct, more distinct and sharp-edged. Even when disparaging the concept itself, they radiate the confidence of certain truth. Although the world of the self that men describe at times includes "people" and "deep attachments," no particular person or relationship is mentioned nor is the activity of relationship portrayed in the context of self-description. Replacing the women's verbs of attachment are the adjectives of separation—"intelligent," "logical," "imaginative," "honest," sometimes even "arrogant" and "cocky." Thus the male "I" is defined in separation and seen as *having* "real contacts" and "deep emotions" or otherwise, wishing for them.

In a randomly selected half of the sample, the men from the same college class as the women, similarly situated in occupational and marital position, give the following initial responses to the request for self-description: How would you describe yourself to yourself?

Logical, compromising, outwardly calm. If it seems like my statements are short and abrupt, it is because of my background and training. Architectural statements have to be very concise and short. Accepting. Those are all on an emotional level. I consider myself educated, reasonably intelligent.

I would describe myself as an enthusiastic, passionate person who is slightly arrogant. Concerned, committed, very tired right now because I didn't get much sleep last night.

I would describe myself as a person who is well developed intellectually and emotionally. Relatively narrow circle of friends, acquaintances, persons with whom I have real contacts as opposed to professional contacts or "community" contacts. And relatively proud of the intellectual skills and development, content with the emotional development as such, as a "not very actively pursued goal." Desiring to broaden that one, the emotional aspect.

Intelligent, perceptive, I am being brutally honest now, still somewhat reserved, unrealistic about a number of social situations which involve other people, particularly authorities. Improving, looser, less tense and hung up than I used to be. Somewhat lazy, although it is hard to say how much of that is tied up with other conflicts. Imaginative, sometimes too much so. A little dilettantish, interested in a lot of things without necessarily going into them in depth, although I am moving toward correcting that.

I would tend to describe myself first by recounting a personal history, where I was born, grew up, and that kind of thing, but I am dissatisfied with that. Having done it thousands of times, it doesn't seem to capture the essence of what I am, I would probably decide after another futile attempt, because there is no such thing as the essence of what I am, and be very bored by the whole thing. . . . I don't think that there is any such thing as myself. There is myself sitting here, there is myself tomorrow, and so on.

Evolving and honest. . .

I guess on the surface, I seem a little easy going and laid back, but I think I am probably a bit more wound up than that. I tend to get would up very easily. Kind of smart aleck, a little bit, or cocky maybe. Not as thorough as I should be. A little bit hard ass, I guess, and a guy that is not swayed by emotions and feelings. I have deep emotions but I am not a person who has a lot of different people. I have attachments to a few people, very deep attachments. Or attachments to a lot of things, at least in the demonstrable sense.

I guess I think I am kind of creative and also a little bit schizophrenic . . . a lot of it is a result of how I grew up. There is a kind of longing for the pastoral life, and at the same time, a desire for the flash, prestige and recognition that you get by going out and hustling.

Two of the men begin more tentatively by talking about people in general, but they return in the end to "great ideas" or a need for distinctive achievement, as follows:

I think I am basically a decent person. I think I like people a lot and I like liking people, I like doing things with pleasure from just people, from their existence, almost. Even people I don't know well. When I said I was a decent person, I think that is almost the thing that makes me a decent person, that is a decent quality, a good quality. I think I am very bright. I think I am a little lost, not acting quite like I am inspired, whether it is just a question of lack of inspiration, I don't know, but not doing . . . [not] accomplishing things, not achieving those things and not knowing where I want to go or what I'm doing. I think most people, especially doctors, have some idea of what they are going to be doing in four years. I [an intern] really have a blank. . . . I have great ideas . . . [but] I can't imagine me in them.

I guess the things that I like to think are important to me are I am aware of what is going on around me, other people's needs around me, and the fact that I enjoy doing things for other people and I feel good about it. I suppose it's nice in my situation, but I am not sure that is true for everybody. I think some people do things for other people and it doesn't make them feel good. Once in a while, that is true of me too, for instance, working around the house, and I am always doing the same old things that everyone else is doing and eventually, I build up some resentment toward that.

At least in this small sample, men's descriptions of self through involvement with others are tied to a qualification of identity rather than seen as its realization. Instead of attachment, individual achievement rivets the male imagination and great ideas or distinctive activity define the standard of self-assessment and success.

Thus the sequential ordering of identity and intimacy through which Erikson describes the transition from adolescence to adulthood better fits, as he recognizes, the development of men than it does the development of women. Power and separation secure the man in an identity achieved through work, but they leave him at a distance from others, who seem in some sense out of his sight.

Your mother must have gone through a good deal of suffering, (Cranly) said then. Would you not try to save her from suffering more even if—or would you?

If I could, Stephen said, that would cost me very little [Joyce, 1916, p. 241].

Then intimacy becomes the critical experience that brings the self back into connection with others, making it possible to see both sides—to discover the effects of action, for others as well as for oneself. The experience of relationship brings an end to isolation that otherwise hardens into indifference, an absence of active concern for others through a willingness to respect their rights. For this reason, intimacy is the transforming experience for men through which adolescent identity turns into the generativity of love and work. In the process, as Erikson (1964) observes, the knowledge gained through intimacy changes the ideological morality of adolescence into the adult ethic of taking care.

Because women, however, define their identity through relationships of intimacy and care, the moral problems that they encounter pertain to issues of a different sort. When relationships are secured by masking desire and when conflict is avoided by equivocation, then the absence of integrity leads to confusion about the locus of responsibility and truth:

Whatever I told them was usually so blurred and glossed, in the effort to meet their approval (for, aside from anything else, I was fond of them and tried to accommodate myself to their perspective), that except when answering a direct question I hardly knew whether what I was saying was true or false. I really tried, or so I thought, to avoid lying but it seemed to me that they forced it on me by the difference in their vision of things, so that I was always transposing reality for them into terms they could understand. To keep matters straight with my conscience, I shrank, whenever possible, from the lie absolute, just as, from a sense of precaution, I shrank from the plain truth [McCarthy, 1946, p. 172].

The critical experience then becomes not that of intimacy but rather of choice, generating the awareness of personal agency and changing the understanding of responsibility.

Thus, in the transition from adolescence to adulthood the dilemma itself is the same for both sexes—the conflict between integrity and care—but it is approached from a different perspective by each and it generates the recognition of opposite truths. These different perspectives are reflected in two different moral ideologies in that separation is justified by an ethic of rights whereas attachment is supported by an ethic of care.

The morality of rights is predicated on equality and centered on the understanding of justice as fairness; the ethic of responsibility is based on the recognition of differences and the perception of the need for response. The ethic of rights is a manifestation of equal respect, balancing the claims of self and other; the ethic of responsibility generates the understanding that gives rise to compassion and care. Thus, the counterpoint of identity and intimacy that marks the time between childhood and adulthood is articulated through two different moralities whose complementarity is the discovery of maturity.

The discovery of this complementarity was traced in the study of moral and ego development through the responses to interview questions about personal experiences involving moral conflicts and choice (Gilligan and Murphy, 1979; Murphy and Gilligan, 1980). Two lawyers chosen from this sample illustrate how the divergence in judgment between the sexes is resolved through the discovery by each of the other's perspective and of the interrelationship between integrity and care.

The dilemma of responsibility and truth that Mary McCarthy describes was reiterated by the lawyer who said she found it too hard to describe herself. She, like Mary McCarthy, considered self-sacrificing acts "courageous" and "praiseworthy," explaining that "if everyone on earth behaved in a way that showed care for others and courage, the world would be a much better place, you wouldn't have crime and you might not have poverty." However, this moral ideal of self-sacrifice and care ran into trouble in a relationship in which the conflicting truths of each person's feelings made it impossible to avoid hurt. Describing how the contradiction arose by indicating how her thinking about morality had changed, she says:

I was more simple-minded then. I went through a period in which I thought there were fairly simple answers of right and wrong in life. I even went through a period that now strikes me as so simplistic, [I thought] that as long as I didn't hurt anybody, everything would be fine. And I soon figured out or eventually figured out that things were not that simple; that you were bound to hurt people, they were bound to hurt you, and life is full of tension and conflict and people are bound to hurt each other's feelings, intentionally, unintentionally, but just in the very way things work out, so I abandoned that idea.

This abandonment occurred during the first years of college when:

I got involved in a love-affair with some guy . . . [who] wanted to settle down and get married and I could not imagine a worse fate but I was really quite fond of him. And we broke up and he was so upset by it that he left school for a year, and I realized that I had hurt him very badly and that I hadn't meant to and I had violated my first principle of moral behavior, but that I had made the right decision.

Explaining that she "could not have possibly married him," she felt that there was, in that sense, "an easy answer" to the dilemma she faced. Yet in another sense, given her moral injunction against hurting, the situation presented an insoluble problem, offering no course of action that would not cause hurt.

This realization led her to question her former absolute moral injunction and to "figure that this principle [of not hurting others] was not all there was to it." The limitation she saw pertained directly to the issue of personal integrity as she recognized that "what that principle was not even attempting to achieve was like 'to thine own self be true'." Indicating that she has "started thinking more about maintaining your personal integrity," she says this experience led her to conclude that "you can't worry about not hurting other people; just do what is right for you."

Yet, given her equation of morality with care, her continuing belief that "acts that are self-sacrificing and that are done for other people or for the good of humanity are good acts," her abandonment of the principle of not hurting others seems tantamount to an abandonment of moral concern. In this light her unwillingness to describe herself while valuing in others their capacity to care, may indicate that she has become unrecognizable to herself, given her current standard of judgment, or perhaps that judging herself by this standard she can only see herself as compromised. In contrast to the account of moral compromise in her professional behavior—her decision not to introduce evidence that would help her opponent win his "meritorious" claim— she describes her husband as "a person of absolute integrity [who] would never do anything he didn't feel was right . . . and will go over backwards to be fair." Given these absolute standards of judgment, she says somewhat apologetically in her own behalf that she has become more tolerant and less willing to blame, more understanding of perspectives she used to condemn.

Thus, the absolute injunction against hurting was found both in relationships and at work to be an inadequate guide to resolving actual dilemmas, given the disparity of intention and consequence. Since her discovery of the disparity between intention and consequence and of the actual constraints of choice, there seemed in some situations no way not to hurt. Having confronted dilemmas to which there was no resolution that was without cost, she did not abdicate responsibility for choice but rather began to claim the right to include herself among the people for whom she considered it moral to care. Her more inclusive morality now contained the injunction to be true to herself, leaving her with two principles of judgment whose integration she could not yet clearly envision. What she recognizes is that both integrity and care must be included in a morality that would encompass the actual dilemmas of love and work that arise in the course of adult life.

The move toward tolerance that accompanies the abandonment of absolutes is considered by Perry (1968) to chart the course of intellectual and ethical development during the early adult years. Perry's nine developmental positions describe the changes in thinking that mark the transition from a dualistic epistemology to a contextually relative understanding of truth and choice. This transition and its impact on moral judgment was discerned by Murphy and Gilligan (1980) in the changes that occurred in the moral understanding of both men and women between the ages of 19 and 27. Although both sexes moved away from absolutes in this time, the absolutes themselves were different for each. In women's development, an absolute of care defined initially as not hurting others came to be seen as complicated through the recognition of the need for personal integrity. This recognition gave rise to the claim for equality embodied in the concept of rights that informed and changed the understanding of relationships and broadened the definition of care. For men, the absolutes of truth and of fairness defined through the concepts of equality and reciprocity came into question through experiences that demonstrated the existence of unresolvable differences. Then the awareness of multiple truths led to the relativizing of equality in the direction of equity and gave rise to generosity. For both sexes the existence of two contexts for decision made judgment by definition contextually relative and led to the realization of responsibility for choice. This recognition changed "the moral environment to the existential," and "ushered in the period of responsibility" (Perry, 1968).

The second context that was discovered by men was the morality of care that informs a different notion of respect than the ethic of justice and rights. The discovery of the reality of differences and thus of the contextual nature of morality and truth was described by a lawyer who began in law school "to realize . . . that you really don't know everything" and "you don't ever know that there is any absolute. I don't think that you ever know that there is an absolute right. What you do is you have to come down one way or the other. You have got to make a decision."

The awareness that he didn't know everything arose more painfully as well in the context of a relationship whose ending took him completely by surprise. In his belated discovery that the woman's experience had been very different from his own, he realized how distant he had been in a relationship he had considered to be close. Then the logical hierarchy of moral values whose absolute truth he had formerly proclaimed came to seem a barrier to intimacy rather than a fortress of personal integrity. As his conception of morality began to change, his thinking focused on issues of relationship, and his concern with injustice was complicated by a new understanding of human attachment. As "the principle of attachment" began to inform his way of looking at moral problems, he realized that justice extends beyond simple equality, given that people have:

. . . real emotional needs to be attached to something and equality doesn't give you attachment. Equality fractures society . . . [and] places on every person the burden of standing on his own two feet.

Although "equality is a crisp thing that you could hang onto," it alone cannot adequately resolve the dilemmas of choice that arise in life. Given a new awareness of responsibility and of consequences of choice, he says, "you don't want to look at just equality, you want to look at how people are going to be able to handle their lives." However, although he recognizes the need for two contexts for judgment, he finds that their integration "is hard to work through" because sometimes "no matter which way you go, somebody is going to be hurt and somebody is going to be hurt forever." Then he says, "you have reached the point where there is an irresolvable conflict" and choice becomes a matter of "choosing the victim" rather than of enacting the good. With the recognition of the responsibility such choices entail, his judgment comes to be more attuned to the psychological and social consequences of action in a historical world.

Starting from very different points, from the different ideologies of justice and care, the men and women who participated in this study came, in the course of becoming an adult, to a greater understanding of both points of view and thus to a greater convergence in judgment. Recognizing the dual contexts of justice and mercy, of the importance of care as well as equality, they came to see that judgment depends on the context in which the problem is framed. In this light, I return to the literature on adult development to show how the depiction of adulthood and of maturity shift when portrayed from a woman's point of view.

A DIFFERENT VIEW OF ADULT DEVELOPMENT

When women construct the adult domain, their fantasies, perceptions, and judgments convey a different social reality. McClelland (1975), having observed sex differences in the projective data of his studies on motivation, turns in his most recent account to elucidate these differences in his description of women's fantasies of power. In these fantasies, a divergence in women's understanding of the relation between self and other emerges to distinctively mark the way women think about having influence on others.

Considering his research on power to deal "in particular with the characteristics of maturity," McClelland addresses the concerns with achievement and reputation that were so salient in Levinson and Vaillant's accounts. Yet, linking his measure of power motivation to Abigail Stewart's (1973) measure of ego development, McClelland goes on to test his theory that the expression of power is indicative of maturing as measured by the level of social and emotional development. In the course of establishing this relationship, however, McClelland stumbles again on the problem of sex differences that had plagued the research on projective imagination from its inception in the study of achievement motivation. Although mean scores of power for each of McClelland's (1975) stages (support, autonomy, assertion, and togetherness) reflected only small sex differences (with women showing a stronger dependent orientation), the modal scores that reflected development indicated a more disturbing effect. According to these developmental measures, derived and standardized on studies of men, adult men appear to be "more mature than a similar sample of married women [p. 40]." Rejecting this conclusion as theoretically "unreasonable," McClelland began to look for sex bias in the theory, the scoring system, and the measures themselves in order to account for these problematic results.

In doing so, McClelland (1975) identified in the n Power scoring system an "expressive modality in which the self, rather than some outside force, is the source of a person's feelings of power [p. 41]." He then considered this modality to express "the Western bias toward self-reliance or toward an acceptance of the individual as the ultimate source of powerful acts [p. 41]." Given this bias, it is hardly surprising that, "the mean n Power score for men is significantly higher than it is for women, a fact which may once more reflect the assertiveness bias built into the scoring system, or at least into the particular picture cues used in this study. [pp. 41–42]." In this light, McClelland considers his findings to show "how the female course of development, while it follows the main outlines of male development, differs in important ways that have not been so clearly defined in the predominantly male-oriented clinical literature [p. 76]."

Thus McClelland returns to amend his definition of power motivation which he had considered as the need "primarily to feel strong and secondarily to act powerfully, having impact on others [p. 77]." Having initially conceived these elements as conjoined, he now begins to trace their separation, observing that at least in the West, "the modes of expressing power have been sex-typed—women traditionally showing more interest in *being* strong (having resources and sharing them) and men in *acting* powerfully [p. 78]." Thus, "women who are high in power motivation appear to focus on building up their resources so that they have more to give." Given this construction, the act of nurturance ("giving as fulfillment") appears to women as an act of strength, whereas assertion and aggression signify powerful activity for men.

On this basis of his findings that "women with a high power need behave differently from men with a high power need," McClelland (1975) then turns to the literature on sex differences in a search for constructs that describe women's functioning. From his search, he reports that, "Overwhelmingly, the evidence points to the conclusion that women are more concerned than men with both sides of an interdependent relationship [p. 85]," a concern that appears to be "most striking in the social field where interrelationships with people are concerned." Women are "quicker to recognize their own interdependence [p. 86]" and "relate to the world in a different style," whereas the male style is "analytic and manipulative," showing "a preference for the simple, the close, the direct [p. 88]." McClelland also says that "women are more interested in the complex, the open, the less defined . . . [they] pay more attention to context, the *whole* picture, while men are abstracting something out of it . . . [ignoring context] for the sake of something they can abstract from it [p. 98]."

Thus, the differences in women's fantasies of power and in the modes of expression to which power relates corroborate the sex differences that appear in other areas of psychological literature. The observations that women are more embedded in lives of relationship than men, more contextual in their perceptual and cognitive style, more oriented toward relationships of interdependence, and more concerned in their judgments with the activity of care are confirmed by more recent studies that report differences in women's judgments and thought (Block, 1977; Gilligan, 1977; Haan, 1978).

This discussion supports Chodorow's (1978) conclusion that the experiences of separation and attachment have different meanings for women and men. Chodorow attributes these differences to the dynamics of female child rearing, which give rise to differences in the formation during early childhood of male and female gender identity. Female identity arises through attachment, through identification with the mother, whereas male identity is contingent on separation from the mother and the reconstruction of the mother – son relationship in more differentiated, sexual, and, thus, Oedipal terms. Whereas male identity is defined positionally through separation from women and connection to society, women's identity is defined personally in the ongoing continuity of relationship.

The mutuality of adulthood of which Erikson speaks, the generativity that informs his conception of maturity, tends to be played out for men in the interdependence of self and society, supported by an ideology that confirms the identity that anchors masculine separation. Conversely, generativity for women is realized in the mutuality of relationships that come to involve the woman in a widening circle of attachments that expand the narrative of self in experience of community.

Turning to women's depictions of adult life, we might then expect to find a different view of adulthood that accords greater importance to ongoing attachment and projects a different integration of autonomy and care.

Hennig and Jardim begin their book on *The Managerial Women* (1976) by saying that, despite the moves toward equal opportunity and the support of the women's movement, on a deeper level for women in management, things have not changed that much. In any event, the women whom they studied grew up long before "things changed." For "the 25 women who by 1970 had reached top management positions in business and industry [p. xv]," success was achieved at a very high price. In contrast to the men Levinson and Vaillant describe, in whose lives marriage was associated with great success, the women in top managerial positions report that, "until their mid-thirties their personal lives were mortgaged to pay for their careers [Hennig & Jardim, 1976, p. xv]."

The descriptions of these careers, however, bear a distinctively female stamp. The managerial women characterize their development as occurring through a sequence of relationships in which father, boss, and husband progressively confirm the woman's sense of competence and success. Furthermore, those who succeeded in management gained, first from their fathers, the knowledge "that women did not need to be men in order to be persons [p. 153]." Later, the boss was reported, like father, to be "her supporter, her encourager, her teacher and her strength [p. 129]," who admired her competence and will to succeed and whom she held responsible for her success: "I really have to thank Jim [the boss] for all of my success. My dad got me to college and Jim took me from there [p. 130]."

However, when in their mid- to late thirties these women moved up to positions in the higher middle levels of management, things "previously held constant began to change [p. 138]." As their fathers grew older, became senile or died and their relationship with their bosses changed consequent to a marked increase of the women's autonomy on the job, these women declared a "moratorium" on success. Then, putting on "the uniforms of women," they began their quest to restore relationship. During this period, half of them married, but all of them actively entertained the idea. Those who married chose men who were at least 10 years older, who themselves held secure professional positions, and whose incomes were "more than double their wives'."

Thus, in these women of remarkable achievement, their identity remained relationally defined; they knew themselves not through societal recognition but as they were known by the men in their lives. That the world looks different to these women than to men in similar high places of power clearly reflects, at least in part, the rarity of the women's achievement and the singularity of their presence in the world they inhabit. Kanter (1977) considers these factors of position as responsible for the differences in corporate women, seeing in their "feminine" behavior the perennial strategies of the subordinate in search of indirect avenues to power.

That women differ from men in their orientation to power is also the theme of Jean Miller's (1976) analysis that begins with relationships of dominance and subordination but finds women's situation in these relationships to provide "a crucial key to understanding the psychological order [p. 1]." This order arises from relationships of difference, between parent and child and woman and man, that create "the milieu—the family—in which the human mind as we know it has been formed [p. 1]."

In these relationships of difference, however, there is in most instances a factor of inequality arising from the differential distribution of resources, fundamentally those of status and power (Miller, 1976, p. 3). Because of this differential in power, these relationships assume a moral dimension that pertains to the way in which power is used to sustain or dissolve inequality. On this basis, Miller distinguishes between relationships of temporary and permanent inequality—the former the context of human development, the latter the condition of psychological oppression. In relationships of temporary inequality, such as parent and child or teacher and student, power is ideally used to foster the development that removes the initial disparity. In contrast, in relationships of permanent inequality, power cements dominance and subordination, and oppression, is rationalized by theories that "explain" the need for its continuation. Miller thus comes to identify the distinctive psychology of women as arising from the combination of their positions in relationships of temporary and permanent inequality. Dominant in temporary relationships of nurturance that dissolve with the dissolution of inequality, women are subservient in relationships of permanently unequal status and power. In addition, although subordinate in social position to men, women are at the same time centrally entwined with them in the intimate and intense relationships of adult sexuality and family life. Thus, women's psychology comes to reflect both sides of relationships of interdependence as well as the range of moral possibilities to which such relationships give rise. Women, therefore, are ideally situated to observe the role of attachment in human development, both as the necessary condition for growth and as the scene of oppression and violence.

This distinct observational perspective can be seen to inform the work of Carol Stack (1975) and Lillian Rubin (1976) who, entering worlds previously known through men's eyes, return to give a different report. In the urban black ghetto where others have seen social disorder and family disarray, Stack finds networks of domestic exchange that describe the organization of the black family in poverty. Rubin, observing the families of the white working class, dispels the myth of "the affluent and happy worker [p. 204]" by charting the *Worlds of Pain* that it costs to raise a family in conditions of social and economic disadvantage. Both women describe an adulthood of relationships that sustain the family functions of protection and care. But they also describe societal relationships of economic dependence and social class and indicate how class, race, and ethnicity are used to justify and rationalize the inequality of an economic system that benefits some at others' expense.

In their separate spheres of analysis, these women find order where others saw chaos—in the psychology of women, the urban black family, and the reproduction of social class. These discoveries required new modes of analysis and a more ethnographic approach in order to find constructs that could give order and meaning to the adulthood they saw. Stack (1975) reports that until she redefined *family* as "the smallest organized, durable network of kin and non-kin who interact daily, providing the domestic needs of children and assuring their survival [p. 31]," she could not find "families" in the world of "The Flats." She states:

> The culturally specific definitions of certain concepts such as family, kin, parent, and friend that emerged during this study made much of the subsequent analysis possible. An arbitrary imposition of widely accepted definitions of the family . . . blocks the way to understanding how the people in The Flats describe and order the world in which they live [p. 31].

Similarly, Miller (1976) calls for "a new psychology of women" that would recognize the different starting point for women's development. She observes:

> that women stay with, build on, and develop in a context of attachment and affiliation with others . . . [that] women's sense of self becomes very much organized around being able to make and then to maintain affiliations and relationships . . . [and that] eventually, for many women, the threat of disruption of an affiliation is perceived not as just a loss of a relationship but as something closer to a total loss of self [p. 83].

This psychic structuring is by now familiar from the descriptions of women's psychopathology, but it has not been recognized that "this psychic starting point contains the possibilities for an entirely different (and more advanced) approach to living and functioning . . . [in which] affiliation is valued as highly as, or more highly than, self-enhancement [Miller, 1976, p. 83]." Thus, Miller points to a psychology of adulthood that would recognize that development does not displace the value of ongoing attachment and the continuing importance of relationships.

The limitation of previous standards of measurement and the need for a more contextual interpretation is evident also in Rubin's approach, which dispels the illusion that family life is everywhere the same or that subcultural differences can be assessed independently of the socioeconomic realities of class. She says that working-class families "reproduce themselves not because they are somehow deficient or their culture aberrant, but because there are no alternatives for most of their children," despite "the mobility myth we cherish so dearly" [p. 210–211]." The temporary inequality of the working-class child thus turns into the permanent inequality of the working-class adult, caught in an ebb tide of social mobility that erodes the quality of family life.

Like the stories that delineate women's fantasies of power and the accounts managerial women give of their lives, women's descriptions of adulthood convey a different sense of its social reality. These differences center on a description of the relationship of self and other that replaces the bias toward separation with constructions of interdependence. By changing the lens of developmental observation from self and work to relationships of care, women depict ongoing attachment as the path that leads to maturity. The parameters of development correspondingly shift toward the progress of affiliative relationship, charting the dissolution of dominance and subordination through the development of relationships toward interdependence.

WOMEN: WORK AND PERSONALITY IN THE MIDDLE YEARS

Given the tendency to chart the unfamiliar waters of adult development with the familiar markers of adolescent separation and growth, it is easy to see the middle years of women's lives as a time of return to the unfinished business of adolescence. This interpretation has been particularly compelling because descriptions of the life cycle, derived predominantly from studies of men, have generated a perspective on human development from which women, insofar as they differ from men, appear to be deficient or deviant. This deviance has been seen as especially marked in the adolescent years when girls appear to confuse identity with intimacy by defining themselves through relationships with others. The legacy left from this resolution of "the second individuation process of adolescence" is considered to be a self that is vulnerable to the issues of separation that arise at midlife.

Yet this construction illustrates the limitation in an account that measures women's development against a male standard and ignores the possibility of a different truth. Seen in a different light, the observation that women's embeddedness in lives of relationship, their orientation to interdependence, their subordination of achievement to care, and their conflicts over competitive success leave them personally at risk in midlife seems to be more a commentary on the society than a problem in women's development.

To consider midlife in adolescent terms as a similar crisis of identity and separation ignores the reality of what has happened since adolescence and tears up the history of love and work. For generativity to begin at midlife, as Vaillant's (1977) data on men suggest, seems—from a woman's perspective—too late for both sexes, given that the bearing and raising of children will have taken place primarily in the preceding years. Similarly, the image of women arriving at midlife childlike and dependent on others is belied by the activity of their care in nurturing and sustaining family relationships (Miller, 1976; Rubin, 1976; Stack, 1974). Thus, the problem appears to be one of construction—an issue of judgment rather than truth.

Given the evidence that women perceive and construe social reality differently from men, and that these differences center around experiences of attachment and separation, life transitions that invariably engage these experiences can be expected to involve women in a distinctive way. Given that women's sense of integrity appears to be entwined with an ethic of care, so that to see herself as a woman is to see herself in a relationship of connection, the major transitions in women's lives would seem to involve changes in the understanding and the activities of care. Certainly the shift from childhood to adulthood witnesses a major redefinition of care when the distinction between helping and pleasing frees the activity of taking care from the wish for approval by others. Then the ethic of responsibility can become a self-chosen anchor of personal integrity.

In the same vein, however, the events of midlife—the menopause and changes in family and work—can alter the woman's activities of care in ways that affect her sense of herself. If midlife brings an end to relationships, of the sense of connection on which she relies, as well as to the activities of care through which she judges her worth, then the mourning that accompanies all life transitions can give way to the melancholia of self-deprecation and despair. The meaning of midlife events for a woman is contextual in the sense that it arises from the interaction between the structures of her thought and the realities of her life.

When the distinction between neurotic conflict and real conflict is made, and the reluctance to choose is differentiated from the reality of having no choice, when the adolescent's understanding is distinguished from that of the adult, then it becomes possible to see more clearly how women's experience provides a key to understanding central truths of adult life. Rather than viewing her anatomy as destined to leave her with a scar of inferiority (Freud, 1931), she can instead see it as giving rise to experiences that illuminate the reality common to both of the sexes: that in life you never see it all, that things unseen undergo change through time, that there is more than one path to gratification, and that the boundaries between self and other are less clear than they sometimes seem.

Thus women not only reach midlife with a psychological history different from men's and face at that time a different social reality with different possibilities for love and for work, but they also make a different sense out of experiences on the basis of their knowledge of human relationships. Because the reality of connection is experienced by women as given rather than as freely contracted, they arrive at a different understanding of the possibilities that inhere in relationships both for oppression and for growth (Miller, 1976). In this sense, women's development delineates the path not only to a less violent life but also to a maturity realized through interdependence and taking care.

In his studies of moral judgment in children, Piaget (1965/1932) describes a three-stage progression through which constraint turns into cooperation and cooperation into generosity and love. In doing so, he points out how long it takes before children from the same class at school, playing with each other every day, come to agree in their understanding of the rules of the game. This agreement, however, signals the completion of a major reorientation of action and thought through which the morality of constraint turns into an ethic of cooperation. Then when the recognition of difference leads to a relativizing of equality in the direction of equity, Piaget notes a rise in generosity that signifies the fusion of justice and love.

There seems at present to be only partial agreement between men and women about the adulthood they commonly share. In the absence of mutual understanding, relationships between the sexes continue in varying conditions of constraint, manifesting the "paradox of egocentrism" in which a mystical respect for rules is combined with everyone "playing more or less as he pleases and paying no attention to his neighbor" (Piaget, 1965/1932). For a life cycle understanding to chart the development in adulthood of relationships of cooperation and care, it is necessary for that understanding to include the lives of women as well as of men.

Among the most pressing items on the agenda for research on adult development are studies that would delineate *in women's own terms* the experience of their adult life. Preliminary work in that direction points toward the need to expand the basic constructs of social understanding to include in the concept of identity the experience of interconnection, to represent in the moral domain the issues of responsibility and care, and to construct an epistemology based not only on the Greek ideal of knowledge as the correspondence between mind and form but the Biblical conception of knowing as a process of human relationship.

Given the evidence of different perspectives in the representations of adulthood by women and men, there is a need for research that elucidates the effects of these differences in marriage, family, and work relationships. My research on moral development suggests that men and women may speak different languages that they assume to be the same, using similar words to encode disparate experiences of self and social relationships. Possibilities arise for a systematic misunderstanding that would impede communication and limit cooperation in the daily life of adult relationships. Studies could elucidate the extent of agreement in men's and women's accounts of the experiences in marriage, parenthood, and work that they commonly share by measuring the congruence in their reports and their ability to understand the other's perspective. Then Piaget's distinction between egocentrism, equality, and generosity could be used to chart the progression of relationships toward generative forms of interconnection.

As we have listened for centuries to the voices of men and the theories of development that their experience informs, so we have begun more recently to notice not only the silence of women but the difficulty in hearing what they say when they speak. Yet in the different voice of women lies the truth of an adulthood of care, the tie between relationship and responsibility, and the origin of aggression in the failure of connection. The failure to see the different reality of women's lives and to hear the differences in their voices stems in part from the assumption that there is a single mode of social experience and interpretation. By positing instead two different modes, we arrive at a more complex rendition of human experience that sees the truth of separation and attachment in the lives of women and men but recognizes as well their differential refraction in the ethical languages of responsibilities and rights. To understand how the tension between these two languages sustains the dialectic of human development is to see the integrity of two disparate modes of experience that are in the end interdependent. Thus, the dialogue of these languages not only informs a better understanding of the relations between the sexes but also provides a basis for a more comprehensive conception of adult work and family relationships.

As Freud and Piaget called our attention to the differences in children's feelings and thoughts, enabling us to respond to children with greater care and respect, so the recognition of the differences in women's experience and understanding expands our conception of maturity and points to the contextual nature of developmental truths. Through this expansion in perspective, we can begin to envision how a marriage between adult development, as it is currently portrayed, and women's development, as it begins to be seen, could lead to a broader understanding of human development and a more generative conception of adult life.

REFERENCES

Bettelheim, B. 1965. "The Problem of Generations." In E. Erikson (Ed.), *The Challenge of Youth*. New York: Doubleday.

Block, J.H. 1977. "Sex Differences in Cognitive Functioning, Personality Characteristics and Socialization Experiences: Implications for Educational Policy." Report to Presidents of Smith, Wellesley, and Mt. Holyoke Colleges.

Chodorow, N. 1978. *The Reproduction of Mothering*. Berkeley: University of California Press.

Daedalus, 1976. **105** (2): "Adulthood."

Douvan, E., and J. Adelson. 1966. *The Adolescent Experience*. New York: Wiley.

Erikson, E.H. 1950. *Childhood and Society*. New York: W.W. Norton & Co., Inc.

———. 1964. *Insight and Responsibility*. New York: W.W. Norton & Co., Inc.

———. 1968. *Identity: Youth and Crisis*. New York: W.W. Norton & Co., Inc.

Freud, S. 1931. "Female Sexuality." In J. Strachey (Ed.), *The Standard Edition of the Complete Psychological Works of Sigmund Freud*. London: The Hogarth Press. 1961.

Gilligan, C. and J.M. Murphy. 1979. "Development from Adolescence to Adulthood: The Philosopher and the Dilemma of the Fact." In D. Kuhn (Ed.), *Intellectual Development Beyond Childhood*. San Francisco: Jossey-Bass.

Gilligan, C. 1977. "In a Different Voice: Women's Conceptions of Self and of Morality." *Harvard Educational Review* **47**. (4):481–517.

Gilligan, C. and S. Langdale. 1980. "The Contribution of Woman's Thought to Developmental Theory: the Elimination of Sex Bias in Moral Development Research and Education." Interim Report: National Institution of Education.

Haan, N. 1978. "Two Moralities in Action Contexts: Relationships to Thought, Ego Regulation, and Development." *Journal of Personality and Social Psychology.* **36**:286–305.

Hennig, M., and A. Jardim. 1977. *The Managerial Woman.* Garden City, NY: Anchor Press.

Joyce, J. 1916. *A Portrait of the Artist as a Young Man.* New York: The Viking Press.

Kanter, R. 1977. *Men and Women of the Corporation.* New York: Basic Books.

Levinson, D. 1978. *The Seasons of a Man's Life.* New York: Ballantine Books.

McCarthy, M. 1946. *Memories of a Catholic Girlhood.* New York: Harcourt Brace Jovanovich.

McClelland, D. 1976. *Power: The Inner Experience.* New York: Irvington Publishers.

Miller, J.B. 1976. *Toward a New Psychology of Women.* Boston: Beacon Press.

Murphy, J.M. and C. Gilligan. 1980. Moral Development in Late Adolescence and Adulthood: A Critique and Reconstruction of Kohlberg's Theory." *Human Development* **23**, (2):77–104.

Osherson, S. 1980. *Holding On or Letting Go.* New York: Free Press.

Perry, W.G. 1968. *Forms of Intellectual and Ethical Development in the College Years.* New York: Holt, Rinehart & Winston.

Piaget, J. 1965. *The Moral Judgment of the Child.* New York: Free Press. (Originally published, 1932)

———. 1970. *Structuralism.* New York: Basic Books.

Rubin, L. 1976. *Worlds of Pain.* New York: Basic Books, 1976.

———. 1979. *Women of a Certain Age.* New York: Basic Books.

Stack, C. 1974. *All Our Kin.* New York: Harper & Row.

Stewart, A.J. 1973. "Scoring System for Stages of Psychological Development." Harvard University, Department of Psychology and Social Relations. Unpublished paper.

Vaillant, G. 1977. *Adaptation to Life.* Boston: Little, Brown.

CHAPTER 4

Women's Work and Family Roles

JANET ZOLLINGER GIELE
Heller School
Brandeis University

In the current period when feminist thought is well established, it is difficult to reconstruct the mood and expectations of just a few decades ago when women married right after college, quickly brought several children into the world, and had little thought of whether they would need or want a job when they were 45. Much has happened since then. Women need to work to fulfill their own interests, to cope with inflation, and in some cases to counter the effects of separation or divorce. In just three decades the social roles of middle-aged women have changed drastically. The challenge to any observer is not only to understand the reasons for change but also to discern the types of life patterns that have been most adaptive under new conditions.

Today it is impossible to project any one pattern that is likely to be most successful in the future. The women who are middle-aged now were making their decisions in a different economic and social context from that which prevails today. Nevertheless, it is the purpose of this chapter to sift out the most successful patterns under a variety of historical and social conditions.

Our account begins with the *historical trends* in women's social roles, particularly their work and family life, since 1950. We then ask how these changes suggest a discernible *life pattern or sequence* of education, work experience, or marriage that has been more adaptive for women in recent years. If such a pattern can be identified, we ask whether its success is likely to continue in the future.

Next we inquire into the types of *family role system* and *work role system* that have been most supportive of women's satisfaction and achievement. Although many contextual factors such as social networks are also relevant, the links between work and family are particularly critical for women. What types of marital and family structure best enable a woman to fulfill herself? Which types of work environment are particularly conducive to her accomplishment? The dual-career family and flexible work arrangements have aroused particular interest. Each takes both family and employment into account.

Ultimately, lessons learned from life course studies and observations of family and employment have implications for practical programs. This chapter concludes with the *social changes for reeducation and reentry* that will help adult women return to the work place. Other specific proposals for change are addressed in the final chapter of this book.

MAJOR CHANGES IN WOMEN'S ROLES, 1950–1980

In his book *Women and Equality*, William H. Chafe (1977) describes the demographic changes since 1950 that continued to shift women's roles away from their traditional anchor in the home. He says:

The birthrate continued to fall, each year setting a new record low. By 1975 the fertility rate of women 15 to 44 years old was only half of what it had been twenty years earlier.

This decline, in turn, coincided with a trend toward later marriages. By 1971 more than half of all women twenty years of age were single in contrast to only one-third in 1960, and the number of unmarried women in the 20-to-24 age bracket had climbed from 28 per cent in 1960 to 37 per cent a decade later.

Simultaneously, the greatest increase in the female labor force occurred among younger women of childbearing age. The proportion of women working in the 20- to-24-year-old group increased from 50 per cent in 1964 to 61 per cent in 1973. Among college women in that age group the employment rate was 86 per cent. But the fastest rise of all took place among women with young children. From 1959 through 1974 the employment rate of mothers with children under three more than doubled, from 15 to 31 per cent, and that for mothers of children three to five years old increased from 25 to 39 per cent [145–146].

Since 1970 every trend that Chafe mentioned has continued in essentially the same direction, and the proportion of women employed has increased by roughly 10 percentage points across all age groups. The employment rate for women with children under six rose from 31 percent in 1970 to 42 percent in 1978. Of mothers with children under 18, 40 percent were employed in 1970 compared with 50 percent in 1978. By 1990 it is predicted that nearly 60 percent of women ages 35 to 54 will be in the labor force. Half of all mothers with children under six will be working, and the pattern of a wife at home will fit only one-fourth of the 44 million women who are expected to be married and living with their children (Smith, 1979; U.S. Dept. of Commerce, 1977; Waldman, Grossman, Hayghe, and Johnson, 1979).

By comparison, women's family roles in 1990 are expected to show a less striking change. The proportion of women aged 16–54 who are married with husband present will rise only slightly from 60 percent in 1978 to 66 percent in 1990 with a corresponding drop in the proportion of never-married (from 26 to 20 percent) and little change in the category of "other ever-married" who represent about 13 percent in both periods. The average size of family will continue to decline from 3.6 in 1970 to roughly 3.0 in 1990.

The proportion of married or ever-married women aged 16–54 with no children present or with very young children will hold constant. There will be a slight increase in proportion of women with children aged 6–17—from 27 percent of all women in the 16–54 age group in 1978 to 32 percent in 1990 (Smith, 1979; U.S. Dept. of Commerce, 1977).

The upshot of these two trends—rising employment and continued family involvements—is that a different mix in women's work and family roles will become increasingly evident. Change in the number of earners per family is an example. In 1950 only about one-third (36 percent) of all families had two earners or more. By 1975 the proportion had grown to nearly half because of the great increase in participation in the labor force by married women (Hayghe, 1976).

An important question for the future is whether these changes will last. At the moment there are two contrasting views on the subject. One view is that the economic situation is about to change drastically and with it will come a return of traditional attitudes. The other view is that structural and attitudinal changes have already been institutionalized and will not easily be reversed.

The economist Richard Easterlin (1978) expects that as economic prospects for the smaller birth cohorts of the 1960s improve during the 1980s, women will marry earlier, have children sooner, and then withdraw from the labor force. He reasons that young males' income relative to older males' will improve, and that the wife's income will no longer be so much needed for the family to live at the standard to which it aspires. As a result, more of the wife's time and effort will go into child rearing and other family work (Collins, 1979).

An opposite prediction comes from demographer Valerie Kincade Oppenheimer (1979). She concedes that the "baby bust" generation born in the 1960s will experience better times, but she takes issue with Easterlin. Oppenheimer particularly questions the wife's predicted withdrawal from the labor force. She believes that young men's "life cycle squeeze" (between heavy financial obligations and limited earning power) will instead continue and that current adaptations such as wives' work and postponement of childbearing will also continue. These patterns have already been institutionalized. There is now an expectation that wives will take paid employment. Moreover, current wage scales for young men take the two-earner family into account. Wages are lower not only because of recent large birth cohorts entering the labor force but also because of job competition from young women in the same cohorts. It is not clear that employers in the future will in fact face any imperative to raise salaries, given demographic changes alone.

Even before future developments unfold, it is possible to assess the actual normative changes that have occurred. There is a clear trend toward greater acceptance of women's employment and achievements outside the home. Each successive generation of women has participated in the labor force at a higher rate than its predecessors. So great is the change that it seems hardly likely to be reversed by demographic or economic cycles.

The place of work in the life cycle has also shifted. Women born before 1900 worked when they were young adults, then withdrew for the rest of their lives. Women born between 1900 and 1930 worked briefly, withdrew to family activity, and then in some instances reentered the work force in middle age. Among younger women, particularly those born since the Depression, the interrupted pattern no longer holds. Instead, women's age curve of participation in the labor force is becoming ever more similar to that of men, with a gradual rise occurring during young adulthood and little sign of withdrawal until retirement age. The graph in Figure 4.1 summarizes the change.

Explanation of these striking patterns requires more than a cyclical demographic or economic theory. Women are now built into the economy in clerical or professional occupations. The pattern is common to all the Western industrial nations. Concentrated in a few occupations (low level sales, high level clerical, etc.), their earnings average only 60 percent of men's. Industrial economies evidently share certain structural features that systematically impose these patterns. Only in those countries such as Belgium and the Federal Republic of Germany, where the service sector is somewhat smaller relative to agriculture and manufacturing, does the rate of

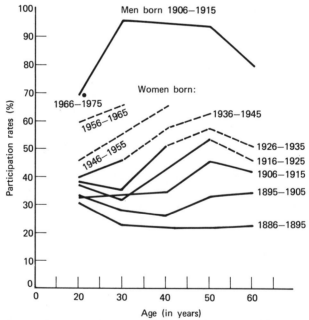

Figure 4.1. Cohort labor force participation: men born 1906–1915; women born 1886–1975.
Source: From the book *Women in the American Economy: A Look to the 1980s* by Juanita M. Kreps. ©1976 by The American Assembly, Columbia University. Published by Prentice-Hall, Inc., Englewood Cliffs, N.J. 07632.

women's participation in the labor force fall much lower than the 45–50 percent rate that is typical of the United States, the United Kingdom, and Canada (Ratner, 1980; Treiman & Roos, 1980).

Evidently many families need two earners, especially in times of employment uncertainty. A longitudinal study of 5000 American families reveals that one-third of all primary breadwinners were out of work at some point between 1968 and 1976 (Hill & Corcoran, 1979). In addition, nearly two-thirds of all employed females in America in 1978 were single, widowed, divorced, separated, or had a husband who earned less than $10,000 in 1977 (U.S. Dept. of Labor, 1979). Under such circumstances, a family need for a wife's earning ability is a key factor in rising rates of participation by women in the labor force.

Yet women's family roles also exert pressures that negatively shape the typical patterns of female employment. Women enter a much narrower range of occupations than men. More than one-third are in clerical occupations alone, and these and other female-typed jobs are typically underpaid and overcrowded. One hypothesis is that typical women's jobs can be more easily combined with family responsibilities. Some occupations like teaching or library work offer scheduling advantages. Others such as clerical work can be entered and reentered with minimum obsolescence of skills (Oaxaca, 1979). But the penalties to women are lower remuneration and less opportunity for advancement.

Thus, structural features of the industrial economy have built women into the labor force. But so also have changes in attitudes. All the major surveys on sex-role attitudes report the same trend—a movement in the direction of more egalitarian beliefs. Gallup polls and other surveys have inquired since 1937 whether the respondent would vote for a woman president. There has been a steady upward trend in the percentage agreeing, from roughly one-third in 1937 to 80 percent in 1978. Similarly, the proportion who approved a woman's working in business or industry, even if she had a husband capable of supporting her, rose from only 20 percent in 1938 to 55 percent in 1969 and 75 percent in 1978 (Duncan & Duncan, 1978; Spitze & Huber, 1979).

Other more detailed surveys have inquired into the desirability of the traditional sex division of labor within the family, the consequences of maternal employment for children's welfare, and the rights of men and women in the labor force. Mason, Czajka, and Arber (1976) compared the results of five surveys conducted between 1964 and 1974 and showed that attitudes had moved in an egalitarian direction on all three dimensions. As time went on, fewer people believed in strict sex-typed roles. Fewer thought that a preschool child would suffer if the mother worked, and more believed that a woman should have exactly the same job opportunities as a man. By 1977 a New York Times–CBS poll reported that more Americans believed in marriage in which partners could share the tasks of breadwinner and homemaker (47 percent) than those who preferred the traditional marriage (43 percent) in which the husband was exclusively a provider and the wife was exclusively a homemaker and mother (Meislin, 1977). The Detroit Area Studies documented a related shift: In 1963 fewer than a third of the respondents disagreed with the statement that "most important decisions of family life should be made by the man of the house." By 1977 two-thirds disagreed (Thornton & Freedman, 1979). Generally speaking, liberal attitudes were more frequent in three groups—the young, the educated, and in those families where women were already working. These were presumably the groups who were most likely to benefit under new conditions.

Actual living arrangements, however, are not perfectly correlated with changes in attitudes. People may believe that couples are more satisfied who share homemaking and breadwinning roles, but this does not ensure implementation of these principles in their own lives. Research to date, in fact, shows that husbands have been slower to share household tasks than changing ideology might suggest. Duncan and Duncan (1978), for example, were unable to discover much change in the number of Detroit couples who shared tasks between 1955 and 1971, or in the types of tasks that they shared.

Yet behavioral changes have certainly occurred in the work place. The changes in women's employment are in fact so dramatic that economists conclude that rewards for women's continuous work participation are outweighing the rewards for work in the home. It may be that the higher opportunity cost for home work in recent years has lowered fertility and stimulated a search for shortcuts in cleaning, cooking, and laundry. Greater use of outside services has perhaps kept the marital division of labor from responding more than it might have (Johnson, 1975; Kreps & Clark, 1975; Sawhill, 1977).

In addition, rather than a major revision of sex roles, it may be that the structure of the family is changing to provide for what Ryan (1979) has called "a disengagement of the sexes." Within the American home "male and female teeter on a delicate imbalance of power" and outside the home "wide margins of inequity separate the sexes in the labor force [232]." Single-parent households now constitute 15 percent of all households whereas the number of single-person households has doubled from about 10 percent of all households in 1950 to 20 percent in 1976 (Barrett, 1979; Kobrin, 1976).

These changes have not yet come together to form a new integrated model of work and family life. No single path to adulthood, no one pattern for the middle years can be recommended over all others. Nevertheless, it is possible to trace three emerging patterns. The first is a new picture of women's life cycle. The second appears in the experimental division of labor between home and work place. A third is the changing national consciousness and new policy frontier that increasingly assumes egalitarian sex roles.

CHANGING THEORIES OF WOMEN'S LIFE COURSE

Women's changing work patterns naturally put a strain on traditional expectations of what a woman's life should be like. Even today, high school counselors frequently note that many girls still primarily look to marriage as their chief career goal. Such young women ignore the present reality that some women will never marry. Perhaps as many as one-third will be separated or divorced. Most women will face at least 30 more years of life after their last child leaves home; and on the average, wives will outlive their husbands by as many as 10 or 15 years. If young women today are still not fully prepared for these realities, how much more understandable it is that older generations were even less prepared. In fact, it is probably true that despite feminism and related changes, each age cohort of women since 1900 has at first modeled its life in terms of the traditional ideal—a brief period of work outside the home, then marriage and settling down, without thought of reentering the work force later on. Education has been valued, and even some career preparation, but more as an insurance policy against emergency or disaster than for an occupation that is to be expected.

Now all this is changing. Some time during the 1970s the norm "tipped" from the previously dominant pattern in which mothers were homemakers to a new pattern in which a majority are employed. The change was particularly noticeable in the suburbs among the college educated. This quiet revolution produced unfamiliar problems. Women were no longer available to serve as den mothers for the Cub Scouts or to work at the church rummage sale. But at the same time, as middle-aged women entering the work force, the women found that their training was inadequate or too general and diffuse. They frequently could not find jobs commensurate with their education and intelligence. Relative to their husbands, many of them had fallen behind because of years out of the work force, lack of graduate work, or lack of special professional training.

Women in this transitional age group were thus particularly disadvantaged because they had grown up with the ideals of their mothers' generation but had to live with a different reality. The question for the future thus became a question of the ideal life cycle. How can present generations of young women face the major life events (education, marriage, births, moves, employment) and negotiate a path that results in a good life? This is the great unspoken quandary for young women in our time. One graduate of the 1970s, Linda Sexton (1980), says young women are caught between two worlds, the femin*ine* mystique of their mother's generation and the femin*ist* mystique of their own. Young women want both career success and family intimacy. The issue is how to get it.

So far as I know, there is no one authority who has come up with an answer. Past experience doesn't give much to go on, and the research results are complex and confusing. Past negative experiences of middle-aged and older women do not automatically reveal an obverse set of positive developmental steps that each young woman should try in the future. Levinson's and Vaillant's theories based on men are no more helpful. The only alternative seems to be induction from piecemeal findings about women. One asks what factors contribute to life satisfaction or career success. What decisions or life events and what timing patterns stand in the way? In the next few pages I examine three major bodies of research with these questions in mind: (1) studies of women and mental health, (2) research on status attainment, and (3) life course theories themselves.

What I conclude is that a new model of the life course is emerging, for women as well as for men. Its structure, rather than holding out a single optimum sequence of life events, is characterized by several possible options, all viable and all potentially capable of giving satisfaction. The significance of this new model of the life course is that it is peculiarly adapted to conditions of modern society. It recognizes a number of individual variations. It accounts for flexibility, redirection, and multiple possible combinations of timing and sequence. It implies that versatility and freedom of choice are to be valued. By the same token, it suggests that certain other patterns should be avoided, particularly those like very early childbearing or school leaving. Such patterns close options and decrease adaptability later on. In my opinion, women who live in such a complex society as our own would do well to have a complex and flexible model before them rather than to believe in marrying and living happily ever after, or to follow simple stairstep guides to maturity. It is fortuitous that a new image of the life course is rising just when the inadequacies of the old model are becoming fully apparent.

Health and Well-Being

One imagines that the people who preserve maximum adaptability and choice are those most happy and at peace with themselves. The unhappy ones, the sick ones, must be those so bound by constraint, stress, and duty that they feel helpless and without hope. Considerable support for this interpretation comes from available research on women's mental health.

Guttentag and Salasin (1977) and Belle (1979) suggest that a sense of helplessness underlies many cases of depression in women. The women who are particularly vulnerable to depression are heads of a single-parent family, have poor education, have responsibility for young children, and at the same time are working but at low wages. A British study of women and depression likewise shows that it is the women subject to high stress and precipitating events (four times as many working-class women as middle-class women) who become depressed (Brown & Harris, 1978). Thus it is the persons who have a lot of responsibility but very little help in meeting strain who are more likely to be unhappy or develop symptoms. Several other pieces of evidence support this conclusion.

In the national survey on quality of American life, Campbell, Converse, and Rodgers (1976) discovered that the highest levels of dissatisfaction appeared in mothers with young children. It was the young married who were still childless and the older married whose children had left home who seemed the happiest. An earlier report by Norval Glenn (1975) based on four national surveys also showed that mothers whose children have left home report somewhat greater happiness. The highest rate of psychiatric and physical symptoms occurs in women who have the greatest care-taking responsibilities, especially those married women with young children and those divorced, separated, or widowed women with dependents (Gove & Hughes, 1979).

Significantly, however, it is not simply the amount of stress or burden that accounts for low satisfaction or high rates of illness. There are in addition certain internal and contextual factors that make some individuals more vulnerable than others. Some are persons with shaky inner resources, such as women in the British study who had lost a mother before the age of 11 and presumably were emotionally more vulnerable as a result (Brown & Harris, 1978). Others are lacking a friend or relative who can help out. This may take the form of living arrangements such as the single-parent family where the nurturer is peculiarly alone. Or the more vulnerable may lack a confidant—or may be in a marriage relationship without intimacy— and thus be more likely to experience depression.

A third factor in women's vulnerability to illness is employment. Brown and Harris found in the British study that *employed* women subject to high stress or low companionship were about *half as likely* to succumb to depression as the women who were not employed. Yet Deborah Belle (1979) observed in a study of Boston women that frequently the depressed are those heading single-parent families, who have poor education, *and* who are working at low-paid jobs. Employment perhaps works as an antidote to depression (as in the British study) when it creates options, gives some leverage against the demands of the nurturant roles, and opens up a new source of social contact and stimulation. Otherwise, it simply adds to total drag. Evidently the employed women in Camberwell, England, gained immunity to symptoms through the options created by multiple roles instead of the hazards of role overload that burdened the poor Massachusetts women. Not just any type of employment is an antidote to depression, but the type of work that supplies adequate earnings, rewards competence, and generally reinforces a sense of self-direction and personal control does seem to be such an antidote.

Conditions to promote women's health apparently require a balance between nurturant and productive roles. This is true not only in the help and resources that such roles generate but also in the role demands they make on the woman herself. For protection against depression a woman needs confidants and emotional support as well as income and material resources. Gratification comes from ties to others as well as from work. Until now we have tended to focus on either nurturance or productive work without taking the question of tradeoffs into account. The result has been a statistical and rhetorical game of showing whether married women were happier than single women, or employed women happier than housewives. The results of these comparisons have been ambiguous, however, because married people generally report higher satisfaction than the single, widowed, divorced, or separated (Bernard, 1972; Campbell et al., 1976). But working women report fewer symptoms than housewives. And single women report greater satisfaction with their *work* life than married women (Sears & Barbee, 1977).

What I believe this all adds up to is that we are just beginning to formulate a new ideal of health and happiness for adult women. In the early stages of the recent feminist movement, women discovered the costs they had paid for concentrating on the nurturant role to the detriment of their work lives and their sense of competence and power. Then a research tradition developed that showed the value of a sense of competence to women. Current studies (Barnett & Baruch, 1979) of women in the middle years hark back to this initial insight:

It is almost a cliché now for people who work long hours at demanding jobs, aware of what they are missing in terms of time with family, long talks with friends, concerts, and all kinds of opportunities for leisure, to express the sentiment that "there is more to life than work." The problem is that life *without* productive work is terrible.

Now, however, a new generation of women has come of age who were imbued with the work and achievement ethic and immunized against the feminine mystique. Like Linda Sexton, "caught between two worlds," they ask how they will find intimacy and connectedness to others. They have their careers; but when will they marry, and will they have children? The second wave of the new women's movement is thus concerned with the rediscovery of nurturant roles and values (Friedan, 1981). Now the question for the individual is how to negotiate the life course to have it all.

Status Attainment

Even more than the studies of mental health, the research on status attainment considers what order of life events may be most conducive to a satisfying and successful life. While psychologists have measured mental health and life situations conducive to it, sociologists have measured who gets ahead. Do women move up the educational and career ladders the way men do? Do they attain the same levels of achievement? If not, why not? These questions have implications for the ideal life course. Ultimately, they can be used to answer whether there is an optimum timing of education, marriage, childbearing, and employment that will maximize the chances for a woman's health and happiness.

First, we must face up to a challenging conceptual and empirical question. What are the major timing patterns, and which ones are associated with the best outcomes? Glen Elder (1975) has defined a career as "a patterned sequence of movements and events [178]." Using this definition, several typologies are possible.

An Australian sociologist, Christabel Young (1978), categorizes women's careers like Mendelian genetic types. She develops several temporal sequences that combine working or not working with different stages of the family life cycle. Out of eight possible role sequences, the five most common are never working (NNN), working only before having a family (YNN), beginning work after children are in school (NNY), working except when the children are of preschool age (YNY), and continuous working (YYY).

A more universal typology (not defined in terms of family life cycle) has been developed by Mary Corcoran (1978) to characterize the work histories of women in the Five Thousand American Family Study. Her findings concisely convey not only the differences between men's and women's career patterns but also the frequency with which each pattern is found among women themselves (see Table 4.1). Perhaps most surprising about these findings is that the continuous work pattern that is most frequent among the men is also the most frequent among the women, even though the proportion who worked continuously is about 1½-times greater for men and the average time they have worked is several years longer. Another surprising finding is that the differences in men's and women's work patterns do not account for the 40 percent difference in their earnings. Can we then say whether the order and time of life events has any effect on life outcomes?

When all is said and done, given our current research findings, two themes stand out. One points to the normative sequences of major life events and the costs of deviating from them. The other emphasizes the complexity of timing, the variety of individual life-styles, and the constantly changing social backdrop. Rather than costs of deviation, this second type of research shows the multiple possible routes to satisfaction. Let us review the evidence on both sides.

Over the years Bernice Neugarten has spoken of the "normal expectable life cycle," a concept that lends itself to research on the effects of being

Table 4.1. Distribution of Five Major Work Patterns Among White Men, White Women, Black Men, and Black Women, 1975 (in percentages)

Work Pattern	White Men	White Women	Black Men	Black Women
Pattern A: continuous work	55	36	61	42
Pattern B: prework interruption	11	29	15	42
Pattern C: work/nonwork/work	29	15	22	5
Pattern D: nonwork/work/nonwork/ work	3	8	1	7
Pattern E: at least five periods of alternating work and non-work or nonwork and work.	3	12	1	4

Source: Table constructed from Figure 2.3 in Corcoran (1978, pp. 59–62). Data from the Panel Study of Income Dynamics.

"on-time" or "off-time," early or late in finishing one's education, establishing a career, starting a family, or reaching the peak of one's achievement (Neugarten, 1979). A great deal of research has shown that people pay a price for deviating markedly from the normal path or the normal pace. Among men, for example, Hogan (1978) has shown that such a disruption in timing as caused by the draft and military service is associated with higher rates of marital disruption later in life. An issue of comparable importance for women is early marriage or childbearing, since numerous studies demonstrate negative consequences. The woman who bears a child very early (before the age of 20 or before or during the first year of marriage) is more likely to suffer a marital breakup, gain limited work experience, foreshorten her education, and become dependent on welfare (Barrett, 1979; Furstenberg, 1976; Moore, Hofferth, Caldwell & Waite, 1980; Taueber & Sweet, 1976). Similarly, early marriage (before 19 in Elder's sample) is more likely to be associated with poorer financial status later on, restricted education, and a heavy burden of child care (Elder & Rockwell, 1976; Freedman & Coombs, 1966; Marini, 1978, 1979). Being late in marriage and childbearing also has its costs. In a small pilot study in western Massachusetts Alice Rossi (1980) found that women who had larger families and later childbearing had more "aging symptoms." They wanted to be a lot younger or to die sooner, and generally they were more dissatisfied than women whose childbearing had occurred at the usual age. Elder and Rockwell (1976) likewise found that women born in 1925 to 1929 who married later (after age 22), when they were interviewed in 1965 and 1970, said they wished they had married sooner. Presumably their views were influenced by their actual life experience.

Yet against this evidence of poorer outcomes associated with "off-time" patterns must be weighed other findings that fail to show any great difference for women who do things one way as compared with those who do them another. It is not at all clear, for example, that work discontinuities hurt women's occupational status or earnings all that much. This curious finding appears in Corcoran's (1978) analysis of women's work histories in the Five Thousand Family Study. It also appears in results from the National Longitudinal Surveys of women analyzed by Sandell and Shapiro who found little evidence that women's work discontinuities had a negative effect. Instead, the large earnings gap between men and women holds even for the never-married women who presumably have experienced continuous work histories like those of men (Kahne, 1977; Sandell & Shapiro, 1976; Sawhill, 1973).

Moreover, life outcomes appear to be determined as much by "tastes" and values (toward a career, further education, or having children) as by the opening or closing of doors that are triggered by the order and timing of life events. At least, this is what I get out of some complicated findings on the relation between participation in the labor force and fertility. Researchers have been trying to answer a question that goes something like this: Does having babies make a woman less likely to participate in the labor force, or does working make her less likely to have a baby? The answer depends on a woman's attitudes and values. If mothering is important to her and if she rates herself high as a mother, a woman will continue to have children even if she is in the labor force (Booth & Duvall, 1980; Smith−Lovin & Tickamyer, 1978). On the other hand, if she has a high initial commitment to a career, she will shape a life-style that ultimately leads to a decision to have few or no children (Houseknecht, 1979; Stolzenberg & Waite, 1977; Waite & Stolzenberg, 1976).

To complicate matters further, there appears to be a reciprocal relationship between tastes and certain life events. Using data from the National Longitudinal Survey (NLS) sample of younger women (aged 19−29 in 1973), Spitze and Waite (1979) discovered that a woman's first marriage lowers her preference for paid (market) work by 10 to 20 percentage points, especially if it occurs in the 14−23 age bracket. The first birth, however, *raises* preference for market work from 10 to 15 percent, especially in the younger age groups of 16 to 27. Divorce also raises preference for paid work by 20 to 30 percentage points. Spitze and Waite clearly imply that, although life choices are shaped by previously held values and attitudes, actual experiences in turn give rise to somewhat different values in the future. It is this complex formula summarizing the interaction of values with experience that perhaps makes the most sense out of the relativity of outcomes observed in women's lives. Daniels and Weingarten (1982) studied the timing of parenthood and found that parents who had had their children later (after the age of 27) experienced certain costs as a result—such as being less youthful, flexible, and energetic than younger parents, but older parents also expressed satisfaction that they were more secure and established when their children were born. Younger parents, on the other hand, were glad for their vitality and flexibility but regretted the financial strain and the educational sacrifice the older parents had not experienced. Evidently, both major temporal alternatives can net roughly equal amounts, although different kinds, of satisfaction.

Much the same point emerges from a study of women's career paths. Perun and Bielby (1980) studied 41 married women with doctorates who were born between 1893 and 1906. Among these women they found three types of accommodation to major life events: Pattern I, marriage then receiving the doctorate; Pattern II, work for the doctorate, then marriage; and Pattern III, simultaneous marriage and work for the doctorate. Some women had children and others did not. When these women's attainments were examined at age 60, few differences could be found either in the status of the institution at which they were employed or in their academic rank. Women with children were employed at institutions of slightly lower rank. When the sample was divided into two groups, one with and the other without children, no differences could be found within groups between those who had followed the three different sequential patterns.

How shall we put together these rich and puzzling findings on status attainment? There appear to be costs for deviation from the normal expectable life course, but satisfaction can also be attained through any one of several other possible routes. Neither fact invalidates the other, in my view. Instead, it is a theoretical challenge to find an overarching conceptual umbrella that makes sense out of both. Such a framework is now in process of development.

The Crossover Theme

All living systems exhibit two processes in the course of change and development. One is differentiation, specialization, and increasing complexity in their component parts. The other is integration and greater interdependence among the specialized parts. The two traditions of life-span research on women reflect both of these tendencies. Efforts to delineate an optimum timing pattern are related to the differentiation tendency; significant life events are enumerated, critical turning points are recognized, and a pattern of optimum development is identified. Skepticism about optimum pattern appears in theories that emphasize integration. Significant life events are also noted in these theories, but they are more likely to be observed according to the way they fit a sequential pattern rather than as being on or off schedule. This second type of research celebrates the number of possible sequential orders of events and emphasizes the variety of combinations that can integrate the whole life course and give it unity.

The crossover theme is the result of both these tendencies. Crossover in sex roles holds that both women and men can usefully perform many tasks that once were primarily assigned to the opposite sex. Crossover in age roles suggests that developmental tasks and significant life events can be taken up at a number of possible different points in the life cycle without undue harm. I find both of these crossover themes throughout contemporary research on the changing roles of women. They did not emerge, I suspect, until the society had become sufficiently specialized so that actual age and sex crossovers could occur. Then social changes were reflected in research and theory. Generally speaking, the differentiation theme appeared in refined stage theories based on a few individuals, and the crossover theme emerged from research on large heterogeneous populations. The crossover theme, in my opinion, however, could not emerge until refined developmental tasks had been described by the stage theorists (Giele, 1980a, 1980b).

In *Childhood and Society* Erikson (1950) charted eight major stages of life. Heavily influenced by his work, Levinson (1978), Gould (1978), and Vaillant (1977) gave highly detailed accounts of the middle years. In *The Seasons in a Man's Life* Levinson described an early adult era (with three distinct phases), a middle adult era (with another three phases), and a late adult era. Such intellectual refinements had not been necessary in simpler colonial and rural society where persons hardly spoke of adulthood other than to distinguish manhood from childhood and old age (Demos, 1978). Now in our post-industrial era, we are refining our categories of knowledge to explore the psychological frontiers of adulthood.

One important discovery during this historical transition was that gross deviations in timing that limited the very complexity of future prospects were in themselves harmful. Thus, very early childbearing and the resulting truncated education and poor job opportunities were out of keeping with a rapidly changing and complex society. Individuals caught in this pattern could not respond flexibly and adaptively to the complicated labor conditions or personal circumstances that they were likely to face.

An unexpected consequence of these refinements, however, was that they made more explicit the developmental tasks to be accomplished, and in the process individuals discovered that such tasks were not necessarily linked to age but could be taken up in any one of several possible orders, with far more complex opportunities for mixing and matching activities than any one "ideal" normal expectable life course could possibly encompass. While stage theorists continued to propound the idea of an optimum life course, other social scientists began to claim that some important life events were "age-independent." Because some major life events are unexpected or unwanted, there may be no particular expectable order or timing of adult development.

Pearlin (1980) finds that developmental issues vary immensely according to a person's socioeconomic location. In research on both middle and working class Americans, Fiske (1980) cannot find evidence to support stage theory. Targ (1979) notes that the current theories built on male experience of middle age frequently do not fit women, in part because the theories fail to recognize the *unexpected events* such as divorce, employment, or unemployment that heavily influence many women's lives. Those studies of women's work and fertility histories that fail to find a difference in attainment that can be attributed to the patterning of life events thus fit the skeptical school of theories of the life span. They recognize the complex society but draw a different lesson. They discover myriad possible combinations of developmental tasks and life events (Best, 1978; Hirschhorn, 1979; Watts & Skidmore, 1978). Perun and Bielby's (1979) discovery that academic women could achieve in any one of several ways is at home in this tradition. So also Daniels and Weingarten's (1982) balanced findings on the advantages of early and late parenthood.

In addition, social roles have changed to reflect increasing complexity and crossover. Tasks have become more differentiated within each sex role. Such women's jobs as cooking or child care have been specialized and rationalized so that they can be done by others. Men's jobs that required greater physical strength have also become more specialized because machinery has taken over some of the heaviest work. As a result, it is now much easier to move across the sex-role boundaries: Men can cook; women can operate power machinery. Quite naturally, these changes are also being reflected in theories of the life course. Writers such as Gutmann (1977) and Brim (1976) have commented on the "unisex of later life." In their middle years, men discover the nurturant aspects of their personality that may have been suppressed in the fight to establish a career. Women, on the other hand, discover their long-delayed desire for assertion and achievement. These theories recognize sex-role crossover in the middle stages of the life course.

At the same time official recognition is growing of the possibilities for what I call "age crossover." Education and employment programs for women take into account the various possible life schedules in which women engage. They may have their children early or late, enter the job market, drop out and reenter, or remain continuously. They may finish their education before establishing a family or getting a job, or they may drop out and continue later. As the variety of patterns gains further acceptance, the challenge to policy makers, educational institutions, and corporations will be to devise programs that meet such a diverse range of needs.

THE NEW FAMILY ROLE SYSTEM

Changing ideas about the typical life cycle of women have affected family structure. No longer is it taken for granted that women's primary task is to be the homemaker and child tender while men earn the money and "bring home the bacon." Instead, what appears to be happening in every major industrial society is a redefinition of men's and women's roles. Change is in the direction of greater equality and sharing in parenting, housekeeping, and making money. The new patterns correspond with greater interpenetration between the worlds of work and family life (Kanter, 1977). They also illustrate crossover in the family roles of women and men.

Recent books and articles on family life indicate a remarkable convergence on a new, more egalitarian form that Young and Willmott (1973) have labeled "the symmetrical family." On the basis of a study of 2600 London families surveyed in 1970, Young and Willmott theorized that family structure had passed through several broad states of development that corresponded with the economic structure of the larger society. In the patriarchal family of the preindustrial era, family activity and economic activity were joined; the whole family worked at the tasks that supported them. The husband had primary authority both as major producer and head of the family. With the onset of the industrial revolution, the patriarchal family was replaced by the nineteenth-century Victorian ideal. The work place was separate from family activity. The husband was the primary breadwinner, and the wife was in charge of the children and the domestic front. In the twentieth century, a third major type of family has appeared. With an advanced industrial economy, even more specialized jobs, and household conveniences, the symmetrical family, found among blue-collar workers and professionals alike, is the result of increasing interpenetration of work and family life. Both husband and wife typically work outside the home; both also share in household tasks. However, the division of labor is still skewed toward greater responsibility of the husband as income producer and the wife as housekeeper and care giver.

Sociological studies from a number of countries reinforce this outline of the emerging symmetrical family. A pilot program in Sweden tries to encourage this type of role sharing by expanding the repertoires of men and women so that each, by incorporating elements of the provider, parent, and citizen roles, can become more of a "whole person" and realize the goal of sex equality (Liljestrom, Mellstrom & Svensson, 1975). Dual-career families in Great Britain are the subject of a major study by Rapoport and Rapoport (1976). Gronseth (1978) analyses the relationships of work-sharing couples in Norway. Holmstrom (1972) documents the dilemmas in career and family choice that face two-career couples in the United States. Lein (1979a) describes American families "in the middle" (working class and lower middle class) who arrange their work time in order to share responsibilities for child care.

In the United States an ever larger number of families include working wives. In 1976 families with both a husband and wife in the labor force made up 41 percent of all husband—wife families, a larger single block than any other form. Families with husbands only in the labor force constituted 34 percent. The remaining 12 percent of husband—wife families had a wife only in the labor force, no employed member, or some other combination (Hayghe, 1976).

Why is the dual-worker family becoming so widespread? Sociologically, the symmetrical family has advantages in a complex and rapidly changing society such as our own because it promotes flexibility and adaptability far better than traditional forms, which dictate rigid role segregation between husband and wife. If husband and wife can substitute for each other, whether in breadwinning or child tending, they are better able to respond to unforeseen circumstances such as loss of health or income, failure in school or work, or some threat to the local economy.

This new type of couple is still likely, however, to put primary emphasis on the husband's job as a basis for choosing residential location or timing major family events. The wife's role more often involves the compromises that keep the family flexible. This perhaps accounts for two penalties that fall on working women: lower pay and a heavier combined burden of paid work and housework.

An international time study by Szalai (1973) extended into Belgium, Bulgaria, Czechoslovakia, France, East and West Germany, Hungary,

Peru, Poland, the United States, the USSR, and Yugoslavia and collected data from 30,000 respondents. Perhaps most telling was the consistent finding that after their contributions to the household employed men still had 50 percent more leisure than the employed women. An earlier time study in the United States by Walker (1969, 1970) showed the same pattern. Women performed more family work than men—4.8 hours a day for married women employed 30 or more hours a week as compared with 1.6 hours for the employed men who were married to working wives. A recent study by Pleck and Rustad (1980) using time budget data from a national survey shows considerable improvement in this picture. Husbands of employed women have doubled the time they give to help around the home (from 1.6 hours in the Walker study to 3.8 hours per day). Still, working wives' family work (6.9 hours per day) is significantly more than their husbands'—almost twice as much. This degree of inequality is a definite improvement, however, over the 3:1 ratio reported by Walker 10 years earlier.

Have these trends toward role sharing and equality now stabilized? Or will the improvement continue in the future? My guess is that additional forward movement is still likely, although perhaps at a slower rate. A more detailed picture of probable changes comes from closer examination of the three major domains that husbands and wives increasingly share: child care, housework, and paid employment.

Child Care

Perhaps the central theme of women's new family roles is that traditional ways need not prevail but can be examined critically and be changed to accommodate people's needs and desires. Nowhere is this more evident than in child care. Among dual-career families, there is a belief that parenting arrangements are most satisfying when they are *chosen*, are the best possible available under the circumstances, and have clear-cut standards and goals (Rapoport, Rapoport & Strelitz, 1977). This new attitude has fostered discovery of men's capacity for parenting, a new willingness for women and men to share more responsibility for child care, and a search for outside supports (day care, cooperative community arrangements, etc.) that will somewhat lighten the traditional burden on the mother.

The father's important role in child development is a relatively recent topic for research. Numerous studies have examined the potentially harmful effects of father absence. More recently there has been an effort to document that fathers *can* ably care for young children, even newborns (Sawin & Parke, 1979). In addition, there is growing evidence that more active participation in child care is both gratifying and beneficial to the fathers themselves (Lewis, Freneau & Roberts, 1979; Rapoport et al., 1977).

Certainly it is a boon to women if they can call on their husbands for relief from the intense demands for care that young children can make. Piotrowski's (1979) sensitive account of one young mother's days spent with her three preschool children suggests the welcome change that a father can provide when the baby is crying, the mother is tired, and each of the other children also needs care and attention. Under such circumstances the father relieves the tension; he is not so caught up with other competing concerns like cooking and the housework. Nor has he the accumulation of a whole day's demands, frustrations, and fatigue when he faces the particular moment at hand. There is a great advantage to be gained from an ideology of parenting and a practical schedule for child care that allows as much sharing as possible.

When children are a little older, they also can be encouraged to help. In their study of dual-career families, the Rapoports (1976) discovered that although there was a good deal of variation in parental roles, *all* the families expected help from their children.

In the current movement toward egalitarian sex roles, I wouldn't be surprised if more progress were made in sharing child care than housework. Children do offer gratification; they cannot be neglected. Using national time study data, Pleck (1979) in fact discovered that husbands of working wives spent 2.7 more hours per week in child care than husbands of nonworking wives and only 1.8 hours more per week in housework. Other national surveys have shown that the personal rewards of a good marriage and family are actually thought to be nearly twice as important for happiness as an interesting job.

Besides more sharing, husbands and wives now also use more outside facilities—formal day care, informal child care, after-school programs, and so on. Between 1964 and 1974 the proportion of all children three to five years old who were enrolled in nursery school and kindergarten rose from one-quarter to nearly half. Of all the care arrangements used for children under six between 1965 and 1971, only one-quarter was provided outside homes in a day-care center or other such arrangement. This compares with a third of all families who have day care in their homes provided by a father or other relative. Another quarter arrange care in their homes to be given by a combination of relatives or nonrelatives. The remaining fraction (17 percent) are cared for in another person's home (Giele, 1978). Whether existing facilities are adequate is a large and unanswered question. Certainly the women's movement and child advocacy groups have shown a sustained interest in providing sufficient high-quality care. Similar interest in adequate child-care programs has surfaced in other advanced industrial nations, and the trend seems likely to continue.

Despite parental role sharing and development of child-care programs outside the family, a familiar asymmetry nevertheless characterizes male and female roles. Increasingly, the observers of two-worker families appear to question whether it will ever be otherwise. Pleck (1979) voices the dilemma:

> In the past, with some stress, one breadwinner in the family could follow the male work model. In the present, with more stress, one breadwinner could emphasize work and another breadwinner plan an ancillary, less-demanding work role. But it is

doubtful whether large numbers of families can function with both partners following the male work model. For both spouses to adopt the male work model, families would have to stop having children, or else household and childcare services would have to be provided on a scale hitherto unprecedented. Without one or the other, two-role living by both men and women will require a new work-role model and for men an expanded family role [409].

In the meantime, as we wait to see the future, it does seem likely that men will participate more in child rearing, and women will seek their help, especially if they are also employed. Yet at the same time women will continue to have a larger role in child tending. It will probably be much as Ferber and Huber (1979) have shown is presently the case with men and women who received their Ph.D.s after 1958. Highly educated women in professional careers in the future will likely have fewer children than their male counterparts. Such is the difficulty of working out a new work–family role system; the opportunity costs for rearing children will still be largely determined by the value of a mother's time.

Housework

Equal sharing of housework in the future is also problematic. The rule of one of the Rapoports' dual-career families seems the ideal direction in which others should follow: When there is family work to do, no one sits down until the work is finished and everyone can sit down. American time budget studies, however, show that employed women are still doing roughly twice as much housework (23.6 hours per week) as their employed husbands (11.4 hours per week) (Pleck & Rustad, 1980). Why is this the case, and what is the likely trend in the future?

Researchers have been surprised that since the 1920s housewives' time spent in household work has not diminished but actually increased. Vanek (1974) found that nonemployed women spent 55 hours a week in family work in 1965–1966 compared with 52 hours a week reported by housewives in 1925–1926, before the widespread introduction of the refrigerator and automatic washing machine. Standards apparently rose: The clothes were washed more often and the house was kept cleaner. In addition, more time was apparently spent in child care because of the increasing emphasis on mothering, and perhaps also because of the absence of older children or others who could help. By contrast, the employed wives spent only about half as much time on family work—26 hours. They evidently had to "cut corners," accept messier houses, and perhaps eat out more. The difference did not result from more help by their husbands or from workers in their households.

There is ample evidence that men resist taking on household chores even when their wives are employed. Both Lein (1979b) and Pleck (1979) attribute the reason to men's feeling that their primary work on behalf of the family is in the breadwinner role. Resistance to housework protects the primacy of their obligation to the provider role. At times it may also be an expression of a stubborn wish that their wives didn't have to work.

Given this bottleneck that slows men's acceptance of responsibility for household chores, several alternatives nevertheless are possible. Chief among them are household conveniences and outside help. Numerous technological advances have streamlined laundry: wash and wear clothing, the automatic washer and dryer, a dependable water supply and plumbing. Cooking is easier because of convenience foods, the refrigerator, freezer, and other mechanical devices for food preparation. Children can eat their lunches in school. Until high rates of inflation, many families frequently ate out. There is still the cleaning, but some families have their children help with vacuuming, dusting, and yard work when they are old enough. Cleaning services visit those who can afford them.

In the meantime there is a slow but steady change in the ideology surrounding men's household work. A husband taking clothes out of the dryer gets pictured in *Newsweek* (1980). Gerald Ford, president of the United States, was known to cook his own breakfasts. The young professional family in which both work are a fashionable symbol of a new age—the advanced, affluent, egalitarian couple who combine personal liberation with responsibility for others. These changes are not yet widespread, however. Some older couples are set in their sex-typed mold. Some younger couples are making do as firemen and keypunch operators, not at all the glamorous managerial or professional pair who can afford day care, dinners out, and a cleaning service.

Yet hopeful signs of more crossover in household roles of men and women come from a variety of quarters. It is claimed that doing things around the home is good for men, helps them to relax and get in touch with their feelings (Tognoli, 1979). The middle-aged companionate marriage actually allows the relationship to mellow. The husband enters more into the emotional relationship, is in some cases less preoccupied with his work, and takes a larger part in housework, especially after he has retired (Hess & Waring, 1978; Keith & Brubaker, 1979). Role theories suggest there may be a value to role expansion and role accumulation, so that a woman, rather than being depleted by employment, may return to her household chores with greater energy and efficiency and also be able to resist the endless demands that would be made on her if homemaking were her only role (Marks, 1977; Sieber, 1974). One recent study even reports a significant decline in the amount of time women spend in family care, 6.6 hours less per week in 1975 than in 1965 (Robinson & Rogers−Millar, 1979). Finally, new generations are coming along. The boys now required to take home economics in the junior high schools will presumably feel more comfortable doing household work as adults. Those around them, including the women they marry, will have a stake in reinforcing their confidence and sense of worth as they help with family work in the future.

The Economic Provider Role

These changes in child care and housework are predicated on the idea that women's increasing participation in the labor force is beneficial to families and should be accommodated wherever possible.[1] Indeed, one of the striking themes of the two-worker family is how important the woman's contribution is to its economic well-being. Families *need* the woman's income. This is particularly true if a divorce or separation occurs; the woman's work, rather than alimony or child support, is what keeps a woman and her children afloat (Burlage, 1978). Even in the intact families unemployment of the major breadwinner is such a common occurrence that the wife's income is badly needed to tide the family over. Lein's (1979a) working family study of 14 dual-worker families in the Boston area found that every family had experienced at least one layoff of either husband or wife in the recession following 1972–1973. Husbands tremendously valued a wife's contribution when her wages helped keep the family income up to the standard they desired.

Yet in the face of this powerful reason to encourage married women's employment, all the evidence points to a strong tendency for the husband's work to take precedence. Even in the professional dual-career families where the ideology of equality is presumably strongest, Holmstrom (1972) found that the wives accommodated to their husbands' careers more than vice versa when deciding where to live. In a study of women and men with the Ph.D. degree Ferber and Huber (1979) found that women were more likely to permit their location to be determined by their spouse's career, even though negative career effects on the woman's eventual employment usually followed.

Perhaps as Pleck suggested, it is difficult to realize full equality when both male and female follow the male work-role model. In order to maintain some flexibility, at least one of the pair must be able to adjust and compromise. The only other solution is to gain room for flexibility in both persons' work roles through adjustable work schedules and other devices. We examine these possibilities in the following consideration of changing work roles.

CHANGING WORK ROLES

The most important single strategy for restructuring work has been the manipulation of scheduling through such devices as part-time jobs, flexible hours, provisions for parental leave, and the like. Between 1948 and 1976 the proportion of part-time workers increased substantially, going from one-fifth to one-third of all women workers and from 9 to 15 percent of all men workers. Flexible hours drew considerable attention as another major

---

[1] I have elsewhere made the case for a diversified set of policies, some designed to aid women who are employed, others to help women who are full-time housewives (Giele, 1978, 1980c). Here I focus on ways to accommodate the employed women because this issue, rather than the needs of the full-time homemaker, is more important to the symmetrical family.

means of accommodating work to family life, and in the late 1970s one estimate reported at least 300,000 workers known to be presently so employed (Giele & Kahne, 1978). The value of women's part-time work was recognized in many quarters and took on certain glamorous possibilities, particularly for the professional or managerial woman. Bell (1976) pictured the accountant who retires from a large firm of auditors but continues to take a few select clients, and the security analyst, operations researcher, or market specialist who works at her former firm as a two- or three-day-a-week consultant and has more time at home with her children. Bell states: "For them, the status of part-time carries none of the stigma, low skills, undependability or lack of motivation attributed to part-time workers at low-income levels [259]."

Gradually, also, the part-time concept expanded. Rather than refer only to women (who make up roughly 70 percent of all part-time workers), social visionaries began to see the possibilities in part-time work for men as well—the students, the retired, and those in the middle years who wish more time with their families. Calls for maternity leaves were transformed into the broader language of "parental leave." The advanced ideas found in Sweden seemed to point the way. Employment services were to help demolish sex barriers in the labor market, train males for "female" jobs, protect the desires of women working part-time who wished to work more, and gain a shorter working day for both men and women (Sandberg, 1975).

Practical details on the dynamics and effects of such changes surfaced in accounts of women who shared part-time professional jobs such as teaching (Giele, 1978), in research on couples who shared a single academic or professional job (Arkin & Dobrovsky, 1978, 1979), and on couples who each worked part-time but sometimes at different jobs (Gronseth, 1978). By all accounts, these joint experiments in part-time work had excellent effects on the family life of the participants: Their roles were less sex typed, marital intimacy increased, and child care was easier and more satisfying.

What was not so clear were the negative effects, but there were some. One was reduced financial gains. Another was the tendency for the part-time job to expand so that each individual was doing much more work than was being paid for. A third disadvantage—especially in high-status occupations in which full time is equated with professionalism and part time with a casual attitude—was the low self-esteem that each part-time person eventually had to confront (Arkin & Dobrovsky, 1978, 1979). Finally, it was difficult to regularize part-time appointments, have them be paid for on a pro-rated basis, and carry pro-rated fringe benefits. Employers were usually afraid to "set a precedent."

At the present moment, part-time work and flexible working hours seem to have only a tenuous place in American working life. They are most common in a few industries (finance, banking, insurance) and among a few occupations (waitresses, cooks, teachers, health workers). Part-time work still carries the dangers of low pay, poor opportunities to gain seniority, and high turnover. Even if it may be good for families under optimum conditions, what likelihood is there that it will spread? And in the long run, what are its prospects for the future work roles of adult women?

The current interest in part-time work is indicative, I believe, of a process that will help bring about greater sex-role crossover in the work place. Experiments with scheduling are essentially signs of a further differentiation of work roles in which discrete bundles of tasks can be moved around and combined in new ways. Discovery that a job can be performed by two part-time people is antecedent to this differentiation process. Such rearrangements cannot occur without sufficient rationality and objectivity to list the job duties and requirements discretely and recognize that they can either be subdivided or be shared with another equally qualified person. When such a breakdown of global attributes has been made, the ascriptive qualities of being a male (able to work full time) or a female (likely to be vulnerable to family demands and to work part time) become less relevant. Thus crossover and equality are facilitated.

Such changes in work demands have obvious implications for family life. A woman's interest in a career can be accommodated more easily. So can a man's interest if he is not fully wrapped up in his work and if he wants more time with his family (Gronseth, 1978). The rigidity of work schedules is relaxed somewhat, and family demands can more easily be met as they arise. Instead of having one full-time worker who follows the male work model, and one flexible worker whose job is secondary, both workers reach an intermediate level of commitment to work and responsiveness to family needs.

Ultimately, the part-time idea has implications for the relative priority of work and family life in the larger society as well as in the lives of individuals. In their study of job-sharing couples, Arkin and Dobrovsky (1979) reported a finding consistent with that of the Rapoports (1976). Occupation for these couples, rather than being a primary source of fulfillment, is either equal to or less important than family and other sources of fulfillment. It is my own hunch that women's equality will not be fully realized until this balanced ideal of relationship and achievement is writ large in the interaction of work and family life. It will be manifest when women see their competence and work as important as intimacy and family life, and when men see close personal ties and family work as important as their occupations and career success. At the moment the realization of this ideal seems a long way off. Women and men still differentiate their primary responsibilities asymmetrically. Yet change is in the direction of a more similar constellation of future duties and rewards.

SOCIAL CHANGES: CONTINUING EDUCATION AND JOB REENTRY

No more dramatic evidence of social change in women's work and family roles can be found than in the crescendo of concern for the so-called *displaced homemaker.* This is a person who has devoted her adult work life to care of family and home and then finds herself economically dependent by loss of a spouse through death or divorce or the maturity of her children (which makes her no longer eligible to receive the child benefits to which she was formerly entitled). Concern for the displaced homemaker, whether she be a middle-class woman threatened by poverty who suddenly must head a single-parent family or a welfare mother whose children have grown, is indicative of two broad converging trends in modern society. One relates to the increasing likelihood of divorce, the other stems from a growing expectation that women cannot (as traditionally expected) depend on others for economic support but must be able to support themselves and their children if the need arises.

The term *displaced homemaker* first appeared in 1974 as a result of a special task force of the National Organization of Women headed by Tish Sommers and Laurie Shields (1978). They defined and publicized the problem of women's dependency and vulnerability if they were suddenly "displaced" from their usual role as full-time homemakers and could no longer depend on a husband or Aid to Families of Dependent Children (AFDC) for economic support. Sommers and Shields proposed counseling services, continuing and vocational education, job placement, and living stipends to tide women over and eventually help them to reenter the work world and become self-supporting. Their naming of the problem was soon followed by a series of legislative efforts by Representative Yvonne Braithwaite Burke (D. California) and Senator Birch Bayh (D. Indiana) that eventually resulted in funding and programs for displaced homemakers under the 1978 amendments to the Comprehensive Employment and Training Act (CETA). Six demonstration projects for retraining CETA-eligible (low income) displaced homemakers, 40 years of age or older, were set up throughout the United States. Experience to date in the Boston area has shown remarkable success in training and placing the low-income, inner-city women enrolled in the program (Bernheim, 1981). The women are strongly motivated to be economically independent and have tackled verbal and mathematical deficiencies, participated regularly in daily training and counseling sessions, and eagerly pursued job opportunities.

For suburban displaced homemakers who are not eligible under CETA, the tasks of retraining and reentry are somewhat different. Very little financial support is available for community services, counseling, and job placement for this group. Yet the problems are still very real: Even women with college degrees who have been out of the labor force 25 or 30 years are frequently so depressed when faced wtih a sudden status change as a result of separation or divorce that they fail to respond even to those outreach efforts that community agencies do make. Such women also then have difficulty following job leads when they materialize. One Boston suburban agency, Affiliates for Adult Development, of Bedford, Massachusetts, does address the needs of this clientele, however. By a combination of efforts to raise funds through corporate contributions, fees for vocational training paid by Blue Cross/Blue Shield, and fees-for-service from job placement this agency has developed a strategy for outreach and service to the middle-class displaced homemaker. In addition to addressing the depression that the displaced homemaker so frequently manifests, the agency develops job leads, and conducts job counseling and group support sessions (Ryser & Hayes, 1981). Such private agencies may become important models for future ways to serve the displaced homemaker if CETA funding is abolished or drastically reduced.

In other countries such as East Germany and the Scandinavian nations, policies on behalf of women's retraining, labor force reentry, and promotions have long been more comprehensive and explicit than in the United States. In the United States over the last decade, however, there has been remarkable change in the direction of actual programs and behavior. Such change indicates increased male and female involvement in both work and the family. The displaced homemaker movement is merely one manifestation of this trend; it excites the interest of both liberals who believe in egalitarian sex roles and conservatives who want to get women off welfare and into the work place.

In additon, in the popular mind there is growing interest in other topics such as continuing education, career change, and an ethic of personal growth and change throughout the life course. All these developments have lessened the stereotyped roles of both age and sex that are applied to men and women over a whole lifetime. It is now increasingly being recognized that children do grow up, that women need not and should not plan for a single role that is solely centered around mothering. At the same time, men may wish to retire early, explore another career, or seek education in another field. The new flexible model of the life course and family division of labor now makes these activities possible (Best, 1980; *Business Week*, 1981). At the same time labor shortages in high technology fields and student shortages in traditional four-year educational institutions are causing innovations that promote job retraining, job reentry, and continuing education. The upshot is that individual choice and institutional response are both furthering the new, more flexible work and family roles and flexible life patterns that are associated with role differentiation and crossover in modern society.

SUMMARY AND CONCLUSIONS

This chapter has described new patterns in women's roles. Since 1900 each major cohort of women has differed from the others in age at marriage, fertility, and work experience. Society also has changed. There are smaller families and more technological aids. The city rather than the countryside has become the environment to which most people are accustomed.

Researchers describing changes in women's lives against the background of a changing society have found it difficult to isolate any single optimum life course that assures adult women of health and satisfaction. A number of different paths are possible and potentially satisfying, provided that they do not cut off options too early and prevent flexible adaptation later on. This conclusion emerges from a review of recent historical change, research on women's mental health and status attainments, and developments in family roles and the work place.

Historically, given demographic changes since 1900, it is clear that women live longer, bear fewer children, and have more time to participate in the labor force. The numbers of working women have grown and will continue to do so. Yet women also remain involved in family life; they continue to marry and have children, even if they are in the labor force. Ways to mesh work and family obligation thus pose a major challenge to women and the larger society. Some solutions of the moment have clear disadvantages. Women are crowded into relatively few occupations (clerical jobs, teaching, nursing, etc.) that are presumably more compatible with the feminine role. Although such jobs frequently have scheduling advantages that permit part-time work, flexible hours, or summers off, they also typically bring lower pay and fewer opportunities for advancement than comparable men's jobs.

Is there some other work pattern that would be more advantageous to women? When one tries to answer this question, the available research seems either contradictory or ambiguous. Some authors claim that marriage and housewifery damage women's opportunities for satisfaction and optimum mental health. Other research results show married women to be happier than single women but single women to be more satisfied with their work. If employment creates options and stimulation, it can in some cases work as an antidote to depression; in other cases, as with low-paying and unpleasant work, it drags a woman further down.

These ambiguous results suggest the possibility that there is little more to be gained from research that tries to answer which life pattern is more satisfying or healthier—employment or nonemployment, marriage or the nonmarried state. Instead, more general dimensions of employment or family life are at issue. Do a woman's work and family roles permit her a balance between nurturant and productive activities? Do her roles open options and encourage adaptive behavior and feelings of personal efficacy? Does employment provide needed limits on the endless demands of family work? Does a woman's family life at times facilitate her achievement?

These questions produce two answers. On the one hand, gross timing deviations appear to have destructive limiting effects on life options. For example, very early childbearing is associated with clear negative effects on a woman's educational attainment and participation in the labor force. On the other hand, several different patterns of life may be equally satisfying.

Work discontinuities, for example, have only minor effects on women's earnings. Whether one has children early or late (within the normal range) apparently does not substantially raise or lower satisfaction. Nor is there any single formula for the ideal sequential order in which a woman should finish her education, start a family, or take up a career.

These complex findings suggest that a new paradigm is needed for understanding *women's life course*. Linear models with clearly delineated steps of development seem too narrow to encompass the facts. A more abstract and universal theory is required that recognizes the relativity of specific life paths. It would focus on whether a person's life course includes or precludes adaptive response and independent action. I have suggested the crossover model as one way of envisioning this new paradigm. The person whose life course includes more differentiated and specialized experiences is in a better position to adapt to new situations by recombining past knowledge in original and flexible ways. Thus, women who have a good deal of education and considerable work and family experience, *no matter in what order experienced*, are well off when it comes to overall adaptiveness. The woman in trouble is one who has early limited her options, cut off opportunities for exposure to more different events, and is thereby trapped. The teenage mother is one example of this latter extreme. The trapped woman is more likely to be depressed than one who has other options. The woman hemmed in from the beginning ranks lower on status attainment than the woman who continues to learn and grow.

Implicit in this new model of the life course is a positive value attached to the number and variety of life experiences, continued learning, and flexible adaptation in the face of new challenges. How is this pattern encouraged? What type of social structure fosters its development? What arrangements in the family and the work place either stimulate it or stand in its way? New family forms and work experiments reveal change in the direction of role sharing and flexible scheduling that are congruent with the crossover model.

In a number of modern countries, the *family role system* appears to be moving toward a more symmetrical structure. There is greater interpenetration of work and family life; at the same time male and female engage in paid work as well as family work. Although the women generally have heavier domestic responsibilities and men still provide major economic support, change is in the direction of greater sharing between the two with respect to income provision as well as household work and child care.

Symmetrical families are having fewer children. Fathers are participating more in their care, and the family is in addition making more use of outside day care or informal arrangements with relatives or neighbors.

With respect to housework, employed women still do more than twice as much as their husbands, but there is an emerging ideal of equal sharing. In the interim, although husbands continue to resist some of the change, families rely on convenience foods, more appliances, and outside help when it is affordable.

Women's role as economic provider is becoming increasingly important. Families need women's earning power whether for bread-and-butter necessities or to put children through college. However, because of low pay, part-time work, and family duties, women's incomes constitute only one-quarter of total family income. Even though the woman's income is needed, the tendency is for the husband's role as breadwinner to take precedence.

The *work role system* also shows signs of change—at least with respect to public awareness of flex-time issues, part-time arrangements, and parental leaves. A majority of part-time workers are female, and the total number of part-time workers has been growing. Experiments in job sharing and regularization of part-time work excite considerable interest, not only among women but among job-sharing couples. It is too early to say whether these arrangements will become more widespread. For the moment experiments in scheduling are particularly instructive. They suggest the kinds of changes needed to facilitate women's flexible movement between work and family life. They also dramatize the costs of part-time work: lower financial rewards, insecurity, and slower career advancement. Unless part-time work can be institutionalized on a more favorable basis, it hardly seems the optimum mechanism to encourage flexibility and crossover in the life course.

In the present era of transition, structural social changes and new social policies on behalf of *continuing education and job reentry* are providing the mechanisms to get from traditional sex-segregated male and female worlds to the future flexible system of crossover between work and family roles. The displaced homemaker movement demonstrates some key social problems that beset women caught between the old and the new. Such solutions as retraining, job counseling, and job reentry that have worked for displaced homemakers have their parallel in programs serving the larger population who are not "displaced." Generally speaking, individuals are learning how to adapt to economic and social change by investigating and trying out new roles. Educational institutions and corporations are learning how to discover the people whose talents they need and who want the changes they offer.

In a book on women in the middle years, the specific function of this chapter has been to explore the interface between women's typical life course and the surrounding social matrix. The picture is complicated because women, who are themselves changing, have to be viewed against a moving historical backdrop. In addition our perceptions at any one moment are shaped by the constantly changing lens through which social observers record these phenomena. Rough outlines emerge, nevertheless. Women's life patterns are becoming more differentiated and various with more opportunities for recombining earlier experiences in useful ways. The society has made use of women's productive energy and built them into the economy. Women also continue to marry and bear children even as they participate in the labor force. The great social change that makes this possible is a shift in the balance of male and female responsibility within the home as well as in the labor market. As more women are employed, more men are expected to help in the home. This new situation is fostering change in traditional family and work roles with experiments in sharing and scheduling. The trend seems clear. Just how long it will last and how far it will go remains to be seen.

REFERENCES

Arkin, W., and L.R. Dobrovsky. 1978. "Job Sharing." In R. Rapoport and R.N. Rapoport (Eds.), *Working Couples*. New York: Harper & Row.

———. 1979. "Job-Sharing Couples." In K.W. Feinstein (Ed.), *WorkingWomen and Families*. Beverly Hills, CA: Sage Publications, Inc.

Barnett, R.C., and G.K. Baruch. 1979. "Career Competence and the Well-Being of Adult Women." *New Directions for Education, Work and Careers* **8**:95−101.

Barrett, N.S. 1979. "Data Needs for Evaluating the Labor Market Status of Women." *Census Bureau Conference on Issues in Federal Statistical Needs Relating to Women*. U.S. Bureau of the Census. *Current Population Reports*, Special Studies, Series P-23, No. 83. Washington, DC: Government Printing Office.

Bell, C.S. 1976. "Working Wives and Family Income." In J.R. Chapman (Ed.), *Economic Independence for Women*. Beverly Hills, CA: Sage Publications, Inc.

Belle, D. 1979. "Depression and Low Income, Female-Headed Families." In E. Corfman (Ed.), *Families Today: A Research Sampler on Families and Children*, Vol. 1. Washington, DC: Government Printing Office.

Bernard, J. 1972. *The Future of Marriage*. New York: World Publishing.

Bernheim, G. 1981. "Services for the Displaced Homemaker by the Displaced Homemaker Network, Inc." Presentation to the Family Policy Study Group. Heller School, Brandeis University, Waltham, MA, March 24.

Best, F. 1978. "The Time of Our Lives: The Parameters of Work−Life Scheduling." *Society and Leisure* **1**(1):95−124.

———. 1980. *Flexible Life Scheduling: Breaking the Education−Work−Retirement Lockstep*. New York: Praeger.

Booth, A., and D. Duvall. 1980. "Sex Roles and the Link Between Fertility and Employment." *Sex Roles*. **7**(8):847−856.

Brim, O.G., Jr. 1976. "Theories of the Male Mid-life Crisis." *The Counseling Psychologist* **6**(1):2−9.

Brown, G.W., and T. Harris. 1978. *Social Origins of Depression: A Study of Psychiatric Disorder in Women*. New York: Free Press.

Burlage, D.D. 1978. "Divorced Mothers: The Decision to Separate and the Transition into Single Parenthood." Paper presented at the annual meeting of the Massachusetts Psychological Association.

Business Week. 1981. "Choosing the Wife as Chief Breadwinner." March 23, pp. 52–54.

Campbell, A., P.E. Converse, and W.L. Rodgers. 1976. *The Quality of American Life: Perceptions, Evaluations, and Satisfactions*. New York: Russell Sage Foundation.

Chafe, W.H. 1977. *Women and Equality: Changing Patterns in American Culture*. New York: Oxford University Press.

Collins, G. 1979. "The Good News about 1984." *Psychology Today*, January, pp. 34–48.

Corcoran, M. 1978. "Work Experience, Work Interruption, and Wages." In G.J. Duncan and J.N. Morgan (Eds.), *Five Thousand American Families—Patterns of Economic Progress*. Ann Arbor, MI: University of Michigan, Institute for Social Research.

Daniels, P., and K. Weingarten. 1982. *Sooner or Later: The Timing of Parenthood in Adult Lives*. New York: W.W. Norton.

Demos, J. 1978. "Old Age in Early New England." In J. Demos and S.S. Boocock (Eds.), *Turning Points: Historical and Sociological Essays on the Family*. Chicago: University of Chicago Press.

Duncan, B., and O.D. Duncan. 1978. *Sex Typing and Social Roles*. New York: Academic Press.

Easterlin, R.A. 1978. "What Will 1984 be Like? Socioeconomic Implications of Recent Twists in Age Structure." *Demography* **15**(4):397–432.

Elder, G.H., Jr. 1975. "Age Differentiation and the Life Course." *Annual Review of Sociology* **5**:165–190.

Elder, G.H., Jr., and R. Rockwell. 1976. "Marital Timing in Women's Life Patterns." *Journal of Family History* **1**(1):34–54.

Erikson, E.H. 1950. *Childhood and Society*. New York: W.W. Norton & Co., Inc.

Ferber, M., and J. Huber. 1979. "Husbands, Wives, and Careers." *Journal of Marriage and Family* **41**(2):315–326.

Fiske, M. 1980. "Changing Hierarchies of Commitment in Adulthood." In N.J. Smelser and E.H. Erikson (Eds.), *Themes of Work and Love in Adulthood*. Cambridge, MA: Harvard University Press.

Freedman, R., and L. Coombs. 1966. "Childspacing and Family Economic Position." *American Sociological Review* **31**(5):631–648.

Friedan, B. 1981. *The Second Stage*. New York: Summit Books.

Furstenberg, F., Jr. 1976. *Unplanned Parenthood: Social Consequences of Teenage Childbearing*. New York: Free Press.

Giele, J.Z. 1978. *Women and the Future: Changing Sex Roles in Modern America*. New York: Free Press.

———. 1980a. "Crossovers: New Themes in Adulthood and the Life Cycle." In D.G. McGuigan (Ed.), *Women's Lives: New Theory, Research and Policy*. Ann Arbor, MI: University of Michigan, Center for Continuing Education of Women.

———. 1980b. "Adulthood as Transcendence of Age and Sex." In N.J. Smelser and E.H. Erikson (Eds.), *Themes of Work and Love in Adulthood.* Cambridge, MA: Harvard University Press.

———. 1980c. "Discrimination, Sex Roles, and Changing Family Structures." Paper presented at the National Research Forum on Family Issues for the White House Conference on Families. Washington, DC, April 10.

Giele, J.Z., and H. Kahne. 1978. "Meeting Work and Family Responsibilities: Proposals for Flexibility." In A.F. Cahn (Ed.), *Women in Mid-life—Security and Fulfillment (Part I)* U.S. House of Representatives Select Committee on Aging. 95th Congress, 2nd Session. Washington, DC: Government Printing Office.

Glenn, N.D. 1975. "Psychological Well-Being in the Postparental Stage: Some Evidence from National Surveys." *Journal of Marriage and Family* 37(1):105–109.

Gould, R.L. 1978. *Transformations: Growth and Change in Adult Life.* New York: Simon & Schuster.

Gove, W., and M. Hughes. 1979. "Possible Causes of the Apparent Sex Differences in Physical Health." *American Sociological Review* 44(1):126–146.

Gronseth, E. 1978. "Work-sharing: A Norwegian Example." In R. Rapoport and R.N. Rapoport (Eds.), *Working Couples.* New York: Harper & Row.

Guttentag, M., and S. Salasin. 1977. "Women, Men, and Mental Health." In L.A. Cater, A.F. Scott, and W. Martyna (Eds.), *Women and Men: Changing Roles, Relationships, and Perceptions.* New York: Praeger.

Gutmann, D. 1977. "The Cross-Cultural Perspective: Notes Toward A Comparative Psychology of Aging." In J.E. Birren and K.W. Schaie (Eds.), *Handbook of the Psychology of Aging.* New York: Van Nostrand Reinhold.

Hayghe, H. 1976. "Families and the Rise of Working Wives—An Overview." *Monthly Labor Review* 99(5):12–19.

Hess, B.B., and J.M. Waring. 1978. "Changing Patterns of Aging and Family Bonds in Later Life." *Family Coordinator* 27(4):313–314.

Hill, M.S., and M. Corcoran. 1979. "Unemployment and Family Men: A 10-year Longitudinal Study." *Monthly Labor Review* 102(11):19–23.

Hirschhorn, L. 1979. "Adult Development and Meta-Policy." Paper presented to National Conference on Social Welfare, Philadelphia, May 14.

Hogan, D.P. 1978. "The Variable Order of Events in the Life Course." *American Sociological Review* 43(4):573–586.

Holmstrom, L.L. 1972. *The Two-Career Family.* Cambridge, MA: Schenkman.

Houseknecht, S.K. 1979. "Female Employment and Reduced Family Size: Some Additional Insight on the Direction of the Relationship." Paper presented at the annual meeting of the American Sociological Association, Boston, August 27–31.

Johnson, S.B. 1975. "The Impact of Women's Liberation on Marriage, Divorce, and Family Life-Style." In C.B. Lloyd (Ed.), *Sex, Discrimination, and the Division of Labor.* New York: Columbia University Press.

Kahne, H. 1977. "Market Participation and Family Life." Paper presented to the SSRC Study Group on Women. Waltham, MA: Brandeis University, Heller School, September 15.

Kanter, R.M. 1977. *Work and Family in the United States: A Critical Review and Agenda for Research and Policy.* New York: Russell Sage Foundation.

Keith, P.M., and T.H. Brubaker. 1979. "Male Household Roles in Later Life: A Look at Masculinity and Marital Relationships." *Family Coordinator* 28(4): 497–502.

Kobrin, F.E. 1976. "The Primary Individual and the Family: Changes in Living Arrangements in the United States since 1940." *Journal of Marriage and the Family* 38(2):233–239.

Kreps, J.M., and R.J. Leaper. 1976. "Home Work, Market Work, and the Allocation of Time." In J.M. Kreps (Ed.), *Women in the American Economy: A Look to the 1980s.* Englewood Cliffs, NJ: Prentice-Hall.

Kreps, J., and R. Clark. 1975. *Sex, Age, and Work: The Changing Composition of the Labor Force.* Baltimore, MD: Johns Hopkins University Press.

Lein, L. 1979a. "Working Couples as Parents." In E. Corfman (Ed.), *Families Today: A Research Sampler on Families and Children,* Vol. 1. Washington, DC: Government Printing Office.

———. 1979b. "Responsibility in the Allocation of Tasks." *Family Coordinator* 28(4):489–496.

Levinson, D.J. 1978. *The Seasons of a Man's Life.* New York: Alfred A. Knopf.

Lewis, R.A., P.J. Freneau, and C.L. Roberts. 1979. "Fathers and the Postparental Transition." *Family Coordinator* 28(4):514–520.

Liljestrom, R., G.F. Mellstrom, and G.L. Svensson. 1975. *Sex Roles in Transition: A Report on a Pilot Program in Sweden.* Stockholm: The Swedish Institute.

Marini, M.M. 1978. "The Transition to Adulthood: Sex Differences in Educational Attainment and Age at Marriage." *American Sociological Review* 43(4): 483–507.

———. 1979. "Sex Differences in the Process of Occupational Achievement." Paper presented at the annual meeting of the American Sociological Association, Boston, August 27-31.

Marks, S.R. 1977. "Multiple Roles and Role Strain: Some Notes on Human Energy, Time, and Commitment." *American Sociological Review* 42(6):921–936.

Mason, K.O., J.L. Czajka, and S. Arber. 1976. "Changes in U.S. Women's Sex-Role Attitudes, 1964–1974." *American Sociological Review* 41(4):573–596.

Meislin, R.J. 1977. "Poll Finds More Liberal Beliefs on Marriage and Sex Roles, Especially Among the Young." *The New York Times,* November 27, p. 75.

Moore, K.A., S.L. Hofferth, S.B. Caldwell, and L.J. Waite. 1980. *Teenage Motherhood: Social and Economic Consequences.* Washington, DC: Urban Institute.

Neugarten, B.L. 1979. "Time, Age, and the Life Cycle." *American Journal of Psychiatry* 136(7):887–894.

Newsweek. 1980. "The Superwoman Squeeze." May 19, pp. 72–79.

Oaxaca, R.L. 1979. "On the Use of Occupational Statistics." *Census Bureau Conference on Issues in Federal Statistical Needs Relating to Women.* U.S. Bureau of the Census, *Current Population Reports,* Special Studies, Series P-23, No. 83. Washington, DC: Government Printing Office.

Oppenheimer, V.K. 1979. "Structural Sources of Economic Pressure for Wives to Work: An Analytical Framework." *Journal of Family History* 4(2):177–197.

Pearlin, L.I. 1980. "Life-Strains and Psychological Distress Among Adults." In N.J. Smelser and E.H. Erikson (Eds.), *Themes of Work and Love in Adulthood*. Cambridge, MA: Harvard University Press.

Perun, P.J., and D.D.V. Bielby. 1980. "Structure and Dynamics of the Individual Life Course." In K.W. Back (Ed.), *Life Course: Integrative Theories and Exemplary Populations*. AAAS Selected Symposium 41. Boulder CO: Westview Press.

Piotrowski, C.S. 1979. *Work and the Family System: A Naturalistic Study of Working Class and Lower Middle Class Families*. New York: Free Press.

Pleck, J. 1979. "Married Men: Work and Family." In E. Corfman (Ed.), *Families Today: A Research Sampler on Families and Children*, Vol. 1. Washington, DC: Government Printing Office.

Pleck, J., and M. Rustad. 1980. "Husbands' and Wives' Time in Family Work and Paid Work in the 1975–76 Study of Time Use." Wellesley, MA: Wellesley College Center for Research on Women.

Rapoport, R., and R.N. Rapoport. 1976. *Dual-Career Families Re-examined: New Integrations of Work and Family*. New York: Harper & Row.

Rapoport, R., R.N. Rapoport, and Z. Strelitz. 1977. *Fathers, Mothers and Society*. New York: Basic Books.

Ratner, R.S. 1980. *Equal Employment Policy for Women: Strategies for Implementation in the United States, Canada, and Western Europe*. Philadelphia: Temple University Press.

Robinson, J.P., and E. Rogers-Millar. 1979. "Housework, Technology and Quality of Life: Implications from Longitudinal Time-Use Surveys." Paper presented at the Annual Meeting of the American Sociological Association, Boston, MA, August 27–31.

Rossi, A.S. 1980. "Life Span Theories and Women's Lives." *Signs: Journal of Women in Culture and Society* 6(1):4–32.

Ryan, M.P. 1979. *Womanhood in America: From Colonial Times to the Present*, 2nd ed. New York: New Viewpoints.

Ryser, C., and A. Hayes. 1981. "Services to Displaced Homemakers by Affiliates for Adult Development, Bedford, Mass." Presentation to the Family Policy Study Group. Heller School, Brandeis University, Waltham, MA, March 24.

Sandberg, E. 1975. *Equality is the Goal: A Swedish Report*. Stockholm: The Swedish Institute.

Sandell, S.H., and D. Shapiro. 1976. "The Theory of Human Capital and the Earnings of Women: A Reexamination of the Evidence." Columbus, OH: Ohio State University, Center for Human Resource Research.

Sawhill, I.V. 1973. "The Economics of Discrimination against Women: Some New Findings." *Journal of Human Resources* 8(3):383–395.

———. 1977. "Economic Perspectives on the Family." *Daedalus* 106(2):115–126.

Sawin, D.B., and R.D. Parke. 1979. "Fathers' Affectionate Stimulation and Caregiving Behaviors wtih Newborn Infants." *Family Coordinator* 28(4):509–513.

Sears, P.S., and A.H. Barbee. 1977. "Career and Life Satisfaction among Terman's Gifted Women." In J. Stanley, W. George, and C. Salano (Eds.), *The Gifted and the Creative: A Fifty Year Perspective.* Baltimore, MD: Johns Hopkins University Press.

Sexton, L. 1980. "Between Two Worlds." *Radcliffe Quarterly* **66**(1):5–14.

Sieber, S.D. 1974. "Toward a Theory of Role Accumulation." *American Sociological Review* **39**(4)567–578.

Smith, R.E. (Ed.) 1979. *The Subtle Revolution: Women at Work.* Washington, DC: Urban Institute.

Smith–Lovin, L., and A. R. Tickamyer. 1978. "Nonrecursive Models of Labor Force Participation, Fertility Behavior, and Sex Role Attitudes." *American Sociological Review* **43**(4):541–557.

Sommers, T., and L. Shields. 1978. "Problems of the Displaced Homemaker." In A.F. Cahn (Ed.), *Women in Mid-life—Security and Fulfillment (Part I).* U.S. House of Representatives Select Committee on Aging. 95th Congress, 2nd Sess. Washington, DC: Government Printing Office.

Spitze, G.D., and J.Huber. 1979. "Changes in Attitudes toward Women's Employment since the 1930s." Paper presented at the Annual Meeting of the American Sociological Association, Boston, MA, August 27–31.

Spitze, G.D., and L.J. Waite. 1979. "Young Women's Preferences for Market Work: Responses to Marital Events." Paper presented at the Annual Meeting of the American Sociological Association, Boston, MA, August 27–31.

Stolzenberg, R.M., and L.J. Waite. 1977. "Age, Fertility Expectations, and Plans for Employment." *American Sociological Review* **42**(5)769–783.

Szalai, A. 1973. "The Quality of Family Life—Traditional and Modern." Paper presented at the United Nations Interregional Seminar on the Family in a Changing Society. London, July 18–31. ESA/SDHA/AC. 3/6.

Taeuber, K.E., and J.A. Sweet. 1976. "Family and Work: The Social Life Cycle of Women." In J.M. Kreps (Ed.), *Women in the American Economy: A Look to the 1980s.* Englewood Cliffs, NJ: Prentice-Hall.

Targ, D. 1979. "Toward a Reassessment of Women's Experience at Middle Age." *Family Coordinator* **28**(3):377–382.

Thornton, A., and D.S. Freedman. 1979. "Changes in the Sex Role Attitudes of Women, 1962-1977." *American Sociological Review* **44**(5):831–842.

Tognoli, J. 1979. "The Flight from Domestic Space: Men's Roles in the Household." *Family Coordinator* **28**(4):599–607.

Treiman, D.J., and P.A. Roos. 1980. "Sex and Earnings in Industrial Society: A Nine Nation Comparison." Washington, DC: National Academy of Sciences.

U.S. Department of Commerce, Bureau of the Census. 1977. *Social Indicators 1976.* Washington, DC: Government Printing Office.

U.S. Department of Labor, Women's Bureau. 1979. "20 Facts for Women Workers." August. Washington, DC: Government Printing Office.

Vaillant, G.E. 1977. *Adaptation to Life.* Boston: Little, Brown.

Vanek, J. 1974. "Time Spent in Housework." *Scientific American*, (November): 116–120.

Waite, L.J., and R.M. Stolzenberg. 1976. "Intended Childbearing and Labor Force Participation of Young Women: Insights from Nonrecursive Models," *American Sociological Review* **41**(2):235–252.

Waldman, E., A.S. Grossman, H. Hayghe, and B. Johnson. 1979. "Working Mothers in the 1970s: A Look at the Statistics." *Monthly Labor Review* **102**(10):39−49.

Walker, K.E. 1969. "Time Spent in Household Work by Homeworkers." *Family Economics Review*, (September): 5−6.

———. 1970. "Time Spent by Husbands in Household Work." *Family Economics Review*, (June): 8−11.

Watts, H.W., and F. Skidmore. 1978. "The Implications of Changing Family Patterns and Behavior for Labor Force and Hardship Measurement." Paper prepared for the National Commission on Employment and Unemployment Statistics. March.

Young, C.M. 1978. "Work Sequences of Women During the Family Life Cycle." *Journal of Marriage and Family* **40**(2):401−411.

Young, M., and P. Willmott. 1973. *The Symmetrical Family*. New York: Pantheon.

CHAPTER 5

Women in the German Democratic Republic: Impact of Culture and Social Policy

JOAN ECKLEIN
Deparment of Sociology
Boston State College

What is the life of women in socialist Germany, the German Democratic Republic? Profound changes have taken place in the last 30 years in the GDR, and many have fundamentally affected the women's lives. This chapter examines the effects of social policies on women's education, occupation, leadership, and family life. Certain questions arise in studying these effects. How do women combine family life and work roles in a country in which 86 percent of all women who are capable of working hold a job? How have social changes come about? What dilemmas have they posed? What effect are these changes likely to have on men's and women's future roles?

Women's roles have changed rapidly as well as profoundly. The result is that not only are the lives of young women significantly different from those of their mothers and grandmothers, but the lives of women of all ages have changed and are continuing to do so. Women during the Fascist period were seen as little more than breeders of children, and few went to universities or became skilled workers. Today, in the 30-and-under age group, equal numbers of men and women receive university diplomas and skilled worker's certificates. There are guaranteed jobs for everyone, equal pay for equal work, abortion on demand, state-supported kindegartens for children between 3 and 6 years old (a provision used by over 92 percent of families with

I wish to thank the following people who helped me write this paper. Dr. Herta Kuhrig of the Academy of Sciences was invaluable in pointing the direction in which I must work. Dr. Dianna Loesser also helped me embark on the study, read drafts, and made suggestions. Herman and Julia Schwendinger discussed many ideas with me as well as read preliminary drafts of the chapter. Professor Erich Leitel of Jena University, GDR made many valuable suggestions. The following people served as interpreters and helped me with translations: Salome Genin, Deborah Lorenz, Irene Runge, Margaret Morse, Margaret Ward, and Thomas DeWitt.

children in this age group), paid pregnancy leaves of up to one year for mothers bearing their second child, special provisions for the further education of working women, full pay to take courses on job time, and special tutors for women. These are only some of the provisions that changes in social policy have made available to women in the GDR.[1]

The GDR is an example of a country which because it is socialist has been able to put into place in a very short time social policies that have had a profound impact on every sphere of women's lives. The aspects of their ideology that have allowed this to happen are many. Among these is the ideological commitment to women's emancipation that is in the socialist tradition. It has always been felt that the building of socialism and the emancipation of women are inseparable. Furthermore, a centrally planned economy in which almost all enterprises are nationally owned means that social policies can be put into place in an organized fashion very quickly. These conditions do not exist in the United States. Nor are they likely to in the near future. Thus, most of the social policies described in this chapter that have had an impact on women's lives in the GDR are but a wish list for American women for the indefinite future.

This is not to imply that all problems regarding women have been solved. Far from it. The various provisions for equality do not automatically change centuries-old attitudes regarding women's roles. Women's attitudes regarding their roles are changing at a faster pace than many men are willing to accept, and the women still do 80 percent of all household and child-care tasks. One consequence of this situation is the rapid rise in the divorce rate. A book of autobiographical sketches of women from all sectors of the population graphically illustrates that women have equal pay and equal opportunities but the same traditional troubles with men (Anderson, 1978; Wander, 1977). Several vignettes from these autobiographical sketches are quoted at length in this chapter to give the reader a graphic sense of the reality of the women's lives.

I spent the 1976–1977 academic year on a sabbatical in East Berlin with my 5-year-old daughter who attended kindergarten there. I taught English conversation half-time at Humboldt University while I studied the changing role of women. The data for this chapter were drawn from thorough and extensive interviews with a wide range of people: colleagues, men and women students, unmarried mothers, child-care workers, and professionals directly concerned with women's issues. In addition, I participated in

---

[1]With the exception of the legal right to abortion, West German women have none of these special provisions. Two detailed studies comparing the GDR women's situation with the West German women's situation found that West German women everywhere are less well trained, paid, respected, and treated (Menschik & Leopold, 1974; Shaffer, 1981). Shaffer concludes the significant dissimilarities are due to social system differences in ideology, social fabric, economic framework, political structure, and resulting differences in society's approach to women's emancipation.

English courses in several cities and gave speeches to various cultural groups. After the speeches I invariably sat down and talked with people.

This chapter shows in what ways social policies have affected women in their adult lives. It details the tremendous impact these policies have had in all spheres of life. To completely comprehend the significance of the changes undergone by women in the last 30 years, it is first necessary to understand the historical and cultural background of the society as a whole: the history of the GDR, the ideology of women's emancipation, instruments of social policy, and the history of women's changing roles.

The impact of policy on women's everyday lives is the major focus of this chapter. It is a fertile area for the study of aging and the middle years. The new policies have differentially affected young, middle aged, and older women. The lives of young women have changed the most. Ultimately, it would be desirable to trace the impact of policy on many aspects of women's lives—the physical and psychological aspects as well as the social roles. Here, however, my summary focuses on what I found through observation and published data on women's social roles in public life, education, employment, family life, and the combination of work and family.

HISTORICAL BACKGROUND

The GDR is not a large country. It has 17 million citizens, in contrast to West Germany's 60 million. It comprises an area of 41,000 square miles compared with West Germany's 90,000 square miles. Following World War II the German Democratic Republic was formed from the Soviet-occupied zone in 1949.

Germany had been heavily industrialized, but its industrial capacity was devastated as a result of the war. Marshall Plan aid from the United States quickly rebuilt the West German economy, but the Soviet Union was in no position to do the same for the GDR. Disparity in the economic recovery rates of the two Germanies created enormous problems for the fledgling socialist government. Between 1955 and 1961, over 2 million people migrated to West Germany where the living standard was much higher, the culture was the same, and most people had relatives. During the same period, 279,000 people, most of them former anti-Fascists, migrated from West Germany to the GDR. In an effort to stabilize its population, the government of the GDR closed its borders in 1961.

The economic situation that prompted the government of the GDR to close the borders can be illustrated by an event that occurred prior to the border closing, when an entire class of medical students received their medical diplomas and immediately entrained to West Germany, where they had jobs already lined up and waiting for them. This was a pattern repeated in other professions. People who had been educated at state expense were leaving the country for West Germany. It was common knowledge that West

German industry "planned" certain areas to be occupied by skilled and professional labor from the GDR. Officials of the GDR perceived that they had no choice but to secure the borders if the country was to develop, because an educated labor force was essential to such development. That subsequent events have proven this correct is shown, for example, by the following facts: the gross national product has risen more than sevenfold from 51,539 million marks in 1949 to 159,834 million marks in 1960, and 369,183 million marks in 1975 (*Statistical Pocket Book of the German Democratic Republic*, 1976).

During the past 30 years, the GDR has developed a socialist society, rebuilt a highly industrialized economy, and overcome the myriad legacies of Fascism. The changes have been sweeping ones. Among the first reforms after the Soviet occupation were the economic reforms of 1945. Private enterprises, starting with the largest, were nationalized. Gradually all enterprises became state-owned until today 95.8% of all enterprises are government owned (*Statistical Pocket Book*, 1976). A second reform divided ownership of land among workers and resettlers until today the land is almost completely cooperatively run. In the administration of the country there has been a third reform, replacing the old state apparatus with a new one, including a completely new judiciary system, (Gransow, 1978a).

Today, the GDR is a socialist society with a planned economy.[2] There is full employment, and as a matter of right everyone is guaranteed a job. (In addition, a person changing jobs is entitled to at least the salary he or she received from the previous job.)

The economy of the GDR has developed rapidly, and the standard of living has gone up accordingly. People who returned from exile in 1949 recall that they found children underfed. Today, the standard of living has kept pace with industrial output. Prices have remained almost stable, and the average income of workers has steadily risen. The average income of office employees and industrial workers was 766 marks in 1970, 927 marks in 1975, and was projected to 1,085 marks by the early 1980s (*What is Life Like in the GDR?*, 1977). In addition, it is estimated that every family in the GDR receives an extra 700 marks per month in the form of a "hidden pay packet"—benefits including kindergarten, rent, transportation, and food that are partially or completely subsidized by the state. Although there is still a severe housing shortage, poverty is virtually unknown in all segments of the population.

The educational system also underwent significant reform. Prior to 1945, 72 percent of all teachers were members of the Fascist party, but these teachers were dismissed in the course of the reform in accordance with the Potsdam agreement. All private schooling was abolished, and ordinary

[2]In the United States it is customary to call the GDR communist. From the standpoint of the participants in the society, however, they are a socialist society and view a communist society as their ultimate goal.

workers were trained as teachers. Boys and girls received identical education, including polytechnical training to combine practical skills with academic work. For the first time children from working-class families received
an education identical with that of children from middle-class families.
Today, 60 percent of all people entering the universities must be from
working-class families.

In the schools, the Fascist period is thoroughly discussed in class and in
history textbooks, and education about the war is not confined to the
classroom. Concentration camps have been made into memorials, and it is
compulsory for children to visit them. Anti-Fascist heroes are honored by
having streets, parks, and public buildings named after them. One woman I
met had spent years in prison for her role in a Jewish resistance group. She
was given a large flat with a beautiful garden in what had been a middle-class
section of Berlin.

Mildred Harnak, an American woman married to a German was part of
the anti-Fascist underground from the beginning of the movement in 1933.
She was captured in 1942 and guillotined in 1943. Today, there is a coveted
annual prize given in her name for outstanding work in Humboldt University's Anglo-American studies department, the department in which I taught.
I was present on the day the chairperson of the department greeted incoming
students and lectured on the history of the school as well as on the significance of the Mildred Harnak Prize. As Allendorf (1975) has stated:

> The women fighters against the Hitler regime who went through hell and survived
> became active the moment they were free, proving themselves wherever they were
> placed. They sat on women's councils, and cared for the wretched women of
> Germany, showing them the way to a new and better democratic country. From the
> beginning there sat together on these councils communists, social democrats, women
> not belonging to any party and members of the old bourgeois women's organizations.
> They put into effect a democratic coalition, such as appeared desirable in all spheres
> of public life [p. 97].

It was these women who in 1947 founded and became the backbone of
the Democratic Women's Federation, Der Demokratische Frauenbund
Deutschlands (the DFD), the mass women's organization in the GDR. The
DFD is represented by 35 members in the People's Chamber, the highest
legislative body. In addition, the DFD has its own parliamentary groups
with 2000 deputies. One of its main tasks has been to get women to participate actively in the new society, especially to join the labor force.

THE IDEOLOGY OF WOMEN'S EMANCIPATION

Although socialist countries differ in their development—depending on
their previous level of industrialization as well as on marked presocialist
cultural differences—the strides toward the emancipation of women have
been dramatic in all of them (Allendorf, 1975; Marquit, 1978). This is true

on a whole range of measures, including placement of women in the labor force, the enforcement of equal pay for equal work legislation, and many others. In part, this progress can be attributed to the socialist ideology regarding women's place in society as women and as workers.

Long before the advent of socialist societies, the earliest socialist thinkers were quite explicit in their belief that in any given society the degree of women's emancipation is the natural measure of the general emancipation. Progress is measured by the emancipation of women, and women's economic activity is believed to be essential to that progress. Marx and Engels saw women's oppression as having its origins in a class society, and they predicted that that oppression would not be completely overcome until the coming of socialist society. The question is not one of women liberating themselves from the domination of men but of the liberation of both men and women from the exploitation experienced in a class society. They further perceived that women were doubly oppressed under capitalism, both as women and as members of the working class.

Irmtraud Morgner (1975), a leading German novelist who deals with women's issues in her writing, does not see the emancipation of women coming about automatically with the advent of socialism. Instead, she adds this qualification:

> This is a problem for mankind. Emancipation for women is unattainable without emancipation for men and vice versa. I believe conversion of women into human beings only happens under socialism—can only really begin after a socialist revolution and this process is not automatic. The abolition of exploitation of man by man does not automatically produce the abolition of exploitation of the woman by "man" [p. M-10].

The founding of a socialist state sets up the preconditions under which it is possible to eliminate the oppression of women, but the work does not end there. The developing socialist society must vigorously pursue this goal if it is to come to pass.

Other writers also affirm that a woman can develop her full potential only if she is working ouside the home. The following statement (*Women in the GDR: Facts and Figures*, 1975) is representative of this conviction:

> Women's equal participation in the professional life of the country ultimately determines her real place in society. Under socialist conditions work helps women develop their creative abilities freely. Women's work not only helps the family live better materially but also creates circumstances enabling the woman to assume a respected place within the family [12].

Morgner (1975) sees work as the key ingredient in changing women's roles: "Women can best change their consciousness and that of the men by means of the self-confidence which comes from finding themselves mainly in their work [p. M-10]."

Women in the GDR are expected to have a family and to work outside the house. This dual role is viewed as necessary for the development of the women's potential as well as for the society as a whole. However, and this is of critical importance, the combination of work and family roles is not felt to be the responsibility of the individual woman. Rather, it is the responsibility of the entire society. It is expected that some day women will have a unified role, free of the strains and contradictions of trying to satisfy conflicting expectations. As Mensh and Mensh (1978) put it, "The socialist countries recognize that at this stage women do have a 'double burden.' This double burden is not the creation of socialism, it is the legacy of capitalism [p. 222]."

INSTRUMENTS OF SOCIAL POLICY

One cannot understand how change takes place in the GDR without understanding the function of the Communist Party (the Socialist Unity Party SED). The SED plays a central role in the direction taken by the society by giving its approval to those policies it feels ought to be fulfilled by planning agencies and other organizations. The SED has been fully committed to the emancipation of women and has acted on that commitment. For example, the central committee report of the Eighth Party Congress of the SED explicitly recognized the progress that women have made, their contributions to the society, and the problems that still exist to prevent them from making use of their rights. Recommendations were made as to how these problems can be overcome in the future.

Social policy regarding women is explicitly laid down in the Family Code and in the myriad regulations of the Labor Code. These are policies on women's issues that are uniformly enforced throughout the country. The trade union, Confederation of Free German Trade Unions (FDGB), and the Women's Democratic Federation (DFD) implement the policies laid down in the Labor Code and the Family Code. Virtually every woman belongs to one or both of these organizations. Women thus have systematic input into policy making and implementation. Every trade union branch has a woman's commission made up of women that helps shape each enterprise's plans vis-à-vis women. There are 35 seats assigned to the DFD in the country's highest legislative body as well as branches of the DFD in every large housing unit and residential area. And it has its own network of parliamentary groups throughout the country.

Changes with respect to provisions for women are being made and thoroughly reviewed in a systematic way (Kuhrig, 1973). For example, there are studies on a wide range of issues, including whether boys or girls do more work around the home, who makes use of the new abortion laws, how to motivate women who are unskilled to obtain skilled worker's certificates, why women work part time, and the problems of women managers. These studies are not merely academic exercises to be written up in books and journals and then ignored. The findings have a direct impact on social policy. As just one example, a study found that unskilled women workers were reluctant to take the training needed to become skilled workers if the courses were given in the evening. Subsequently, courses specifically for women were developed to be attended during working hours with no loss in pay.

According to Kuhrig (1973), equality of women can be attained only if the following problems in socialist development are solved:

1.   It is necessary to create and continually improve material conditions as far as the economy is able, so that women can make use of their equal rights.

2.   Men and women must change their attitudes toward the women's role "in harmony with the character of socialist humanism."

3.   "Special protection of women in their capacity as mothers must be ensured. The consequences of centuries of discrimination must be eliminated step by step by appropriate promotional measures [pp. 10−11]."

CHANGING ROLES OF WOMEN IN THE GDR

The change in the role of women during the socialist period is especially remarkable when one considers women's position prior to 1945. Before the Fascists took power in 1933, there had been a vigorous feminist movement. Thönnessen (1973) describes the women's movement within the context of German bourgeois democracy between 1863 and 1933. Discussing the dilemmas faced by women trying to effect a fundamental change under capitalist conditions, he concludes that fundamental changes are possible only under socialism. He attempts to demonstrate that reforms under capitalist conditions did not meet the objectives sought by the reformers. His book ends with the ascendency of Fascism in 1933, when the workers' movement in Germany perished and with it the most important achievements of the women's movement (Thönnessen, 1973).

Slepack (1976) states perceptively and concisely the position of women during the half century before 1945. She distinguishes the Fascist from the pre-Fascist period while placing the role of women in a total context:

Until 1945 Germany was essentially a man's world. Public life was characterized by a strict hierarchy with levels of authority and submission clearly defined. . . . [T]his hierarchy in public life spilled over into the family and educational system. In the family women were the victims of men's absolute superiority. During the kaiser-reich (1871−1919) with its authoritarian tradition the hierarchy of values was founded on the Pillars of God, the Kaiser and the Father. Young citizens were responsible to these three male giants. It was at this time that the role of women was defined by the kinder-kuche-kirche slogan. . . . The women's movement of the Weimer Republic (1919−1933) sought to reverse this . . . and transform sex roles of the early 20th Century. The advancement of women's rights was associated with the socialist and communist parties. Some progress was achieved. When the Nazis came to power, women's new status was challenged again.

During the Third Reich (1933–1945) the progress that women had made was undermined and even greater degradation of women took its place. Hitler restricted woman's activity to her husband, her family, her children, and her house.

During the Third Reich only 10% of the Gymnasium graduates were allowed to be women. Since woman's chief function was to breed potential soldiers, her education combined a minimum of intellectual training with a maximum of physical development. Besides being breeders women were also expected to do the heavy farm work. Young girls were sent to compulsory labor camps. . . . When the war broke out, women's employment became indispensable. However, women were limited to simple mechanical work and were placed under male supervision [p. 17].

Thus, in 1945 when the economy was in ruins and it was necessary to rebuild the country, the female population was almost completely unskilled and inadequately educated. Furthermore, there was a tremendous labor shortage because of the number of men killed in the war. Women far outnumbered men, a disparity in numbers that was further aggrevated by the emigration of skilled men to West Germany. It was essential not only that women join the labor force but that they become educated and skilled workers.

Today there is still a distinct imbalance in the sex ratio in the population of the country. The female:male ratio is 117:100, and the difference is especially marked in women 40 years old and older. There are 4.4 million women to 2.8 million men. Presently there is a marked labor shortage. The shortage of labor is expected to be alleviated by 1987 (Slepack, 1976).

In 1946 the Soviet occupying forces, according to Allendorf (1975), issued an order requring equal pay for equal work, initiating "the first and decisive step towards complete equality of women in East Germany [p. 98]." Equality had been demanded by generations of German women before 1933. When the Soviet-occupied zone became the GDR in 1949, laws were immediately enacted decreeing full equality in all spheres of life. According to Allendorf (1975), Article 7 of the constitution states: "Men and women have equal rights. All laws and decrees contrary to woman's equality are repealed [p. 98]," and Article 17 states: "Men and women, adults and youths, have the right to receive the same pay for the same work. Woman enjoys special protection in the working relationship. The law of the republic will create institutions to guarantee that woman can combine her task as a citizen and creative person with her duties as wife and mother [p. 99]." In the ensuing years, laws have been enacted to implement what the constitution has set down as basic rights of individuals. Ever since 1946, however, equal pay for equal work has been an enforced social policy and is today considered a completely settled issue.

During the early years after the war, it was the women who cleared the rubble. There are monuments in Berlin to women's industry and sacrifices during that period. Both the economy and women's conditions are extraordinarily different today. These historic changes have necessarily affected women of different age groups. According to Slepack, a third of the people living in the GDR today played a role in the Nazi war effort with its ideology about the "master race" and "masculine superiority," a second third of the population was below 15 years of age at the end of the war, and the last third was born after the war was over (Slepack, 1976).

The differences among these generations are reflected today in differences in education, occupation, marital relations, and in women's attitudes toward housework and child rearing—in short, in every aspect of women's and men's roles. The oldest group is not nearly as equal to men in terms of education or occupational achievement as the youngest generation, who exhibit few differences from men. And no wonder, considering the different lives each generation has led and the different factors conditioning their lives.

When we speak of women in the GDR, we must be very careful to specify which women we are talking about. That is not to say that the older women have not experienced a great change in their lives from the roles their mothers played or even from their own roles and role expectations as young women. They have—and dramatically so. However, it is the youngest group, growing up entirely under socialism, that gives the strongest indication of what the future will be like (Ecklein, 1982).

The following vignette from *Guten Morgen, Du Schoene* (Wander, 1977) illustrates the contrast in women's lives from one generation to the next as well as the tremendous hardships faced by the older generations that younger people growing up entirely under socialist conditions have simply not experienced.[3]

Yes, yes, things were very difficult after this stupid ol' war. Instead of going forwards we went backwards. We were just building before the war, then everything was destroyed again. At first I had four men to house who had been bombed out. One then asked me: can't I bring my bride here, she has no roof over her head either. And then one's own grandchildren came, one every year from Anna. Anna had a difficult time of it too. Her mother had taught her nothing, just told her: sit down children, be very quiet or the cake will collapse in the oven. That was the mother of our Anna. But what you don't know you can learn. . . . Anna then experienced the complete development of the village. She fought for a kindergarten, that a school be erected and a laundry. I didn't believe that we would achieve that. I carried water in pails hanging by chains from a pole across my back; we had no running water. Yes, yes, it is an entire novel. But I still walk erect, yes! It really angers me to see the youth shuffling along and slouching. Our Berndt walks very gracefully; he learned that in the military.

In 1952 the young folks received new farmland for planting and started with a cow harness. It was a great change with lots of noise and fighting. Anna was always pregnant. Once she was injured unloading wood. I got her on her feet again, but it seemed as if her last hour had come. I raised her eight children and one died, only a few weeks old. Anna was in the cow-shed and then in the field. Now she drives

---

[3]I am indebted to Thomas DeWitt for the translations from *Guten Morgen, Du Schoene*. The translations are in a stream of consciousness style that reflects the style of the interviews.

the new threshers. She could only do all these things because grandma was there. But Anna had it rough. So many children; so many cares, right? The oldest was half dead once, with a motorcycle. Anna ran to the hospital at night, and at home the partly completed Christmas tree. The dolls had no heads, only new clothes; the heads were not delivered by the factory until January. Now they all have a real profession and don't understand how hard we had it [243–244].

In the following analysis in which we discuss women's roles vis-à-vis leadership, education, occupation, and family life, three factors must be constantly kept in mind. One is the present-day reality of the lives of the people; another is the tremendous changes in the lives of women in the last 30 years; the third is the difference among the age groups in the population.

WOMEN IN PUBLIC LIFE

Considerable numbers of women are elected to office at all levels of public life. Although they are not present in equal proportion to men, especially at the very top levels, their numbers have been increasing year by year. Morgner (1975) aptly describes the current situation. "The GDR is naturally still a man's state—the leading positions in the state, the economy and the cultural field are all overwhelmingly occupied by men. This is in no way surprising. Our state is not even 30 years old yet. However its legislation can be described as decisively pro-woman and this is due not simply to the solidarity and understanding of male communists, but predominantly to the political work and initiative of female communists in the Socialist Unity Party, in organizations and commissions [M-10]."

Every third elected deputy in the GDR, whether to local assemblies or to the People's Chamber, the highest legislative body, is a woman. In the elected bodies of the districts, towns, boroughs, and communities, 65,000 of the 193,735 elected officials are women. Similarly, in the People's Chamber, the highest legislative body, women number 165 out of the 500 deputies. Thirty-five of the women are representatives of the DFD, the large national women's organization, which has these seats reserved for them. The number of women in the People's Chamber has steadily increased. For example, in the first electoral period 23.8 percent were women (*Women in the GDR*, 1975).[4] A sizeable percentage of all the mayors in the GDR are women. As of 1977 25 percent of all the mayors were women as compared with 11 percent in 1965. Today women are mayors in more than 1600 communities (Einheit, 1978).

Women are active participants at all levels in the trade union, FDGB. Everyone who works belongs to the union. Almost half of the elected officials are women although there is some variation in the type of office. For example, 47 percent of the FDGB national executive are women, whereas

[4]The analysis of women in leadership positions takes all of its data from *Women in the GDR: Facts and Figures*, 1975, pp. 17–23 with the exception of the figures on women in the Communist Party and those on women mayors.

40 percent of the trade union department committees are women. There are many opportunities for women to play a role in the union, and about one woman in three holds some position of responsibility. As the number of working women has risen, so has the number of women holding an elective position in the trade union.

Every third judge is a woman elected by the local assemblies. There is also a system of lay judges, 48 percent of whom are women elected by factory employees and other workers.

The National Front is an important political entity composed of neighborhood-level organizations of people from all political parties and large organizations. There are 335,000 elected positions in 170,000 committees. Of these, 30.7 percent are held by women. Of the 289 members of the National Council, 83 are women.

Among all the organizations, membership in the Communist Party (SED) is the most important. Dr. Volker Gransow analyzed documents of the Ninth Party Congress and found that 31 percent of all party members are women, 30 percent of the basic party leadership are women, and 30 percent of the delegates to the party congress are women. However, only 12 percent of the members of the Central Committee are women, and there are no women in the Politburo, the highest decision-making body. Two out of 10 Politburo candidates are women. Candidates have no right to vote but are very influential. One woman is a cabinet minister (Gransow, 1978b).

In his study of socialist countries, Marquit very aptly analyzes this pyramid effect—the lack of women in the very top positions of leadership. His analysis could apply to other decision-making bodies as well as to the Communist Party. Marquit (1978) states:

Membership in the Communist Party places severe demands on a person's time. Not only are Communists expected to be among the most active persons in the mass organizations, parents' committees in the schools, tenants' councils, and the like. With the factual situation being that women still carry excessive household and child-care burdens (in comparison with the men) it is more difficult for women to engage in activity on this level although a great many manage to do it. When it comes to the highest echelons of Party and government another factor enters. Here one finds older persons whose entire adult lives were generally dedicated single-purposedly, day and night, to social activism, starting at a time when the conditions in their countries were less favorable for women playing more active roles in public life [179].

Given these facts the number of women in elected office is remarkable. The trends are quite clear. With each election more women obtain office. Furthermore, young women are increasingly being elected. For example 36 percent of the female deputies in the local assemblies are under 31. There is thus every likelihood that the percentage of women will increase in all levels of leadership, but it will take many years before complete parity with men is achieved.

EDUCATION

Education is a good topic through which to examine conditions and opportunities for women in the GDR. Education can have a decisive impact on women's economic and political achievement. Educational opportunities and achievements of women today must be understood against a background in which a mere 30 years ago, during the Fascist period, few women were even allowed to receive higher education. How do women now compare with men in terms of education? How has this changed over the years? How can women workers in a full-employment society combine a family and further education? What has been the experience of women receiving higher education?

Today there is virtually no difference between men and women in the education they receive. For example, in 1976 47.7 percent of all persons graduating from colleges or universities were women, according to *What is Life Like in the GDR?* (1977), and 69 percent of all those graduating from technical schools were women. (The very high percentage of women graduating from technical schools may reflect the fact that in 1974 there were newly founded technical schools for paramedical professions, which have a high concentration of women. Furthermore, technical schools also now include programs for crèche and kindergarten teachers. I am extrapolating my conclusion from the fact that in 1973—before these fields were added to technical school programs—out of 162,900 students, 87,000 were women. By 1975, just two years later, out of 156,400 students, 122,000 were women.) More striking is the fact that "the proportion of women studying technological or natural science subjects has risen over the past few years from 4.6 to 61.7 percent (*Women and Socialism*, 1976). As of 1974, 99 percent of female school graduates received vocational training. In effect, hardly anyone graduates today from secondary school in the GDR without vocational training. Figure 5.1 shows the differences in education among the different age groups.

The number of unskilled workers has reversed itself in very dramatic fashion. By 1971 80 percent of women under 30 had skilled workers' training or a postsecondary education, whereas only 22 percent of women 60 years old and older had such an education. For each corresponding five-year age differential, there are sizeable differences in the number of women who are at least skilled workers.

One of the most significant facts illustrated in Figure 5.1 is the reversal in the ratio of skilled to unskilled workers in the 35-and-under age group. That is, it is in the 35-and-under age group that for the first time more than 50 percent of the women have been trained to be at least skilled workers. These are women who were 12 years old or less when the war ended and who were the first to receive a sizeable proportion of their initial education under a socialist system.

Another way of analyzing the data is to look at the proportion of women who received their training after the war ended. In 1971, out of every 100 women, the following number had acquired their respective educational level after 1945: college graduates, 92 percent; technical school graduates, 90 percent; supervisors, 79 percent; skilled workers, 74 percent (*Women in the GDR*, 1975, p. 33). Thus, the vast majority of women received their education after 1945.

The changes in the differences in education between men and women (by age), as shown in Figure 5.2, are also quite striking. Today, educational differences between men and women are all but wiped out. Although the

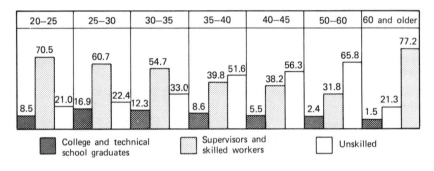

Figure 5.1. Educational level of working women according to age groups as of 1971 (in percentages). *Source: Women in the GDR: Facts and Figures.* Dresden: Zeit im Bild. 1975:33.

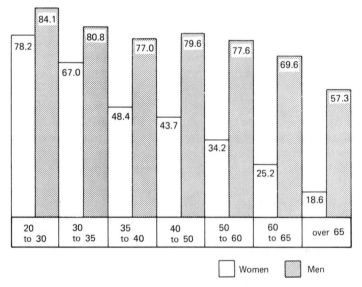

Figure 5.2. Percentage of employees classified by age groups who have undergone complete vocational training (data for 1971). *Source: Women in the GDR: Facts and Figures.* Dresden: Verlag Zeit im Bild. 1975:34.

level of educational achievement was greater for both men and women during each 10-year interval, the women moved ahead at a much faster pace than the men did. Again, the most dramatic increase in educational level occurred in the 30-to-35 age group, the first group to come to maturity under socialism.

In summing up the data on the education of women, three facts stand out:

1. Today, everyone receives at least skilled workers' training.
2. Educational differences between men and women 30 years old and younger have been eliminated.
3. Almost all women who have had a skilled worker's or professional education—whatever their age—have attained it during the socialist period.

Although education of men and women has reached parity in the younger age group, a great deal has been done to make it possible for older women to upgrade their skills. Adult education for the entire population is extensive, with both men and women participating by the hundreds of thousands. According to *Women in the GDR* (1975), every year 300,000 to 400,000 working women take part in course work to complete their education. A man told me that so many courses were offered at his work place that he could not possibly take advantage of all of them.

The economy of the GDR is developing at a rapid rate, and there are constant technological improvements in all areas, making it necessary to continually upgrade the skills of all workers so that they can operate the equipment of advanced technology. For this and other reasons, the introduction of more and more women into the production process has always been combined with special efforts to improve their qualifications (Kuhrig, 1976). In fact, in the future it is projected that production processes will be automated to such an extent that no unskilled workers will be needed. Unskilled labor is seen as detrimental to increased production as well as to the welfare of workers who must do boring, repetitive work. Consequently, the GDR is looking for ways to adapt technology to eliminate the necessity of unskilled labor.

The Eighth Party Congress of the SED specifically stated that the number of unskilled women workers should be reduced and that the quality of courses to train skilled women should be improved. The Congress focused on unskilled women for several reasons. In the first place, there was a very high percentage of women who were unskilled both absolutely and in relation to the number of unskilled men. In 1971 51.8 percent of all women workers were unskilled (*Women in the GDR*, 1975). The party emphasized the value of an educated working class; such a class increases the possibility of placing women in leadership positions and enabling them to contribute creatively to the production process.

These goals have been accomplished in several ways. The Central Institute for Job Qualifications has been set up to develop skilled jobs from unskilled ones. Furthermore, in order to upgrade women from unskilled to skilled positions, state-owned industries have created jobs for women that demand higher qualifications, encouraging the women to become skilled workers (*Effektive Facharbeiter-ausbildung von Arbeiterinnen*, 1976).

Following the Eighth Party Congress, a number of provisions were made to enable women to combine obligations to family with continuing education. These provisions applied to all working women regardless of their level of qualification, although they were aimed at encouraging unskilled workers to study for skilled worker's certificates. The broad question is, of course, how to encourage working women to further their education.

For a number of years the major project of the scientific advisory council of the Academy of Science was research concerning the improvement of the technical and vocational as well as the political and ideological qualification of women (Kuhrig, 1974, 1976). This research concentrated primarily on the further education of unskilled women. Women workers in 38 factories were studied by a team of 23 people to determine what would motivate unskilled women workers to take further training. The research team used survey research techniques and developed special courses in several industries. These courses consisted not only of training in specific skills but instruction in Marxism—Leninism and economics. How each industry fit into the overall economy and its goals was also an integral part of the courses. Some of the courses are now required for all people receiving a skilled worker's certificate; others are specific to workers in specific industries.

One of the major objectives of the original research project was to determine what motivates unskilled women to take further training. The study found that the most important motives for readiness for further training included an appreciation of the necessity of the training and the desire for more money. The most important motives for refusing further training were that the training was not actually necessary for the job, family responsibilities were not compatible with the demands of the programs, a lack of self-confidence on the worker's part, or that further training was no longer possible because of age or ill health. Interestingly, the women studied did not identify either the attitudes of their husbands or the fear that their children would not be properly cared for while they were taking the courses as factors in their readiness for further training. Generally, the study showed that the more education and training a woman had, the more willing she was to take on more.

Policy decisions have been made to put these findings to practical use (though some had been in force before). Many provisions encourage working women to continue their education. Women are given released time from work to study at no loss in pay, with the amount of released time depending on the type of course. A firm may organize a full-time course, in which case a woman may be given up to 60 days for study with no loss in pay. If she attends a course outside her firm, she may be given two to three days off from her firm. At full-time courses especially adapted for women, she is given 190 marks per month as a grant plus 80 percent of her net average wage (*Women and Socialism*, 1976).

Most factories have education institutes that enable women to take courses within the factories during working hours. Tutors are available to help women with intellectual and personal problems. There is an assurance that a woman can finish a course even if she must interrupt it because of family illness or pregnancy. And there are written agreements between a woman and her firm specifying the job she will return to after a course is completed (*Women in the GDR*, 1975; *Women and Socialism*, 1976). When appropriate, these same provisions apply to men who have custody of their children or who have wives who are ill.

There are also various provisions specifically designed to encourage older women to take additional training. These women are given recognition for skills and knowledge acquired through many years of work. Since 1973, women over 35 have not had to take written examinations if they have worked three years on the job for which they are taking special courses. *Women and Socialism* states: "Women over 40 who have been 10 years or more carrying out the work of a skilled worker, who have been to courses of advanced education, and work in a particularly responsible manner may receive their qualifications through recognition without having to attend any further courses of study [p. 30]."

Partly as a result of the application of the findings from the research project and the directives of the Eighth Party Congress, 13,609 women received skilled worker's certificates in 1974, 65 percent more than did so in 1972. Between 1971 and 1973, the number of skilled male workers increased by 2 percent, whereas the number of skilled women workers increased by 17 percent—a difference in numbers that was partly the result of the new provisions for women (Kuhrig, 1976).

As one might expect with the introduction of anything new, there are difficulties to be ironed out in implementing these policies. When the new provisions for education of women were introduced, for example, production quotas were not reduced accordingly. Factory managers are thus concerned about meeting quotas with a reduced labor force, although it has been shown that the more education a woman has, the more likely she is to remain in the labor force throughout her child-bearing years on a full-time basis. In addition, other workers may feel that they are being penalized with extra work to make up the hours lost by women who take time out for education courses. Finally, the women themselves, even with all the support of official policy, must have the assertiveness, courage, and extra energy to take advantage of the opportunities offered to them.

An additional problem, in terms of social planning, is that many women take training in several fields, and these training courses are very expensive for the state. I met one woman who had trained in three different fields: as a nurses' aide, a librarian, and a swimming instructor. Another problem arises when women abandon work for which they have been trained in favor of unskilled but better-paying jobs.

I had occasion to observe some results of these policies and some of their problems because several of my students at Humboldt University were on leave from their enterprises to learn English.[5] One of my students, a woman in her mid thirties who had never married, was extremely shy, although she worked very hard to learn English. She took the course because the import – export firm for which she worked needed someone to conduct its English correspondence. The woman became quite proficient in English, more than enough to satisfy the needs of her enterprise. When she wanted to continue her education in English, however, she found that many of her co-workers were jealous of her efforts and spoke harshly about what she was doing. She had to have the courage to continue in spite of their attitudes—no small accomplishment for a shy, sensitive woman. The fact that 300,000 to 400,000 women each year take part in such education is a testament to their eagerness to develop their potential and to their determination to take advantage of their new opportunities.

The following vignette[6] from *Guten Morgen, Du Schoene* (Wander, 1977) illustrates the difficulties one woman encountered when she took advantage of the new educational opportunities:

. . . then came affirmative action plans (to promote women). My boss actually had no ambition, said it was all silly and that one should qualify oneself on the job. But another thought why not, he is constantly asking and we only have women in the department. For God's sake, my boss cried, at your age; do you even have a high school degree [Abitur]? No, I said. Well then, he cried, it's silly; but the other one remained firm and I just said: I'll do it. I didn't even know what I was getting into.

I went to the Volkshochschule and met a woman. We spoke for an hour and then she said: it is amazing, all the things you don't know. You will never make the entrance examination to the eleventh grade. . . . In the evenings I told my husband: I have no time, I have to read. He did not ask what I read and why I read, he only complained constantly that his shirts had no buttons. And he watched television. And I sat in the kitchen and studied. Read Heine. . . . A world opened up for me. But my husband only told stories of how an education can ruin a marriage. I never took it seriously because I thought a man as jealous as that won't try anything. . . .

I worked and worked and worked at home. Sometimes I deliberately provoked a quarrel . . . I was so angry at him because he never asked: can I help with the household, can I check the children's homework? Nothing, absolutely nothing. The

---

[5]There are various types of leave arrangements. Some women go to a university full time on leave from their enterprise. Others take special courses at a university. In either case, a woman receives a paycheck covering the time she is at school.

[6]Professor Erich Leitel of Jena University commented on this passage. He felt this woman's experience was not necessarily typical. A great many older women who received their diplomas are accepted for further study, and many husbands are very sympathetic and helpful while their wives are studying.

only thing he ever said: now you finally realize how little you know . . . short and sweet, I completed the Abitur with a 1 (A) after a year. . . .

But would you believe it, I was not accepted for a course of studies! I only received a letter: Dear Mrs. S. Your interview and written work did not, regrettably, produce the result we expected. Your age is actually also . . .Well, thank you! Now you finally had the proof that you are just stupid. . . .

Now something terrific happened to our marriage. It suddenly thrived again. After twenty years such a lift! I ran home, I was happy not having to take that course of studies because now I had time for him. We did an incredible number of things in this year, and we could afford a great deal since I also working. It was a time, when everything was right: husband, children, work, the world. He was more and more tender, that was the crazy part, and began talking in the following manner: whatever happens, nothing will tear us apart. . . . Until one day he asked: what would you say if a new woman had entered my life? [178–181].[6]

EMPLOYMENT

The number of working women has doubled since 1949. Out of all women who are capable of working, 86 percent actually work, and women make up 49 percent of the labor force. Women are not working primarily out of economic necessity. Married couples, for example, can maintain an adequate standard of living on one salary, and they can rely on the security of that salary because everyone is guaranteed a job and a person changing jobs is guaranteed at least the salary received in the previous position.

The general attitude of the public toward working women has changed dramatically in the last 30 years. Renate Mitchell, interpreter and mother of three, recalls (1974): "In 1957 husbands could still persuade their wives to stop working and might look down on others who could not 'provide for' their wife and family [3]."

According to Irmtraud Morgner (1975), however, men in the GDR today see their own respect as tied up with their wives' working; it is practically a matter of honor. "Wives who are simply housewives may make life more comfortable, but they are not held in particularly high regard by men [M-10]."

This change in attitudes toward women's working has not been accomplished without considerable struggle. One of the Democratic Women's Organization's (DFD) most important functions has been their ideological and political effort to get nonworking women out of their homes and into the labor force. Women work in all branches of industry, but they are concentrated in certain areas, as shown in Table 5.1.

Only 15 percent of the building industry and 27 percent of the transport industry are composed of women, but 71 percent of those persons employed in education and culture, 85 percent in health and social services, and 71 percent in commerce are women. To put these figures in perspective, we must also bear in mind that of all working women, only 27 percent are in

Table 5.1.   Percentage of Employees Who Were Female, by Sector, 1974 (percent)

Transport	27
Agriculture and forestry	43
Industry	44
Producing crafts	38
Building industry	15
Post and telecommunications	71
Commerce	71
Other productive industries	55
Nonproductive fields	72
Education and culture	71
Health and social services	85

Source: Women in the GDR: Facts and Figures. Dresden: Verlag Zeit im Bild. 1975:45.

education, health, culture, and social services, whereas 36 percent of them are in industry and construction. However, when the industry category is further broken down, we find that women are overrepresented in some industries and underrepresented in others. For example, we find that only 28 percent of the work force in the energy and fuel industry and 27 percent in the metallurgical industry are women, whereas women comprise 71 percent of workers in the textile industry and 62 percent in other light industry (*Women in the GDR*, 1975).

To understand the significance of these statistics about women in the labor force, we must take into account certain facts. First, it would be unrealistic and utopian to expect a 50−50 distribution in all occupational categories at this stage. A socialist society inherits its occupational structure from the capitalist society that precedes it, and after only 30 years it is still a fact that a large proportion of workers began their working lives under capitalism. Furthermore, it is to be expected that within such a short time a large number of women will still be inclined to go into more traditional women's occupations.

Second, the GDR has very strict prohibitions concerning the kinds of work women can engage in, prohibitions based on women's physiology and the child-bearing functions. For example, women are not allowed to be miners underground, to work under conditions of higher than atmospheric pressure, under the effects of mechanical vibration caused by air compressors, or under conditions of high temperatures (*Gesetzblatt des DDR*, 1973). Thus, women are excluded from many occupations in heavy industry and construction as well as mining. Other industries have adapted their facilities to better accommodate women workers. Factory managers are urged to see to it that machinery is automated in such a way that women can do the work and still comply with safety regulations. This adaptation occurred to a large extent in agriculture where equipment has been designed and built specifically so that it is free from vibrations and women can handle and repair it themselves.

Third, although there are no published statistics concerning differences in median wages between men and women, women workers tend to cluster in the lower paying jobs. The trade union organization has been trying to rectify this situation by changing the wage scale (Slepack, 1976). However, such a process is extremely difficult. It is more likely that the pay differential will be overcome as the technology becomes more automated and women are able to go increasingly into jobs now dominated by men, rather than as a result of an overhaul in wage structure (Marquit, 1978).

Dr. Herta Kuhrig pointed out to me that policy makers seek eventually to have an equal proportion of men and women in all occupations and to eliminate high concentrations of women in certain areas. Frau Wetterhahn of the Haus des Lehrers expressed the same sentiment with regard to teachers. Noting the high proportion of women teachers, she told me that plans are under way to give preference to young men in training to become teachers. She expressed great confidence that a balance between men and women teachers could be achieved.

Athough much remains to be done before equal numbers of men and women work in all occupations, certain changes have taken place already: (1) an increased emphasis on upgrading the level of skill of women working in production, (2) an increase in the numbers of women receiving technical training and going into fields traditionally dominated by men, and (3) a general shift in the occupational structure in terms of where women are concentrated.

A considerable emphasis has been given to upgrading the level of skill of women working in production. As mentioned previously, the training of unskilled women workers has been given high priority since 1971. Between 1971 and 1975, the number of skilled women workers in production jobs rose from 26 to 36 percent (*Einheit*, 1977). In the age group 25–30, the vast majority (75 percent) are now skilled workers. During the same period, the number of female graduates of college and technical schools working in industry doubled (Slepack, 1976).

Women receiving technical training are going into technical fields previously dominated by men. They are also entering new areas of technology and professions of high prestige. For example, whereas 27 percent of the people employed in the building material industry are women, 52 percent of the students admitted to technical schools in 1974 were women (*Women in the GDR*, 1975). In the same year 82 percent of the new apprentices in data processing, 69 percent in chemical engineering, and 60 percent in electrical engineering were women (*Women and Socialism*, 1976). Women are also gaining a strong foothold in such occupations of high prestige as medicine (46 percent), law (30 percent), and high public office (31 percent) (Slepack 1976).

These statistics do not mean that women are going into all fields in the same proportion as men. For example, only 27 percent of those persons studying mathematics and 25 percent studying mechanical engineering are women. However, the trends are clear. And with such a concerted effort being made to encourage women to go into the same fields as men, the day may not be too far off when women and men go into almost all fields in the same proportion.

There has also been a sizeable shift in the overall occupational structure. Agriculture has had a great proportion of working women in it. Since the mechanization of agriculture, however, far fewer persons of both sexes are working in that sector. Thus, although in 1949 more than half of all working women were employed in agriculture and crafts and only 17 percent in industry, today only 10 percent work in agriculture and 34 percent in industry. It should also be noted that in 1960 only 27 percent of the women working in agriculture were skilled, but that by 1974, 71 percent had vocational training (*Women in the GDR*, 1975). Another area in which there have been sizeable shifts of women workers is in commerce; the number of women in commerce (saleswomen, cashiers, and goods handlers) has doubled since 1949.

Another aspect of women's employment is their position as supervisory personnel or as managers. As might be expected, given the foregoing discussion, women in management have not yet reached parity with men. However, their numbers are definitely on the rise, and they are encouraged to take training to be managers. Of all persons in managerial positions, 30 percent are women; of these only 17.3 percent are in industry, and 49.1 percent are in health and education (Felgentreau, 1977). Felgentreau told me in an interview, "It's no secret a lot has to be done still to get women into leading positions."

A lengthy interview with Eva Birnbaum (1976), head of education at a large cable combine employing 8000 workers, gave me a great deal of insight into some of the problems in this area: for example, that there are structural constraints on women as well as problems with both men's and women's attitudes toward leadership positions. She told me that many women do not want to take the courses because they lack self-confidence. They are afraid of failing the course or failing in their position as managers. Although they are given all kinds of extra support as they participate in the training course, after the course is completed and they become managers they are given no special consideration. Birnbaum feels that women in their capacity as managers should be given special support because managerial positions mean extra responsibilities, which women are reluctant to take on.

Another factor is men's attitudes toward women managers. Although men accepted women in management positions, Birnbaum said that they watched women managers very critically: to measure up, a woman had to be three times as qualified as a man and continually justify herself.

Birnbaum confessed that she herself felt like quitting at times. She also recognized that she had made various mistakes. She was quite young, in her late twenties, when she became head of education at the combine about 15 years ago. She supervised the work of older men who resented her. She now sees that one mistake she made was to feel that she always had to be superior, so that even if someone made a good suggestion, she would feel she had to come up with an even better one herself.

Birnbaum made another interesting observation about her own feelings as a manager, one that indicates what might be called a "feminine" approach to handling authority. When she first took on her job, she didn't want to hurt people's feelings by telling them they had made a mistake, and it was difficult for her to find the correct relationship with people. She received support from several sources. She said she had a very good relationship with her husband, who shares family responsibilities with her. She said she would always be grateful to her good work team and that as a Communist Party member she found her party collective very supportive in her struggles to be a good manager.

For the younger generation of women, Birnbaum explained, these problems are not so sharp. She gave me examples of how she personally has encouraged talented young women. Also younger men are far more supportive and accepting of women managers. An example of the help men are willing to give so women can be managers was reported in the *Democratic German Report* (1975). A young woman manager related: "The most effective help came from the economic director in the factory; for a whole year he shared with my husband the task of taking our young daughter to the kindergarten in the morning and picking her up in the evening (*Democratic German Report*) [12]."

Throughout the trade unions there are what American women would call "affirmative action" programs, which are very extensive and strictly enforced. Within each trade union branch committee is a woman's commission made up of women members elected every two years. These commissions have played a crucial role in the rapid advancement of women. The women's commissions shape the content and application of women's promotion plans that are part of the agreement signed each year between the management of an enterprise and the trade union committee. The manager and the trade union committee of a firm are then answerable to the women for carrying out the terms of this agreement. At least twice a year the head of a factory and the trade union must report to the women's commission on how they have fulfilled the plan. These promotion plans stipulate the increased participation by women in management and planning, further education for women, and the improvement within the enterprise of women's working and living conditions. In addition, there are special plans for each individual woman who has children that encourage the women's future education and occupational advancement. In effect, this means that there is systematic encouragement for every woman worker with children to overcome the handicapping family obligations to career advancement.

The women's commissions also bring pressure to bear on factory management to develop equipment that is legal for women to handle, a crucial factor in women's movement away from traditional jobs and light industry into more highly skilled, highly paid work.

Various amenities are provided by the place of employment. In the GDR the place of employment is not confined only to job tasks. Specific facilities might vary from place to place, but almost all enterprises serve full course meals at extremely low rates. Children also receive hot, well-balanced meals at kindergartens and schools. This means that the family does not have a big meal in the evening, and women do not have to go home after work and face the task of preparing it. A great many enterprises also have libraries, saunas, beauty shops, and cosmeticians. All enterprises with more than 6000 employees have their own health service complete with specialists. Managers are required to see to it that the women they supervise have a yearly physical examination.

Many enterprises have food markets on the premises. Most have child-care facilities for very young children (aged six months to three years) as well as for kindergarten children (aged three to six years). Because many parents prefer to send their children to child-care facilities close to their place of residence so that the chldren do not have to travel long distances, the people using the child-care facilities in the enterprises are more likely to live nearby, or to be nursing mothers. People in nearby communities may also use a firm's child-care facilities, if there is room.

Workers participate as a group in many after-work activities. An enterprise's plans for the year may include plays, concerts, and sporting activities that the workers may attend with or without their families. There are sports clubs, art clubs, drama groups, and other cultural organizations connected with each enterprise. Through the union branch connected with each enterprise, workers also attend holiday homes and the children attend summer camps. All these facilities are rapidly expanding. The women's commissions within the unions play a major role in deciding which of these facilities should be expanded or developed to meet the needs of women workers.

THE FAMILY

The changing role of the family and of the relationships within the family unit are an extremely complex process in the GDR. This section deals with the following areas: (1) the concept of the socialist family, (2) support of the family by the state, (3) new roles for men, women, and children,

(4) divorce, (5) birth control, and (6) the rights of unwed mothers and children born out of wedlock.

The Socialist Family

Until 1945 bourgeois law gave the man the right to decide all matters in the marriage while the wife had the right and obligation to manage the joint household. These laws were abolished in 1945, and the GDR constitution of 1949 abolished all other laws contrary to women's equality. According to article 30 of the GDR constitution (Allendorf, 1975): "Marriage and family are the foundation of community life. They enjoy the protection of the state. Laws and decrees that impair the equality of man and woman in the family are repealed [98]." A law on the Protection of Mother and Child and the Rights of Women, also passed in 1949, was revised in 1966 and is now called the Family Code. The Family Code establishes the position of the family within the society and provides for the protection and promotion of marriage and family life. Contained in the Family Code are the laws relating to relationships of married couples, the right to education, and laws concerning names, property, and divorce. Both the constitution and the Family Code support two important principles: equal rights for men and women, and protection and promotion of married and family life (Kuhrig, 1973). Both principles are regarded as a single entity, and measures are designed so that they can be integrated with each other.

The policy aim of strengthening the family is not for the sake of preserving the family *per se*; instead, preserving harmonious family relations is seen as the best way to allow people to develop themselves to their full potential. This is especially true in the case of children. One of the specific functions of the family is to help children make use of the opportunities open to them. As Kuhrig (1973) puts it, the aim of the family code "focuses on the strengthening of relations of equality between married partners, motivated by the ideas of comradely help and support, mutual understanding, love and trust, responsibility for the personal development of the partner and the education of the children [25]." According to Grandke, Kuhrig, and Weisse (1966), the Family Code "considers the marriage a long-lasting and reliable community which is based on very close connections resulting from the emotional relations between man and woman and the relations of mutual love, respect and confidence between all members of the family [p. 12]." Marriage in the GDR is free of many of the external considerations prevalent to a greater or lesser extent in all countries, such as economic dependence of women on their husbands, discrimination against divorced women, and the inferior social position of single women within the society (Kuhrig, 1973). However, the transition from a bourgeois to a socialist form of marriage is filled with contradictions and difficulties. Both men and women are finding it difficult to discard traditions and behavior handed down through generations.

Support of the Family by the State

The state has attempted both to help in this transition and to strengthen the family as a unit. This help has included (1) specific social measures, (2) the involvement of the entire society in the development of the new Family Code, and (3) public education.

The family unit is supported by the state through specific social measures. These include virtually free child care immediately after maternity leave. There is a paid maternity leave of 26 weeks for the first child and a year for the second and successive children. The state pays families a lump sum maternity benefit on the birth of each child, and provides a monthly allowance to each family on the basis of the number of children in the family. There are also special housing and clothing benefits for families with many children, as well as special benefits for single-parent families.

All the provisions have steadily as well as rapidly increased. For example, by 1972 a lump sum benefit of 1000M was paid to a family on the birth of each child; in 1958 couples having their first child received 500M and only couples having their fifth child received 1000M. Winkler (1978), a leading social demographer, states: "Financial burdens arising from the birth, care, and upbringing of children will, to an increasing extent, be recognized and borne by the whole community [3]."

To help young couples, an interest-free 5000M loan is extended to all newly married young people. To qualify for this loan, couples must be in their first marriage, be under the age of 27, and have gross monthly earnings not exceeding 1400M. They can receive an additional loan in the same amount if they want to build a house or purchase shares in a workers' housing construction cooperative. The loans must be paid back in eight years, but they are remitted in part with each child and are erased entirely on the birth of a third child to the family (*Youth-Education-Profession*, 1978).

Housing is heavily subsidized. Rent and utilities are only about 4 percent of a family's income. However, there is still a severe housing shortage as a result of vast destruction during the war and the need to develop first a more balanced industrial base (Marquit, 1978). As a linchpin of the social policy of the SED, it was planned that between 1976 and 1980, 750,000 dwelling units were to have been constructed or modernized (*Directives of the Five-Year Plan for the GDR's National Economic Development, 1976–1980*). It now appears that 100,000 additional units will be completed by 1980 (*GDR Review*, 1979). Since 1971 a quarter of the entire population has been rehoused or had their dwelling units modernized. It is planned that the housing question as a social problem will be solved by 1990.

The manner of developing the new Family Code has also helped to strengthen the family as a unit. Adopted in 1966, the Family Code was developed from a Draft Law that was extensively discussed by a wide section of the population before it was put into effect. These discussions were felt to be very important for a number of reasons. Internal relations in the family can be developed only by family members themselves, and such laws can be carried out only with the cooperation of family members. This means that for the law to be successful, the people themselves must be intimately connected with drafting the law, and it must reflect their feelings and ideas. In developing the Family Code, discussions led to many changes in the draft as well as decisions *not* to change certain sections of the law that some people wanted.

Accordingly, although the draft law was written by experts from many fields on the basis of extensive data concerning the development of the family and of the society as a whole, many sections of it were rewritten after extensive discussions with all segments of the general population. All the political parties had a role in drafting the law, and the whole draft law was published in the daily press. There were many forms of discussion. Press, radio, and television took an active part. Public discussion lasted four months. In all, 33,973 meetings took place, in which 752,671 people participated. There were 23,737 comments on the draft law recorded (Grandke et al., 1966). From these extraordinarily detailed figures, as well as the careful accounting of them, we can appreciate how serious an effort was made to involve the entire population.

A plan was worked out on the basis of the structure of the population so that every segment of the population would take part in the discussions. On the basis of these investigations, a number of changes were made. The discussions made it quite clear that people felt young people needed to be better prepared for marriage. It was felt young people were left too much on their own and that important areas of intellectual and psychological education concerning family life had been neglected. Many people also wanted improved and enlarged marriage guidance centers so that people could consult with specialists in this area. The outcome of these discussions was a law requiring the establishment of a broad network of marriage and family guidance institutions where everyone can ask for advice from teachers, doctors, lawyers, and other specialists (Grandke et al., 1966).

The Draft Law stipulated that on marriage, a couple could choose either the husband's or wife's name, or each could maintain his or her original family name. People objected to the latter provision, however, because they felt that the unity of the partners and the family should be expressed by a common name. In the final version of the law, a couple can choose either name but do not have the option to maintain different family names.

A similar situation arose with respect to the ownership of property. In the original laws passed in 1949, women were given the right to control their own property and to make independent decisions about taking up a profession and choosing a domicile. These rights were felt to be necessary first steps in giving women control over their own lives and making a complete break with the traditions and laws in the old German Civil Code. The discussions of the draft of the Family Code in 1965 made it clear that couples did not consider the property they obtained after marriage to be individually owned by either husband or wife but to be joint property. Thus, the need for the earlier separate ownership of property was no longer necessary, as it was no longer in fact being practiced.

The Draft Law and the final Family Code specifically stipulate that husband and wife are equally responsible for management of the household and care of the children. Kuhrig (1973) quotes Article 10 of the Family Code:

(1) Both married partners share in the upbringing and care of the children and in the management of the household. The relations between the married partners are to be so organized as to enable the wife to combine her occupational and social activity with motherhood. (2) Should the partner, who was previously not gainfully employed, decide to take up an occupation or should one of the partners decide to continue his education or engage in social work, the other partner gives considerate and comradely support and helps in the realization of his marital partner's plan [pp. 58—59].

Many people felt that the law should go further and apply sanctions against a husband who was not willing to share in these responsibilities. This provision was excluded, however, because it was felt to be impossible for the state to enforce it even though it was extremely important to express the legal principle of common responsibility in family affairs (Grandke et al., 1966).

The exclusion of this provision follows from a general principle of the Family Code applicable in other areas—namely, that administrative decisions of the state cannot relieve people of their responsibilities in developing relationships. The state can guarantee social security and a steady increase in the standard of living, and it can provide the family counselling centers already discussed. But internal relations within the family can be developed only by the family members themselves.

The media and the arts, which are completely and lavishly supported in the GDR, offer yet another avenue through which the state supports the family as well as promotes equality between the sexes. Culture is a very vibrant and significant part of GDR society, and tickets to all cultural events are very inexpensive.

Harry and Elaine Mensh (1978), two Americans who have extensively studied the arts in the GDR, describe in some detail the plots of plays, television dramas, and movies that deal with many facets of the male—female relationship. They point out: "Helping to redefine women's new role and to overcome these patriarchal survivals is an important role of socialist art. . . . At each stage of socialist development, GDR art has treated the new conflicts confronting women [pp. 246—247]." Earlier novels and television dramas dealt with problems women faced in deciding to go to work and seek further education. Currently, they deal with the issue of the woman alone.

Christine Romero (1978) of Tufts University analyzed the themes in recent novels written by GDR women in the 1970s. Three such novels portray women "who have become more emancipated, more independent and more demanding of themselves than is good for individual happiness. In these novels the men are more inadequate and left behind." Romero points out that many of these novels deal with the failure of marriage. They portray the conflicts of an unequal relationship—one in which men feel no obligation to share the load.

Irmtraud Morgner (1975), a leading novelist has this to say on the role of the professional writer in changing people's lives:

> It is only possible to change the traditions by making people conscious of the fact that they are odd and unfitting; in the literary field this can be done by encouraging the readers to take part in a creative process of thought and to become surprised at themselves. A change in customs is a creative process both for society and for each individual, a process which brings with it discoveries. Literature can stimulate people to make such discoveries, and in particular to discover themselves [pp. M-10].

Another cultural medium is *Für Dich*, a weekly magazine for women, which has a circulation of 1 million and goes to 25 percent of the households in the GDR. Men write a third of the letters to the editor. The magazine attempts to overcome stereotyped sex roles in every way it can by featuring stories and letters on men who participate in household tasks and men who share equally in the responsibility of the household.

Thus, cultural forms in the GDR deal with all aspects of the changing roles of men and women. There is a genuine attempt to help people move on to the next steps in women's emancipation and at the same time to cope with current difficulties. In a very real sense, cultural forms in the GDR have had a significant impact on changing male–female relationships.

New Role for Men, Women, and Children

As might be expected, changing traditional relationships within the family has proved extraordinarily difficult. Even with the backing of governmental social supports, laws, and propaganda, the couples must still work things out themselves. Men are being asked to give up privileges that they have had for generations. Many are reluctant to do this. As Menschik and Leopold (1974) point out, "Women have the law and propaganda on their side, while men have tradition on theirs [p. 193]." Traditional roles within the work place have changed more rapidly. At work, enforceable union rules and regulations and the sheer number of people involved make it easier to change traditional relationships.

The shift in roles taking place within the family is profound. Couples of all ages and walks of life are sensitive and analytical about their relationships with each other. It must be remembered that there are no German socialist models of family life for people to follow. There is not yet one generation of people who have lived their entire lives under socialist conditions.

The significance of the family itself is changing. For men, the family is becoming more important; for women, less. A woman's place of employment is beginning to occupy a more prominent place in her life.

For all these reasons a new type of relationship between men and women is coming into being. According to the authors of *Gretchens Rote Schwestern*, a new interpretation of love relationships is occurring. Couples are no longer as possessive of their spouses. They don't think in terms of *my* husband or *my* wife. The partners respect each other as individuals and attempt to develop together (Menschik & Leopold, 1974).

This new form of marriage has raised a number of conflicts and contradictions that are proving difficult to overcome. The sharing of household tasks is one of the major stumbling blocks to women's equality. Women spend an average of 37 hours a week on household tasks, but men contribute only around 6 hours a week. Two safe generalizations can be made regarding the sharing of work in the home. First, there is a tremendous range within the society. In some couples child rearing and household tasks are shared equally; in others the woman bears the entire burden. Second, among younger couples there is far more sharing. Typical is the comment made to the Menshes (1978): "Husbands forty and fifty years old and older are lazybones. . . . and wives will do everything for these husbands without complaining. But my twenty-seven year old daughter won't give her husband supper if he doesn't shop. Once he came home without potatoes. The store was too crowded. 'Will it be less crowded' she asked, 'if *I* shop there?' They went to a restaurant [p. 244]."

The discrepancy between the way a woman is treated on the job and at home is another source of conflict. Women are increasingly achieving genuine equality on the job. It is not at all rare to find that men who accept women as equals at work do not want that same kind of equality in the household. On the other hand, a woman who had a certain amount of responsibility on the job and is respected by men as an equal at work does not want to tolerate a husband who wants a more traditional relationship.

The absorption of each of the spouses in an occupational life also means that they have less time and energy for family relationships, even though they care for each other a great deal. Rueschemeyer (1977), an American sociologist, found this to be true for East Berlin couples when both of the partners were professional. She found the men and women she interviewed to be tense in their relationships and to feel overburdened. They attributed this in part to their absorption in their professional lives. She states: "Men and women are absorbed in different worlds, with different people and sometimes a different spirit [p. 253]."

Because the external constraints that traditionally bound couples together in a marriage have been removed, differences in character, temperament, and inclination are playing an increasingly greater role. Under presocialist conditions, couples felt compelled to accept these personal differences. However, under the new conditions these personal differences become much more important (Kuhrig, 1973).

Another difficulty is the uneven acceptance of changing roles in society as a whole. Women are far more eager than men to accept the new roles, which often leads to all manner of difficulties, especially if each has changed at a different pace since they were first married. Women feel few constraints to stay in a marriage with a partner they feel is backward. Almost 70 percent of divorce proceedings are initiated by women.

The contradictions and conflicts arising from the rapid changes in women's roles have resulted in a dramatic increase in the divorce rate. In 1955 there were 25,736 divorces; in 1966, 26,576; and by 1975, 41,620 (*Statistisches Jahrbuch*, 1976). In 1976 there were 27 divorces to 10,000 marriages (Anderson, 1978). Even though the nuclear family of husband, wife, and children is still seen as preferable, there are few obstacles in the way of couples who wish a divorce. It is felt to be unseemly for a couple to remain in an undignified marriage. On the other hand, there is some feeling that many people obtain a divorce rather than work at making a success of their marriage. This is thought to be especially true of couples who marry young and divorce within a few years—a not uncommon phenomenon in the GDR.

The high divorce rate is viewed as a genuine problem. Divorce severely disrupts people's lives and is especially difficult for the children. Furthermore, the severe housing shortage often forces divorced couples to live together after the divorce, sometimes for several years, until new housing arrangements can be made. This situation creates tremendous stress for everyone in the household. However, the high divorce rate is viewed as a temporary result of the problems caused by new family roles under socialist conditions. It is definitely not viewed as a permanent feature of socialist family life.

Morgner (1975) puts the issue of the rising divorce rate and the tempo of the changes in male–female relationships in perspective when she says:

It is not a question of continuing the war between the sexes, something we have had for long enough; it is a question of finally ending this war and what may appear as a sharpening of this war can, I believe, be the prologue to peace. . . . Customs which have grown up over thousands of years cannot be changed in decades. This is an unpleasant prospect, since our lives are short. Impatience is understandable, but unfortunately not suited to great historical moments. Great historic moments last a long time. Anybody who suggests illusions about time is consciously or unconsciously working towards a nostalgic setback, which must follow disappointed hopes [p. M-10].

As the changing roles of men and women within the family are complex and difficult, so too are new roles for boys and girls. Because sex-role stereotyping begins almost at birth, roles must be changed at a very early age if genuine equality is to be achieved, and this must be accomplished within the family. There is explicit recognition that the old stereotypes have negative consequences for adult life. Kuhrig (1973) points out: "For the socialist society it is not in the first place a question of bringing up girls or boys but of developing socialist personalities conscious of their rights and responsibilities in all spheres of public life . . . [p. 29]."

The media, public lectures, and discussion for parents, as well as meetings with parents in the school, all stress the need to treat boys and girls equally. It is especially stressed that girls must be given the same opportunity for career development as boys. Changing the roles of boys and girls is complicated by the fact that children witness the stereotyped roles of their mothers and fathers. It is felt that this problem could be alleviated if, for example, more boys saw their fathers doing traditional women's work (Grandke, 1976).

Changes within the family are slowly taking place. Girls now see their future not merely in terms of marriage and a family but in terms of a lifelong career. However, it is now recognized that changes in many aspects of sex-role sterotyping in children will come about only in several generations and with great effort.

Family Planning and Single Mothers

Because the GDR is a socialist country and has a planned economy, the birth rate is of special importance. The birth rate in the GDR is very low, and women have access to all forms of birth control. At age 16 women who request it are give contraceptives. In 1972 the GDR passed laws permitting women to have abortions on demand at a time when the birth rate was at one of its lowest points. Abortion is treated as a medical procedure and is completely free. The provisions for sick leave from employment are the same as for any other medical problem.

Prior to 1972 women had to apply to a commission of doctors and DFD representatives (the large women's organization) for an abortion. Since the 1972 laws, however, abortion is viewed by medical and legal experts as being within the context of the health protection of women, which includes the physical, psychic, and social components of health. Accordingly, the 1972 law has the following specific provisions: Women up to the twelfth week of pregnancy can request an abortion independent of marital considerations. They alone have the right to make this decision. They have the right to free medical care, and there are no moral judgments involved. After the twelfth week, or if the woman has had an abortion within the previous 6-month period, or if there is a history of repeated abortions, then a commission must decide. Under these circumstances, abortions are performed only to save the life of the mother or for other special reasons. For example, if a patent has had an abortion within 6 months, an abortion is possible only if she was raped and the criminal act is being investigated or prosecuted. Abortion is never legal if for any reason it will endanger the health of the mother. These conditions are spelled out in detail in the law. For women under age 16, the parents must decide. If the parents can't agree, then a judge decides (Fritsche and Roth, 1975).

Abortion is not considered the desired method of family planning because there is some risk of medical complications. As of 1976, about 40 percent of all GDR women took contraceptive pills. Doctors follow these women closely to ascertain if there are any negative side effects. All women who have abortions are given information on contraceptives.

Changing the law to allow abortion on demand was a controversial step. Unlike most laws in the GDR, the law was not passed unanimously in the People's Chamber, the highest legislative body. It was understood, before the law came to a vote, that several of the religious parties would vote against it. Nevertheless it passed. Furthermore, the law passed at a time of a serious decline in the birth rate. The birth rate was only 13.9 in 1970, down from 16.5 in 1965 (Winkler, 1978).

There were a number of reasons why the law was passed despite opposition and the misgivings of planners. In an extensive interview, Dr. Klaus Peter Orth (1977) a professor of family law at Humboldt University, told me that one of the main reasons the law was passed was that women made it quite clear they wanted the option of legal abortion. More and more women applying to the commissions for permission to have an abortion were using reasons that satisfied the legal requirements but that had no basis in reality.

Anita Grandke, another family law professor at Humboldt University, explicitly stated that equal rights for women demands the end of dependence on biological accident (Grandke, 1972). It had become clear that the need for population and the protection of women's health were not furthered to any great extent by the antiabortion laws. Unwanted pregnancies were being terminated illegally in great numbers. According to Allendorf (1975), the following ideas concerning abortion had been crystallized by 1972: "Unwanted pregnancies have always been terminated (in millions of cases in a doubtful way). The question should therefore not be: termination, yes or no? Rather it should be: interruption with the best possible protection of women's health, yes or no? [p. 182]."

Grandke (1972) pointed out that the conflict caused by an unwanted pregnancy takes on a qualitatively different character under socialism from that under capitalism. The conditions for the development of the family are different under socialism. All children are assured of equal education, guaranteed employment, social status, health care, and the like regardless of whether the mother is married. However, the number and spacing of children in harmony with the parents' wishes was seen as an unmet need before the new abortion laws. It was felt that to force women to apply for an abortion was placing in the hands of a commission a decision that properly belonged in the family.

Immediately after the 1972 laws went into effect, there was a dramatic increase in the number of abortions. They went up 600 percent, and the birth rate dropped by 24 percent, or 57,000 births (Marquit, 1978). This rate has leveled off, and now there are fewer abortions. Since 1975 the birth rate has gone up following the implementation of two new social policies: (1) Young, newly married couples were given interest-free loans in 1976, after which the birth rate immediately rose 10 percent; (2) women having their second child were given a paid one-year's leave of absence in 1977.

From this discussion certain factors stand out with respect to family planning in the GDR. Women have complete freedom of choice as to the number and spacing of their children, which reflects the philosophy that family planning should be voluntary, not compulsory. This concept is seen as essential for women's equality and is in harmony with the spirit of equality embodied in the Family Code. The GDR instituted abortion on demand at a time when the birth rate was at one of its lowest points. To raise the birth rate, economic stimuli, rather than coercion or pressure, were used.

There is absolutely no stigma on either the mother or child if a woman decides to have a child and not marry the father. This was not always the case. During the 1950s, a couple could be forced into marriage to "give the baby a name" and the girl might have to give up her schooling or vocational training (Mitchell, 1974). Public opinion on both these matters has completely changed. The government has always given preferential treatment to mothers without husbands. Among the forms this treatment has taken are extra pay if the single parent must stay home with a sick child, preference in available crèche space, and income to support the family if there is no crèche space available.

WORK AND FAMILY

One major goal of GDR policy makers is to eliminate role conflict for women who work and have a family, just as men experience relatively little conflict between working and being a parent. This reduction in role conflict is viewed as the responsibility of the entire society, not just of individual women. Paragraph 3 of the Labor Code (*GDR Review*, 1978) stipulates, for example, that "The socialist state ensures that conditions are created which enable women to measure up to their equal status at work and in vocational development, and which help them combine their professional activities with their family duties ever more successfully [p. 41]."

This ideal of a conflict-free, unified role has not yet been realized in practice. At the *present* stage of development of women's emancipation in the GDR, women carry a double burden and thus must work especially hard. The Institute for Market Research in the GDR found, for example, that in 1900 households housework took an average of 47.1 hours a week, of which women did 37.1 hours (or more than 80 percent), husbands did 6.1 hours, and other family members 3.9 hours (Allendorf, 1975).

Nevertheless, the GDR has done as much to help women combine a family with a full-fledged career as any country in the world. In this section I discuss (1) social policies that have been implemented to enable women to work and have a family, (2) the as-yet-unsolved problems of combining the two roles, and (3) the prospects for the future.

The following excerpt from *Gutne Morgen, Du Schoene* (Wander, 1977) illustrates some aspects of the daily routine of a working mother.

I'm the first to get up, before 5 A.M., wash up, curl my hair, you know, moisten it and put it in curlers. Then while I'm busy it dries; I make sandwiches and the kids slowly get up. Dieter helps to get them dressed, looks out for everything, and then we have breakfast together. I still wash up and Catherine takes out the garbage pail. Dieter leaves at 6:45. I take Andre and Sven along; the kindergarten and nursery are located next to each other. My working hours normally run until 3:30 since I work three-quarters of an hour less than others because of three children. Usually Catherine is home before I am, I pick up the two small ones, then we have coffee together. Andre, I tell you, is very considerate, he runs through the apartment when I am exhausted: "Mom, lie down on the couch, I'll do everything for you today." I call on the two bigger ones more now, you know, Dieter is gone much of the time. We get the Trabant [car] next year, and the garden costs money too. So he moonlights. . . . Things just pile up at home, which makes me nervous. I mean, we wanted the garden; where else with the children, they have to be able to move around. It used to be just land outside of town; now we have cleared it, dug a well, built an arbor for sleeping, all with our own hands, what do you think?! [p. 118].

Special Provisions for Women Workers

Child care is critical because, without child care, it is simply not possible for the vast majority of women to work. In the GDR the problem of child care for working mothers is all but solved, and child-care facilities have been systematically expanded as can be seen in Table 5.2.

By 1980 92 percent of all kindergarten-age children (ages 3 to 6) were in state-supported kindergartens. Presently, places for crèche-age children, who may be as young as several weeks, are still relatively scarce, with preference being given to infants of women without husbands and of students. Many parents have to travel long distances to a crèche with an

Table 5.2. **Percentage of All Children Cared for in State-Supported Child-Care Facilities**

	1965	1970	1975	1977	1980
Crèche (under 3 years)	18.7	29.1	50.8	60.1	61
Kindergarten (3 to 6 years)	52.8	64.5	84.6	89.2	92
After-school programs (7 to 10 years)	44.0	48.6	69.8	77.4	

Source: Einheit, 1978; Olivier, 1981; Statistical Pocketbook of the GDR, 1979).

available space. This is not true of kindergarten programs, however; kindergarten facilities are in abundant evidence in all residential areas, and most kindergartners can attend school within a few minutes' walk from home. Kindergarten facilities are also located in places of employment.

All the child-care centers are virtually free of charge. There is a nominal fee for food; for three meals a day, the cost is 20¢. Kindergartens and crèches are open from 6:30 A.M. to 7 P.M. to accommodate parents with varying work schedules. Breakfast is served at 8:00 A.M., so children must arrive no later than 8:00. Most parents pick up their children by 4:00 P.M. or shortly thereafter, although children can stay later if necessary.

Child care in kindergartens and crèches is seen as an opportunity for education as well as care and is organized according to a central plan. In the early years of the GDR, the teachers devised their own programs. It was soon found, however, that the children learned only things that were the teacher's special strengths, such as music or art. Now a broad, well-balanced program is centrally planned.

In the kindergarten my daughter attended, great stress was placed on helping other children, cleanliness, and sharing various responsibilities for the routine care of the kindergarten—setting the tables for meals, taking out and putting back the cots for nap time, and so on. There were many beautiful toys and games. The playground in the back contained a garden where each kindergarten section had a plot of land and grew vegetables or flowers. And the children went on trips to puppet shows and children's plays. The teacher met with the parents on a regular basis, and there was a group of parents who helped out in special ways. Holidays were celebrated with great festivity; the rooms were decorated gaily, and there were many presents for the children provided by the kindergarten. Of all the parents I talked with, there was universal agreement about the excellent quality of the kindergartens.

The care of children in the crèches poses certain problems that have not yet been solved. For example, although a doctor sees the children on a weekly basis (they receive all their shots from crèche doctors), illnesses among children of that age spread quickly throughout the group.

When a child is sick, it is still usually the mother who stays home because, aside from tradition about the mother's role, her pay is usually lower than her husband's. Parents do receive sick pay for the time they are at home with sick children, and some fathers do stay home for extended periods to care for children who are ill.

Another problem that arose with crèche children—one that has been solved—concerns the developmental progress of children who attended crèches as opposed to children who did not attend them. It was found that the crèche attenders were developmentally behind the noncrèche attenders: As a result, there are now definite day-by-day plans worked out to enhance the development of crèche attenders. The most recent comparison of crèche and noncrèche children shows that crèche children now are more developmentally advanced than noncrèche attenders.

Another problem that has been solved, at least partially, is that of infants who are not suited to crèche attendance. Researchers have found that in some instances babies do not thrive in crèches but only at home. According to one head of a crèche with whom I had an extensive discussion, the researchers have now developed tests that can determine for which babies this is the case.

There is the question of the woman's satisfaction with her mother role if her infant is taken care of full time in a crèche. I saw no survey data on this. Most women whose children were age 12 and over had not used crèches because there were few of them when their children were infants. However, the central issue is that with the advent of plentiful child-care centers that are practically free and well run women are able to make the decision as to whether to work, unrestricted by lack of these facilities. Clearly, the decision will always involve many factors, including the mother's personality, the particular child, the state of the mother's career, and her career commitment.

Other social policies that help women to reconcile family and work roles are pregnancy provisions and maternity leaves. Marquit (1978) states: "When a woman learns she is pregnant, any number of protections immediately go into effect; her job cannot be phased out or terminated until some minimum time has elapsed after her return to work from maternity leave. If her job is particularly arduous or involves occupational hazards that would adversely affect her health or the future of the child, she must be transferred (at no loss in average pay) to lighter work or a safer environment [p. 168]." The new Labor Code in the GDR extends a number of protective regulations hitherto covering only expectant and nursing mothers, to all mothers with children under one year of age (*GDR Review*, 1978).

Care during pregnancy and at the birth of a child, as with all medical expenses, is completely free of charge. New in the 1978 Labor Code is the provision for working mothers to be paid their average wages while attending ante- and post-natal centers when this cannot be arranged outside of working hours. Infant mortality in the GDR has been reduced from 13.1 percent in 1946 to 1.7 percent in 1973; maternal mortality is practically nonexistent. Both infant and maternal mortality are among the lowest in Europe (*Women Under Socialism*, 1974).

Maternity leaves are designed so that women are able to resume work after the birth of their children with as little disruption as possible in their work. During a mother's maternity leave, she can continue training and education courses. The enterprise that employs her treats her as a full-time worker there, and she can use all the facilities and is invited to social functions and club activities. This is true even if the mother takes an extended maternity leave of up to three years.

There have been considerable changes in the duration of maternity leaves granted since 1950. In 1950 a woman received 11 weeks of paid maternity leave to which she could add her vacation pay. In 1963 this was raised to 14 weeks of paid leave, and in 1972 it was raised again to 18 weeks of paid leave. At the end of the leave and vacation time, the mother could stay home without pay until the child's first birthday or until the child's third birthday if no crèche space could be found. As of May 1976, maternity provisions were again changed. A woman having her first child receives 26 weeks' paid maternity leave (six weeks before the birth and 20 weeks after the birth). Mothers having a second or further child are entitled to 26 weeks of maternity leave on full pay and then the equivalent of sick leave pay until the child is one year old. Thus, in 1976 the GDR adopted a policy for a year's paid maternity leave when women give birth to second or further children.

   Maternity benefits were extended for a number of reasons. Among these are the shortage of crèche space and some feelings that very young babies may be better off in a home setting. Extended maternity benefits were designed not only to help women reconcile their employment role with their role of motherhood but to encourage families to have more children as well. Policy planners recognized that the GDR's low birth rate, one of the lowest in Europe, was in part caused by the difficulties of combining the various roles and in part by the economic considerations. Prior to May 1976, for example, a woman who stayed home a year with her second baby lost the income she would have earned if she had not had a baby. The present government policy of paying almost a full year's salary to women having a second child is thus viewed as a way to lessen the economic discrimination for families having several children. The first full year that the new policy was in effect saw a dramatic increase in the birth rate, which rose from 11.6 per thousand in 1976 to 13.3 per thousand in 1977, an increase of 24 percent (Winkler, 1978).

   A number of other special provisions for women are set forth in the Labor Code (*Joint Decision*, 1976). As of 1976, the working week for mothers with two or more children under age 16 has been reduced from 44 to 40 hours with no loss of pay. (Prior to 1976 this provision was available only to mothers with three or more children.) Another new provision extends the monthly paid day off (the household day) to all full-time working women, whether or not they have children. (Previously, this provision applied only to women with children.) Presently, an employed, single father can also take a monthly household day, provided he has the consent of the union and the enterprise manager.[7]

   These provisions have produced some negative effects. Renate Mitchell, (1974), GDR mother of three and an interpreter, puts it very well, as follows:

---

[7]Women with two children were not the only workers to receive a 40-hour week. People working in a three-shift or a rotating-shift system received a 40-hour week simultaneously. Government planners expect that, as the economy develops, working hours will be systematically reduced for all workers to a 40-hour week and eventually to an even shorter week, all with no loss in pay.

Of course, socialism does not mean that everything in the garden is lovely. Things well-meant in themselves can sometimes bring unforeseen difficulties. In 1973 the government granted mothers with three or more children shorter working hours with full pay, to give them more time with their children. Everybody was delighted until they found that the old-fashioned concept of 'mother's special role' was actually strengthened by this. Discussion is on the way as to how to right the balance again [4].

Thus, although these measures were instituted to ease the burden of women, they also had the effect—not anticipated by their planners—of locking the women ever more tightly into their domestic roles. Among the solutions that are being suggested is that no more of these special provisions be accorded women and/or that families choose which member—husband or wife—should take the reduced work (Grandke, 1976).

It must be emphasized that the role of men is changing with respect to helping with children and household chores. Younger men are doing far more domestic work than older men ever did. Thus, if in the future, families are given the choice of which person, husband or wife, is to have household time off, it is quite likely that they will increasingly choose the husband.

Household Work

There has been a marked improvement in a whole range of services and facilities in recent years that help reduce the burden of domestic work on families, especially on women. The number of supermarkets has doubled since 1968 (*Women in the GDR*, 1975). In 1977 95 percent of all families had refrigerators compared to only 7 percent in 1960. In the same year 78 percent of all families had washing machines, compared to 6 percent in 1960 (*Einheit*, 1978). Commercial laundry services had been greatly expanded by 1975; 25 percent of all families sent their linen to laundries. In Berlin, this figure is now up to 50 percent. Dry cleaning services have also been greatly expanded.

Most people have their large meal of the day at their place of work or at school. In 1977 75 percent of all students ate a hot meal at school (Zadek, 1978). These meals are so heavily subsidized that they cost the workers and students very little money. In addition, this means that the family meal in the evening can be a light one and the burden of cooking at home is lessened. On weekends families have large meals together.

It was thought that substantial improvements in facilities, services, and electrical equipment would reduce the amount of time required for household duties by women. Yet recent investigations show that the time women spend on household chores has remained constant in spite of these improvements. Two factors are involved. First, certain aspects of material life have not kept pace with these improvements. Shopping, for example, remains very time-consuming; there are long waiting lines at many stores and a shortage of employees to wait on customers (this shortage is a reflection of the broader shortage of labor throughout the GDR). Few families have cars (32 percent in 1976), and although public transportation is excellent, the lack of a car means that errands are all the more time-consuming. This situation has improved with the opening of supermarkets in almost all neighborhoods and the inclusion of a variety of stores in all new housing developments. Even so, material conditions will have to continue to improve if the time involved in household work is to be substantially reduced.

A second factor is subjective: Just how clean is a clean house? This is a matter of dispute. Many women told me they thought other women they knew were too "house proud" and spent more time than necessary in keeping a spotless house. However, there was also a great deal of ambivalence about this. A recently divorced man had great scorn for women who did what he saw as unnecessary housework. He felt that some women were "house proud" only because they had nothing else to be proud of; that if a woman was creative in her career, she wouldn't need to measure her self-worth by how good a housekeeper she was.

The issue is more complicated than this comment suggests, however. It is a Northern European cultural tradition to have a spotless house; order, neatness, and cleanliness are emphasized from the time children are very young. Although GDR living space per family is small, immaculate housekeeping is inevitably very time-consuming. It may be that in time this tradition won't have such a hold on people, especially as women increasingly identify themselves with their occupations outside the home.

As a temporary solution to time-consuming housework, other household members, especially the husbands, are enjoined to "share the slavery." In the long range, however, the equal sharing of household work by husband and wife is not viewed as the ultimate solution, because household tasks are considered ennervating and uncreative, a domestic slavery. Thus, as Allendorf (1975) puts it, "A genuine solution can only be reached if most domestic work can be done outside the home [193]." Planners foresee the day when household service will become a highly developed branch of modern industry.

Part-Time Work

Not all women workers work full time. Fully 30 percent of the women who work are part-time workers. This is one way women have of reconciling their family roles and their employment. Yet part-time work is not considered a satisfactory solution, and there is considerable encouragement through the mass media for women to work full time.

Among the major negative side effects of part-time work is the fact that women are not fully integrated into the life of the factory, office, or school. Furthermore, part-time work may consolidate the traditional division of labor in the family. On the other hand, in a marriage in which the husband does not want his wife to work and refuses to help in the home, part-time work may be the only avenue through which the woman can work at all.

There has been some fluctuation in the number of women who work part time. These fluctuations seem to be the direct result of changes in social policy. For example, in 1967 the GDR reduced the working week from a 45-hour, six-day week to a 43¾-hour five-day week, thus lengthening each work day. Many women felt the impact of the lengthened day and switched to part-time work. In 1972 when women with three or more children were given a 40-hour week, 20 percent of those working part-time switched to full-time work (Menschik & Leopold, 1974). It is foreseen that the number of women choosing part-time rather than full-time work will diminish only when more of the problems associated with the double burden are alleviated.

The double burden is perceived as temporary. Morgner (1975) puts it very well when she says, "Unfortunately there is no road to emancipation which can avoid, for a time at least, the double load [M-10]." Women entered the labor market before the conditions existed for them to combine their different roles with ease. Yet participation in the labor market was seen as a necessary first step, as a precursor to real emancipation. It is through work in the economic sector that a woman gains self-confidence in herself and is more respected by men. Partly as a result of her employment outside the home, women are seen today as complete people, able to live on their own without men.

The double burden for women will be a thing of the past only when the following conditions are more fully realized: Men must more equally share the running of the household. Material conditions must be raised to such a level that running a household is less time-consuming. Women must become more invested in their careers and less invested in a spotless home. There is considerable progress in all these areas, and every reason to believe it will continue. It is just a matter of time until the ideal of a unified role is realized.

SUMMARY AND CONCLUSIONS

Remarkable changes have taken place in the role of women in the GDR in the last 30 years. These changes are a direct result of the socialist government's commitment to women's equality and its ability (because it has a centrally planned economy) to rapidly put into place social policies affecting people's lives. That the government is completely committed to the emancipation of women is reflected in every aspect of life. Menschik and Leopold (1974) express the essence of this process in the conclusion to their book: "There was not one economic plan, law or regulation which did not set up a new image of a working woman and at the same time take social measures to make the new image possible even when the GDR was hardly able financially to do this [p. 191]."

Tremendous inequalities in all areas of life have been significantly reduced, if not eliminated. Differences in education between men and women under 30 have been eliminated. The number of unskilled women workers was reduced by 17 percent between 1971 and 1973 after the implementation of measures making it possible for women to receive training without interfering with other aspects of their lives.

Almost 90 percent of all women of working age are employed. They are definitely not part of a reserve labor force. The number of women in paid work has doubled since 1949. Women are not working out of absolute necessity. It is still possible to have a good standard of living with only one member of the family employed. Equal pay for equal work has been a reality in the GDR since 1949.

Women are employed in all branches of industry and are moving in significant numbers into fields traditionally dominated by men. They have also gained a strong foothold in such prestigious fields as medicine, law, and high public office. Effective and strictly enforced affirmative action programs for women are systematically increasing their participation in management, furthering their education, and improving their working conditions.

With respect to family life, the Family Code and the constitution wipe out all statutory inequalities between men and women within the family. Husband and wife are enjoined to share equally in household tasks and child rearing and to help each other to develop to their full potential in all aspects of life. Furthermore, the state has accepted as its responsibility the creation of institutions and provisions whereby a woman can combine a full professional life with that of wife and mother. Accordingly, there is virtually free child care, paid maternity leave, guaranteed jobs at the end of maternity leaves, and many other provisions designed to help women mesh their roles as mother and homemaker with their careers.

Tremendously impressive in their own right, these accomplishments help put into perspective the many problems that must still be overcome. In times of great social change it is not possible for all sectors of the society to change simultaneously, in harmony and at the same pace. The GDR has attempted to end all inequalities between men and women, create a highly educated population, develop a highly industrialized economy, and elevate the standard of living for the entire population. These goals have by and large been accomplished in the 30 years since the founding of the GDR. However, changes in some of these areas are out of phase with changes in others. Furthermore, solving one set of problems often creates further problems that then must be dealt with.

One of the most persistent problems is that, although formal problems of inequality between men and women have been solved, changes in people's attitudes and feelings have not occurred to the same extent. This is particularly true of men who find it difficult to give up their male superiority and to share equally in household tasks and decision making. Consequently, women still do 80 percent of all the work in the home. This situation may actually be exacerbated by some of the social policies designed to lessen women's current double burden. For example, women with two children work shorter hours, and all women have one paid household day a month. These measures may have inadvertently contributed to strengthening women's traditional role within the family.

Although a number of women also have quite traditional views of their roles, the majority have made the shift to the emancipated role model. This is particularly true among younger women. The difference in the rate of attitude change between men and women has caused tremendous strains in marital relationships, resulting in increasingly high divorce rates. The high divorce rate in turn has exacerbated an already severe housing shortage and created many one-parent households with attendant problems for the women and children involved.

Women entered the labor force in large numbers before there were material supports for them to do so easily. Today, child-care facilities for children aged 3 to 10 are so plentiful that care for children in these age groups is no longer an issue. Care for children under age 3, however, is still a problem because there are not enough facilities.

Household duties still consume almost 40 hours a week because labor-saving devices and shopping facilities are not yet plentiful and "house-proud" attitudes persist among women.

Women are still concentrated in traditional female occupations in health, education, and light industry. As a consequence their average income is lower than men's. Women are not allowed to work at jobs that are viewed as detrimental to their health. These issues will not be completely resolved until there are more attitude changes regarding women's work and until technological developments make it safe for women to work in all aspects of heavy industry.

New social policies giving women extended leave or fewer working hours were not instituted without difficulties at their places of work in part because of the severe labor shortage. When women having second children were given a year's leave with pay, the work quotas were not necessarily cut. This is a particular problem in enterprises with a high percentage of women workers. Similarly, work quotas were not cut when women with children were given shorter weekly working hours. Maternity leave for a woman may mean that other members of her work team must postpone leaves for advanced education and research. In all these instances women have the unquestionable right to maternity leave and shorter working hours. It is co-workers and management who have the responsibility of coping with her absence.

When progress for women in the GDR is balanced against difficulties and contradictions, it is nevertheless clear that the most significant accomplishment is freedom women have in the three most important areas of their lives.

They have the right to employment and are given every opportunity for advancement and further education. They have the right to determine the number and spacing of their children. They have the right to marry, divorce, or remain single with or without children with no alteration in social status. Thus, women are no longer dependent on men for either social status or economic support.

The changing role of women is a process that is still evolving. At first, many men as well as women were opposed to women working, the placing of children in child-care centers, and women in positions of leadership. Today, all these are taken for granted by all segments of the population, but the acceptance of these role changes came about gradually.

Three generations of women are living side by side in the GDR who have developed into adults under extremely different social conditions. Each generation of women has experienced considerable changes in the female role but in different ways. A composite picture of how the generations have responded to the changes would look something like this. Older women, working and respected in their work roles, are delighted with their new position; a whole new world has opened up for them. They are resigned and rather philosophical about the lack of help they receive from their husbands. It is difficult to generalize about women in the middle group. Some have found it easy to combine work and a family while others feel the double burden weighing heavily on them. Young women take for granted equal employment opportunities and all the amenities of free child care and other benefits. But they are impatient when anything keeps them from advancing in their careers, and they fully expect to be able to combine a career and a family. They also expect a more equal partnership with their husbands in all matters and are not resigned to accepting men in their traditional roles.

The life course perspective described by Giele is applicable to GDR women. Although all the women will remain in the labor force during their entire adult lives, the meshing of their roles as wives and mothers with a career means at the present time that the energy they devote to their careers is tempered by the timing of other events in their lives. For example, it was my observation that the age and number of children a woman had influenced whether she worked full or part time, continued her education, or volunteered to take additional training to become a manager. This is true despite the fact that the GDR has instituted numerous social policies designed to minimize the effects of family on a woman's career.

It has not been possible in this chapter to trace the impact of social policy on the physical and psychological aspect of women's lives In her chapter Gilligan postulates that men and women in the United States develop differently psychologically. It remains for another study to determine to what extent this is true in the GDR. Presently, women in the GDR are still expected to take the primary responsibility for nurturance of the family. However, role sharing of nurturing is certainly much more widespread in the 30 and younger age group. It is quite probable that for those people growing up entirely under socialist conditions the psychological development of men and women is more similar than in the older group.

What of the future? There is every reason to expect that the changing role of women will continue in the same direction it has taken in the last 30 years. Women will continue to move into more diverse occupations, some of which are now dominated by men. This process may accelerate in the future because the gap between men and women's education is closed for the under-30 generation and industry is rapidly automating. I completely agree with the assessment of Menschik and Leopold (1974) when they say: "The day is not far off when one asks not whether a man or woman is suitable for the job but which of the two is most capable of the job [p. 192]." The development of a unified woman's role combining participation in the labor market with a family will also be easier as a result of the increased emphasis on changing men's roles and the steady increase in material goods and services for the household.

Projected increases in productivity will also mean higher standards of living not only in terms of labor-saving devices for the home but shorter working hours, longer vacations, and more vacation places. This will make a qualitative difference in people's lives, allowing families more time to enjoy each other's company. For all these reasons there is every reason to expect that the two most serious problems still facing GDR women—the gap between formal equality and people's attitudes, and the double burden for women—will be solved.

REFERENCES

Allendorf, M. 1975. *Women in Socialist Society*. New York: International Publishers.

Anderson, E. 1978. Review of *Guten Morgen, Du Schoene* by Maxie Wander. "In These Times" **22** (March 8–14): p. 22.

Birnbaum, E. 1977. Education Director of Cable Factory. Interview. March 28.

Democratic German Report. 1975. "Women as Managers: Is It Easy?" January 29, p. 12.

Directives for the Five Year Plan for the GDR's National Economic Development, 1976–1980. 1976. Issued by the 9th Congress of the Socialist Unity Party of German. Dresden: Verlag Zeit Im Bild.

Ecklein, J.L. 1982. "Obstacles to Understanding the Changing Role of Women in Socialist Countries." *Insurgent Sociologist* (in press).

Effective Facharbeiter-ausbildung von Arbeiterinnen. 1976. Berlin: Verlag Tribune: 5–18.

Einheit. 1977. March, p. 230.

Einheit. 1978. July/August, p. 848.

Felgentreau, M. 1977. Deputy Head of the Women's Commission of the FDGB. Interview. April 27.

Fritsche, M. and Rothe, J. 1975. "Sozialmedizinische Aspekte in der Schwanger-schaftsunterbrechung" (Socio-Medical Aspects in the Interruption of Pregnancy). *Zeitschrift für Arzliche Fortbildung*, pp. 1131–1136.

GDR Review. 1978. "Special Rights for Working Women and Mothers." March, p. 41.

GDR Review. 1979. "Our State Keeps Its Word: A Review of Social-Welfare Policy in the GDR." January, p. 1.

Gesestzblatt des DDR. September 27, 1973.

Grandke, A., H. Kuhrig, W. Weise. 1966. "Public Opinion in the German Democratic Republic on the Development of the Family and Family Law and Its Influence on the Content of the New Family Code." Unpublished pamphlet.

Grandke, A. 1972. "Firming Up Equality and Furthering Conscious Parenthood about the Law on Abortion." *Neue Justiz* November, pp. 313–319.

———. 1976. "Women in Education of the Family." At Colloquium on Women in Family Upbringing. March, Humboldt University: Berlin.

Gransow, V. 1978a. "Cultural Needs and the Working Class in the German Democratic Republic." GDR Symposium at the World Fellowship Center, Conway, NH. June 16–23.

Gransow, V. 1978b. Personal Communication to Joan Ecklein, July 1, 1978.

"Joint Decision on the Further Systematic Improvement of Working and Living Conditions in the GDR from 1976 to 1980." Adopted by the SED Central Committee, the FDGB National Executive, and the GDR Council of Ministers May 27, 1976. Pamphlet. Berlin: Panorama.

Kuhrig, H. 1973. "Equal Rights for Women in the German Democratic Republic." Berlin: GDR Committee for Human Rights.

———. 1974. "On the Development of the Social Conditions for the Training of Women Workers in the GDR." 8th World Congress of Sociology. Toronto, Canada. August 17–24.

———. 1976. "Das Internationale Jahr der Frau und Probleme der Qualifizierung von Arbeiterinnen". *Effektive Facharbeiter-ausbildung von Arbeiterinnen*. Berlin: Verlag Tribune, pp. 5–18.

Marquit, E. 1978. *The Socialist Countries*. Minneapolis: Marxist Educational Press.

Menschik, J. and E. Leopold. 1974. *Gretchens Rote Schwestern*. Frankfurt am Main: Fischer Taschenbuch Verlag.

Mensh, E., and Harry Mensh. 1978. *Behind the Scenes in Two Worlds*. New York: International Publishers.

Mitchell, R. 1974. "As Good As You Make It." Berlin: Unpublished.

Morgner, I. 1975. Interview in *Frankfurter Rundschau*. FRG: August. Quoted in *Daily World*, November 8, 1975: M-10.

Olivier, K. 1981. Statistics Based on a Report from Central Office of Statistics for the GDR. Personal communication to Joan L. Ecklein, June 18.

Orth, K.P. 1977. Professor of Family Law Humboldt University, Berlin. GDR. Interview. February 17.

Romero, C. 1978. "The Fiction of Marriage—On the Treatment of Love and

Marriage in the GDR Novel." GDR Symposium at the World Fellowship Center, Conway, NH. June 16–23.

Rueschemeyer, M. 1977. "The Demands of Work and the Human Quality of Marriage: An Exploratory Study of Professionals in Two Socialist Societies." *Journal of Comparative Family Studies* (2):243–255.

Shaffer, H. 1981. *Women in the Two Germanies: A Comparison of a Socialist and a Non-Socialist Society.* Elmsford, NY: Pergamon Press.

Slepack, D. 1976. "Women in the German Democratic Republic: A Field Study and Comparative Analysis of Sex Bias in USA and GDR Children's Readers." Ph.D. Dissertation, University of Cincinnati. Ann Arbor: University Microfilms International.

Statistisches Jahrbuch der Deutschen Demokratischen Republik. 1976. Berlin: Staatsverlag der Deutchen Demokratischen Republik.

Statistical Pocket Book of the German Democratic Republic. 1976 and 1979. Berlin: State Central Administration for Statistics. State Publishing House of the German Democratic Republic.

Thönnessen, W. 1973. *The Emancipation of Women: The Rise and Decline of the Women's Movement in German Social Democracy 1863–1933.* Glasgow: Robert MacLehose and Co.

Wander, M. 1977. *Guten Morgen, Du Schoene* (Good Morning, My Beauty). Berlin: Der Morgen.

What Is Life Like in the GDR?: Living Standards and Way of Life Under Socialism: 1977. Berlin: Panorama.

Winkler, G. 1978. "Principles and Aims of the GDR's Population Policy." 9th World Congress of Sociology, Uppsala, Sweden. August 14–19.

Women and Socialism, 2nd edition, rev. 1976. Berlin: Panorama.

Women in the GDR: Facts and Figures. 1975. Dresden: Verlag Zeit im Bild.

Women Under Socialism, 1974. Berlin: Panorama.

Youth-Education-Profession. 1978. "What is Being Done for Young Marriages." May 22, p. 80.

Zadek, A. 1978. "Frauen im Gesellschaftlichen Leben der DDR" *Einheit.* July/August, pp. 849–850.

CHAPTER 6

Future Research and Policy Questions

JANET ZOLLINGER GIELE
Heller School
Brandeis University

In 1962 Thomas Kuhn wrote an influential book about the history of science, *The Structure of Scientific Revolutions*. Kuhn's thesis was itself revolutionary. Science, according to Kuhn, rather than representing the simple accretion of known facts, is governed by its central organizing paradigms. Facts that fail to fit a predominant paradigm are either overlooked or explained away; only the compatible findings are codified. The old paradigm prevails until discrepant facts become so numerous and alternative theories so compelling that a new paradigm replaces the old. A good example is the Copernican revolution that substituted a model of the solar system for the reigning earth-centered theory of the universe.

On a smaller scale such a scientific revolution has occurred in the study of women's roles. The central organizing paradigm has had to shift because it can no longer be assumed that women's place is in the home. Women's presence in the labor force, the rising divorce rate, and the growing numbers of older women living alone have strained Parsons and Bales' (1955) established model of the nuclear family in which a man was the instrumental leader and a woman the expressive leader. Instead, a new theory is called for that will help researchers identify and explain the pressing problems of women in coming decades. How can women gain equal treatment in the labor force? What will happen to children if mothers work? Can men's roles change also? What will become of older women, and how can their lives even now be planned so that they can avoid poverty and isolation?

These pressing current questions were not foreseen by the sociological theorists of the 1950s. Their model of women's lives was based on the changes that had accompanied industrialization over a century before. The development of textile factories had forced apart the traditional identity between work and family life. Men went into the work place, women stayed in the home. The years after World War II merely reinforced this model.

199

After the hardships and sacrifices of the wartime era, young couples turned with relief to a celebration of family life and the goal of suburban comfort. The model presupposed a husband/father in school or a career and the wife/mother at home or in a merely temporary job that would tide the family over while the man finished his education. Parsons and Bales' instrumental-expressive dichotomy helped to interpret this new phenomenon, a type of marital partnership that was heretofore uncommon in rural and small town society where couples were supported by farms and small business. The burgeoning professions and technical occupations of the 1950s and 1960s actually represented an advance in the occupational specialization of modern society.

For a time it appeared that, like the occupational world, the family too was becoming more specialized, only that its focus was in the expressive or socioemotional realm of stabilizing adult personalities and socializing children rather than in the economy or production. The socioemotional functions of the wife/mother and the tasks of the nuclear family had become more specialized. During the 1950s the family shed many aspects of household production—gardening, sewing, canning, and preserving. Entertaining increased, however, and, most of all, the investment in reproduction and childrearing. The 1950s thus appeared to be yet another refined variation on a theme first sounded during the Industrial Revolution. The functions of the family that had earlier included both economic and reproductive tasks were being separated or differentiated into two streams, one that was now diverted into the work place and was associated with the male role, the other that remained in the home and became the reason-for-being of the female role.

The great trouble with this concept of instrumental and expressive roles was that it utterly failed to predict the further changes in sex roles that were already in motion. Young women graduating from college in the 1950s were supposedly members of a silent generation, dutifully marrying quickly, putting their husbands through school, and then having lots of children and staying home for the rest of their lives. Yet today this generation has higher continuous rates of participation in the labor force than any women of their age in American history.

The failure of the earlier functionalist paradigm (it was "functional" to have a separation of the male instrumental and female expressive roles) to predict and explain this massive migration of women into the labor force created precisely the conditions that were ripe for a scientific revolution. The old theoretical model had outlived its usefulness. A new paradigm had to be found.

At just this point a concept introduced earlier in this volume began to assume growing importance. This was the idea of a potential for equality between the sexes accompanied by *crossover between specialized roles*. The crossover metaphor suggested bridges between different territories that connected domains never entirely merged with each other but that permitted movement to occur across the boundaries. The crossover concept represented a sociological advance not only in popular understanding but in role differentiation theories as well. First, it implied that equality need not result in de-differentiation, or movement back to a simpler society, but can be built on the specialization and boundaries between territories that are already in place. (In fact, specialization may be a prerequisite to the flexibility and interchangeability of tasks that permits crossover.) Second, the crossover concept made room for coexistence of a variety of values, roles, and functions, all of which are necessary to the larger social system. Thus movement into one type of role or function need not, and indeed probably should not, always take place in only one direction.

Convergence on the crossover concept has come slowly and painfully. Its two major implications are still subjects for controversy: (1) that equality builds on further differentiation as well as de-differentiation, and (2) that equality can be built on recognition of differences as well as sameness. Nevertheless, the course of research on changing sex roles since 1960 bears out my contention that the crossover theme is the major new paradigm now used for understanding contemporary sex role change and shaping future policies (Giele, 1980c).

The evidence for this new paradigm may be found first in the major feminist writings of our era. In 1963 Betty Friedan was the first to criticize the "functionalist freeze" in the theory of sex roles for which Parsons and others were responsible. Close on her heels came Alice Rossi with her "immodest proposal" for equality between the sexes. Rossi also in 1964 criticized the functionalists for emphasizing differences between the sexes to the disadvantage of women. Rossi was among the first contemporary feminists to call for men's participation in housework and child rearing along with women's participation in the world of work. Equality between the sexes thus presupposed a crossover or interpenetration of the functions heretofore assigned to one gender or the other. The way out of the functionalist freeze was not to return to a simpler society (de-differentiation) but progress toward an even more flexible and interchangeable array of roles. In her book on work and family published in 1977 Rosabeth Moss Kanter in fact demonstrated that such interpenetration of the instrumental and expressive worlds has already begun. Informal expressive ties exist in the work place; rationality, planning, and instrumental activities in the home.

My own interpretation of these shifting intellectual currents is that not just the sociological theories have changed, but society and sex roles have also changed. In the postwar era many tasks, whether cooking a meal in the home with packaged foods or driving a big bus with power steering, became more specialized; many jobs were broken into several more precise operations, some of which could be done by nonexperts or by machinery. The result was that many tasks could then be performed by persons who under the old system were unqualified.

It is now recognized that there is no necessary connection between being of one sex or another and performing instrumental or expressive roles. It is quite common for women to go into the labor force. And it is getting to be less unusual for men to take a larger role in child care and household tasks. The process of crossover has gone so far that it may be the healthiest situation for everyone if each woman can express and combine instrumental and expressive qualities in her own life pattern, and men likewise. The really big questions are how a fuller realization of this ideal can be brought about, given the structural constraints, the scheduling routines, and current unequal rewards to men and women.

Briefly, scholars may make two major responses to women's changed situation. One is research: to ask what are the apparent deadends and promising future questions. The other is a contribution to policy: to ask what kinds of social change should be encouraged in education, employment, and the family. This chapter treats these two dimensions in turn, by showing some of the research and policy implications in current knowledge of women in the middle years.

THE NEW RESEARCH AGENDA

Before listing the new methodologies and the content areas that the crossover paradigm suggests, it is useful to make explicit what now seem some deadends in past research efforts. The whole laborious attempt to prove one way of life happier or more satisfying than another seems a relatively fruitless research strategy. As documented in Chapter 4, there is contradictory evidence on the relative happiness of working wives, housewives, married, and single women. One recent research study confronts this issue and finds that there is no evidence of significant difference between the satisfaction of employed and nonemployed women (Wright, 1978).

Proving differences in happiness by marital status is also problematic. Zill (1978) found in a large survey of children and their families that very happily married women report less tension and depression and have children who report significantly fewer difficulties and psychological problems. But women in less happy marriages were not very different from the divorced, separated, or never married. Yet the overwhelming majority of married women reported being "very happy." Such findings are difficult to convert into any remedy for distress of either mothers or children. Should the less happily married try to make their marriages "very happy"? Should the unmarried, divorced, and separated try to enter the married state? Like employment, the marriage variable has limited capacity for explaining the process of successful life adaptation.

In place of this "old" type of question, the new research substitutes questions about life events. It calls for a finer-grained analysis of the interconnections between specific experiences in concrete settings and their overall effect on the life course. Gone are the gross ascribed categories of "married" or "single", "employed" or "nonemployed" for tagging the different levels of happiness or satisfaction that people achieve. Instead, the current focus is on refined studies of work histories, expected and unexpected life events, and the many possible facets of life experience that determine outcomes.

At the same time, the new research poses broader questions about coping styles, adaptation, and quality of life rather than wrestling with rough distinctions between the happy and unhappy. *The Quality of American Life* by Campbell, Converse, and Rodgers (1976) represents a major landmark in this more refined analysis of happiness. Using national survey data, the investigators show clearly how concepts of happiness must be refined to ask about specific objective domains of satisfaction and well-being. Questions touch daily realities ranging all the way from work, marriage and family life to housing and personal resources. The authors show that satisfaction varies across these several domains and gives rise to more global feelings of dissatisfaction or well-being.

Other recent works probe the capacity for coping and adaptation. In his investigation of Harvard men's *Adaptation to Life,* Vaillant (1977) concludes that individuals develop different styles of dealing with stress, success, and difficulties. Some persons rise above their circumstances and give back to the world more than they receive. Others never achieve such transcendence. What accounts for the difference? In their studies of depressed women Brown and Harris (1979) show the crucial importance of early family experience and later support networks in helping the individual to ward off depression and cope with stress effectively. Also of importance is the total amount of stress (caused by poverty, role overload, marital disruption, etc.) that the person must bear.

In sum, the difference between the "old" and "new" research is in the refinement of the conceptual model for tracing the connections between an individual's earlier experience and later fate. Rather than relying primarily on marriage or employment status as principal explanatory variables, scholars now chronicle specific life events and career histories. In place of global outcomes like "happiness," they probe the many different components of a sense of well-being. Finally, they look for intervening structural conditions (such as having a confidant) or adaptive mechanisms (such as coping, mourning, etc.) that enable a person to adapt successfully.

What has transformed the research outlook is partly the changing social structure surrounding women's lives. More women are in the labor force; more women are divorced. Often within a single lifespan, several types of status are experienced by an individual woman. The crude categories of employment and marital status used in the past are inadequate for dealing with such complexity. So also are such static measures as global happiness. Instead, room must be made to accommodate not only the variety of social roles that any individual may occupy but also the twists, occasional backward turns, and ever-present possibility of accidental events that may be encountered within a single lifespan.

To better document this complexity, economists and sociologists advocate more precise measurement of work histories. Spilerman (1977) is interested in the individual's changing tastes for different facets of the work setting. Kahne (1977) would examine details of the work environment, scheduling, and interruptions in paid work. Joanne Miller (1980) has used highly sophisticated measures of job conditions and job satisfaction to discover links that are valid for each sex. She finds that time pressure and risk of job loss are associated with lower satisfaction in both sexes, but women are more sensitive to substantive complexity, dirtiness, number of hours worked, and job income than men. Men are more sensitive to job protection, closeness of supervision, organizational structure, and their position in the supervisory hierarchy than women.

In addition there is a growing interest in the predictability or accidental nature of major life events, and whether their effect is positive or negative when they occur. Gail Sheehy (1981) in a *Life* magazine article on the return of the American hostages from Iran shows the changes in the hostages' wives who had to cope with the extraordinary accident of their husband's captivity. Their normal lives were disrupted; they found themselves in turn angry, depressed, and galvanized into action. In some instances they experienced role innovations that probably would not have occurred otherwise. Sheehy's focus on the accidental nature of these events draws a distinction between normal predictable life events and unexpected crises that has recently become common in the scholarly literature (Brim, 1979; Giele, 1980a; Neugarten, 1979; Perun, 1981; Perun and Bielby, 1979; Rossi, 1980). It is not yet well understood how the impact of the two kinds of events may differ, but it appears that the individual faces greater stress and finds less help with coping in the case of the accidental than the expectable life event. The common culture lacks tried and true remedies, and new ones either have to be invented or to be done without. The result may be that friends rally around and the person copes, but anomie and isolation with destructive effects on the person are also very real possibilities.

Even among relatively predictable life events, some are inherently positive such as getting a promotion, whereas others, like loss of good health or widowhood in old age, are negative. Duncan and Morgan (1980) note that the two types of events have very different effects on the person's sense of ability to control her destiny. A preponderance of negative life events such as those found in the lives of older women is associated with a much lower sense of personal efficacy.

The New Focus on Work and Family Linkages

Past research on women, with its rough distinctions between married and nonmarried, employed and nonemployed, sought explanations for happiness in the choice *between* work and family life. The new research increasingly recognizes the *interpenetration* of work and family life and traces the activities and life events within the individual's life course that either connect or polarize these two worlds.

In her book on *Work and Family Life in the United States* Rosabeth Moss Kanter (1977) was one of the first to make explicit this theme of connection rather than separation between work and family life. It is currently a key issue in the study of women's lives. In a review of literature on the well-being of women in the middle years, Barnett and Baruch (1978) concluded that a theory was needed to link women's work conditions, their role patterns, and the stage of their family's life cycle. Kahne (1978) showed a similar convergence on the work–family theme in the economic literature. And in a more detailed bibliography Kahne and Hybels (1978) explicitly list research related to paid work, to family and nonmarket work, and related life cycle issues.

Actual empirical studies are now beginning to capitalize on this new formulation of the central questions. Barnett and Baruch (1980) are themselves engaged in an interview study of several hundred midlife Boston women, some employed, others not. They are gathering retrospective information about the women's lives and connecting past and present situations to their current sense of well-being. Elder (1974) and Bennett and Elder (1979) have used historical methods based on detailed longitudinal information from two cohorts of women born in Berkeley and Oakland, California, in the 1920s. By linking childhood experience of economic deprivation, mother's employment inside or outside the home during the Depression, and a girl's own education and subsequent experience, they show the connections between earlier life events and later outcomes such as a woman's present family and employment status. With a similar historical interest, Perun and I, using cross-sectional data on college alumnae of different ages, are reconstructing women's changing life patterns since the turn of the century (Giele, 1973; Perun & Giele, 1982).

All these recent or ongoing studies demonstrate a common focus on relations between women's work and family lives and how the two are integrated over the life course.

Needed Methodologies

To advance the study of life events under the new theoretical model at least three types of research are needed—longitudinal, cross-cultural, and naturalistic.

1. *Longitudinal research* observes lives across time. The ideal method is to collect data from subjects at several successive points in time, as did the intensive Oakland and Berkeley studies analyzed by Elder. Surveys of the type known as *panel studies* can also be conducted, asking respondents for

information at periodic intervals. Examples of this genre include the National Longitudinal Surveys of young and mature women that began in 1967 or the Five Thousand Family Study that also began in 1967. Still another possibility, although not strictly longitudinal, is to construct life patterns retrospectively, using data collected at a single point in time.

A number of researchers have recently called for more longitudinal research of one sort or another. Specifically, persons interested in women's promotion, pay, and attachment to the labor force have suggested that detailed information on women's work histories and work environments will help to explain women's consistently lower pay (Barrett, 1979). Such a refined knowledge of actual work experience will help reveal sources of satisfaction and why women limit their work to certain occupations (Miller, 1980; Kahne, 1977).

A similar claim has been made for the need to document the history of a woman's family involvements and their impact on her work, health, and self-concept. A joint research conference sponsored by the National Institute of Mental Health (NIMH) and the National Institute on Aging (NIA) called for special attention to women's changing life patterns as a factor in the poverty, health, and mental health of the older woman (U.S. Department of Health, Education, and Welfare, 1979a). The workshop particularly noted the difference in the experience of older and younger cohorts and remarked on the serious gap in information on older women. This gap is especially troublesome in the area of income maintenance where a combination of past history, demographic change, and women's changing roles and family patterns makes it difficult to gauge the likelihood of security in the later years.

For the understanding of the psychological process of maturing and adult development, a great wealth of data is potentially available. Antonucci's chapter in this volume lists six major longitudinal studies beginning in childhood that cover personality variables as well as issues of work and satisfaction. It should be noted, however, that all of these began in a very narrow time period, 1928–1931. Gathering comparably rich data on tomorrow's midlife adults is also necessary if scholars are to have the basis for future cohort comparisons. These efforts must even now be under way.

Future longitudinal research will be able to benefit from two types of methodological advances made during the past decade: first, theoretical clarification of the logical connections between age, period, and cohort effects; and second, technical improvements in research design and analytic strategies for measuring these effects. Sociologists like Riley (1973) and Mason, Mason, Winsborough, & Poole (1973), as well as psychologists led by Neugarten and Datan (1973), Baltes and Willis (1976), and Schaie (1977) have pointed to the potential fallacies that lurk in explanations that attribute age differences either to generational differences or to maturational changes over the individual life course. The problem is that historical changes are also involved, and all three dimensions of age—individual development, generational differences, and the historical era—may be responsible for the phenomena observed.

Good longitudinal research, to avoid the danger of attributing to maturation or aging what in fact is peculiar to a certain generation, must build in safeguards that whenever possible allow for comparison of the shape of life patterns or learning curves across different birth cohorts (Baltes, Reese, & Nesselroade, 1977). In addition, new techniques for analysis of data now permit explanations and predictions of behavior change within specific subgroups of the population (Nesselroade & Baltes, 1980). By examining compositional changes within cohorts and considering differential probabilities of given responses associated with particular attributes, changing rates of behavior can be explained.

2. *Cross-cultural research* makes possible comparisons across nations. Important variables are economic and demographic conditions, prevailing life patterns of women, and innovative social forms and social policies. A good deal of information has already been gained but in patchwork fashion. The next step is to codify and integrate what is already known and at the same time collect further data that will help to explain national differences in women's labor force ratio, occupational distribution, promotion, and pay. In addition, it is important to learn more about the connection between family support policies (day care, maternity leaves, etc.), women's role in the labor force, and their impact on fertility, child rearing, and poverty.

Right now we can point to some good building blocks for the codification process. A few works treat the political variable and consider how women's roles vary in socialist and nonsocialist societies (Giele & Smock, 1977; Iglitzin & Ross, 1976; Kamerman & Kahn, 1978; Scott, 1977). Several recent studies examine differences in women's labor force participation associated with economic structure—whether a country is more or less agricultural, production, or service-oriented (Rainwater, 1979; Ratner, 1980; Treiman & Roos, 1980). Comparisons along other lines are also possible. For example, Fogarty and the Rapoports (1971) have compared countries with different types of schedules and dual-career family patterns. Another potential comparison is between women's life-cycle patterns that have evolved in different times and places. One could use data from Australia (Young, 1978), the contemporary United States (Kreps & Clark, 1975), nineteenth-century Europe (Scott & Tilly, 1975), or different eras of the feminine role in U.S. history (Giele, 1978).

An almost totally unexplored realm is cross-cultural research on the psychological, physiological, and developmental aspects of women's lives. Do sex differences in health and illness behavior reported by Nathanson and Lorenz in this volume appear in other countries? Does the kind of developmental sequence that Gilligan (Chapter 3) finds in young American women have its counterpart in other societies? What broad cross-cultural differences and similarities are evident in the middle and later years of the life span? Answering these questions is a crucial step in addressing the broad issue that Alice Rossi (1980) has raised about the human aging process: What features seem more or less universal across cultures and across historical time periods? These are the features assumed to be most closely tied to the biological nature of women. Only in the events that are quite variable does it seem likely that culture and social structure are the primary determinants rather than sex-linked physical and biological characteristics.

3. *Naturalistic studies* permit exploratory work and allow for the expansion of qualitative description and fresh insights into the connectedness of life events and social context. Some years ago the psychologist Julia Sherman (1971) complained that "Studies of normal mothering are surprisingly few. Little objective data is available concerning the correlates and antecedents of succourant behavior in women [p. 226]." Despite outstanding work by ethnologists and the comparative work of such scholars as Beatrice Whiting (1963) in simpler societies, naturalistic and observational studies of women's work and family roles in modern societies are still few and far between. A recent outstanding example that would surely please Julia Sherman is the detailed observation of parenting behavior by Chaya Piotrowski (1979). Piotrowski notes all the little interactions between mother and father, the aggravations of fatigue, the relief of a walk or an ice cream cone, and the complex impact of siblings on each other that affect and help to describe women's role in the care and socialization of young children.

Qualitative studies have also been done by the Rapoports (1976) on dual-career families. Lein (1979), an anthropologist, has used field work techniques to describe the scheduling, the tensions, and the social networks that are part of the child-care arrangements of two-worker families. In a beautiful narrative Beatrice Whiting (1977) draws contrasts between women's lives in rural and urban Kenya and in the United States. She comments on the remarkable ability of the rural Kenyan women to engage in conversation and sociable exchange, and the hurried life, the tense interaction with children, and calculated interactions and use of time when people move to the city. After reading Whiting, one realizes how sparse have become ordinary terms to describe human behavior in our modern social science literature on women. Words like conversation, sociability, and irritability are indeed rare. Yet they refer to significant dimensions of human life. To the extent that qualitative, naturalistic studies of normal life can restore such familiar but powerful concepts to research on women's lives, they are an important supplement and corrective to be encouraged alongside quantitative analysis and experimental research designs.

Life Outcomes and Dimensions of Well-Being

The new model of the life course requires a somewhat different approach to specialized substantive fields from the model that prevailed in the past.

First, definitions of women's work and family activity must be expanded and refined. Second, rather than focus on a typology of life-styles (married, divorced, employed, nonemployed, childless, etc.) as the guarantors or threateners of a woman's future satisfaction, new research must put more emphasis on critical examination of outcomes and indicators of well-being. Finally, the new investigations must trace the interconnections between discrete life events to show how they affect these outcomes. The work involves collection of histories not only of a woman's work and family involvements but also of her physiological pattern of aging and her intrapsychic development. These new departures are even now evident in the latest research on adult women's health, mental health, work, and family life. There is a redefinition of the principal antecedent and outcome variables and a search for general theories that will explain the connections.

1. *Women's sickness and health* are the objects of an assessment of past and needed research by Nathanson and Lorenz in Chapter 2. They critically examine the common indicators of illness and health and reconceptualize the outcome variable (good or bad health) to show that it is made up of several components, some of which are related to "real" organic conditions, but others of which may be heavily influenced by social factors such as whether or not one goes to the doctor when feeling sick. Statistics that suggest women are in poor health must be critically examined to sort out how much is due to women's "illness behavior" that brings their cases to attention and thus causes them to be counted rather than ignored.

Nathanson and Lorenz also outline the several major antecedent variables that affect health outcomes. Some are related to biological factors (genetic, hormonal, and reproductive); others are related to women's special roles in marriage, parenting, and employment. Their work points to a need for further information on such topics as menstruation, menopause, pregnancy, contraception, and health care of women. But in addition a theory is needed that will highlight the interconnections between women's physical states, their social roles, and their ultimate health outcomes. Nathanson and Lorenz believe we are now at the point where we need "to determine how both the biologically defined, relatively invariant, component of women's roles, and the variant component, associated with culture and social conditions . . . influence indexes of health, illness, and death."

2. *Women's mental health* is also the object of extensive research activity. This volume does not contain a chapter directed to this topic. However, current work in this field is also advancing along lines suggested by the life course perspective. Of special interest has been the question of sex differences in the epidemiology of mental illness. Throughout the world the sexes are similar in prevalence of schizophrenia, but a higher proportion of men exhibit personality disorders and a higher proportion of women show manic-depressive disorders (Dohrenwend & Dohrenwend, 1976). Women's rates

for depressive disorders are roughly two to three times greater than men's (Weissman & Klerman, 1977).

Considerable effort has gone into explaining these differences. The life-course perspective has surfaced as researchers have given increasing attention to the etiological role of stressful life events, the several possible ways of measuring mental health outcomes, and the complex variety of intervening variables that mediate such stress. Such simple distinctions as marital or employment status do not satisfactorily account for observed differences in mental illness or general sense of well-being. Women's lives are most exposed to stressful life events such as disruption of attachment bonds, and they are more profoundly affected by them (Weissman & Klerman, 1977; Depner & Kulka, 1979). Yet various explanatory factors such as response bias or differences in men's and women's social roles affect positive outcome measures (well-being) differently from negative outcomes (psychological distress or illness) (Depner & Kulka, 1979).

As to the protective value of being married or being employed, there is also no clear or unitary relationship. Fidell (1980) found no great differences in emotional health between employed women and satisfied housewives; the group who stood out were the dissatisfied housewives whose mental health was clearly more problematic. Kessler and McRae (1980) report that sex differences in mental illness declined between 1957 and 1976. They attribute part of the change to a compositional factor—the growing participation of women in the labor force. But their prediction that compositional changes in marriage and child-bearing rates would also have an effect was not borne out. They conclude that the key reason that sex differences in mental illness declined is that women's role opportunities expanded so that they had a greater opportunity to do what they prefer. Similarly, Riessman and Gerstel (1980) reject any bald statements that marriage is protective for males and destructive for females. In their review of the impact of separation and divorce on mental health they find a complex interaction of many factors that have to be differentiated and placed in a larger social context to result in meaningful social analysis.

As in studies of other dimensions of the midlife period, these new research findings on women's mental health and illness display an increasingly complex and differentiated paradigm for investigating the interplay between life events. Key basic needs for a sense of competence, social integration, new experience, physical comfort, and predictability may or may not be met (Barnett and Baruch, 1978; Whiting, 1978). In addition, environmental factors influence the ability to adapt or cope. The outcomes are a product of all these factors.

3.　*Women's work outcomes* have recently also attracted new interest. What are the major factors that affect a woman's ultimate work destination? What is the relative importance of unpaid or nonmarket work in shaping her career? Kanter (1977) and many others have already noted the interpenetration of work and family spheres. Kahne (1979) has suggested that there be some way to credential all work experience so that women's time out of the paid labor force would not count so heavily against them. Melvin Kohn has recently broadened his research on the reciprocal effects of work on personality to include household work as well as paid work; presumably nonmarket work can also be analyzed in terms of substantive complexity, time pressures, dirtiness, or position in the job hierarchy (Kohn & Schooler, 1978; Miller 1980).

Besides broadening the concept of work, scholars are also now reexamining what constitutes success. The traditional criteria for evaluating women's work status are labor force participation, employment versus unemployment, earnings compared to men's, and degree of occupational segregation. Recently these criteria have been questioned. Critics of inflation and the capitalist system contend that women's high rates of labor force participation are a symptom of the de-skilling of work, lower real incomes for men, and the necessity for families to have two incomes to survive (Braverman, 1974; Oppenheimer, 1979). Those who find lower pay in "women's jobs" are beginning to question whether the only solution is greater diversification of women's job choices, or whether instead there should be rethinking of pay scales to reflect "equal pay for work of comparable value" (Ratner, 1980). Finally, there is growing skepticism about the traditional economic explanations of why women have received lower pay and fewer promotions. The difference is greater than can be explained by work discontinuities, lesser education, or differences in women's initial job choice. More investigators are wondering whether the effects of work rhythm (such as working part time) or different work conditions (by type of industry) are in part responsible (Kahne & Hybels, 1978; Barrett, 1979; Oaxaca, 1979).

4. *Women's family roles* importantly affect women's total life patterns and thus deserve special theoretical and empirical effort. Family researchers are reinterpreting time spent in the family to define it as work and to measure it by type and amount of activity. They are also confronting the fact that there are many possible alternative definitions of what constitutes successful performance in family roles, largely because family structure is changing to include a variety of forms and a variety of definitions of women's proper role. Even among feminists, leaders like Betty Friedan (1979) have openly questioned whether an earlier emphasis on women's work achievement has perhaps sacrificed too much of the satisfaction that women gain from intimacy, leisure, and family life. Now it is time to examine the valuable integrative work that women perform in the networks, friendships, and family activities that constitute what Bernard (1981) has termed "the female world."

In addition, the concept of nonmarket work is being further refined to distinguish between several types of activity (e.g., home and volunteer work) and their antecedents and consequents. Women's family roles are shaped by a number of factors: the variety of family forms, the stage of the family life-cycle, a woman's own career history. Thus it is not surprising that in one review of economic literature on women's work and family issues the following topics appear under the family rubric: dual-earner families, female family heads, marital instability, fertility and childrearing, and child care (Kahne & Hybels, 1978). A factor such as family location or migration also bears on work. Yet, in general, it is fair to say that examination of women's life course in terms of nonmarket work is still rather primitive. As Mortimer and Simmons (1978) recently noted, there is as yet no systematic research on adult socialization and family roles. As the pattern of women returning to school and work becomes more common, however, it is likely that research on this topic will also advance.

5. *Adult development, education, and job reentry* in a climate of changing sex roles now raise questions about widely accepted models of adult psychology and experience. The static orientation of many vocational and personality tests, their tendency to type persons as one sort or another, and the further likelihood that counselors may try to reinforce stereotypically feminine styles of behavior rather than encourage change toward assertiveness, autonomy, and choice is increasingly a subject for critical review (Gutek, 1979).

At the same time, encouraged by government interest in the elderly and the plight of aged women, economists and sociologists are probing causes of the high incidence of poverty among older women. Women's greater longevity, marital status, and shorter and more discontinuous work histories are all associated with the fact that they receive lower incomes from earnings, private pensions, and social security than their male counterparts (Congresswomen's Caucus, 1980; Kahne, 1981). Basic knowledge of these causative factors is crucial to the successful design of policies that can correct the problem.

A new model of adult development can itself have practical value for women if it clearly questions the stereotyped stages of the life-cycle and reveals the actual rather than supposed sources of satisfaction and well-being in women's lives. Fred Best (1980) shows that currently a sizable proportion of the working population would prefer more flexibility in scheduling of education, work, leisure, and family activity—not just within a week or month, or year, but between youth, middle age, and old age. If such a model were widely institutionalized in schools, firms, and families, women would have greater likelihood of equal success and rewards because a flexible pattern would be normative rather than an exception to the rule. In addition, it would become clearer just what combination of employment and family responsibility is desirable to women at different stages of family life. Waite (1980), using data from the National Longitudinal Surveys of Young Women, confirms a familiar observation that women with young children who have not yet completed their childbearing are less likely to be in the labor force *even if* their husband's income or their own wage potential is of the type associated with participation in the labor force. However, before this stage and after it is complete, these two traditional positive factors carry greater weight again.

The difficulty for most people is that they have frozen an image of women and their needs at one stage of the family life-cycle—when women are bearing and rearing young children. As a result, most people underestimate the importance of autonomy, accomplishment, and competent performance in realms other than child rearing as sources of women's happiness and satisfaction. Recent research on attitudes of continuing education students at the University of Michigan, however, suggests that wanting a job and not having one may exert more negative effect on satisfaction than wanting and not having a love relationship (Manis, 1980). Of those students wanting a job, only 34 percent fell into the satisfied category compared with 48.5 percent who mentioned the lack of a love relationship.

In concluding this review of the emerging agenda for research on women in the middle years, it is useful to pause briefly and consider the extent to which any current and future research can shape policy toward women. Tangri and Strasburg (1979) explicitly consider this question, and they identify three specific ways in which research can be useful in formation of policy. First, research can be *intellectually* useful by establishing the facts. Second, it can be *intrinsically* useful by targeting goals relevant to policy. Finally, it can be *politically* useful when it identifies critical variables over which policymakers have some control. A great deal of social science research is useful in relation to the first function of establishing the facts. Very frequently, however, scientific studies are so conceived that they fall wide of the mark of being helpful in formulating practical goals and the means to attain them.

To avoid being irrelevant to policy and practical programs, Scott and Shore (1979) advocate that researchers be in close touch with policymakers and service deliverers. Over the past decade great ferment has occurred in practical programs related to women's education and development, work, and family life. To formulate research questions relevant to policy, researchers must keep abreast of these developments. The remainder of this chapter reviews emerging issues of social policy for women.

THE EMERGING POLICY AGENDA

The realities of women's changing roles have already forced a paradigm shift in the social sciences. Crossover theory better accommodates women's participation in the labor force than traditional theory that justifies women's place as being entirely in the home. Similarly, new social policies now support the crossover model of sex roles and the life course. Arrangements that once tacitly segregated men's and women's duties are presently subject to question; flexibility and interchange are instead in vogue—at least among the visionaries and activists who seek change. Consistent with greater diversity in life patterns and family forms, the new programs represent an emerging policy agenda that covers employment, family, education, community, and security throughout the life course, as follows:

1.   *Equal employment opportunity*: anti-discrimination in hiring; flexible schedules; revaluation of comparable work.
2.   *Supportive family policies*: pro-choice family planning; expansion of child-care facilities; encouragement of men's participation in the family; recognition of homemaker contributions.
3.   *Equal educational opportunity*: expansion of career options; vocational training; apprenticeship; continuing education; women's centers.
4.   *Community supports for women's multiple roles*: better housing design; integration into social networks, credit and encouragement for volunteer and political activity; integration of social services.
5.   *Security throughout the life course*: equitable distribution of family income between women and men and accumulation of credits for Social Security; supports for the displaced homemaker; adequate pension and benefit coverage regardless of occupation or marital status.

What is interesting about all these proposals is that they seek to promote greater choice, not only by encouraging women's entry into new roles but also by lending support and giving recognition to women's traditional occupations. As Shelia Kamerman (1979) has noted, in response to women's rising labor force participation, modern countries have had three major alternatives: (1) to reinforce traditional sex role segregation; (2) to institute special policies for working women such as maternity leave or protected leaves for mothers of infants and young children (with job guaranteed on return); and (3) to encourage men and women to share breadwinning and homemaking responsibilities. Most modern countries have tended to reinforce either traditional or modified sex segregation through special policies for women's work, hours, and wages (Land, 1979). A few, such as Sweden, have actually encouraged the most egalitarian alternative; even then actual practice tends to fall short of the goal. Ecklein's account of relevant policies in the German Democratic Republic shows how concerned that country is to move beyond sex-typed policies to more fundamental reforms of the division of labor in work and family; but there, again, clear differences persist in women's and men's work and family roles.

The crossover model, however, suggests that the preferred policy should be Kamerman's third strategy: to promote task sharing between men and women. But the prevailing solution in European countries, with special provisions for "women's work" and maternity leaves and child care attached to the mother's (but not the father's) job is closer to the second alternative. Evidence on current policy developments in Europe, Canada, and the United States nevertheless suggests that future programs will indeed move toward the task-sharing mode. One sign is the current willingness of a few leaders to question the current heavy emphasis on work at the expense of care for families and children. Blumberg (1979) observes that women must gain the "poker chips" of power—education and jobs—to reorder the priorities and gain more representation and reward. In an extensive review of equal opportunity programs in Europe, Canada, and the U.S., Ratner (1980) also notes the higher value accorded productive rather than reproductive and socialization tasks. She suggests that women must gain power through unionization, action at the bargaining table, or other organizational representation to monitor and advocate programs and policies that will better serve women's interests.

In the meantime, like a rising tide, other developments—such as changes in the typical individual's life pattern—bear the crossover trend forward despite lags in explicit policies for equal opportunity. In connection with the typical life-cycle, for example, there is recognition that the timing of major life transitions may be somewhat arbitrary. Rather than make policies for certain target groups such as "midlife women," it may be more reasonable to foster what Hirschhorn (1979) calls a "meta-policy" on behalf of the fluid life-cycle.

Although the family and the work place *used to be* the major mechanisms for synchronizing people's lives, today greater flexibility in both of these worlds has disrupted traditional timetables. Hirschhorn advocates a meta-policy to develop fluidity and thereby organize life-cycle transitions such as moving, finding a new job, or adapting to changing family composition. Self-help groups can give individuals support during critical periods and help families by getting members consciously to coordinate their personal developmental schedules. Policies at the macroeconomic level could foster a tax structure responsive to various developmental tasks and crises such as family formation and divorce.

Entirely consistent with Hirschhorn's work is that of Fred Best (1978, 1980), who describes and advocates policies to permit work – leisure trade-offs, thereby promoting flexibility in the timing of education, work, and leisure activity. As early as 1973 the Swedish writer Göste Rehn propounded a visionary plan for the Common Market countries in which persons could accumulate their leisure time credits in a "bank" to be drawn out as needed for some special project such as reeducation, child rearing, career change, or part-time work. The individual would deposit all those "fees, taxes (unemployment, Social Security), study-loan payments and other compulsory savings" in a single unified account. In periods of nonemployment, child-bearing, child care, education, leisure, and retirement, the person could draw on the account, much as a person has the right to borrow on private life insurance (Giele, 1978; Ratner, 1980). Such ideas have special appeal for women. They are entirely compatible with the crossover model of social roles. Individuals may have a choice as to the age at which they take up specific tasks, and this added flexibility furthers the process of task sharing between the sexes.

One implication of the fluid life cycle is that there is no homogeneous age−sex target group such as "midlife women" for whom distinct policies can be made as for children, youth, or the elderly. Instead, the fluid life-cycle implies that adult women comprise many different subgroups, with different educational histories, employment, and family experience. Policies are therefore more useful when attuned to such special subgroups as displaced homemakers or educated women with part-time careers. Policies for adult women are perhaps more effective if aimed at institutions—work, family, and community—than at women as a special target group. In fact, it is probably not accidental that a richer literature is available on the changing roles of women and men in the work place and the family than under the rubric labeled "women's policy." Such development is consistent with the crossover trend. It points to Kamerman's third strategy for policy development—one that promotes task sharing between the sexes—rather than special women's jobs or women's benefits.

The newest developments in the work place and the family are consistent with this fluid model of the life course and task sharing between men and women. What is particularly prominent in current family policy discussion is emphasis on the variety of family forms (female-headed, married couple with wife in the home, married couple with wife in the labor force, etc.). Policy analysts have pointed to the dangers of favoring one of these forms over another and the need for neutrality in dealing with each of them (Giele 1980b; Kamerman & Kahn, 1978; MacDonald & Sawhill, 1978; Schorr & Moen, 1979). This theme reinforces the view that women's roles take many forms and that no one family type is necessarily *the* right one for all people in all times and circumstances. Rather, all these analysts argue that the special needs of each family type should be differentiated from one another; then each type can be treated in the manner appropriate to its particular strengths and deficits.

Recent research on work design and employment similarly recognizes the need for differentiated policies that address specialized target groups. Most important, however, the reformers of the work place would broaden the options available. They contend that whether working part time, or full time, on an assembly line, or in a small production unit, the worker should have the possibility of self-direction as well as cooperation. There should be enough flexibility to permit movement between different types of jobs and part-time and full-time work (Committee on Alternative Work Patterns, 1976; Giele, 1978; *Work in America,* 1973). Here again the emphasis on diversity and choice in the work place reinforces the crossover paradigm.

All these themes related to the life cycle, family, and the work place come together in the emerging policy agenda to promote equity for women. Two key government documents give the broad outlines of the agenda. The first, *American Women Workers in a Full Employment Economy,* prepared for the U.S. Congress Joint Economic Committee (1977) contains major articles on women's work, family roles, and education, as well as policy implications of current tax and Social Security regulations. The second document, *Women in Midlife—Security and Fulfillment,* prepared for the U.S. House of Representatives Select Committee on Aging (1978) continues within these broad outlines. It, however, adds two other dimensions: life course issues (psychological factors, new careers, counseling, continuing education) and community participation (volunteer work, social networks, housing, political involvement). These topics also appear in the work of other authors, in a policy agenda for women as wives and mothers that includes expansion of Social Security benefits, flexible hours, preschools and child health care, innovative housing design, and community and youth programs (Kamerman, 1977; Adams & Winston, 1980), and in economic analysis of the implications of women's rising employment for child care, tax, and pension systems (Smith, 1979).

It is still too soon to say how this emergent policy agenda on behalf of flexible sex roles will fare in the face of cutbacks in the federal budget. With the advent of the Reagan administration, feminist groups began to warn that federal pressure for affirmative action in employment and education would weaken (*National NOW Times,*1981; *WEAL Washington Report,* 1981b). Unless individuals and corporations of their own volition continue to engage in desegregation of sex roles, an alternative ideology based on the re-enforcement of sex-typed roles could gain ascendance, and with it a different set of policy directions. At the moment, however, the predominant trends are oriented to increasing age- and sex-role flexibility as described in these pages.

Equal Employment Policy

A good deal of equal opportunity legislation is already in place. What is still wanting is full implementation and realization of principle in practice. The Equal Pay Act was passed in 1963; the Civil Rights Act of 1964 prohibited discrimination in employment on the basis of sex. Since then other federal laws have banned job discrimination based on pregnancy, extended the provisions of the Equal Pay Act to cover administrative and professional occupations, and amended the Comprehensive Employment Training Act (CETA) to accommodate women more easily (Giele, 1978: 68-69; Waldman, Grossman, Hayghe, & Johnson, 1979). Nevertheless, recent figures show women's pay to be only 59 percent of men's and women workers to be still concentrated in a few less well paid occupations. To address these issues, scholars and policymakers have had to redefine discrimination to include differences in treatment that are not always intentional or are not intended to be invidious (Ratner, 1980). In fact, in some instances exactly the *same* treatment of women and men may turn out to be disadvantageous to women (when, for example, a person is considered too old to be hired or promoted). Thus, at the moment, the central issues of equal opportunity policy revolve around two opposing themes: the need to give women the *same* opportunities as men, and yet the simultaneous need to accord equal recognition and reward to alternative schedules or patterns of work that are different but no less valuable. These themes appear in policies covering unemployment, job segregation, flexible schedules, and equal pay.

1. *Employment policy at the macroeconomic level* affects women's work opportunities by influencing the number and kind of jobs available. Unemployment has a somewhat heavier impact on women than on men. Between 1947 and 1959, unemployment averaged 11 percent higher for women than men, and between 1960 and 1976, 31 percent higher (Keyserling, 1977). One possible inference is that to improve women's status, it is necessary to stimulate employment (Smith 1979), or at least not to accept higher rates of unemployment simply because relatively more females make up the ranks of the unemployed.

Connected with women's employment opportunities are the nature and kinds of jobs available. Economist Anne Carter (1978) suggests that the "tilt" of the U.S. economy toward white collar work has perhaps stimulated women's entry into the labor force. Jobs would have been less attractive to women if the economy were preeminent in heavy industry. On the other hand, concentration of women in secretarial and clerical occupations may spell doom if massive technological change (word processing, for example) drastically reduces the number of clerical workers needed. Sally Hacker (1979) in a study of technological change at American Telephone and Telegraph in fact argues that more women's jobs will be lost through technological change than will be gained through affirmative action.

A more immediate issue is the operation and results of employment training programs. Currently there is concern that CETA training programs under the Comprehensive Employment Training Act of 1972 may subtly discriminate by sex. Even though unemployment falls more heavily on women, the available remedies tend to provide more opportunities to males through public service employment. Women represent nearly half of the target population for youth employment programs, yet they constitute only one-fourth to one-third of the participants, probably because available slots tend to provide "male" jobs. (Ratner, 1980; Underwood 1979).

2. *Job segregation* is a special object for equal employment policy because it is the key structural constraint that limits women's opportunities for promotion and equal pay. Job segregation is reflected in the sex typing of occupations and thus influences girls' and boys' early choices about educa-

tion and vocational preparation. It is also evident in employers' distinctions between primary and secondary jobs, between those jobs that carry greater security and remuneration, and those that are seasonal or temporary and thus ineligible for the best promotions, salaries, and fringe benefits. Women workers are disproportionately underrepresented in the primary sector and overrepresented in the secondary (Blau & Jusenius, 1976; Reagan, 1977).

A number of remedies for job segregation have been tried: educational reform to decrease sex stereotyping and broaden career choice, affirmative action to hire females in formerly male positions, and greater attention to women as potential candidates for managerial and professional positions. Ruth Shaeffer (1980) of the Conference Board reports some encouraging results within female-intensive industries such as publishing, financing, banking, insurance, and communications. Between 1970 and 1975 the numbers of female officials and managers in some large firms representative of this group increased from 17 to 28 percent compared with a change from only 2 percent to 3 percent among comparable large male-intensive industrial firms. In the face of these positive gains, however, it cannot be forgotten that a great deal remains to be done. That American women who work full-time all year earn only 59 percent of what their male counterparts earn is largely caused by their being in certain types of jobs and industries, a striking manifestation of job segregation.

3. *Flexible schedules* excite the imagination of many observers who would better women's work lives. Many types of flexibility are possible— part time, part year, flexible hours, parental leaves, work sharing (Greenwald, 1977; Giele & Kahne, 1978). If women could see that certain professional or other jobs that they had formerly avoided were compatible with family responsibility, they might choose among a more varied range of occupations. If employers and government could see that part-time work, rather than being an inconvenience merely to accommodate the workers, can also be a valuable device for sharing available work among a wider population, often with higher productivity, then not only women might benefit from flexible schedules but corporations as well (Best, 1978; Levitan & Belous, 1977). Ultimately, flexible schedules, especially if available to men also, could support the redifferentiation of productive tasks that is necessary for greater sharing of work and family responsibilities between the sexes.

4. *Comparable worth* is the newest concept in equal employment policy; the term refers to the possibility of reevaluating jobs for the actual skills required and work produced rather than by using existing wage rates or job classifications that may have a built-in sex bias. Why should a foreman who oversees blueprints on a construction site necessarily have a higher job classification and pay than a woman who manages an office and oversees the work of fifteen secretarial and clerical workers? This is the kind of question being asked under the job evaluation process. It requires rethinking such

criteria for judging performance and commitment as time put in, willingness to move, ability to bring in new business, and responsibility assumed. The new standard of comparable worth thus requires some method of job analysis and evaluation to determine "worth".

Results so far have been discouraging, however (Ratner, 1980). Women are still poorly paid even when a high degree of skill is required, and the courts have been unsympathetic, even hostile, to the concept of a standard of comparable worth. Yet Bailyn (1979) reports that standards for job evaluation (e.g., willingness to move) are being questioned by young managers. The impetus for change comes as much from men as from women. Until further experience accumulates, however, the future of the concept of comparable worth is still in doubt.

Family Policy

Another possible strategy for integrating women's work and family responsibilities is to restructure family roles. The term *family policy* has been familiar in Europe for some time, but only recently has it been used with any frequency in the United States. Initially, family policies developed in European countries such as France and Sweden during the Depression in order to slow falling birth rates and give basic support to families with children. More recently, the term has been broadened to include a variety of programs created by the larger society to support and supplement family functions. The list of relevant programs ranges from child care and family planning to income maintenance and housing, with many other medical, economic, and educational activities potentially involved. In the women's movement in the latter part of the twentieth century, family policy is also seen as a tool for realigning and equalizing traditional work and family responsibilities of men and women (Giele, 1978; Kamerman, 1979; Keniston, 1977; Land, 1979). The programs that have received the most attention assist the family with nurturance and economic support yet at the same time challenge traditional sex roles. Principal examples include fertility control, day care, encouragement of men's family work, and reevaluation of women's roles in unpaid family labor.

1. *Fertility and family planning* represent the most basic dimension of family policy. Family planning can promote integration of women's work and family roles by limiting family size and making possible women's continued employment. A full range of measures includes contraception, abortion, aids to infertility, and control of teenage pregnancy. With such alternatives available, women can choose where to spend their time. On the other hand, pronatalist policies in some instances discourage women's attachment to the labor force by encouraging higher birth rates and heavier responsibilities in the home. Land (1979) notes the continuing importance of such pronatalist policies in Europe. By and large, however, the advocates of women's equality have ranged themselves on the side of women's freedom

to choose, and in recent history, this has more often meant the right to prevent motherhood or avoid large families rather than a positive choice of more family responsibility (Adams & Winston, 1980; Kamerman, 1979).

2. *Day care* is probably the single most popular issue in feminists' policy agenda for altering women's family roles. The traditional assumption that a mother should be a child's exclusive caretaker is being widely challenged. Various observers have suggested that both child and mother may be better off if they can take advantage of good available child-care programs. The mother can then continue her other interests (perhaps including a job or career), and the child can experience social stimulation and other benefits not always available in the ordinary home (Cook, 1977; Glazer, Majka, Acker, & Bose, 1977; Smith, 1979; Strober, 1977). The great difficulty with this agenda is that mounting evidence reveals a chronic dearth of good available child-care facilities. Critics like Selma Fraiberg (1979) worry that mothers may be parking their children in poor overcrowded preschools while they work, with irreparably harmful consequences for the child. And even when parents may have good child care available, the vulnerability of young children to sickness and the difficulty of finding sitters on short notice to keep the child at home, leaves many problems to be worked out even under the best of circumstances.

Other observers argue that too much has been made of the child-care issue—that families work out their own informal arrangements (Feinstein, 1979; Woolsey, 1977). These commentators, however, do not so much focus on the results for women as for children. Those who persist in their concern for women's status advocate a variety of measures that expand available options: the use of informal networks and referral systems, expansion of after-school care and use of school facilities, subsidized child-care services, direct cash transfers to enable parents to purchase child care, or tax credits or some combination of the foregoing (Feinstein, 1979; Kamerman, 1979). In the United States, unlike the European countries, it may be a combination of such incremental improvements rather than a more radical universal program that will eventually result.

3. *Expansion of men's family roles* is a means for realigning the division of labor between women and men so that both sexes can share equally in nurturance and economic support of the family. Presumably if men can take a larger part of family work, their wives can more easily participate in the paid labor force. The job of supporting a family will then not fall so heavily or exclusively on the male breadwinner; women will also be spared an exclusive preoccupation with family affairs that risks cutting them off from productive outside work. The means for producing this transformation are unfortunately elusive. Nor is everyone in complete agreement that traditional sex roles should be changed. Yet current popular proposals include parental leaves for fathers as well as mothers (Keniston, 1977), more equity between men's and women's family work (especially in couples where the woman is also employed) (Pleck & Rustad, 1980), and continuing support

and sympathy for experimental dual-career arrangements with more involvement by men in family life (Bailyn, 1978).

4. *Recognition of the homemaker* is the newest and in some ways the most surprising addition to family policy initiatives for changing women's status. Rather than merely devalue women's family work in an effort to broaden their options, feminists have recently learned to appreciate the unpaid contributions that women have made to family and community life. In 1979 the National Organization for Women published a "Bill of Rights for Homemakers" listing economic rights that should obtain within marriage, types of economic recognition that homemakers should enjoy, and safeguards for homemakers who are widowed or divorced (*National NOW Times,* 1979). Similar concern to give recognition and protection to homemakers had earlier appeared in the special compendium on women in midlife prepared for the U.S. House of Representatives in 1978, especially in Sommers' and Shields' (1978) list of possible programs to help the displaced homemaker, and in Giele and Kahne's (1978) review of proposals for giving Social Security credit to work of the homemaker (see also Hauserman, 1980).

In actuality it is difficult to develop realistic proposals for homemaker benefits that are fair and yet beneficial to the women who need them most. Eligibility requirements are one issue. One proposal would permit homemaker "drop-out years" (used for calculating the earnings record on which Social Security is based) only when a child is present under age 7 and when a woman's earnings have been reduced by at least 60 percent below her previous average earnings when no child was present. Such a provision would not cover the homemaker caring for aged parents or handicapped family members. Another issue is paying for the costs of such a program. For all practical purposes, it is likely that homemaker credits for calculation of Social Security can be given only as a form of spousal benefits. Although such a program would help to establish an independent earnings record for women, it would not drastically alter the relative disadvantage of widows, the formerly married, and the low-paid women workers in comparison with married women in well-off couples (Kahne, 1981).

Educational Policy

Both in the nineteenth century and today education has been a key tool for changing women's roles. After the massive educational growth of the 1960s, male and female rates of college attendance are converging. The choice of field of study appears to be less sex-typed than in the past. There is more equal distribution of advanced degrees between males and females, and male and female rates of part-time study are becoming more similar. Economic returns for women's college education have never been greater, although for men they have somewhat declined (Heyns & Bird, 1979).

These encouraging changes primarily affect the young, however. What about older women who are past the college years? A number of innovations are in process: expansion of educational entitlement, programs for continuing education, counselling of mature women, and credentialing experiments to give credit for nonacademic learning.

1. *Educational entitlements* in the past were available only to the school-age child. After World War II the G.I. Bill that gave soldiers benefits to continue their education represented a major new departure. Recently Alice H. Cook (1975) has suggested that the nation institute a Maternal Bill of Rights to recognize interruption of work for maternity and child-rearing as a service to the country. The bill would recognize that such interruption results in some loss of skill and productivity. It would provide compensation through vocational or general education, counselling, and guidance, or subsidies to employers for on-the-job training. The system could also justify a woman's right to unemployment compensation and help with child care and support during her training period. Like Alice Cook, others have proposed similar but less comprehensive proposals. In their plans, women could receive deductions or credits to support continuing education and counselling (Entine 1978; Blau, Rogers, Stephens, and Oser, 1978).

2. *Continuing education and vocational education* provide the general background and specific training needed by many women who either quit school before finishing or presently find themselves with rusty or irrelevant skills. New kinds of curriculum, scheduling, and a host of supportive services are needed to recruit, counsel, and give women such help as child care (Briggs, 1977; Giele, 1978; Mitchell, 1977; Roby, 1977). Particular scrutiny is now being given to government training programs for displaced home-makers or unemployed youth to be sure that needed support services are actually being provided to women in the programs. Without such help women's needs are in danger of being unmet (Association of American Colleges, 1980; Underwood, 1979).

Experiments in credentialing represent another innovation in the continuing education movement. Because life experience outside academia may be every bit as useful in a job as a formal education, some educators advocate new techniques for certifying or giving educational credits for that experience. The difficult issue is how to evaluate work experience and education in relation to each other. And since much of women's work is unpaid (as family managers, community volunteers, etc.), the matter is particularly complicated. In the past two decades a variety of devices have developed, from use of the College Level Entrance Program examinations (CLEP) to work–study programs for disadvantaged women such as are found in New York City at the College for Human Services (Campbell, 1973). One economist has suggested that all work, paid and unpaid, be translated into credentialed work experience for determining productive accomplishment and economic reward, and similarly that skills gained in education be translated into experience credits (Kahne, 1979). Another approach is to consider how employers can give credit to volunteer work when a woman reenters the labor market (Hybels & Mueller, 1978).

3. *Counseling and guidance* help women to direct their interests toward needed training and available job opportunities. Women in midlife who have been out of the labor force often feel overwhelmed by their lack of specific skills or specific goals. They need to take stock, chart a fresh course, learn about the realities of the job world, and develop their own capacities to advantage. Yet who is to take responsibility for developing such services? A number of colleges and universities provide help in connection with programs of continuing education. As women's roles continue to change, it is becoming ever more apparent how necessary these counselling and guidance programs are (DuBrin, 1978; Schlossberg & Waters, 1978).

In the past decade women's centers have developed at a number of universities. Their mission is complex. At the Center for Continuing Education of Women at the University of Michigan, for example, counseling, advice on career development, and administration of financial assistance to returning women coexist along with research on women's roles and a liaison to the academic faculty in women's studies. Some women's centers are also particularly concerned with day care and the provision of other support services. Women's centers are often the official representatives of women's presence on a university campus. In this capacity they show interest in research and teaching about women as well as advocacy and support for women (Campbell, 1973; Chamberlain, 1979).

Community Supports

One of the recurring yet still amorphous themes of women's contemporary policy agenda revolves around social networks and community supports. Informal helping arrangements, often made exclusively by women, have established nursery schools in churches, come to the aid of the bereaved, or otherwise mobilized local efforts on behalf of worthy projects (Giele, 1978; Lopata, 1978).

Persons interested in women's volunteer contributions have made specific policy suggestions to foster this work. Glazer and her coauthors (1977) suggest the establishment of neighborhood centers to serve visitors, coordinate needed transportation, to develop clinics, and so on. Like Kamerman (1977) they envision housing and community design that could facilitate women's work in the household and beyond. With the nineteenth-century feminist visionary, Charlotte Perkins Gilman, they picture a whole new neighborhood and household ecology that might be more supportive of women's (and now also men's) family work: local food, laundry, cleaning, and child-care services that realize economies of scale and that socialize what have sometimes been isolating and lonely tasks for the individual housewife.

It is noteworthy that a number of these ideas have now achieved a place on an implicit policy agenda for women. Volunteer work, social networks, housing, and political participation are all topics addressed in the compendium of papers on *Women in Midlife—Security and Fulfillment* submitted to the U.S. House of Representatives Select Committee on Aging (1978). The women's centers based at some large universities represent one concrete form in which the idea has partly been realized.

At the same time, a new approach for mobilizing community support has just recently emerged: coordination of a variety of entitlements and social services under the Vocational Educational Act of 1976 or the Comprehensive Employment and Training Act (CETA amendments of 1978). New programs for entering women at community colleges, for example, have learned how to coordinate entitlements to day care, transportation assistance, and opportunities for job training so that women can move successfully from dependency to employment (U.S. Department of Labor, 1979). In addition, as colleges and universities accept more nontraditional students, they are discovering ways to help such special populations as women covered by CETA, the Aid to Families with Dependent Children program (AFDC), and the Work Incentive program (WIN). In this connection the Project on the Status of Women under the auspices of the Association of American Colleges (1980) has developed background materials to publicize these new programs and thus facilitate women's reentry to member colleges and employment opportunities.

In a climate of cutbacks in federal social programs, however, it is likely that AFDC and CETA funds will no longer be available in the same amounts to support women's reentry to the work force. Two-thirds of all new CETA demonstration programs for displaced homemakers, for example, were slated to close down in March of 1981 (*National NOW Times,* 1981; *WEAL Washington Report,* 1981a). Early results show, however, that women who are already working will try to make ends meet, even if it means taking two jobs, rather than stay at home full time to qualify for welfare (Schorr, 1981). The current question is how to maintain the necessary supports and incentives to enable those still at home to gain needed training for job reentry. Without aid from public programs, providing such support will be more difficult.

Economic Security through the Life Course

At the end of life, the balance sheet of women's activities determines whether they will live in security or in poverty, and whether their situation in middle and old age will be better, worse, or about the same as men's. The life course concept has recently made observers aware that there are several ways to assess women's relative position. One can conclude that full-time homemakers are relatively favored compared to working wives, or alternatively, that homemaking receives so little explicit reward under the present system that a woman is vulnerable to poverty when she is widowed or divorced. The fact that a disproportionate number of poor old people are women raises such questions. What features of women's life patterns doom them to this end? Is it their work histories—that they tend to be in poorly paid occupations with few extra fringe benefits, that they work intermittently or part-time, or that they simply live longer? Is it their marital status—the fact that they are unmarried, or that they are dependents who receive benefits on their husband's earning records, and that they are vulnerable to gaps in coverage dictated by eligibility rules concerning age, length of marriage, or presence of children? It is probably some combination of all these factors that determines women's present economic status in middle and old age.

Several recent conferences and reports have documented the variety of factors that shape women's economic status through the life course. Two recent Congressional reports on women contain data on their treatment under Social Security and current tax policy (Blumberg, 1977), their coverage by private pensions (Schulz, 1978), their condition as homemakers (Sommers & Shields, 1978; Giele & Kahne, 1978), and in retirement (Atchley, 1978). A 1978 conference on "The Older Woman" jointly sponsored by the National Institute on Aging and the National Institute of Mental Health considered work, health, family relations, living arrangements, and retirement income as factors in the economic status of older women. The Social Security Administration and interested scholars have engaged in a series of reports and discussions on the present Social Security system (Burkhauser & Holden, 1982; U.S. Department of Health, Education, and Welfare, 1979a, 1979b; University of Wisconsin, 1980).

Clearly, women's economic status through the life course is on the national policy agenda. Besides scholarly consideration of the determining variables and practical alternatives, both the National Organization for Women and the Women's Equity Action League have featured these issues prominently in their recent publications. Four topics surface throughout the academic and political debate: taxation, Social Security, private pensions, and poverty—especially for the women "who fall through the cracks" of our present system.

1.   *Taxation policy* is of particular concern in those situations in which it inequitably treats one- and two-earner couples, and married and single individuals. The so-called "marriage penalty" refers to the fact that marriage may increase the total tax bill of two wage earners over what they would have paid had they remained single. It apparently results from an inadequate differentiation in the tax law between the traditional worker—housewife couple and the emergent two-earner couple. Compulsory joint filing by the couple aggregates their income and thus taxes the second earner at the first earner's highest marginal tax rate. As more married women enter the labor force, more couples will be experiencing this marriage penalty.

Those who would improve the present law recommend some form of individual filing (either mandatory or optional) to remove the marriage penalty and lessen the work disincentive for married women (Blumberg, 1977; Gordon, 1979a; O'Neill, 1980). Legislation currently before Congress allows a couple a 5 percent deduction on the income of the lower paid spouse up to a maximum of $1500, in 1982 and a 10 percent deduction, up to a maximum of $3000 after that (*WEAL Washington Report,* 1981c).

2. *Social Security,* of all the means for providing economic security for women, has received the most attention. In recent years, as two-earner couples have increased and divorce has become more common, the existing taxation and benefit rules of Social Security have come under question. Generally speaking, the "top tier" of earners has been most concerned about equity—the fact that a married working woman pays redundant Social Security taxes, that the dependent spouses of high wage earners get higher benefits, that a married couple with two earners may get lower benefits than a couple with one earner, and so on. Of course, there are also questions about the adequacy of coverage for this group—cases involving a divorced homemaker who has been married 10 years and cannot claim coverage on the basis of her husband's earnings record, the fact that disability benefits are not available to homemakers, and that a surviving widow or divorcee under 60 without children gets no benefits (Lampman & MacDonald, 1980).

Most of the proposals for remedying these problems involve some form of earnings sharing by which the joint income of a couple would be equally attributed to each partner. Such a rule would impose no penalties on the one-earner family, would treat two-earner families more equitably, and would provide protection for the divorced homemaker by establishing a separate earnings record of her own (Gordon, 1979b).

There are, however, "bottom tier" adequacy considerations that are not addressed by the proposals for earnings sharing. In a conservative commentary on efforts to change the Social Security system, Robert J. Myers (1980) holds that preserving adequacy of coverage is more important than equity in a *social* insurance program. He therefore rejects earnings splitting, homemaker credits, and related schemes as costly, unnecessary, and administratively infeasible. Instead, he recommends benefit splitting (rather than earnings splitting) for the one-worker family, elimination of marriage and remarriage as a cause for termination of benefits, reduction of the duration-of-marriage rule from 10 to five years, additional child-care dropout years for calculation of a woman's earnings record, and an additional working spouse benefit to enhance equity between the one- and two-worker couples.

In a trenchant review of the major suggestions for reforming Social Security, Munnell and Stiglin (1980) contend that even at present women workers are treated better than men by Social Security. Benefits for women are about one-fourth higher than for men workers, if one considers wage records alone. Care is thus required in reform of the system not to reduce women's benefits. One also has to calculate Supplemental Security Insurance (SSI) payments (for the poor and near-poor) along with Social Security to obtain a true picture of how women are doing under the present system. To balance equity and adequacy considerations Munnell and Stiglin suggest a two-tier system based first on broad use of SSI to provide a basic benefit and second on earnings sharing (between members of a couple) as a basis for calculation of an additional benefit that reflects wages earned. Such a system would (1) increase equity between one- and two-earner couples and between married and single persons, (2) eliminate the danger of high-income workers receiving negative rates of return on their investments, (3) alleviate pressure on the payroll tax by reallocating the income maintenance burden (for SSI) to general revenues, and (4) establish a means-tested first benefit tier that would more efficiently distribute funds to low-income individuals than does the present system.

Clearly, the variety of current proposals for altering the Social Security system reveals the immense ferment in this field. The issue of women's treatment is on the national agenda; it is still too soon to say how it will be resolved.

3. *Private pensions* are an important additional element in older persons' economic security that have received much less attention than Social Security but are no less a vital factor in adequate income for the retirement years. Schulz (1980) has dramatically shown that older people with two pensions have adequate replacement rates (in the range of 60 to 80 percent of their preretirement income). Those with Social Security *only,* however, are much more likely to fall in the poor or near-poor category—23 percent of couples with Social Security only and 67 percent of nonmarried individuals. Add to this the fact that many fewer women are covered by private pensions than are men, both as workers in their own right and as dependents. Only 36 percent of full-time employed women are covered by private pensions compared with 52 percent of men (Schulz, 1978). In addition, the extent of women's coverage as survivors under their husband's pension plan is not fully known. Before the 1974 Employee's Retirement Income Security Act (ERISA), a good many husbands did not elect the joint-and-survivor option for payment of benefits. Since ERISA, many small plans have folded, and coverage for some has thereby been eliminated (Halverson, 1978). Dissolution of a marriage also raises troublesome questions about the homemaker's rights in her husband's pension (King, 1980).

Some of the principal policy implications of these issues include the need for a combined system of retirement security that takes both Social Security and private pensions into account, the need to extend private pension coverage to more employed women, and the necessity of tackling the difficult issues of coverage for the homemaker.

4. *Poverty of women* is a gross indicator of women's lesser financial security throughout the life course, because women are disproportionately represented in the ranks of the poor. Of the aged poor in the United States, 72 percent are women. Three million women live in poverty, and

one-half of all women 65 and over receive an annual income of $1800 or less (Buerket, 1979a, 1979b). These facts have caused a review of the many variables that contribute to women's poverty—poor wages, intermittent work histories, their status as dependent beneficiaries, and so on.

One of the key new strategies for tackling these problems has been to focus on the women who "fall through the cracks" of the present system, that is, the women who by virtue of their age, marital or parental status, work history, or health fail to gain needed coverage because of gaps in the pension system, Social Security, or marriage and property laws. The so-called displaced homemaker has gained attention because her problems illustrate these difficulties. Since the early 1970s, when a NOW Task Force headed by Tish Sommers first called attention to their needs, displaced homemakers have been the object of Congressional legislation to help them become self-sustaining and have gained limited rights to vocational education and CETA training and employment (Jacobs, 1980; Vinick & Jacobs, 1980). Programs developed so rapidly that the Department of Labor has supported research to review and evaluate what has been accomplished so far.

Probably other approaches should also be developed to understand women's poverty. They would focus on problems in women's educational and employment histories. Or they would focus on the implications of remaining single, which along with the homemaker status, are probably just as important in determining whether a woman is poor at the end of her life.

SUMMARY AND CONCLUSIONS

Not only this final chapter but all the chapters in this book attest to the changing social structure and social consciousness surrounding women's lives. The segregated model of women's home life separated from men's work life is being strained by the growing participation of women in the labor force, the rising divorce rate, and a changing ideology about what should constitute a satisfying life. As a result, a new paradigm is emerging that has consequences for research and policy. The paradigm recognizes the increasing complexity of all modern roles. Moreover, it allows for the interchanges and crossovers that bridge realms once thought separate and distinct from one another. New crossovers are being discovered between men's and women's roles, and also between different stages of the life cycle.

The consequences for research are that old categories of analysis are no longer adequate to describe the new situation. Social scientists can no longer rely on rigid typologies of married and nonmarried women, or employed and nonemployed women to understand crucial differences in life satisfaction and well-being. Instead, a more fluid and dynamic model must be constructed to analyze the *events*—their nature and sequence—that each person has experienced. Women move in and out of the work force, in and out of marriage and parenting. Experience in work and the family bear on each other and change over time. Only this revised picture of the life course, with all its flexibility, backward turns, and crossovers, can encompass the complexity of adult women's current life patterns.

As new research categories and a new theoretical model are developed, certain methodologies hold particular promise. Longitudinal research can document the complex interplay of work and family events in women's lives and their impact on well-being. Cross-cultural research can point up the variety of social and economic settings in which particular life patterns appear to be more successful than others. By looking at women's lives across societies, one can also observe what may be universal themes and patterns. Finally, naturalistic studies of mothering, working, the operation of social support networks, or different types of families (such as the dual-career mode) can provide rich qualitative insight into the connections between events and outcomes, and can thus generate hypotheses for more systematic study.

More complex modes of analysis are also needed in a variety of specialized fields: health, mental health, work outcomes, family life, and continuing education. Each area is developing through broader definitions of relevant topics, new efforts to define outcomes that are of interest, and more sophisticated efforts to trace the connections between outcomes and antecedent experience. These advances in part result from using the new life-course perspective described in Chapter 1. As women's roles and life patterns have become more complex, less amenable to rigid categorization, and more subject to the interplay of work, family, and other influences, the analytic models used to describe them have also become more differentiated, complex, and reflective of the interaction among the many relevant variables.

The emerging national policy agenda for middle-aged and older women reflects this new paradigm. In the realm of men's and women's roles, policy appears to be moving from specific "women's policies" toward more general efforts to encourage flexible task sharing between men and women. In the realm of education and human development, the new idea of fluidity in the life course has brought a wider acceptance of continuing education, job reentry, and changes in family life-style.

The themes of sex role equality and flexibility over the life course are borne out in five basic areas for program and policy development: (1) equal employment opportunity, (2) family policy, (3) educational programs for women, (4) community supports, and (5) economic security. In each field there is a two-pronged exploration of ways to help women improve their situation. One strategy seeks the same opportunities that men enjoy. The other strategy tries to recognize, facilitate, and reward those aspects of women's lives that may be different from men's. Equal employment policy through attempts to overcome job segregation would enable women to approximate men's employment conditions more closely. Yet flexible scheduling and evaluation of women's jobs on the basis of comparable worth accept the differences in women's situations and try to adapt work conditions to their needs. Family planning and day care move women's family responsibilities somewhat closer to men's, but expansion of men's family roles and provision of credit to the homemaker recognize the value of family-related work that women have always done. Efforts to get for women educational entitlements similar to the GI Bill or to encourage more vocational education would help women by following the male models of educational and occupational achievement. New types of counselling for the returning woman and credentialing experiments to credit women's volunteer experience introduce a female model of life experience that attempts to change existing career structures as much as the individual woman. All these opposing tendencies are expressed in reform efforts to assure women economic security throughout their lives. Some proposals for improving taxation, Social Security, and pensions emphasize equal treatment of men and women through earnings sharing or individual filing. Other proposals would give homemaker credit, increase child-care drop-out years, or institute other forms of special treatment.

Although seemingly contradictory, the two roads to change—helping women to follow the male pattern, or asking the world to make a better place for the female pattern—are both logical policy implications of the crossover paradigm. They express the actual interpenetration and complexity of the new worlds of women and men. They assume a flexible ordering of life events and thereby implicitly extend the crossover motif to the life course.

These new research and policy agendas remain to be implemented and tested. Other data must be collected. Alternative policy recommendations must be evaluated. Eventually, each agenda must be revised in light of new findings. Until that time, the directions charted here give an orientation that is promising at least for now.

REFERENCES

Adams, C.T. and K.T. Winston. 1980. *Mothers at Work: Public Policies in the United States, Sweden, and China.* New York: Longman.

Association of American Colleges. 1980. Field Evaluation Draft for "Women's Re-Entry Project." Washington, DC: Association of American Colleges, Project on the Status and Education of Women.

Atchley, R.C. 1978. "Retirement Preparation for Women." In U.S. House of Representatives, *Women in Midlife—Security and Fulfillment.* Washington, DC: Government Printing Office.

Bailyn, L. 1978. "Accommodation of Work to Family." In R. and R.N. Rapoport (Eds.), *Working Couples.* New York: Harper & Row.

———. 1979. Presentation at Wellesley College Center for Research on Women, Wellesley, MA, March 20.

Baltes, P.B., H.W. Reese, and J.R. Nesselroade. 1977. *Life-Span Developmental Psychology: Introduction to Research Methods.* Monterey, CA: Brooks/Cole.

Baltes, P.B. and S. Willis. 1976. "Toward Psychological Theories of Aging and Development." In J.E. Birren and K.W. Schaie (Eds.), *Handbook of the Psychology of Aging.* New York: Academic Press.

Barnett, R.C. and G.K. Baruch. 1978. "Women in the Middle Years: A Critique of Research and Theory." *Psychology of Women Quarterly* **3** (2): 187–197.

Barnett, R.C. and G.K. Baruch. 1980. "Toward Economic Independence: Women's Involvement in Multiple Roles." In D.G. McGuigan (Ed.), *Women's Lives: New Theory, Research and Policy.* Ann Arbor, MI: University of Michigan, Center for Continuing Education of Women.

Barrett, N.S. 1979. "Data Needs for Evaluating the Labor Market Status of Women." *Census Bureau Conference on Issues in Federal Statistical Needs Relating to Women.* U.S. Bureau of the Census. *Current Population Reports,* Special Studies, Series P-23, No. 83.

Bennett, S.K. and G.H. Elder, Jr. 1979. "Women's Work in the Family Economy: A Study of Depression Hardship in Women's Lives." *Journal of Family History* **4** (2): 153–176.

Bernard, J. 1981. *The Female World.* New York: The Free Press.

Best, F. 1978. "Preferences on Worklife Scheduling and Work–Leisure Tradeoffs." *Monthly Labor Review,* June, pp. 31–37.

———. 1980. *Flexible Life Scheduling: Breaking the Education–Work–Retirement Lockstep.* New York: Praeger.

Blau, F.D., and C.L. Jusenius. 1976. "Economists' Approaches to Sex Segregation in the Labor Market: An Appraisal." *Signs: Journal of Women in Culture and Society* **1** (3): 181–199.

Blau, Z.S., P.P. Rogers, R.C. Stephens, and G.T. Oser. 1978. "School Bells and Work Whistles: Sounds that Echo a Better Life for Women in Later years." In U.S. House of Representatives, *Women in Midlife—Security and Fulfillment.* Washington, DC: Government Printing Office.

Blumberg, G.G. 1977. "Federal Income Tax and Social Security Law." In U.S. Congress, *American Women Workers in a Full Employment Economy.* Washington, DC: Government Printing Office.

Blumberg, R.L. 1979. "Paradigm for Predicting the Position of Women: Policy Implications and Problems." In J. Lipman-Blumen and J. Bernard (Eds.), *Sex Roles and Social Policy.* Beverly Hills, CA: Sage Publications.

Braverman, H. 1974. *Labor and Monopoly Capital: The Degradation of Work in the Twentieth Century.* New York: Monthly Review Press.

Briggs, N. 1977. "Apprenticeship." In U.S. Congress, *American Women Workers in a Full Employment Economy.* Washington, DC: Government Printing Office.

Brim, O., Jr. 1979. "On the Properties of Life Events." Kurt Lewin Memorial Address presented at the annual meeting of the American Psychological Association, New York, September 3.

Brown, G.W. and T. Harris. 1979. *Social Origins of Depression in Women.* New York: Free Press.

Buerket, K. 1979a. "Social Security Needs Reform." *WEAL Washington Report,* October, p. 2.

———. 1979b. "The Social Security System: A Disincentive to Marriage." *WEAL Washington Report,* December, pp. 3, 6.

Burkhauser, R.V., and K.C. Holden (Eds). 1982. *A Challenge to Social Security: The Changing Roles of Women and Men in American Society.* New York: Academic Press.

Burlage, D. 1978. "Divorced Mothers: the Decision to Separate and the Transition into Single Parenthood." Paper presented to the Massachusetts Psychological Association, Spring.

Campbell, A., P.E. Converse, and W.L. Rodgers. 1976. *The Quality of American Life: Perceptions, Evaluations, and Satisfactions.* New York: Russell Sage Foundation.

Campbell, J.W. 1973. "Women Drop Back In: Educational Innovation in the Sixties." In A.S. Rossi and A. Calderwood (Eds.), *Academic Women on the Move.* New York: Russell Sage Foundation.

Carter, A. 1978. "Priorities for Economic Research on Women in the Middle Years." Memo to SSRC Study Group on Women in the Middle Years. Waltham, MA: Brandeis University.

Chamberlain, M.K. 1979. "Centers for Research on Women." New York: Ford Foundation, April.

Committee on Alternative Work Patterns. 1976. *Alternatives in the World of Work.* Washington, DC: National Center for Productivity and Quality of Working Life.

Congresswomen's Caucus. 1980. *Older Women: the Economics of Aging.* Washington, DC: Women's Research and Education Institute of the Congresswomen's Caucus and Women's Studies Program and Policy Center, George Washington University.

Cook, A.H. 1975. *The Working Mother: A Survey of Problems and Programs in Nine Countries.* Ithaca, NY: New York State School of Industrial Relations, Cornell University.

———1977. "Working Women: European Experience and American Need." In U.S. Congress, *American Women Workers in a Full Employment Economy.* Washington, DC: Government Printing Office.

Depner, C.E. and R. Kulka. 1979. "Sex Differences in Psychological Distress and Use of Professional Help as a Function of Social and Social-Psychological Factors." Unpublished manuscript, Survey Research Center, University of Michigan, Ann Arbor.

Dohrenwend, B.P. and B.S. Dohrenwend. 1976. "Sex Differences and Psychiatric Disorders." *American Journal of Sociology* **81** (6): 1447–1454.

DuBrin, A.J. 1978. "Psychological Factors: Reentry and Mid-Career Crises." In U.S. House of Representatives, *Women in Midlife—Security and Fulfillment.* Washington, DC: Government Printing Office.

Duncan, G.J., and J.N. Morgan (Eds.). 1980. *Five Thousand American Families— Patterns of Economic Progress,* Vol. 7. Ann Arbor, MI: Institute for Social Research.

Elder, G.H., Jr. 1974. *Children of the Great Depression: Social Change in Life Experience.* Chicago: University of Chicago Press.

Entine, A.D. 1978. "The Role of Continuing Education." In U.S. House of Representatives, *Women in Midlife—Security and Fulfillment.* Washington, DC: Government Printing Office.

Feinstein, K.W. 1979. "Directions for Day Care." In K.W. Feinstein (Ed.), *Working Women and Families.* Beverly Hills, CA: Sage Publications.

Fidell, L.S. 1980. "Employment Status, Role Dissatisfaction and the Housewife Syndrome." Psychology Department, California State University at Northridge.

Fogarty, M.P., R. Rapoport, and R.N. Rapoport. 1971. *Sex, Career, and Family.* London: Allen and Unwin.

Fraiberg, S. 1979. *Every Child's Birthright: In Defense of Mothering.* New York: Bantam Books.

Friedan, B. 1963. *The Feminine Mystique.* New York: W.W. Norton.

———. 1979. "Feminism Takes a New Turn." *The New York Times Magazine,* November 18, p. 40ff.

Giele, J.Z. 1973. "Age Cohorts and Changes in Women's Roles." Paper presented at the annual meeting of the American Sociological Association, New York, August.

———. 1978. *Women and the Future: Changing Sex Roles in Modern America.* New York: Free Press.

———. 1980a. "Adulthood as Transcendence of Age and Sex." In N.J. Smelser and E.H. Erikson (Eds.), *Themes of Work and Love in Adulthood.* Cambridge, MA: Harvard University Press.

———. 1980b. "Discrimination, Sex Roles, and Changing Family Structures." Paper presented at the National Research Forum on Family Issues for the White House Conference on Families. Washington, DC: April 10.

———. 1980c. "Crossovers: New Themes in Adult Roles and the Life Cycle." In D.G. McGuigan (Ed.), *Women's Lives: New Theory, Research and Policy.* Ann Arbor, MI: University of Michigan, Center for Continuing Education of Women.

Giele, J.Z. and H. Kahne. 1978. "Meeting Work and Family Responsibilities: Proposals for Flexibility." In U.S. House of Representatives, *Women in Midlife—Security and Fulfillment.* Washington, DC: Government Printing Office.

Giele, J.Z., and A.C. Smock (Eds.) 1977. *Women: Roles and Status in Eight Countries.* New York: Wiley.

Glazer, N., L. Majka, J. Acker, and C. Bose. 1977. "The Homemaker, the Family, and Employment." In U.S. Congress, *American Women Workers in a Full Employment Economy.* Washington, DC: Government Printing Office.

Gordon, N.M. 1979a. "Institutional Responses: The Federal Income Tax System." In R.E. Smith (Ed.), *The Subtle Revolution.* Washington, DC: Urban Institute.

———. 1979b. "Institutional Responses: The Social Security System." In R.E. Smith (Ed.), *The Subtle Revolution.* Washington, DC: Urban Institute.

Greenwald, C.S. 1977. "Part-Time Work." In U.S. Congress, *American Women*

Workers in a Full Employment Economy. Washington, DC: Government Printing Office.

Gutek, B.A. (Ed.). 1979. *New Directions for Education, Work and Careers; Enhancing Women's Career Development.* San Francisco: Jossey-Bass.

Hacker, S.L. 1979. "Sex Stratification, Technology and Organizational Change: A Longitudinal Analysis of AT&T." Paper presented at the annual meetings of the American Sociological Association, Boston, August 27–31.

Halverson, G. 1978. "Despite ERISA, More Pension Plans Have Folded." *Christian Science Monitor,* December 18, p. B10.

Hauserman, N.R. 1980. "The American Homemaker: Policy Proposals." In D.G. McGuigan (Ed.), *Women's Lives: New Theory, Research and Policy.* Ann Arbor: University of Michigan, Center for Continuing Education of Women.

Heyns, B. and J.A. Bird, 1979. "Recent Trends in the Higher Education of Women." Paper prepared for the Research Conference on Educational Environments and the Undergraduate Woman. Wellesley, MA: Wellesley College Center for Research on Women, September 13–15.

Hirschhorn, L. 1979. "Adult Development and Meta-Policy." Paper presented to the National Conference on Social Welfare, Philadelphia, May 14.

Hybels, J.H. and M.W. Mueller. 1978. "Volunteer Work: Recognition and Accreditation." In U.S. House of Representatives, *Women in Midlife—Security and Fulfillment.* Washington, DC: Government Printing Office.

Iglitzin, L.B. and R. Ross (Eds.) 1976. *Women in the World: A Comparative Study.* Santa Barbara, CA: ABC–Clio Press.

Jacobs, R.H. 1980, "Integrating Displaced Homemakers into the Economy." Wellesley, MA: Wellesley College Center for Research on Women.

Kahne, H. 1977. "Market Participation and Family Life: The Contributions of Economics to Life Cycle Issues for Women in the Middle Years." Presentation to the SSRC Study Group on Women in the Middle Years. Waltham, MA: Brandeis University, September 15.

———. 1978. "Economic Research on Women and Families." *Signs: Journal of Women in Culture and Society* **3** (3): 652–665.

———. 1979. "Women's Occupational Choices and Life-Time Work Rhythms: Are We Still Making Progress?" *Journal of Employment Counseling* **16** (2): 83–93.

———. 1981. "Economic Security of Older Women: Too Little for Late in Life." Monograph. Waltham, MA: Brandeis University, National Aging Policy Center on Income Maintenance.

Kahne, H. and J.H. Hybels. 1978. "Work and Family Issues: A Bibliography of Economic and Related Social Science Research." Wellesley, MA: Wellesley College Center for Research on Women.

Kamerman, S.B. 1977. "Public Policy and the Family: A New Strategy for Women as Wives and Mothers." In J.R. Chapman and M. Gates (Eds.), *Women into Wives.* Beverly Hills, CA: Sage Publications.

———. 1979. "Work and Family in Industrialized Societies." *Signs: Journal of Women in Culture and Society* 4 (4): 632–650.

Kamerman, S.B. and A.J. Kahn. (Eds.) 1978. *Family Policy: Government and Families in Fourteen Countries*. New York: Columbia University Press.

Kanter, R.M. 1977. *Work and Family in the United States: A Critical Review and Agenda for Research and Policy*. New York: Russell Sage Foundation.

Keniston, K.H. 1977. *All Our Children: The American Family Under Pressure*. New York: Harcourt Brace Jovanovich.

Kessler, R.C. and J.A. McRae. 1980. "Trends in the Relationship between Sex and Mental Illness: 1957–1976." Unpublished manuscript, University of Michigan, Ann Arbor.

Keyserling, M.D. 1977. "Women's Stake in Full Employment: Their Disadvantaged Role in the Economy." In U.S. Congress, *American Women Workers in a Full Employment Economy*. Washington, DC: Government Printing Office.

King, F.P. 1980. "Occupational Pension Plans and Spouse Benefits." Paper presented at the Conference on Social Security and the Changing Roles of Women. Madison, WI: University of Wisconsin, April 11–12.

Kohn, M.L., and C. Schooler. 1978. "The Reciprocal Effects of the Substantive Complexity of Work and Intellectual Flexibility: A Longitudinal Assessment." *American Journal of Sociology* **84** (1): 24–52.

Koten, J. 1978. "Aged and Alone, Many Elderly Women Fight Ill Health, Fear of Crime, Loneliness." *Wall Street Journal,* October 17, pp. 1, 22.

Kreps, J.M., and R. Clark. 1975. *Sex, Age, and Work: The Changing Composition of the Labor Force*. Baltimore, MD: Johns Hopkins University Press.

Kuhn, T.S. 1962. *The Structure of Scientific Revolutions*. Chicago: University of Chicago Press.

Lampman, R., and M. MacDonald. 1980. "Underlying Concepts and Institutions." Paper presented at the Conference on Social Security and the Changing Roles of Women. Madison, WI: University of Wisconsin, April 11–12.

Land, H. 1979. "The Changing Place of Women in Europe." *Daedalus* **108** (2): 73–94.

Lein, L. 1979. "Working Couples as Parents." In E. Corfman (Ed.), *Families Today: A Research Sampler on Families and Children,* Vol. 1. Washington, DC: Government Printing Office.

Levitan, S.A., and R.S. Belous. 1977. *Shorter Hours, Shorter Weeks: Spreading the Work to Reduce Unemployment*. Baltimore, MD: Johns Hopkins University Press.

Lopata, H.Z. 1978. "Changing Roles, Projections for the Future, and Policy Implications." In U.S. House of Representatives, *Women in Midlife—Security and Fulfillment*. Washington, DC: Government Printing Office.

MacDonald, M., and I.V. Sawhill. 1978. "Welfare Policy and the Family." *Public Policy* **26** (1): 89–119.

Manis, J. 1980. "Transition to Work: Who is Satisfied and Who is Not." In D.G. McGuigan (Ed.), *Women's Lives: New Theory, Research and Policy*. Ann Arbor, MI: University of Michigan, Center for Continuing Education of Women.

Mason, K.O., W. Mason, H. Winsborough, and W. Poole. 1973. "Some Methodological Issues in Cohort Analysis of Archival Data." *American Sociological Review* **38** (2): 242–259.

Miller, J. 1980. "Individual and Occupational Determinants of Job Satisfaction: A Focus on Gender Differences." *Sociology of Work and Occupations* **7** (3): 337–366.

Mitchell, A.M. 1977. "Facilitating Full Employment of Women Through Career Education." In U.S. Congress, *American Women Workers in a Full Employment Economy*. Washington, DC: Government Printing Office.

Mortimer, J.T., and R. Simmons. 1978. "Adult Socialization." *Annual Review of Sociology* **4**: 421–454.

Munnell, A.H., and L.E. Stiglin. 1980. "Women and a Two-Tier Social Security System." Paper presented at the Conference on Social Security and Changing Roles of Women. Madison, WI: University of Wisconsin, April 11–12.

Myers, R.J. 1980. "Incremental Changes in Social Security Needed to Result in Equal and Fair Treatment of Men and Women." Paper presented at the Conference on Social Security and Changing Roles of Women. Madison, WI: University of Wisconsin, April 11–12.

National NOW Times. 1979. "Smeal Reiterates NOW Position on Social Security." August, p. 7.

———. 1981. "Reagan Budget Cuts Hit Women Hardest of All." April, p. 1.

Nesselroade, J.R., and P.B. Baltes. 1980. *Longitudinal Research in the Behavioral Sciences*. New York: Academic Press.

Neugarten, B. 1979. "Time, Age, and the Life Cycle." *American Journal of Psychiatry* **136** (7): 887–894.

Neugarten, B.L., and N. Datan. 1973. "Sociological Perspectives on the Life Cycle." In P.B. Baltes and K.W. Schaie (Eds.), *Life-Span Developmental Psychology: Personality and Socialization*. New York: Academic Press.

Oaxaca, R.L. 1979. "On the Use of Occupational Statistics." *Census Bureau Conference on Issues in Federal Statistical Needs Relating to Women*. U.S. Bureau of the Census, *Current Population Reports*, Special Studies, Series P-23, No. 83.

O'Neill, J. 1980. "The Marriage Penalty." *Urban Institute Policy and Research Report* **10** (2): 14–16.

Oppenheimer, V.K. 1979. "Structural Sources of Economic Pressure for Wives to Work: An Analytical Framework." *Journal of Family History* **4** (2): 177–197.

Parsons, T., and R.F. Bales. 1955. *Family, Socialization and Interaction Process*. New York: Free Press.

Perun, P.J. 1981. "Age and the Woman: A Comment on Rossi's 'Life-Span Theories and Women's Lives'." *Signs: Journal of Women in Culture and Society* **7** (1): 243–248.

Perun, P.J., and D.D.V. Bielby. 1979. "Midlife: A Discussion of Competing Models." *Research in Aging* **1** (3): 275–300.

Perun, P.J. and J.Z. Giele. 1982. "Life after College: Historical Links Between Women's Education and Women's Work." In P.J. Perun (Ed.), *The Under-*

graduate Woman: Issues in Educational Equality. Lexington, MA: Lexington Books.

Piotrowski, C.S. 1979. *Work and the Family System: A Naturalistic Study of Working Class and Lower Middle Class Families*. New York: Free Press.

Pleck, J. and M. Rustad. 1980. "Husbands' and Wives' Time in Family Work and Paid Work in the 1975–76 Study of Time Use." Wellesley, MA: Wellesley College, Center for Research on Women.

Rainwater, L. 1979. "Mothers' Contributions to the Family Money Economy." *Journal of Family History* **4** (2): 198–211.

Rapoport, R. and R.N. Rapoport. 1976. *Dual-Career Families Re-examined*. New York: Harper & Row.

Ratner, R.S. (Ed.) 1980. *Equal Employment Policy for Women: Strategies for Implementation in the United States, Canada, and Western Europe*. Philadelphia: Temple University Press.

Reagan, B.B. 1977. "De Facto Job Segregation." In U.S. Congress, *American Women Workers in a Full Employment Economy*. Washington, DC: Government Printing Office.

Riessman, C.K. and N. Gerstel. 1980. "Marital Status and Health and Illness: A Critical Review of the Literature on Sex Differences in Adaptation to Marital Separation and Divorce." Paper presented at the Annual Meeting of the American Sociological Association, New York, August 31.

Riley, M.W. 1973. "Aging and Cohort Succession: Interpretations and Misinterpretations." *Public Opinion Quarterly* **37** (1): 35–49.

Roby, P.A. 1977. "Vocational Education." In U.S. Congress, *American Women Workers in a Full Employment Economy*. Washington, DC: Government Printing Office.

Rossi, A.S. 1964. "Equality Between the Sexes: An Immodest Proposal." In R.J. Lifton (Ed.), *The Woman in America*. Boston: Beacon Press.

———. 1980. "Life Span Theories and Women's Lives." *Signs: Journal of Women in Culture and Society* **6** (1): 4–32.

Schaie, K.W. 1977. "Quasi-Experimental Research Designs in the Psychology of Aging." In J.E. Birren, and K.W. Schaie (Eds.), *Handbook of the Psychology of Aging*. New York: Van Nostrand.

Schlossberg, N.K. and E.B. Waters. 1978. "Counseling: Shifting the Balance from Problem to Possibility." In U.S. House of Representatives, *Women in Midlife—Security and Fulfillment*. Washington, DC: Government Printing Office.

Schorr, A.L. and P. Moen. 1979. "The Single Parent and Public Policy." *Social Policy* **9** (5): 15–21.

Schorr, B. 1981. "Canceled Checks: Reagan Team Weighs Impact of Welfare Cuts on Working Parents." *Wall Street Journal,* October 21, p. 1.

Schulz, J.H. 1978. "Private Pensions and Women." In U.S. House of Representatives, *Women in Midlife—Security and Fulfillment*. Washington, DC: Government Printing Office.

Schulz, J.H. 1980. "Assessing the Adequacy of Pension Income." Testimony before the President's Commission on Pension Policy, January 11.

Scott, H. 1974. *Does Socialism Liberate Women? Experiences from Eastern Europe.* Boston: Beacon Press.

———. 1977. "Women's Place in Socialist Society: The Case of Eastern Europe." *Social Policy* **7** (5): 32–35.

Scott, J.W. and L.A. Tilly. 1975. "Women's Work and the Family in Nineteenth Century Europe." *Comparative Studies in Society and History* **17** (1): 36–64.

Scott, R.A. and A.R. Shore. 1979. *Why Sociology Does Not Apply: A Study of the Use of Sociology in Public Policy.* New York: Elsevier North-Holland.

Shaeffer, R. 1980. "Improving Job Opportunities for Women from a U.S. Corporate Perspective." In R.S. Ratner (Ed.), *Equal Employment Policy for Women.* Philadelphia: Temple University Press.

Sheehy, G. 1981. "The Private Passages of the Hostages and Their Wives." *Life* **4** (3): 34–40.

Sherman, J. 1971. *On the Psychology of Woman: A Survey of Empirical Studies.* Springfield, IL: Charles C Thomas.

Smith, R.E. 1979. *Women in the Labor Force in 1990.* Washington, DC: Urban Institute.

Sommers, T. and L. Shields. 1978. "Problems of the Displaced Homemaker." In U.S. House of Representatives, *Women in Midlife—Security and Fulfillment.* Washington, DC: Government Printing Office.

Spilerman, S. 1977. "Careers, Labor Market Structure, and Socioeconomic Achievement." *American Journal of Sociology* **83** (3): 551–593.

Strober, M.H. 1977. "Economic Aspects of Child Care." In U.S. Congress, *American Women Workers in a Full Employment Economy.* Washington, DC: Government Printing Office.

Tangri, S.S. and G.L. Strasburg. 1979. "Where Research and Policy Connect: the American Scene." In J. Lipman-Blumen and J. Bernard (Eds.), *Sex Roles and Social Policy.* Beverly Hills, CA: Sage Publications.

Treiman, D.J. and P.A. Roos. 1980. "Sex and Earnings in Industrial Society: A Nine Nation Comparison." Washington, DC: National Academy of Sciences.

Underwood, L.A. 1979. *Women in Federal Employment Programs.* Washington, DC: Urban Institute.

U.S. Congress, Joint Economic Committee. 1977. *American Women Workers in a Full Employment Economy.* Washington, DC: Government Printing Office.

U.S. Department of Health, Education, and Welfare. 1979a. *The Older Woman: Continuities and Discontinuities.* Report of the National Institute on Aging and National Institute on Mental Health Workshop, September 14–16, 1978. Washington, DC: Government Printing Office.

———. 1979b. *Social Security and the Changing Roles of Men and Women.* Washington, DC: Government Printing Office.

U.S. Department of Labor, Women's Bureau. 1979. *A Guide to Coordinating CETA/Vocational Education Legislation Affecting Displaced Homemaker Programs.* Washington, DC: Department of Labor, Office of the Secretary.

U.S. House of Representatives, Select Committee on Aging. 1978. *Women in*

Midlife—Security and Fulfillment. Washington, DC: Government Printing Office.

University of Wisconsin. 1980. Conference on Social Security and the Changing Roles of Women. Madison, WI: The Institute for Research on Poverty and the Women's Studies Research Center.

Vaillant, G.E. 1977. *Adaptation to Life.* Boston: Little, Brown.

Vinick, B.H. and R.H. Jacobs. 1980. "The Displaced Homemaker: A State-of-the-Art Review." Wellesley, MA: Wellesley College, Center for Research on Women.

Waite, L.J. 1980. Working Wives and the Family Life Cycle." *American Journal of Sociology* 86 (2): 272–294.

Waldman, E., A.S. Grossman, H. Hayghe, and B. Johnson. 1979. "Working Mothers in the 1970's: A Look at the Statistics." *Monthly Labor Review* **102** (10): 39–49.

WEAL Washington Report. 1981a. "Women and the Budget: Cuts Threaten Key Programs." (April/May): 2.

———. 1981b. "Reagan Questions Federal Role: Hiring Goals For Women Reviewed." (June/July): 1.

———. 1981c. "Tax Reform to Ease, Not Eliminate Marriage Penalty." (August/September): 1.

Weissman, M.M., and G.L. Klerman. 1977. "Sex Differences and the Epidemiology of Depression." *Archives of General Psychiatry* **34** (1): 98–111.

Whiting, B.B. 1963. *Six Cultures: Studies of Child Rearing.* New York: Wiley.

Whiting, B.B. 1977. "Changing Life Styles in Kenya." *Daedalus* **106** (2): 211–225.

Whiting, B.B. 1978. "Probems of American Middle Class Women in Their Middle Years—A Comparative Approach." Paper prepared for the SSRC Study Group on Women: Work and Personality in the Middle Years. Waltham, MA: Brandeis University.

Woolsey, S.H. 1977. "Pied Piper Politics and the Child-Care Debate." *Daedalus* **106** (2): 127–145.

Work in America: Report of a Special Task Force to the Secretary of Health, Education, and Welfare. 1973. Cambridge, MA: MIT Press.

Wright, J.D. 1978. "Are Working Women Really More Satisfied? Evidence from Several National Surveys." *Journal of Marriage and Family* **40** (2): 301–313.

Young, C.M. 1978. "Work Sequences of Women during the Family Life Cycle." *Journal of Marriage and Family* **40** (2): 401–411.

Zill, N. 1978. "Divorce, Marital Happiness, and the Mental Health of Children: Findings from the Foundation of Child Development National Survey of Children." Paper prepared for the NIMH Workshop on Divorce and Children, Bethesda, MD, February 7–8.

APPENDIX:

Longitudinal and Cross-Sectional Data Sources on Women in the Middle Years

TONI C. ANTONUCCI

Institute for Social Research,
The University of Michigan

As this volume indicates, we have reached a point in scientific inquiry where it is necessary to consider the individual within the context of his or her life course. This focus is perhaps more evident as we turn to the study of middle-aged women. Chapters in this book (see Gilligan) and elsewhere have begun to point to the uniqueness of the life experience of women. It may seem as if we have only just discovered that man continues to grow and develop through adulthood. Nevertheless, it is time to modify this statement and attend to the fact that both men and women continue to grow and develop over their life course and not necessarily in a similar fashion. Although the questions are new, the data that might be useful, for at least preliminary examinations of these questions, are in some cases already available.

The following compendium is designed to give the reader, perhaps a social scientist who has become very excited by the questions and issues raised in this book, some idea of the resources that are available. In the main, there are five types of data sets presented: large data sets, fertility-related studies, longitudinal data sets, research on college and professional women, and miscellaneous regional data sets. Some of these data sets are representative of the national population, and some are more specific. Others were designed to include people with some unique quality of interest (e.g., women with Ph.D.'s in sociology). Still other data sets have followed the same people over 10 to 20 years. As you will see, the exact nature of the data sets included in this compendium varies considerably. They were chosen in large part for the vast array of resources they represent. Although the original purpose of the study might not at first glance seem particularly relevant to our present concerns, it is frequently the case that the right or nearly the right questions have already been asked, but no one has yet looked at just the right combination of answers. So, for example, in a national study of the *Quality of Life in America* both men and women were asked about their feelings of satisfaction in various domains of life, but until recently no one has looked at how these satisfactions differ for men and women over the family life-cycle. Similarly, as data were collected from the boys and girls in California and their parents in the 1920s and followed over many years, no one was thinking about the impact of history and social experience on their parents. It remained for someone 50 years later to examine this particular question (see Glen Elder's *Children of the Great Depression*, 1974). As Glen Elder asked a different question, so too do we want to ask different questions about women in middle age. We are now interested in understanding what the formative factors in the life course of women are and how do these affect personality, changing work histories, and life satisfaction. The data sets I have outlined in this appendix are meant to provide ammunition for a first inquiry. The list includes a great variety of types of data, although there is no claim that this compendium is in any way exhaustive. Again, these are meant to be suggestive, to whet your appetite to explore the questions that might have been raised as a result of your reading this book. It is important to recognize that what is included here represents only a small fraction of the data that are actually already collected and available for use. It is also important to note that if the exact data to answer a particular question do not seem available, it is possible to begin with preliminary or approximate data and with the advantage of such pilot work, then to collect primary data.

Very few large data sets have focused exclusively on women in their middle years. National surveys that are representative of the population do, of course, include middle-aged women, and these are an important data source. I have included a few of the largest and most relevant data sets here. In particular, the Morgan study of 5000 families and the Parnes National Longitudinal Surveys are enormous sources of information. These two data sources alone represent some of the most inclusive studies presently available. The fact that the women in these surveys were interviewed independently as were members of their families is particularly relevant for the study of the middle-aged woman within the context of her life course and of her family. Other large data sets are included that have various unique or distinctive qualities. For example, the *Quality of Life, Americans View Their Mental Health*, and *Parent-Child Socialization* studies each offer at least two cohorts at different periods in time. The *Market Opinion Research Study of Women* and the *Virginia Slims Women's Opinion Poll* represent the only two large scientifically conducted surveys that focus on women. These are also unique. The *National Study of Black Americans* and *The National Study of Chicanos* are included as the first large representative data sets on minorities in this country. The *Quality of Employment, Work History,* and *Retirement History* studies provide special and unique perspectives on the work experience. The *Social Networks of Adults* and the *Study of Women's Attitudes* are each unusual studies. The social networks study explores the network characteristics of men and women over 50, and the study of women's attitudes examines women's sense of identity as females as well as members of various other groups. In short, the data sets are very diverse representatives of the large national surveys frequently considered appropriate for secondary analyses. A large majority of these data sets are now or should soon be available for public use.

The next group of studies included is large data sets related to fertility. These data sets are included as examples of a unique kind of research related to women. Indeed, at one point, this was the only kind of data that focused exclusively on women. In some ways, this research was avant garde because it attempted to take into account the special life-cycle and family life-cycle considerations that dominate the lives of many women. These data sets represent a large tradition in research that has been often recognized, in fact legitimized, through associations with Departments of Population Studies, Demography and/or Sociology. These data sets are interesting for several reasons. They are frequently longitudinal in nature, and in that way permit one to trace the development and change of women and women's roles in the twentieth century. However, equally true is the fact that the data sets frequently also trace the development of the researchers. Thus, in some early studies women's work history or experience was not considered an important area of inquiry. Instead, one asked about the work history of the spouse. Similarly, many studies simply assumed "the joy of parenting." More recent studies such as Hoffman's on *Attitudes About Children* and Chilman's on *Parental Satisfaction* consider these uncharted territories as appropriate areas for inquiry. These studies are included in the hope that they will provide a unique source of information on the norms, expectations, and experiences of women in their child-bearing/child-rearing years.

Another unusual data source is the longitudinal studies that began in childhood and continued through adulthood. Many of these studies were initiated in the early part of the century. Most of them are regionally based and tend to focus on the West Coast. Although in some ways these data are the least rigorous because they include smaller samples and suffer nonrandom attrition, recent analysis of them has benefited from advances in psychometric techniques. There have also been several changes in the main thrust of such studies that coincide with the evolving interests of the principal researchers. Yet these studies are also unique. One cannot deny the time and tedium that must be invested in a longitudinal study. With the soaring costs of research it is not clear that we will ever be able to replicate these studies. They are therefore included not only because they are unique unto themselves but also because they provide what may be an increasingly rare type of data.

Of late, there has been much developing interest in the work and educational experiences of adult women. Professional women have become a focus for an intense research effort that is aimed at understanding and documenting the experience of female professionals. In part, this research activity has been motivated by affirmative action. People, both men and women, seek to document inequities in professional experiences (promotion, salary, etc.). Similarly, research that focuses on the educational experiences and achievement patterns of women is beginning to identify the different factors that affect women's professional and educational achievement. These data sets are included for those persons interested in exploring this relatively recent pattern of adult development among women.

Finally, the last section labeled "Miscellaneous Regional Data Sets" consists of a variety of interesting studies that have content related to women in the middle years. Here are included investigations of neighborhood informal networks, housewives, widows, role conflicts, transitions, retirement, and life stress. Although each of these studies is useful in its own right, the only common theme tying them together is their regional nature. It should be noted, however, that regional limitation does not necessarily imply that the sample is small because these "miscellaneous data sets" include as few as 100 middle-aged women in the Chicago area and as many as 2499 men and women in the Detroit area.

As stated earlier, the purpose of this compendium is to provide the interested researcher with some idea of the kind of data that are already available. It is hoped that these data will help answer questions about work- and personality-related issues of middle-aged women. This is clearly an important new area of research. As we face the changing social, economic, and political times, it is becoming evident that women are experiencing, affecting, and influencing these changes to a degree that is perhaps greater than any other time in history. We need to proceed with the most intensive and yet cost-effective research effort possible. This summary list is designed to aid that process.

In order to provide an overview of the data sets reported, a series of tables follows that summarizes the relevant information about each data source. The tables include the director or principal investigator of the study, the year the data were collected, the present location of the data, the type of data and type of sample, the number of people in the study and the sex of the participants, whether or not new data are expected in the future, and finally whether personality, work, and/or satisfaction variables are included.

Following the tables is a brief summary of each data set. The data sets, both in the tables and in the brief summaries, are grouped into five categories: (1) large data sets, (2) large data sets related to fertility, (3) longitudinal studies beginning in childhood or early adulthood, (4) professional women/ college women, and (5) miscellaneous regional data sets. Although the content of the summaries varies, it is especially the distinctive features of the data that are described. When possible, I have given the original purpose of the study and details on other information that are relevant to women in midlife but that are only tangentially related to the purpose of the original study. By cross-referencing the information in the summaries and the tables, the reader should be able first to ascertain whether the data set contains information of interest on personality, work, and/or satisfaction issues, and then to locate the data and obtain further information about the data set.

Large Data Sets

Study	Director	Year	Location of Data	Type of Data	Type of Sample	N Male/Female	New Data Expected	Personality Variables	Satisfaction Variables	Work Variables
National Longitudinal Survey	Parnes	1968+	Ohio State University	Long. cohort[a]	Nat'l	22,157mf	Yes	Yes	Yes	Yes
5000 American Families	Morgan	1968+	ICPSR[c]	Long.	Nat'l	5,000mf	Yes	Yes	Yes	Yes
Project Talent	Flanagan/AIR	1960+	AIR[d]	Long. cohort	Nat'l	400,000mf	Yes	Yes	Yes	Yes
Quality of American Life	Campbell, Converse, Rodgers	1971 1978	ICPSR	C–S[b]	Nat'l	2,164mf 3,692mf	No	Yes	Yes	Yes
Social Indicators of Well-being	Andrews, Withey	1973	ICPSR	C–S	Nat'l	5,422mf	No	Yes	Yes	Yes
Americans View their Mental Health	Gurin, Veroff, Feld Veroff, Douvan, Kulka	1957 1976	ICPSR	C–S cohort	Nat'l	2,460mf 2,264mf	No	Yes	Yes	Yes
Parent–Child Socialization	Jennings	1965/1973+	ICPSR	Long.	Nat'l	2,099mf	Yes	Yes	Yes	Yes
Time Use	Juster	1976+	ICPSR	Long.	Nat'l	1,500mf	No	No	Yes	Yes
Quality of Employment	Quinn	1969/73/77	ICPSR	C–S cohort Long. in part	Nat'l	1,500mf each wave	?	Yes	Yes	Yes
Work History	Social Security Administration	1957+	SSA[e]	C–S Long. cohort	Nat'l	2,000,000mf	Yes	No	No	Yes
Retirement History	Social Security Administration	1969–1979	SSA	Long. C–S	Nat'l	11,153mf	Yes	No	No	Yes
Study of Women's Attitudes	Gurin	1972 1976 1979	ICPSR	C–S Long.	Nat'l	2,705mf 2,000mf 273mf	No	Yes	Yes	Yes

246

Market Opinion Research Study of Women	Bryant	1975	Detroit	C–S	Nat'l	1,522f	No	Yes	Yes	Yes
Virginia Slims Women's Opinion Poll	Harris, Roper	1970/72/73 1974	ICPSR Roper	C–S C–S	Nat'l Nat'l	4,020mf 4,000mf	No	Yes	Yes	Yes
Black Americans	Jackson	1978–	ISR[f]	C–S	Nat'l	2,103+mf	?	Yes	Yes	Yes
Chicanos	Arce	1978–	ISR	C–S	Nat'l	991mf	No	Yes	Yes	Yes
Quality of Life of Older Americans	Flanagan	1978–	AIR	C–S/ cohort	Nat'l	3,000mf	Yes?	Yes	Yes	Yes
Study of Groups	Jackman	1975	ISR	C–S	Nat'l	1,914mf	No	Yes	No	Yes
General Social Survey	NORC[g]	1972/73/ 74/75/76	ICPSR	C–S cohort	Nat'l	around 1,500mf each year	No	Yes	Yes	Yes
American Family Reports	Yankelovich	1974 1977	Minneapolis	C–S C–S	Nat'l Nat'l	2,194mf 2,102mf	? ?	No Yes	Yes Yes	Yes No
Support Networks in Adult Life	Kahn, Antonucci	1981	ISR	C–S	Nat'l	718mf	?	Yes	Yes	Yes

[a]Long. = longitudinal.

[b]C–S = cross-sectional.

[c]Inter-University Consortium for Political and Social Research, Institute for Social Research, University of Michigan, Ann Arbor.

[d]American Institutes for Research, Palo Alto, CA.

[e]Social Security Administration.

[f]Institute for Social Research, University of Michigan, Ann Arbor.

[g]NORC = National Opinion Research Center, Chicago.

Large Data Sets Related to Fertility

Study	Director	Year	Location of Data	Type of Data	Type of Sample	N Male/ Female	New Data Expected	Personality Variables	Satisfaction Variables	Work Variables
Growth of American Families	Freedman, Whelpton	1955 1960	U. of Wisc. Madison	C-S[a]	Nat'l	2,713f 3,322f	Yes	No	Yes	Yes
National Fertility Study	Ryder, Westoff	1965 1970>panel 1975	U. of Wisc. Madison	C-S Long.[b]	Nat'l	5,617f 6,752f	Yes	No	Yes	Yes
Princeton Fertility Study	Westoff	1957/60 1963–1967	Princeton	Long.	Nat'l Metro	1,165f	No	Yes	Yes	No
Detroit Family Growth/ Study of American Families	R. Freedman, D. Freedman, Thornton	1962/63/66/ 77/80	ICPSR[c]	Long. cohort	Reg.	1,304f 935f	Yes	No	Yes	Yes
Sex Roles, Life Styles and Childbearing	Scanzoni	1971/1975	Nat'l Analysts/Phila.	C-S +Long.	Reg.	3,100mf	No	Yes	Yes	Yes
Attitudes about Children	L. Hoffman	1975	ICPSR	C-S	Nat'l	1,569f	No	Yes	Yes	Yes
Parental Satisfaction	Chilman	1977	Wisconsin	C-S	Reg.	454mf	No	Yes	Yes	Yes

[a] C-S = Cross-sectional.
[b] Long. = Longitudinal.
[c] Inter-University Consortium for Political and Social Research, Institute for Social Research, University of Michigan, Ann Arbor.

Longitudinal Studies Beginning in Childhood

Study	Director	Year	Location of Data	Type of Data	Type of Sample	N Male/Female	New Data Expected	Personality Variables	Satisfaction Variables	Work Variables
Study of Gifted Children	Terman, Sears	1928	Stanford	Long.[a]	Reg.	1,470mf	Yes	Yes	Yes	Yes
Berkeley Growth Study	Bayley	1928	Berkeley	Long.	Reg.	61mf	Yes	Yes	Yes	Yes
Oakland Growth Study	Stolz, Jones	1931	Berkeley	Long.	Reg.	200mf	Yes	Yes	Yes	Yes
Guidance Study	MacFarlane	1928	Berkeley	Long.	Reg.	123mf	Yes	Yes	Yes	Yes
From 30 to 70	Maas, Kuypers	1928	Berkeley	Long.	Reg.	142mf	No	Yes	Yes	Yes
Fels Study	Sontag	1929	Yellow Springs	Long.	Reg.	300+mf	Yes	Yes	Yes	Yes

[a]Long. = Longitudinal.

Professional Women/College Women

Study	Director	Year	Location of Data	Type of Data	Type of Sample	N Male/Female	New Data Expected	Personality Variables	Satisfaction Variables	Work Variables
Political Science	Converse	1970	ICPSR[c]	C–S[a]	Special	40%f	?	No	No	Yes
Microbiologists	Kashket	1971	Cambridge	C–S	Special	815mf	?	No	No	Yes
Modern Language Dept.	Howe	1970	Baltimore	C–S	Special	595dept.	?	No	No	Yes
Sociology	Rossi	1969	Washington DC	C–S	Special	189dept.	Yes	No	No	Yes
Social Work	Fanshel	1972/75	Washington DC	C–S	Special	21,755mf	Yes	No	No	Yes
Couples in Psychology	Butler	1958/1973	Stanford	C–S	Special	870mf	Yes	No	No	Yes
Women Doctorates	Astin	1966	ACE[d]	C–S	Special	1,547f	?	Yes	No	Yes
Women in Academe	Astin	1969	ACE	C–S	Special	6,892mf	?	Yes	No	Yes
Social Workers	D. Herberg	1967	Ann Arbor	Long.[b] cohort	Special	1,037f	No	Yes	Yes	Yes
National Survey of Higher Education	Carnegie Commission	1969	Minnesota	C–S	Nat'l	60,000mf	?	No	No	Yes
College Alumnae in Midlife	Stycos	1975	Ithaca	Long.	Nat'l	1,512f	?	Yes	Yes	Yes
Vassar	Brown	b.1953+ –1974	Ann Arbor & Vassar	Long.	Special	108f	Yes	Yes	Yes	Yes
Continuing Education of Women	Markus	1978–79	Ann Arbor	Long. cohort	Reg./ Special	1,145f	Yes	Yes	Yes	Yes
	Manis	1981	Ann Arbor	Long. cohort	Reg./ Special	2,000f	?	Yes	Yes	Yes

[a] C–S = Cross-sectional.
[b] Long. = Longitudinal.
[c] ICPSR = Inter-University Consortium for Political and Social Research, Institute for Social Research, University of Michigan, Ann Arbor.
[d] ACE = American Council on Education, Washington, DC.

Miscellaneous Regional Data Sets

Study	Director	Year	Location of Data	Type of Data	Type of Sample	N Male/ Female	New Data Expected	Person- ality Variables	Satis- faction Variables	Work Variables
Neighborhoods	Warren	1976	Oakland, Mich.	C–S[a]	Reg.	2,499mf	No	Yes	Yes	Yes
Jobs and Gender	Bose, Rossi	1972	NORC[c]	C–S	Reg.	392f	No	No	No	Yes
Housewives	Lopata	1950–60	Chicago	C–S	Reg.	571f	No	No	Yes	Yes
Widows	Lopata	1969	Chicago	C–S	Reg.	301f	Yes	Yes	Yes	Yes
Widows	Lopata	1974	Chicago	C–S	Reg.	1,169f	No	Yes	Yes	Yes
Time Use/Housework	Walker	1967/68	Cornell	C–S	Reg.	1,296f	No	No	No	Yes
Middle-Aged Women	Neugarten	1963/75	Chicago	C–S Long.[b]	Reg.	100f	?	Yes	Yes	Yes
Role conflicts	Nevill	1971	Florida	C–S	Reg.	518f	No	Yes	Yes	Yes
Retirement	Atchley	1977+	Scripps Found.	Long.	Reg.	1,106mf	Yes	Yes	Yes	Yes
Adaptation Study	Maddox	1968+	Duke	Long.	Reg.	502mf	Yes	Yes	Yes	Yes
Adult Phases	Gould	1972	Los Angeles	C–S	Reg.	524mf	Yes?	Yes	Yes	Yes
Transitions	Lowenthal	1975+	San Francisco	Long. cohort	Reg.	216mf	Yes	Yes	Yes	Yes
Life Activity	Schaie	1977	USC[d]	Long./C–S cohort	Reg.	1,400mf	Yes?	Yes	Yes	Yes
Life Stress	Pearlin	1977	NORC	C–S	Reg.	2,300mf	No	Yes	Yes	Yes
Life Events	Myers	1967/69	Yale	C–S	Reg.	938mf	No	Yes	Yes	Yes

[a]C–S = Cross-sectional.
[b]Long. = Longitudinal.
[c]NORC = National Opinion Research Center, Chicago.
[d]USC = University of Southern California, Los Angeles.

LARGE DATA SETS

The National Longitudinal Surveys—Herbert S. Parnes

The National Longitudinal Surveys are one of the most extensive data sets available on men and women and their labor market experience. The study began in 1968 and is currently ongoing. The original sample consists of 5518 men between the ages of 45−59, 5393 women between the ages of 30−44, 5713 "boys" aged 14−24, and 5533 "girls" aged 14−24. In addition, a new cohort of 12,000 young men and women aged 14−21 was added in 1979. The sample has been continually reinterviewed, eight or nine times thus far, either in person, by telephone, or by mail. Continued reinterviews are planned. Although complete details of the study would be impossible to report, the handbook lists the following as foci of interest: labor market experience, socioeconomic and human capital variables, financial characteristics, military service, job attitudes, aspirations and expectations, attitudes toward high school and college, other social psychological variables (including Rotter's I−E Scale, mental ability, labor market information, retrospective evaluation of labor market experience), and environmental variables. Research based on these data is so extensive that a newsletter exists that reports on what areas are currently being explored and by whom. This is called the NLS Newsletter (Center for Human Resource Research, The Ohio State University), and would be useful for anyone interested in this data set. A 10-year report of the mature women cohort has recently been completed.

Sources:

Shaw, L. (Ed.). *Dual Careers: A Decade of Change in the Lives of Mature Women*, 1981, a report to the Department of Labor, soon to be published with MIT Press.

A special issue of *Journal of Economics and Business* has been published on the topic of "Longitudinal Research and Labor Force Behavior" with articles by D. Featherman, B. Singer, H. Watts, F. Skidmore, and J. Peterson and an overview by P. Andrisani on the NLS data, 1980.

Chenoweth, L. and E. Maret, 1980. "The Career Patterns of Mature American Women." *Sociology of Work and Occupations, An International Journal,* **7** (2): 222.

The Changing Economic Status of 5000 American Families: The Panel Study of Income Dynamics—James N. Morgan

This panel study began in 1968 with a sample of approximately 3000 families, oversampled for poor families. Interviews have been conducted yearly, incorporating into the study new families that have been formed from the original 1968 sample. Detailed information has been collected about income, family composition, as well as information on child care, housework, age, education, sex, race, work history, and work experiences. This sample includes families with husbands, wives, and children as well as various other possible family combinations (e.g., single parent families, extended families living together, etc.). In addition, in 1976 wives were specifically interviewed. The emphasis in this study is clearly economic although there have been some personality-related questions asked at various times. The study is expected to continue perhaps for 5 or 10 years. This is a unique and extensive data set.

Source:

Morgan, J.N., G. Duncan, and the staff of the Economic Behavior Program. *Five Thousand American Families, Vols. I, II, III, IV, V, VI.* Institute for Social Research. Ann Arbor, MI. 48106.

Project Talent—John C. Flanagan, Original Project Director, American Institutes for Research, Present Base of the Study

Project Talent, a longitudinal study of American youth, was conceived as a means of developing a national inventory of human resources that would allow the identification of the educational and life experiences most important in preparing individuals for their life work. The original sample, collected around 1960, included over 400,000 ninth, tenth, eleventh, and twelfth grade students: 205,972 males and 202,159 females. Follow-up studies with various sample sizes have been collected at one, five and 11 years from the respondents' high school graduation. In addition, John Flanagan has begun a study entitled *Identifying Opportunities for Improving the Quality of Life of Older Age Groups* (see separate listing for this study), which includes 1000 30-year-olds (500 women) drawn from the Project Talent sample. When the Project Talent students were in high school, their ability, knowledge, and achievement were assessed as were their dispositional traits and interests; background information on their family, health, current activities, and future plans were also gathered. Follow-up survey data include an examination and assessment of educational experiences, occupations, marriage, and family, as well as global measures of life satisfaction. This data set is important not only because it provides background information for a large sample of women who might presently be defined as in their middle adult years, but also because subsequent studies are likely to be conducted across the entire lifetime of the respondents.

Although data sets can be prepared by the American Institutes for Research according to the specifications of the researchers, a public use file has also been prepared by AIR that is available at considerably less cost.

Sources:

Russ-Eft, D. and J.C. Flanagan. 1976. *Contribution of Vocational Guidance, Vocational Training, and Employment to the Quality of Life of 30 Year Olds.* Palo Alto, CA: American Institutes for Research.

Shaycoft, M.F. 1975. *Careers in Science: A Project Talent Study.* Palo Alto, CA: American Institutes for Research.

The Quality of American Life—Angus Campbell, Philip Converse, and Willard Rodgers

The Quality of American Life study is based on a national probability sample and survey designed to measure the respondents' perceptions of their sociopsychological condition, their needs and expectations from life, and the degree to which these needs are satisfied. Particular topics include the community and neighborhood, current conditions of life in the United States, educational and work experiences, leisure activities, and personal relationships. Questions measure general life satisfaction as well as satisfaction for specific life domains. Life satisfaction and work issues are explored, but personality is not. In 1978 Campbell and Converse conducted a replication of the original study.

Sources:

Campbell, A., P.E. Converse, and W.L. Rodgers. 1976. *The Quality of American Life: Perceptions, Evaluations, and Satisfactions.* New York: Russell Sage Foundation.

Campbell, A. 1981. *The Sense of Well-Being in America: Recent Patterns and Trends.* New York: McGraw-Hill.

Social Indicators of Well-Being—Frank Andrews and Steven Withey

Social Indicators of Well-Being is a national probability study designed to measure the quality of life through subjective and objective social indicators. This survey focused on the concerns of the American people and their relevance to a feeling of well-being; how each concern relates to another; how Americans arrive at a general sense of well-being; how readily people can identify and report their feelings about well-being; and how comparable are various subgroups within the American population with respect to each of these issues. Life satisfaction is explored in depth, work issues are explored somewhat, and personality issues not at all.

Source:

Andrews, F.M. and S.B. Withey. 1976. *Social Indicators of Well-Being: Americans' Perceptions of Life Quality.* New York: Plenum Press.

Americans View Their Mental Health—Gurin, Veroff and Feld/1957, Veroff, Douvan and Kulka/1976

This survey was designed to assess people's own evaluations of their mental health and the way they handled their problems. The questionnaries focused on various areas of life in which problems may develop, including marriage and parenthood, the work situation, and general social relationships. Several questions tap general happiness; others tap happiness or satisfaction within specific areas such as marital and work roles. An extensive set of health-related variables and measures of social activities, as well as numerous background variables, were assessed in these studies. The 1976 replication includes 70 percent of the questions asked in 1957.

Sources:

Gurin, J., J. Veroff, and S. Feld. 1960. *Americans View Their Mental Health.* New York: Basic Books.

Veroff, J., and S. Feld. 1970. *Marriage and Work in America.* New York: Van Nostrand Reinhold.

Veroff, J., E. Douvan, and R. Kulka. 1981. *The Inner American.* New York: Basic Books.

Parent–Child Socialization Study—Kent Jennings

This is a unique and multilevel study, but the most relevant sample includes 2099 high school seniors and their parent or parents who were interviewed in 1965 and then reinterviewed in 1973. At the time of the reinterview, the spouse of the child was also interviewed if he/she had married. This study focused on socialization of the child and parent with respect to a variety of issues including politics, family life, education, and attitudes toward the other generational member. M.K. Jennings and G. Markus hope to collect a new wave of data from both parents and their now adult children.

Sources:

Jennings, M.K., and R.G. Niemi. 1981. *Generations and Politics: A Panel Study of Young Adults and Their Parents.* Princeton: Princeton Universtiy Press.

Niemi, R., R. Hedges, and K. Jennings. 1977. "The Similarity of Husbands' and Wives' Political Views." *American Political Quarterly* **5** (2): 133–148.

Time Use in Economic and Social Accounts—F.T. Juster et al.

This study is actually a series of surveys conducted during a 12-month period from fall 1975 through summer 1976. These data are unique in that they consist of four samplings of the same individuals, controlling for season and including two weekdays, a Saturday and a Sunday. These data include the respondents' account of what they did at each moment of the previous 24-hour day, whom they were with, and where the activity took place. On the basis of these data, the researchers have constructed a synthetic week, which represents the general behavior pattern of the respondent. The study also includes life-state questions as well as general background information. The primary respondents are a representative sample of American adults living in the coterminous United States. In addition, the spouses of the original sample members were also included.

Source:

Juster, F.T., P. Courant, G.J. Duncan, J.P. Robinson, and F.P. Stafford. 1979. *Time Use in Economic and Social Accounts, 1975–1976.* Survey Research Center, Institute for Social Research Archives. The University of Michigan (ICPSR study #7580) Ann Arbor, MI, 48106.

Quality of Employment—Robert Quinn

This is a national representative sample of people in the labor force who work 20 hours a week or more. The major purpose of this study is to provide a description, interpretation, and continuous monitoring of the quality of people's employment. The principal aims of the survey were (1) to assess the impact of working conditions on the well-being of workers, (2) to establish baseline statistics, and (3) to permit comparisons from other studies. Data were gathered cross-sectionally in 1969 and 1973. In 1977, another cross-sectional wave of 1500 people was conducted as well as a five-year follow-up interview of those interviewed in the 1973 Employment Survey. Some people in this latter group are also participants in the third cross-sectional wave of 1977.

Sources:

Quinn, R.P. and G.L. Staines. 1979. *The 1977 Quality of Employment Survey: Descriptive Statistics with Comparison Data from the 1969–1970 Survey of Working Conditions and the 1972–1973 Quality of Employment Survey.* Ann Arbor, MI: Institute for Social Research, The University of Michigan.

Staines, G.L. and R.P. Quinn. 1979. "American Workers Evaluate the Quality of Their Jobs." *Monthly Labor Review* **102** (1): 3–12.

Work History 1957—Social Security Administration

The Social Security Administration is constantly gathering economic and demographic data in the course of administering the Social Security system. The *Work History* sample is part of this and contains basic demographic, employment, earnings, and benefits data for a sample of over 2 million workers currently or previously in paid employment covered under the provisions of the Social Security system. This data base provides complete and accurate information on both earnings and benefits and also permits following migration and employment patterns of covered workers in relation to earnings on a yearly basis. These data have been gathered since 1957 on an annual basis.

Source:

Hirschberg, D.A. 1975. "The continuous Work-History Sample." *Review of Public Data Use,* **3** (3): 11–14.

Retirement History Study, 1969–1979—Social Security Administration

This is a 10-year longitudinal study of men and women on the threshold of retirement. The purpose of the study is to assess the adequacy and effects of the Social Security program's provision for retired workers. Detailed questions about work experience, financial circumstances, consumption patterns, and standard demographic variables, living arrangements, and changes in residence are asked. The sample includes 11,153 men and women aged 58–63. The first interviews were conducted in 1969 and have been recurring every two years.

Source:

Irelan, L.M. 1972. *Retirement History Study: Introduction.* Retirement History Study Report No. 1 (November).

Studies of Women's Attitudes—Patricia Gurin

Portions of this study were conducted as part of the 1972 and 1976 election study. The sample consisted of 2705 men and women in 1972, 2248 men and women in 1976, and 273 women in 1979. All the 1979 sample represent three-panel respondents', a greater number of two-panel respondents are available from 1972 and 1976. During the election studies the representative sample was interviewed both pre- and post-election. The pre-election interview contained demographic questions and personal efficacy questions;, a random half of the sample also received Rotter's I−E Scale and some questions about life satisfaction. In the post-election surveys individuals were asked about job self-confidence, employment expectations for the future, causal attributions for success, and failure in efforts to improve one's market situation. Housewives were asked additional questions about career commitments, intentions of getting a job in the next year, and whether they had worked for pay in the last 12 months. Both interviews contained questions about women's issues, abortion, politics, and equality. The third and smallest wave of this study included only women and focused on women's attitudes about women and their feelings of group identification with women.

Sources:

Townsend, A., and P. Gurin. 1981. "Re-examining the Frustrated Homemaker Hypothesis: Role fit, personal dissatisfaction and collective discontent." *Sociology of Work and Occupations.*

Gurin, P., and B.M. Morrison. 1976. *Education, Labor Market Experiences, and Current Expectancies of Black and White Men and Women.* Report to the National Institute of Education. Institute for Social Research, The Universtiy of Michigan, Ann Arbor, MI 48109.

Gurin, P. 1976. "The Role of Worker Expectancies in the Study of Employment Discrimination." In P. Wallace, (Ed.), *Women, Minorities and Employment Discrimination.* Boston, MA: Lexington Books.

Market Opinion Research: A National Survey of Women— Barbara Everitt Bryant

This study was undertaken by the National Commission on the Observance of International Women's Year, 1975. It is a national survey of women that is designed to assess women's attitudes and opinions, record their current activities, and examine the patterns of their lives and their views about the future. The sample includes 1522 adult women and represents a geographically stratified probability sample of the United States. The areas covered in the survey are as follows: the life work of women (including non-paid as well as paid employment, work in and outside the home), education, work patterns, marital status, motherhood, family planning, child care, leisure activities, mass media use, media image of women, and involvement in and attitudes about the women's movement.

Source:

Bryant, B.E. 1977. *American Women Today and Tomorrow.* Washington, DC: Government Printing Office.

Virginia Slims American Women's Opinion Poll— Louis Harris and the Roper Organization

This is a series of surveys that Virginia Slims, the cigarette manufacturers, commissioned Louis Harris and the Roper Organization to conduct. The first survey in 1970 dealt with how women perceived their role and status in American society. The 1972 survey measured women's views of themselves in politics and the economy, and men's views of women with respect to these same issues. The 1972 respondents were asked about their attitudes toward a variety of women's issues: political involvement, handling of a variety of situations, problems facing the nation, organizational membership, and income as well as personal demographic issues.

In 1974 Virginia Slims commissioned the Roper Organization to conduct a third study on women's thoughts and feelings. This poll covered such areas as love, marriage, sex roles and stereotypes, family relationships, the working wife, divorce, changing sex values, children born outside of marriage, and other personal areas.

Sources:

Several publications are available from: Virginia Slims American Women's Opinion Poll, Philip Morris U.S.A., 100 Park Ave., New York, N.Y. 10017. See for example:
The 1972 Virginia Slims American Women's Opinion Poll: A Study Conducted by Louis Harris and Associates.
The Virginia Slims American Women's Opinion Poll. Vol. III. *A Study Conducted by the Roper Organization Inc.* 1974.

National Survey of Black Americans—James S. Jackson

This is the first national representative study of Black Americans and is now being completed. The substantive areas of investigation include: the inter-relationships among identity, formal and informal support systems, mental health indexes, and use of mental health resources. Information is also being gathered about participation in the labor force, income, educational background, family composition, housing, and health. These data will provide a national resource and comparative base for research on the Black American. In addition, a three-generational sample is also being interviewed. No publications are available at this time.

Source:

Jackson, J.S. 1977–. *National Surveys of Black Americans.* Current research studies at the Institute for Social Research, The Universtiy of Michigan, Ann Arbor, MI.

National Chicano Identity and Mental Health—Carlos Arce

This national study of Chicanos has recently been completed. The survey focuses on ethnic identification, ethnic consciousness, cultural consciousness, political consciousness and associational preferences. Information about structural aspirations for self and children and indicators of mental health status such as personal efficacy, self-esteem, psychophysical symptoms, responses to life stresses, self-definition of problems, attitudes, and use of help resources has also been collected. No publications are available at this time.

Source:

Arce, Carlos. 1978–. National Chicano Identity and Mental Health Project. A current research study at the Institute for Social Research, The University of Michigan, Ann Arbor, MI.

Quality of Life of Older Age Groups—John Flanagan

This sample includes 1000 people (500 men, 500 women) from each of three age groups: 30, 50, and 70. The 30-year-olds represent a sample of the Project Talent population; the other two age groups are representative samples of the 48−52 and 68−72 age groups respectively. The topics covered in the interview include leisure activities and interests, organizational activities, friends, health, occupation, economic conditions, marital history, quality of life, family relationships, parents, and some general questions about the respondents' past life. The total number of people in this survey should be 3000. It is possible that these people will be reinterviewed in the future.

Only a few papers are presently available (see below). However, data from the Project Talent study have been published and represent the 30-year-olds in this sample during their young adulthood (see separate listing for Project Talent). The study is being conducted by the American Institutes for Research, Palo Alto, California 94302.

Sources:

Flanagan, J.C. 1978. "The Major Contributors to Quality of Life for the Elderly." Paper presented at the APA meeting in Toronto, Canada, September.

Flanagan, J.C. 1979. "Life's Last 20 Years: How to Improve Them." Paper presented at the APA Convention in New York City, September.

General Social Surveys—National Opinion Research Center

This is a series of studies conducted in 1972, 1973, 1974, 1975, and 1976. Approximately 1500 men and women were interviewed each time as part of this national survey. A variety of topics was covered each time. Generally, basic demographic data were collected each year. Questions on changes in behavior related to the life cycle, social control, morale, social mobility, quality of work, life satisfaction, and attitudes about women's roles were asked in some years and not in others.

Source:

Davis, J.A. 1972−. General Social Surveys. Data and descriptions of the General Social Surveys, 1972−1978, are available through the Inter-University Consortium for Political and Social Research. *See its Guide to Resources and Services, 1979−1980.* University of Michigan, Ann Arbor, MI.

General Mills American Family Reports—Yankelovich, Skelly, and White, Inc.

General Mills has commissioned two studies of American family life. The first reports how Americans cope with and adapt to their financial situation. It is an attempt to analyze the impact money has on the family in a time of economic stress. The study explores several aspects of American life including family structure, intrafamily relationships, the value system, money management, money hopes and pleasures, money problems, and money's relationships to institutions, health and well-being, life-styles, outlooks, and goals. The interviews included men and women, sometimes husbands and wives in the same family.

The second report concerns how American families cope with problems of raising children. The results are based on a national probability sample of 1,230 families and a total of 2,102 interviews including 403 interviews with the other parent in the same household and 469 interviews with children between the ages of 6 and 12 in the households surveyed. Major topics covered with parents include demographic profiles, attitudes toward parenting, sex roles, discipline, and handling of problems. Among topics covered with children are satisfactions and dissatisfactions, sources of arguments, and parents' requirements.

Sources:

Yankelovich, Skelly, and White, Inc. 1975. *The General Mills American Family Report, 1974–1975: A Study of the American Family and Money.* Minneapolis: General Mills.

Yankelovich, Skelly, and White, Inc. 1977. *The General Mills American Family Report, 1976–77: Raising Children in a Changing Society.* Minneapolis: General Mills.

Social Networks in Adult Life—Robert L. Kahn and Toni C. Antonucci

This study includes a national sample of 718 adults, 50 years of age and older. The study was designed to explore the role of social relationships in the lives of adult Americans. Extensive information was obtained on the individual's support network, those people he or she felt close to, what functions network members actually performed for one another, and whether any negative support existed. In addition, people were asked about several domains of life satisfaction: their health, their opinion on a variety of issues relevant to older people, and general work history and demographic questions. A complementary study was conducted at the same time that involved the interview of approximately two members of the social network of people over 70 in the sample.

Sources:

Antonucci, T.C. and C.E. Depner. 1982. "Social Support and Informal Helping Relationships." In T.A. Wills (Ed.), *Basic Processes in Helping Relationships.* New York: Academic Press.

Depner, C., and B. Ingersoll. 1982. "Employment Status and Social Support: The Experience of the Mature Woman." In M. Szinovacz (Ed.), *Women's Retirement: Policy Implications of Recent Research.* Sage Publications, Beverly Hills, CA.

LARGE DATA SETS RELATED TO FERTILITY

The Growth of American Families Study and the National Fertility Study

These two studies are related. The second is an offshoot of the first, with some continuity between the two. Both include large numbers of women who are in their middle years. The samples are both national and cross-sectional, with the exception that the 1970–1975 samples are longitudinal. However, the studies are only briefly mentioned here because there are almost no personality and satisfaction measures included and only a small number of questions concerning the work history of the women. As one might imagine, the major emphasis of these studies was the fertility and fertility plans of the respondents, their methods of contraception, attitudes toward abortion, and the like. Data concerning women's socioeconomic status, education, religion, and area of residence were customarily collected. Further information on these data sets can be obtained from Larry Bumpass at the University of Wisconsin, Madison.

Sources:

Freedman, R., P.K. Whelpton, and A.A. Campbell. 1959. *Family Planning, Sterility and Population Growth.* New York: McGraw-Hill.

Ryder, N.B., and C.F. Westoff. 1971. *Reproduction in the United States 1965.* Princeton: Princeton University Press.

Princeton Fertility Study—Office of Population Research, Princeton University

The Princeton Fertility Study is based on 1165 couples who had a second child in September 1956. The wives were interviewed in person, and both husband and wives were sent follow-up questionnaires. Three years later these couples were interviewed again, and a final follow-up occurred when the women were near the end of their child-bearing years. The study was designed to examine the relationship between fertility planning behavior and socioeconomic status, social mobility aspirations, adherence to traditional values, religious beliefs, marital adjustment, education, and feelings of personal adequacy. The sample was drawn from the largest standard metropolitan areas of the country excluding Boston. Further sample characteristics are both spouses were white, born in continental United States, once married, and still living together, with no births before marriage, no plural births, adoptions, child deaths, nor more than one miscarriage, and at the time of the first interview the wife did not believe she was pregnant.

Sources:

Westoff, C.F., R.G. Potter Jr., P.C. Sagi, and E.G. Mishler. 1961. *Family Growth in Metropolitan America.* Princeton: Princeton University Press.

Westoff, C.F., R.G. Potter Jr. and P.C. Sagi. 1963. *The Third Child.* Princeton: Princeton University Press.

Bumpass, L.L., and C.L. Westoff. 1971. *The Later Years of Childbearing.* Princeton: Princeton University Press.

Ryder, N.B., and C.L. Westoff. 1977. *Contraceptive Revolution.* Princeton, New Jersey: Princeton University Press.

The Detroit Family Growth Study and The Study of American Families— R. Freedman, D. Freedman, and A. Thornton

This longitudinal study was begun in 1962 and has recently become intergenerational. The original sample consisted of wives living in the Detroit metropolitan area who either had just married or had just had a first, second, or fourth birth. These women have been reinterviewed six times, most recently in 1980. During the course of the interviews, extensive information has been obtained from the wives about the organization of the families as well as the characteristics, attitudes, and behaviors of both husband and wife. The 1980 follow-up study involved the children of the original respondents, who were approximately 16 years old at the time of the interview.

Sources:

Freedman, R., and D. Goldberg. 1962. *Detroit Family Growth Study.* Institute for Social Research, University of Michigan, Ann Arbor, MI.

Thornton, A., and D. Freedman. 1979. "Changes in the Sex Role Attitudes of Women, 1962–1967: Evidence from a Panel Study," *American Sociological Review,* **44** (6): 831–842.

Freedman, R., D.S. Freedman, and A.D. Thornton. 1980. "Changes in Fertility Expectations and Preferences Between 1962 and 1977: Their Relation to Final Parity." *Demography* **17** (4): 365–378.

Sex Roles, Life Styles, and Childbearing—John H. Scanzoni

This study involved 3100 adults (half husbands and half wives) from 10 midwestern cities, oversampled for blacks, working wives, and younger persons. Questions concerned the effect of the sex role norms of these men and women on the number of children they planned to have, the age they married, and the effectiveness of their contraceptive use. Wife's employment, religion, age, race, education, marital satisfaction, and economic satisfaction were also examined. The sample involved men and women who had been married only to each other and was drawn from nonpoverty areas. The wives' ages were designated to span the child-bearing years and ranged from 18 to 44. The central focus of the study was to examine the relationship between the role structures of modern marriage and fertility control. The white women aged 19–29 in this sample were reinterviewed in 1975.

Source:

Scanzoni, J.H. 1975. *Sex Roles, Life Styles and Childbearing: Changing Patterns in Marriage and the Family.* New York: Free Press.

Attitudes about Children—Lois Hoffman

In 1975, 1569 married women between the ages of 15 and 39 (about 600 over 30 years old) and 456 husbands were interviewed. The study was designed to examine people's perceptions about the advantages and disadvantages of having children, attitudes about family size, the cost of raising children, people's goals for their children, and women's work experience and expectations. The value of having children was explored within nine categories which were identified as related to each of the following areas: adult status and social identity, expansion of self, moral values, primary group ties and affection, stimulation and fun, accomplishment, achievement and a form of creativity, social comparison, power and influence, and economic utility. The sample included both people with children and people with no children.

Sources:

Hoffman, L.W., and J.D. Manis. 1978. "Influences of Children on Marital Interaction and Parental Satisfactions and Dissatisfactions." In R.M. Lerner and G.B. Spanier (Eds.), *Child Influences on Marital and Family Interaction: A Life-Span Perspective.* New York: Academic Press.

Hoffman, L.W., and J.D. Manis. 1979. "The Value of Children in the United States: A New Approach to the Study of Fertility." *Journal of Marriage and the Family,* **41** (3): 583–596.

Hoffman, L.W., A. Thornton, and J.D. Manis. 1978. "The Value of Children to Parents in the United States." *Journal of Population* **1** (2): 91–131.

Parental Satisfaction—Catherine Chilman

This study includes 261 mothers and 193 fathers, most of whom were between the ages of 30 and 45. The study was designed to investigate the influence on parental satisfactions of external factors such as income, employment, housing, neighborhood, friends, and community resources and internal factors such as demographic family characteristics, marital happiness, family health and planning, social support, sex role behaviors, and family communication.

Source:

Chilman, C.S. 1977. *Parameters and Correlates of Parent Satisfaction and Dissatisfaction.* Condensed report of study conducted under a grant from the Wisconsin State Department of Health and Social Services.

LONGITUDINAL STUDIES BEGINNING IN CHILDHOOD

The Terman Study of Gifted Children—Begun by Lewis M. Terman and Presently Directed by Robert R. Sears

This famous study began in 1922 with 857 boys and 671 girls in grades 3 through 8 whose IQ was 135 or more. These individuals were followed up as children in 1928 and as adults in 1936, 1940, at five-year intervals until 1960, and most recently in 1972. At this last follow-up, 486 men and 430 women averaging 62 years of age constituted the sample. Thus, a large, regionally specific (California) data set exists that spans almost the entire lifetime of the participants. Early adult data include the Terman Marital Happiness Test, the Terman Marital Attitude Test, the Concept Mastery Test and, for men, the Strong Vocational Interest Blank. In general, the foci of the adult follow-up studies are personality, work, and overall adjustment. Terman reported in a 25-year follow-up that there were some personality problems in this group but that overall many were successful at fulfilling their earlier promise. General issues such as occupational satisfaction, occupational persistence, family-life satisfaction, marriage and divorce, and retirement were examined. Some testing has been done of 1600 offspring of the original sample.

Sources:

Sears, P.S. and A.H. Barbee. 1978. "Career and Life Satisfaction among Terman's Gifted Women." In J. Stanley, W. George, and C. Solano (Eds.), *The Gifted and the Creative: A Fifty-Year Perspective.* Baltimore: Johns Hopkins University Press.

Terman, L.M. and M.H. Oden. 1959. *Genetic Studies of Genius: V The Gifted Group in Mid-Life.* Stanford: Stanford University Press.

Willemsen, E.W. "Terman's Gifted Women: Work and the Way They See Their Lives." In K.W. Back (Ed.), *Life Course: Integrative Theories and Exemplary Populations.* Boulder, CO: The Westview Press, 1980.

The Berkeley Longitudinal Study—Nancy Bayley

Berkeley Growth Study—Nancy Bayley The BGS study included 31 boys and 30 girls enrolled in this longitudinal study from the first two months of life. They have been followed up fairly consistently, and the study is still active. The early measures included mental tests, projective tests, and personality—interest inventories. The children were also interviewed at 9½ and 12½ years of age concerning likes, dislikes, and activities. Adult data similar to the foregoing have also been collected.

Oakland Growth Study—Begun by Herbert Stolz and Harold Jones This project was begun in 1931 with 200 boys and girls (half each) who were 11 or 12 years old. They were tested fairly intensively through their adolescence, and then approximately 100 were followed up again between the ages of 30 and 40. The adolescent data include intelligence and achievement tests scores, personality inventories, projective tests, interviews with mothers and child, observations in the classroom and in a free play situation with peers, sociometric information, and background material on the family. The adult assessment data include projectives, inventories, and interviews. The original sample all resided in the Oakland, California area, and most of them attended a specific junior high school. Some of these follow-up assessments have been reported in combination with other Berkeley longitudinal data. An interesting cohort comparison was conducted by Elder in 1974 (see below).

Guidance Study—Jean Macfarlane This project contains extensive personality information on 123 males and 125 females who have been followed from birth. Two-thirds of the sample were reassessed at 30 and again at 40. The subjects were originally from the Berkeley area and were selected by enrolling every third child born in Berkeley in 1928—1929. Childhood and adolescent information included mental tests and academic achievement tests, projective tests and personality interest inventories, interviews, behavioral observations, and growth data. As adults, the subjects have been given mental tests, physical examinations, and x-rays. In addition, health histories and personality assessments have been obtained. It should also be noted that, as in the case of Maas and Kuypers (see separate citation for *From Thirty to Seventy*), the parents, especially the mothers, of the subjects were frequently included in the studies through interviews and questionnaires. More recently, as the "children" became adults and then parents, their children have sometimes been the subjects of studies.

Sources:

Block, J. 1971. *Lives Through Time*. Berkeley: Bancroft Books.

Haan, N., and D. Day. 1971. "A Longitudinal Study of Change and Sameness in Personality Development: Adolescence to Later Adulthood." *International Journal of Aging and Human Development* **5** (1): 11–39.

Peskin, J. 1972. "Multiple Prediction of Adult Psychological Health and Preadolescent and Adolescent Behavior." *Journal of Consulting Psychology* **38** (2): 155–160.

Livson, F.B. 1975. "Sex Differences in Personality Development in the Middle Adult Years: A Longitudinal Study." *Gerontologist* **15** (5): 70.

Elder, G.H., Jr. 1974. *Children of the Great Depression*. Chicago: University of Chicago Press.

Haan, N. 1977. *Coping and Defending: Processes of Self-Environment Organization*. New York: Academic Press.

From Thirty to Seventy—Henry Maas and Joseph Kuypers

This is a longitudinal study of 142 parents (men and women) of children who had been included in either the Berkeley Growth Study or the Guidance Study, both begun in the 1920s by the Institute of Human Development at the University of California, Berkeley. At the time, the focus of these studies was the children, but the parents were often interviewed extensively. The last phase of the study began in 1958 and included 95 mothers and 47 fathers. The average age of the parents at the time of the last interview was 69 for women and 71 for men. The sample is generally upper middle class, economically advantaged, and above average in general health. The study focused on three general issues: life styles, personality, and contexts of the respondents. A lengthy interview schedule was used to gather information on what Maas and Kuypers call "12 arenas of living:" questions about home and neighborhoods, work, retirement and leisure activities, parenting, grandparenting, brothers and sisters, marriage, friendships, formal organizational membership, health, death and life perspectives or life review. In their book *From Thirty to Seventy* Maas and Kuypers outline four life-style clusters of the fathers: family-centered fathers, hobbyists, remotely sociable fathers, and unwell-disengaged fathers. They outline six life-style clusters of the mothers: husband-centered wives, uncentered mothers, visiting mothers, work-centered mothers, disabled-disengaging mothers, and group-centered mothers. This data set is interesting because it provided early and mid-adult comparisons to later adult responses. Also interesting is the possibility of comparisons of the children as they grow older with their own parents' responses.

Source:

Maas, H.S., and J.A. Kuypers. 1974. *From Thirty to Seventy: A Forty Year Longitudinal Study of Adult Life Styles and Personality*. San Francisco: Jossey-Bass Publishers.

Fels Study of Human Development—Lester Sontag

This study began in 1929 and continues still. New infants are added each year. The sample consists of about 300 people, half male and half female.

The families are predominantly middle class and live within a 40-mile radius of Fels Research Institute in Yellow Springs, Ohio. They are rural farmers, and small town and large city dwellers. Data collection has remained relatively consistent with continuous administration of mental and personality tests, observations of the child at home and at the Institute, interviews with the mother and the child, and observations and ratings of the mother–child interacton. In the early 1960s a lengthy assessment of the subjects between 20 and 29 was obtained. Because the study has continued, the data should now be available for men and women in their middle years.

Source:

Kagan, J., and H.A. Moss. 1962. *From Birth to Maturity.* New York: Wiley.

PROFESSIONAL WOMEN/COLLEGE WOMEN

A large number of studies have recently been conducted by various professional organizations to examine the status of women within their professions. Only a few of these studies are briefly listed below because they represent very specific interests:

Women in Political Science—P.E. Converse

This study consisted of a mail survey of graduate students and postgraduate professionals and was conducted in the spring of 1970. The questionnaire explored issues such as sex discrimination, and it broadly addressed the numerous difficulties facing any women interested in a career in political science.

Source:

Converse, P.E., and J.M. Converse. 1971. "The Status of Women as Students and Professionals in Political Science." *Political Science* **4** (3): 328–348.

Women Microbiologists—Eva Ruth Kashket

A questionnarie was distributed to all the registrants of the 1971 annual meeting of the American Society for Microbiology to assess the present status of women in the profession and to inquire into the possible reasons for the status. The sample consisted of 237 women and 578 men and is clearly biased in that only microbiologists who attended the national meetings were included. Areas covered in the questionnaire included job performance, discontinuities in professional career, salary and employment status, supervisory responsibilities, extramural recognition, career guidance, attitudes of respondents, and attitudes of spouses.

Source:

Kashket, E.R., M.L. Robbins, L. Leive, and A.S. Huang. 1974. "Status of Women Microbiologists." *Science* **183** (4124):488–494.

Women in Modern Language Departments—Florence Howe

This study is a survey of modern language departments and the status of women within each department. Information gathered include all levels of involvement (i.e., graduate schools, junior and senior faculty positions). Data were also collected on salaries, teaching assignments, and tenure. Information was gathered about both men and women.

Source:

Howe, F., L. Morlock and R. Berk. 1974. "The Status of Women in Modern Language Departments: A Report of the Modern Language Association Commission on Status of Women in the Profession." *Publication of the Modern Language Association* **86** (171): 459–468.

Women in Sociology

At least three different data sources are available for women in sociology. The American Sociological Association has been surveying departments roughly every other year since Alice Rossi began in 1969 with a survey of graduate departments of sociology to gather information on the rank distribution by sex of the faculty in these departments.

Sources:

Rossi, A.S. 1970. "Status of Women in Graduate Departments of Sociology, 1968–1969." *American Sociologist* **5** (1): 1–11.

Hughes, H.M. 1973. *The Status of Women in Sociology 1968–1972.* Washington: American Sociological Association.

Patterson, M. 1971. "Alice in Wonderland: A Study of Women Faculty in Graduate Departments of Sociology." *American Sociologist* **6** (4): 226–234.

Social Workers—Paul Schreiber/ David Fanshel

The data for this study are derived from the files on members of the National Association of Social Workers. The study addresses two questions: Are female social workers underrepresented in leadership jobs relative to males? And, are females paid less than males in the profession? The professional membership includes 12,760 women and 8995 men.

Source:

Fanshel, D. 1976. "Status Differentials: Men and Women in Social Work." *Social Work* **21** (6): 448–454.

Professional Couples in Psychology—Matilda Butler

This study is an attempt to compare data from 1958 and 1973 American Psychological Association membership directories on married couples in psychology. In 1958 139 couples were found and, in 1973 296 couples were included. Data concerning sex, birth year, year of graduation, status of university from which highest degree was obtained, current employer, status of employer if an academic institution and current employer were coded.

Source:

Butler, M., and W. Paisley. 1977. "Status of Professional Couples in Psychology." *Psychology of Women Quarterly* **1** (4): 307–318.

Women with Doctorates/Women in Academia—Helen Astin

Helen Astin has conducted several studies that explore issues related to women in academia. A study of doctorates granted to women included 1547 women who had completed their doctorates between 1957 and 1958. These women returned a questionnaire mailed to them in early 1966. The area of specialization, demographic variables, career patterns, family background, early educational background, educational funding, work activities, and employer information represent the types of information collected. Another study examined sex discrimination in academia and involved 6892 questionnaires from faculty members at a variety of institutions of higher learning. From those with a regular faculty appointment and full time teaching responsibilities, 3438 women and 3454 men were randomly chosen. Academic rank, tenure status, and basic institutional salary constituted the criterion variables. Demographic characteristics, educational histories, professional/work experience, teaching/research interests, and institutional affiliations were considered as possible predictor variables.

Sources:

Rossi, A.S., and A. Calderwood. (Eds.) 1973. *Academic Women on the Move.* New York: Russell Sage Foundation.

Astin, H.S. 1969. *The Woman Doctorate in America: Origins, Career, and Family.* New York: Russell Sage Foundation.

A Study of Social Workers—Dorothy Chave Herberg

This study included 1037 women who graduated from one of 10 schools of social work in the two years 1907 and 1927. They were surveyed by means of a mailed questionnaire. The study represents an attempt to predict the work participation by graduate female social workers. Among the variables explored are early sex role ideology and sequencing of marriage and professional education.

Source:

Herberg, D.C. 1973. *Career Patterns and Work Participation of Graduate Female Social Workers.* Ann Arbor: University Microfilms.

National Surveys of Higher Education—Carnegie Commission

This is a study commissioned to provide a wide range of data bearing on various aspects of academic life. The faculty survey was conducted by questionnaire in 1969 and included faculty members in some 300 American colleges and universities. Data were obtained from over 60,000 men and women. Information about sex, age, educational institutions, and other background variables was obtained as well as present status and income and the individual's present situation within the reward structure of academia.

Sources:

Fulton, O. 1973. *Rewards and Fairness: Academic Women in the United States.* Occasional paper. Edinburg: Center for Research in the Educatonal Sciences, University of Edinburg, June 15.

The Carnegie Commission also publishes periodic reports that provide details of their studies.

The Vassar Studies—Donald Brown

There are at least two studies of Vassar College women. The alumnae study is the smaller of the two (N = 50) and is focused on the effect of the Vassar experience on later lives. These data were collected in 1955 and 1960 and included women who were members of the classes of 1925 through 1935. The second study included the entering classes in the years 1953 through 1962 (N = 4000). The women from the classes of 1957 and 1958 were reinterviewed (N = 108) in 1962, and the class of 1958 was reinterviewed in 1974 (N = 50). The socialization of the college students and the effects of these experiences on later life constitutes the main thrust of this study.

Source:

Brown, D. 1962. "Personality, College Environments and Academic Productivity." In Nevitt Sanford, (Ed.), *The American College.* New York: Wiley.

College Alumnae of 1964 in 1975—J. Mayone Stycos

This study follows those women who were studied by Westoff and Potvin as college seniors. The women were sent a questionnaire by mail and were asked a variety of questions about their fertility, labor force participation, child care, further education, marriage, and attitudes toward women's roles.

Source:

Reynolds, R.T. 1976. "Sex Roles and Fertility of 1964 College Alumnae." Paper presented at the Conference on Women in Middlelife Crises. Cornell University, October 30.

Continuing Education of Women—H. Markus, J. Manis

One study on this subject has already been completed and another is just beginning. The first study followed up those women who came back to school during their adult years and sought advice or counsel from the University of Michigan's Center for Continuing Education of Women during its first 10 years of existence. Mailed questionnaires were returned by 1145 women. The areas targeted by the questionnaire and telephone interview include educational history, the women's original hopes and aspirations for the future and whether these have been met, their family and work roles, plans for the future, information about their parents, spouses, their childhood, and their children. The women are about equally divided in age between three groups ≤34, 35–44, ≥45. A new study is in progress that is aimed at surveying women who have visited CEW between 1974–1977. They anticipate a sample of about 2000 from this new cohort of women. In addition, a separate portion of this study involves about 1000 women who received graduate degrees four years ago. This substudy will compare men and women of similar degree status.

Sources:

Markus, H. 1980. "Work, Women and Well-Being: A Life Course Perspective." In D.G. McGuigan (Ed.), *Women's Lives: New Theory, Research and Policy.* Ann Arbor, University of Michigan, Center for Continuing Education of Women.

Manis, J.D., and H. Markus. 1980. "Combining Families and Careers: Views from—and of—Different Points of the Life Cycle." In D.G. McGuigan (Ed.), *Changing Family, Changing Workplace: New Research.* Ann Arbor, University of Michigan, Center for Continuing Education of Women.

MISCELLANEOUS REGIONAL DATA SETS

Neighborhood and Community Contexts in Help Seeking, Problem Coping, and Mental Health—Donald Warren

The major thrust of this research was to investigate how the individual draws on others to cope with a range of frequently experienced problems. The problems were selected because they did not seem to require professional help or were not perceived as recognized attributes of poor mental health. The list of recently felt concerns was derived from a "pretest" sampling. People were asked how frequently these issues were concerns of theirs and what they did about such concerns, specifically to whom they turned for help. The categories of helpers included spouse, relative, friend, neighbor, co-worker, clergy, teacher, police, doctor, and counselor. The race, sex, marital status, and employment status of the respondents were obtained. A subsample was reinterviewed to assess the helpfulness of the persons to whom the respondent had turned for assistance.

Source:

Warren, D. 1976. *Neighborhood and Community Contexts in Help Seeking, Problem Coping and Mental Health.* Ann Arbor: Program in Community Effectiveness, University of Michigan.

Study of Groups—Mary Jackman

The purpose of this research was to examine the attitudinal dynamics of sex, class, and race. Intergroup attitudes and group consciousness, patterns and quality of intergroup contact and intragroup associations, and the ramifications of multiple group membership are explored. These data were collected in 1975.

Sources:

Jackman, M.R., and M.S. Senter. 1980. "Images of Social Groups: Categorical or Qualified?" *Public Opinion Quarterly* **44** (3): 342–361.

Jackman, M.R., and M.S. Senter. 1981. "Different Therefore Unequal: Beliefs about Trait Differences between Groups of Unequal Status." In D.J. Treiman and R.V. Robinson (Eds.), *Research on Social Stratification and Mobility.* Greenwich, CT: JAI Press.

Jobs and Gender—Christine E. Bose and Peter H. Rossi

This is a study of people's perception of occupational status and prestige. The sample consisted of 197, preferably working, women of varied income levels and 195 college women. The research was designed to explore the relationship between the status of a job and the sex of the incumbent, if jobs held by women and identified as "women's jobs" have less prestige, if the payoff of a job varies in terms of prestige and income by sex of the incumbent, if there is institutional sexism, and the evaluation of women in unusual jobs.

Source:

Bose, C.E., and P.H. Rossi. 1973. *Jobs and Gender: Sex and Occupational Prestige.* Baltimore: Center for Metropolitan Planning and Research, The Johns Hopkins University.

Housewives—Helena Znaniecki Lopata

This is a study of 571 women from the Chicago area. The in-depth interviews were obtained over a wide period of time beginning in the 1950s and continuing into the 1960s. The women were chosen to represent three groups: suburban housewives, nonworking housewives, and working wives. In addition to background data, information was gathered about the perceived characteristics of the social role of the housewife, the effects of changes in role of the husband on the wife, the community, relations with neighbors, and other social roles.

Source:

Lopata, H.Z. 1971. *Occupation: Housewife.* New York: Oxford University Press.

Widows—Helena Z. Lopata

Lopata has conducted two studies on widows. The first study included a representative sample of 301 widows in the Chicago area. The mean age of the widows was 50. A variety of open-ended as well as closed-ended questions were asked of the sample. The areas of interest include life prior to the husband's death, roles, social isolation, frequency of social contact, and various types of social relations. This study is reported in the first publication listed below. The second study is considerably larger. The sample was drawn from former or current Social Security beneficiaries, again in the Chicago area. Lopata interviewed 1169 women in person for approximately two and a half hours. The main focus of this study was the resources and support systems of widows. The findings of this study are reported in the second publication listed below.

Sources:

Lopata, H.Z. 1973. *Widowhood in an American City.* Cambridge: Schenkman Publishing Company.

———. 1979. *Women as Widows: Support Systems.* New York: Elsevier, North-Holland.

Time Use/Housework—Kathryn Walker

This is a sample of 1296 households consisting of a husband and wife, with or without children, in the Syracuse area. The study was conducted during 1967–1968 and involved the examination through the use of a diary by a wife of how time was spent and who actually took care of the home. The areas of interest included household chores generally, as well as separate tasks such as food preparation, care of family members, care of the house, care of clothing, marketing and management.

Source:

Walker, K.E., and M.E. Woods. 1976. *Time Use: A Measure of Household Production of Family Goods and Services.* Washington, DC: Center for the Family, American Home Economics Association.

Middle Age Studies—Bernice Neugarten

Extensive longitudinal data gathered by Neugarten and her colleagues comprise the Kansas City study. These data were collected in the 1950s and 1960s and have been reported widely. However, several other studies have been undertaken that concentrate on the middle years. One study in 1963 was an exploratory description of 100 "highly placed" middle-aged people in Chicago, and another involved 100 mothers in their late forties and fifties in 1963 who had children in selected high schools. This study focused on attitudes toward menopause, social role change and self concept. These same mothers were reinterviewed in 1975.

Source:

Neugarten, B. 1968. *Middle Age and Aging.* Chicago: University of Chicago Press.

Role Conflicts—Dorothy Nevill

This study involves 518 women in a university community in the southeastern United States. Groups were selected for inclusion in the study to provide a range of age, interests, and life styles likely to be found in such a community. The areas of conflict examined included time management, relations with husband, household management, financial affairs, child care, expectations for self, expectations of others, and guilt. Demographic data collected included marital status, age, number and age of children, occupation of self and spouse, education of self and spouse.

Source:

Nevill, D. and S. Damico. 1975. "Role Conflict in Women as a Function of Marital Status." *Human Relations* **28** (5): 487–498.

The Impact of Retirement—Robert Atchley

This is a study of 1106 men and women aged 50 or over and the impact of retirement on their lives. People were initially interviewed by means of a mailed questionnaire in 1975, and they were reinterviewed in 1977. The impact of pending retirement, actual retirement, income, life satisfaction, confidence, and morale were the major foci of this study. A variety of demographic data were collected, and it is possible that new data will be collected in the future.

Sources:

Atchley, R.C. 1976. *The Sociology of Retirement.* Cambridge, MA: Schenkman.

———. 1977. *The Social Forces in Later Life.* Belmont, CA: Wadsworth.

The Adaptation Study—George Maddox

This study is part of the Duke Longitudinal Studies and is of particular interest because it includes people in their forties and fifties as well as people over 60. It is an interdisciplinary study designed to gain information about how people adapt to the normal process of aging. The study is ongoing, and reports are being published periodically. The sample includes approximately 40 persons from each of 10 five-year age, sex, and cohort groups, thus allowing a variety of analyses. Areas investigated include physical aging, health care, mental aging, mental illness, social roles and self concepts, leisure, sexual behavior, and longevity.

Source:

Palmore, E. (Ed.). 1974. *Normal Aging II: Reports from the Duke Longitudinal Studies, 1970–1973.* Durham, NC: Duke University Press.

Adult Life—Roger Gould

In this study of 524 middle-class, white, educated people who were not psychiatric patients and were available through a network of acquaintances, Roger Gould examined a variety of aspects related to adult life. He explored people's sense of time, their relationships to family and friends, decision making, their feelings about their own personality, job, and sex. Also studied were their major concerns about life and the companionship, approval, and the general influence of people important in their lives. This study was preceded by a longitudinal study of patients in an outpatient clinic.

Sources:

Gould, R.L. 1972. "The Phases of Adult Life: A Study in Developmental Psychology." *American Journal of Psychiatry* **129** (5): 521–531.

———. 1978. *Transformations: Growth and Change in Adult Life.* New York: Simon and Schuster.

Study of Transitions—Marjorie Fiske Lowenthal

This is a longitudinal study of 216 men and women in four stages of life. Twenty-five boys and 27 girls who were high school seniors, 25 newlywed couples (both husbands and wives) entering their first marriages, 27 men and 27 women who were middle-aged parents, and 30 men and 30 women who were of preretirement age constituted the sample. All subjects lived in the San Francisco area. Life-styles, life course perspectives on family and friendships, self concept, well-being, stress, value continuities and discontinuities were all assessed. These age categories were chosen because they represent particular periods of life stress. The study involved people before they entered key transitional periods and will continue to follow them through these transitions and posttransition intervals.

Source:

Lowenthal, M.F., M. Thurnberg, and D. Chiriboga. 1975. *Four Stages of Life: A Comparative Study of Women and Men Facing Transitions.* San Francisco: Jossey-Bass.

Life Activity Study—K. Warner Schaie

This is part of a 21-year sequential study and is particularly relevant because of its emphasis on the interaction of birth cohort and aging in the prediction of intelligence and other traits in old age. Fourteen hundred men and women from the Seattle area have been interviewed, and a subsample have been asked a variety of questions about women's issues. Longitudinal data on some of this sample have been collected, and there is a possibility that data will be collected in the future. Work, personality, life satisfaction, and IQ data have all been gathered.

Sources:

Schaie, K. W., and I. A. Parham. 1980. "Cohort-Sequential Analyses of Adult Intellectual Development." *Developmental Psychology* **13** (6): 649–653.

Gribbin, K., K.W. Schaie, and I.A. Parham. 1980. "Complexity of Life Style and Maintenance of Intellectual Abilities." *The Journal of Social Issues* **36** (2): 47–62.

Life Strains—Leonard I. Pearlin

This study includes 2300 men and women between the ages of 18 and 65, representative of those living in the Chicago area. The interview deals extensively with the strains experienced by people—the conflicts, frustrations and threats. Particular foci include the strains occurring in the roles of occupation, marriage, childbearing, and economic life. The interview also investigated peoples' methods of coping with these stresses and symptoms of disturbances, such as depression, and anxiety.

Source:

Pearlin, L.I., and J.S. Johnson. 1977. "Marital Status, Life-Strains, and Depression." *American Sociological Review* **42** (5): 704–715.

A Longitudinal Study of Stress in Life Events—Jerome K. Myers

This study involves a detailed examination of relationships between life events, social class, and mental status in a large community sample over time. The sample consists of 938 men and women randomly chosen from within a specific area of metropolitan New Haven. These people were originally interviewed in 1967, and 720 were reinterviewed two years later. Basic demographic variables, physical and mental health status, social and instrumental roles, help-seeking behavior, and life crises were explored.

Source:

Myers, J.K., J.J. Lindenthal, and M.P. Pepper. 1974. "Social Class, Life Events, and Psychiatric Symptoms: A Longitudinal Study." In B.S. Dohrenwend and B.P. Dohrenwend (Eds.), *Stressful Life Events: The Nature and Effects*. New York: Wiley.

Index

Abortion, 56, 57, 58, 151, 182-184, 220
Absolutes, abandonment of, 102-104
Accidental major life events, 204
Accidents, 39
Achievement, importance of, 11, 22, 138
  in adult development, 91, 92, 93, 97, 100, 105
Adaptation to Life (Vaillant), 92, 203
Adult development, 89-113
  areas for future research, 112-113, 212-213
  study of moral and ego development, 96-104
    abandonment of absolutes, 102-104
    conflict between care and integrity,
      100-104
    men's self-descriptions, 98-100, 101
    women's self-descriptions, 96-98
  theories, 91-110
    based on men's lives, 91-94, 110
    different view, 104-110
    restoring missing text of women's
      development, 94-104
  work and personality of women in middle
    years, 110-113
Adult Life study, 273
Affiliates for Adult Development, 139-140
Age crossover, 128-130, 212-213
Aging, 55, 126, 209
  disease risks and, 52
Aging research, 12-13, 212
Aid to Families of Dependent Children
  (AFDC), 139, 140, 225
American Gynecological Society, 37
Americans View Their Mental Health, 242, 254
American Telephone and Telegraph, 218
*American Women Workers in a Full
  Employment Economy,* 217
Arthritis, 42, 43
Association of American Colleges, 225

Asthma, 42, 43
Attachment, 89, 94, 95, 97, 98, 106-111,
  113, 210
  see also Relationships, importance of;
    Separation (concept)
Attitudes About Children, 243, 262-263

Back problems, 42, 43
Bayh, Birch, 139
Belgium, 118, 131
Berkeley Longitudinal Study, 264-265
"Bill of Rights for Homemakers," 222
Birth control, 57, 58, 220
  see also Fertility control
Black family, urban, 108-109
Blood pressure levels, employment status
  and, 65
  see also Hypertension
Breast cancer, 52, 58
British Columbia, 66
Bronchitis, 39
Bulgaria, 131
Burke, Yvonne Braithwaite, 139

Canada, 46, 74, 119, 215
Cancer, 50, 55
  breast, 52, 58
  cervical, 58
  endometrial, 56, 59
  lung, 39, 40, 66, 68, 72
Cardiovascular disease, 39, 40, 42, 43, 59,
  60, 73
  employment and, 65, 66
  menopause and, 51-52
Care, *see* Relationships, importance of
Careers, *see* Family roles; Housewife role;
  Labor force, women in

Cervix, cancer of, 58
Cesarian section, 59
Chicago Area Studies, 244, 271
Childbearing, 16, 17, 41-42, 44-45, 56, 57,
    58, 59
  correlation between working and, 126-127,
    212-213
  early, 122, 126, 127, 129, 141, 142
  postponement of, 117, 126, 127, 129, 142
  see also Child care; Fertility control;
    Parental leave; Parenthood
Child care:
  by parents, 27, 121, 126
    in German Democratic Republic, 152,
      178, 189, 192, 194
    new family role system, 130, 131, 132-134,
      142, 202, 221
  public facilities for, 22, 27, 133, 142, 217,
    221, 231
    in German Democratic Republic,
      151-152, 154, 174, 176, 185-187,
      192, 194
  see also Childbearing; Family roles;
    Parenthood
Childhood and Society (Erikson), 2, 128
Children of the Great Depression (Elder), 242
China, 74
Cirrhosis of the liver, 39, 68
Civil Rights Act of 1964, 217
College Alumni of 1964 in 1975, study of, 265
College Level Entrance Program (CLEP)
  examinations, 223
College of Human Services, 223
Community supports, 214, 217, 224-225, 230
Comparable worth concept, 219-220
Comprehensive Employment and Training
  Act (CETA), 139, 140, 217, 218,
    225, 229
Condom, 58
Confederation of Free German Trade Unions
  (FDGB), 157, 161-162
Conference Board, 219
Continuing Education of Women studies,
  269-270
Contraception, see Birth control; Fertility
  control; specific forms of
  contraception
Cooperation, 111-112
Coping mechanisms, 203, 204, 210
Counseling services, 224, 231
Créche, 174, 176, 185-187

Credentialing, 223-224, 231
Cross-cultural research, 207-208, 214-215, 230
Crossover theme, 128-130, 135, 138, 142,
    200-202, 212-213
  social policy agenda and, 213-229, 230-231
Czechoslovakia, 131

Data sources, 28-29, 112-113, 241-274
  see also specific sources
Day-care centers, 133, 142, 217, 221, 231
  see also Child care, public facilities for
Death rates, see Mortality
Demokratische Frauenbund Deutschlands
    (DFD), 155, 157, 169, 182
Depression, 19-21, 65, 122, 123, 202, 203,
    209-210
Detroit Family Growth Study and The Study
    of American Families, 120, 244,
    261-262
Development, 89, 94, 101
  adult, see Adult development
  of moral judgment in children, 111-112
Diaphragm, 58
Disease, see Health; Psychological issues
Displaced homemaker, 138-140, 143, 216, 222,
    223, 225, 229
Divorce, 22, 25, 27, 115, 121, 123, 124,
    210, 222
  entrance into labor market and, 127, 136,
    139
  in German Democratic Republic, 152,
    181-182, 193
  Social Security benefits and, 227
  see also Marriage; Separation (of a
    marriage)
Drugs, psychotropic, 45

"Ecology of development," 8
Economic provider role, 136, 143, 214, 221-222
  see also Family roles; Labor force, women in
Economic security, social policy and, 214,
    225-229, 230, 231
Education, 121, 126, 129
  continuing, 140, 143, 223-224
  entitlement programs, 223, 231
  equal opportunity for, 214, 222-224, 230
  in German Democratic Republic, 151, 152,
    154-155, 163-169
  physical, 18
  to reenter labor market, 27, 121, 140, 143,
    223-224, 225

sex, 18
timing of, 129, 130, 212
Educational achievement, data sets related to,
    243-244, 250, 266-270
*Effecktive Facharbeiter-ausbildung von
    Arbeiterinnen*, 166
Egocentrism, 111, 112
Ego development, 96-104
    see also Adult development
"Eight Stages of Men," 2, 19
Emancipation of women, 155-157
Employee's Retirement Income Security Act,
    228
Employment, *see* Labor force, women in;
    Work; Work histories
Endometrial cancer, 56, 59
Equal educational opportunity, 214, 222-224,
    230
Equal employment opportunity, 22, 26, 214,
    217-220, 230
Equal Pay Act, 217
Equal pay for equal work, 151, 156
Estrogen, 51-52
    estrogen replacement therapy, 17, 52-53,
        55-56, 59
Europe, 214-215, 220
    see also specific countries
Exercise, 16, 18

Family planning, *see* Fertility control
Family roles, 22, 108-109, 110, 112
    combined with working roles, 22-23,
        115-144
    changes in attitude toward, 119-120
    changes in theories on women's life
        course, 120-130, 142, 212-213, 215, 216
    changes in work roles, 22, 136-138, 143,
        214
    emerging policy agenda and, 213-229,
        230-231
    new family role system, 120, 130-136,
        142-143, 221-222
    new research on, 204-205, 212
    social changes and, 138-140
    summary and conclusions, 140-144
    future of the family, 116-117, 216
    in German Democratic Republic, *see*
        German Democratic Republic
    new research on, 211-212
    new system of, 120, 130-136, 142-143,
        221-222

child care, 130, 131, 132-134, 202, 221
economic provider role, 136, 214, 221-222
housework, 131-132, 134-135, 202, 221
in patriarchal family, 130
social policy and, 26, 27, 214, 220-222, 230,
    231
symmetrical family, 130-136, 142
Victorian family, 130-131, 199-200
see also Childbearing; Child care;
    Generativity; Housewife role; Labor
    force, women in; Parenthood; Roles of
    women
Federal Republic of Germany, *see* West
    Germany
Fels Study of Human Development, 265-266
Feminine Mystique, The (Friedan), 10
Fertility, large data sources related to, 243,
    248, 260-263
Fertility control, 12, 46, 56-59, 73, 220-221,
    231
    in German Democratic Republic, 182-184
Fertility rate, 116, 120
    in German Democratic Republic, 183, 184,
        188
    of working women, 126-127, 134
Five Thousand American Family Study, 125,
    126, 206, 242, 252-253
Flexible working hours, 22, 136-137, 143, 217,
    219
Ford, Gerald, 135
France, 15, 46, 55, 74, 131, 220
Friendship, 90, 93, 203, 204, 211
From Thirty to Seventy, 265
Für Dich, 179

Gallup polls, 119
Gandhi, Mahatma, 94
General Mills American Family Reports,
    259-260
General Social Surveys, 259
Generativity, 92, 106, 110
Generosity, 111, 112
Genetic differences between sexes, 50, 59
German Democratic Republic, 10, 11, 14, 25,
    131, 140, 151-195, 214
    the arts in, 178-179
    education in, 151, 152, 154-155, 163-169,
        171, 172, 187, 191, 192, 195
    employment in, 151-152, 169-174
        combining family life with, 166, 173-174,
            184-191, 192

education for, *see* German Democratic
  Republic, education in
equal pay for equal work, 151, 156, 159
guaranteed, 151, 154, 192
occupational status of women, 169-172,
  191-192, 193
paid pregnancy leave, 152, 176, 187-188,
  192, 193
part-time, 190-191
reduced working hours, 188-189, 193
women as managers, 172-173
family life in, 151, 174-191
abortion on demand, 151, 182-184
aids to household work, 189-190, 193
child care responsibility, 152, 178, 189,
  192, 194
combining work with, 166, 173-174,
  184-191, 192
divorce in 152, 181-182, 193
family planning and single mothers,
  182-184, 194
household division of labor, 152, 189, 190,
  191, 192
new roles, 179-182
public child care, 151-152, 154, 174, 176,
  185-187, 192, 193
socialist family, 175-176
support by the State of, 176-179
historical background, 153-155
ideology of women's emancipation
  in, 155-157
roles of women in, 156-157, 178-179, 184
attitudes of men toward, 168-169,
  172-173, 180, 181-182, 189, 192-193,
  194
attitudes of women toward, 152, 169, 172,
  173, 181-182, 187, 193, 194
changes in, 158-161, 194, 195
sex ratio in, 159
social policy in, 26, 27, 151-152, 159,
  163-195
instruments of, 157-158
summary and conclusion, 191-195
women in public life in, 161-162
women's groups in, 155, 157, 158, 169,
  173, 174, 182
Gretchen's Rote Schwester, 180
Growth of American Families Study, 260-261
Guten Morgen, Du Schoene (Wander), 160,
  168, 185
Guttentag, Marcia, 10

Happiness, *see* Psychological issues
Harnak, Mildred, 155
Hay fever, 42, 43
Health, 12, 14-18, 37-74
biological and social roles and, 15, 38,
  49-69, 71-74, 209
employment, 63-69, 123
fertility and its control, 56-59
genetic factors, 50, 59
marital status, 60-62, 122-124
menstruation and menopause, 50-56, 59,
  62-63
parenthood, 62-63, 122-124
summaries, 59, 69-70
illness and illness behavior, 15, 40-44,
  47-49, 58-59, 60-73
invariant role dimensions, 49-59
mortality, *see* Mortality
perspectives and issues for research, 70-74,
  209
issues of method and meaning, 70-71
research issues and designs, 71-74
preventive measures, 46, 48, 71
psychological, *see* Psychological issues
variant role dimensions, 60-69
see also Health delivery system
Health delivery system, 18
women's use of, 44-46, 58-59, 62, 70-71,
  72, 73
employed women, 63, 64, 65-66
see also Hospitalization; Physicians
Health Interview Surveys, *see* U.S. Health
  Interview Surveys
Heart disease, *see* Cardiovascular disease
History's impact on life course, 12-14, 24,
  115, 116-120, 206, 207
Hospitalization, 15, 16, 44-46, 47, 62
see also Health delivery system
Housewife role, 121
choice of, 22-23
depression and, 19-21
displaced homemaker, 138-140, 216, 222,
  223, 225, 229
health and, 64, 65, 66, 68
mental, 65, 124, 210
intellectual performance of, 21-22
recognition of, 222, 231
social policy and, 26, 27, 222, 231
see also Family roles
Housewives in Chicago area, study of, 244,
  271

Housework, division of, 130-132, 134-135, 142, 202, 214, 221
  in German Democratic Republic, 152, 189, 190, 191, 192
Housing design, 217, 224, 225
Humboldt University, 155, 168, 183
Hungary, 131
Hypertension, 42, 43

Identifying Opportunities for Improving the Quality of Life of Older Age Groups, 253
Identity, 89, 90, 94, 95, 112
  achievement and, 100
  intimacy and, 97, 98, 106
  separation and, 98, 106
Illness, *see* Health
Individuation and adult development, 5, 91, 92, 93, 94
Infant mortality, 50
Integrity, 95, 96, 100-104, 110-111
Intellectual performance 21-22
Intimacy, 89, 90, 92, 94, 96, 100
  identity and, 97, 98, 106
  see also Attachment; Relationships, importance of
Intrauterine devices, 58

Japan, 52
Jobs and Gender, 270-271
Job segregation, 219
Job-sharing, 137, 143, 219

Kenya, 208
Kindergartens, 151-152, 154, 174, 185-186

Labor force, women in, 11, 12, 14, 131
  changing theories on women's life cycle, 118, 120-130, 212-213, 215, 216
  changing attitudes toward, 119-120
  occupational status and, 118, 119, 126
  changing work roles, 22, 136-138, 143, 214
  compensation inequalities, 118, 119, 125, 126, 211, 212, 217
  comparable worth concept, 219-220
  employment programs, 129, 130, 218
  reentry and, 26, 27, 116, 121, 139-140, 143, 223-224, 225
  equal employment opportunity, 22, 26, 214, 217-220
  family roles of women and, *see* Family roles,

  combined with working roles
  fertility of, 126-127
  in German Democratic Republic, *see* German Democratic Republic
  health of, 15, 63-69
  mental, 20, 21, 22, 123, 202, 210
  husband's career taking precedence for, 131, 136, 143
  in management, 107
  see also Professionals
  mortality rates and, 63, 66-69
  new research into, 210-211
  outlook for, 116, 117-118
  role models and, 22-24
  social policy and, 25-27, 116, 139-140, 143, 213-229, 230-231
  statistics on, 25, 63, 116, 117, 118-119
  work histories, 204, 206, 210-211, 212, 223-224
  see also Roles of women
Lactation, 16, 17
"Learned helplessness," 20
Leisure time credits, 215-216
Life Activity Study, 274
Life expectancy, 39
Life magazine, 204
Life outcomes, research into, 208-213
Life-span perspectives, 2-8, 24, 209, 210
  changing theories on women's life course, 118, 120-130, 142, 212-213, 215, 216, 231
    crossover theme, 128-130
    health and well-being, 122-124
    status attainment, 124-128
  crossover theme, *see* Crossover theme
  defining the middle years, 3-4
  "normal expectable life cycle," 125
    deviations from, 126-128 140, 141-142, 212-213
  stage theories, 4-6, 8, 128, 129
  synthesis of theories, 8
  timing models, 4, 6-8, 125
Life Strains study, 274
Longevity, 50
Longitudinal research, 205-207, 230
  data sets from childhood, 243, 249, 263-266
Love, 89, 100, 110
  see also Attachment; Intimacy; Relationships, importance of
Lung cancer, 39, 40, 66, 68, 72

Luther, Martin, 94

Managerial Women, The (Hennig and
    Jardim), 107
Martial status, health and mortality and,
    60-62, 122-124, 210
*Market Opinion Research: A National Survey
    of Women*, 242, 257
Marriage, 112, 119-120, 121
    deviation from normal life cycle and, 126,
        127
    early, 126
    in German Democratic Republic, 152,
        175-176, 179-182, 184, 193
    health status and, 60-62, 122-124
    mental health and, 20-21, 202, 210
    statistics on, 116
    see also Divorce; Family roles; Separation
        (of a marriage)
Maternity leave, *see* Parental leave
Memories of a Catholic Girlhood (McCarthy),
    94, 95
Menarche, 52, 53
Men in adulthood:
    differences from women in adulthood,
        10-11, 19, 38
    adult development theories, 89-110
    biological differences, 16, 50
    in career patterns, 125, 126
    in illness and illness behavior, 15, 40-44,
        47-49, 60-73
    in mental disorders, 209-210
    mortality, 39-40, 46-47, 49, 60-69, 71,
        72-73
    in orientation toward power, 104-108
    stage theories, 5-6
    trends in research and, 2
    in use of health services, 44-46, 64,
        70-71, 73
    in German Democratic Republic, *see*
        German Democratic Republic
    new family role system and, 120, 130-136,
        142-143, 221-222
    precedence of career of, 131, 136, 143
    sex-role crossover, 128, 129-130, 135, 138,
        200-202
    social policy and, 213-229, 230-231
Menopause, 14-15, 16-17, 50-56, 59, 73, 111
    parenthood and symptoms of, 62-63
Menstruation, 16, 46, 50-56, 59, 62-63
Mental health, *see* Psychological issues

Middle Age and Aging, 272
Middle years, defining, 3-4
Morality, 96-104, 111-112
Mortality, 39-40, 46-47, 49, 60-69, 71
    changing sex roles and, 72-73
    employment and, 63, 66-69
    infant, 50
    marital status and, 60-62
    maternal, 57-58, 59, 187
    parenthood and, 62
    among physicians, 67-68
    among professionals, 68-69

National Ambulatory Medical Care Survey,
    47
National Center for Health Statistics, 41, 42,
    44, 46, 47, 60
National Chicano Identity and Mental Health,
    258
National Fertility Study, 260-261
National Front, 162
National Institute of Mental Health, 225
National Institute on Aging, 226
National Longitudinal Surveys, 23, 127, 206,
    212-213, 242, 252
National Organization of Women, 139, 222,
    226, 229
National Survey of Black Americans, 242, 258
National Surveys of Higher Education, 268
Naturalistic studies, 208, 230
*Neighborhood and Community Contexts in
    Help Seeking, Problem Coping, and
    Mental Health*, 270
Neighborhood centers, 224
Networks, women's, 22, 26, 115, 211, 224, 225,
    243
New England Journal of Medicine, 55
Newsweek, 135
New York City, 223
New York Times-CBS poll, 119-120
Norway, 131
Nursing a child, 17

Oakland Growth Study, 24
Occupational stress, 65, 66
Occupation: Housewife, 271
"Older Woman, The," conference on, 226
Oral contraception, 58, 59
Osteoporosis, 52, 53

Panel studies, 205-206

see also specific studies
Parental leave, 136, 137, 143, 214, 219, 221
    in German Democratic Republic, 152, 176,
        187-188, 192, 193
Parental Satisfaction, 243, 263
Parent-Child Socialization study, 242, 255
Parenthood, 92, 126-127
    health and mortality rates and, 62-63,
        122-124
    see also Childbearing; Child care; Family
        roles
Part-time work, 136, 137-138, 143, 216, 219
    in German Democratic Republic, 190-191
Passages (Sheehy), 1
Patriarchal family, 130
Pension coverage, 22, 26, 212, 217, 226, 228,
    231
Peru, 132
Physical changes, *see* Health
Physicians:
    expectations of menopausal women, 56
    mortality rates of, 67-68
    women's visits to, 45-46, 58, 59, 62
        employed women, 64, 65
Poland, 132
Portrait of the Artist as a Young Man
    (Joyce), 94, 95
Poverty among women, 212, 226, 228-229
Power, sex differences in use of, 104-108
Predictable major life events, 204
Pregnancy, *see* Childbearing
Princeton Fertility Study, 261
Professional Couples in Psychology, study
    of, 267
Professionals, 134, 136
    data sets related to, 243-244, 250, 266-270
    mortality among, 68-69
Project on the Status of Women, 225
Project Talent, 253
Psychological issues, 18-22, 42, 43, 53
    depression, 19-21, 65, 122, 123, 202,
        209-210
    mental health and roles of women, 122-124,
        202
    new research on, 203, 209-210
Psychotropic drugs, 45

Quality of American Life study, 21, 203, 242,
    253-254
Quality of Employment study, 242, 255-256
Quality of Life of Older Age Groups, 259

Reentry programs, 26, 27, 116, 121, 139-140,
    143, 223-224, 225, 231
Regional studies, 244, 251, 270-274
Regression models, statistical, 7
Relationships, importance of, 6, 10-11, 19, 138
    adult development and, 89, 90, 95, 97, 98,
        108-113
    conflict with integrity, 100-104
    power and, 104-108
    subordination of, 92, 93-94
    roles of women and, 123-124
    see also Attachment; Intimacy; Love;
        Separation (concept)
Reproduction, *see* Childbearing; Fertility
    control; Sexuality and sex activity
Research on women in adulthood, 1-29,
    199-213
    basic assumptions, 2-14
        differences between men and women,
            10-11
        impact of history on life course, 12-14
        life-span perspectives, 2-8
        major dimensions of the life course, 8-9
    data sources and future questions, 28-29,
        241-274
        on adult development, 112-113
        large data sets, 242-243, 246-248, 252-263
        longitudinal studies beginning in
            childhood, 243, 249, 263-266
        miscellaneous regional studies, 244, 251,
            270-274
        on professional and college women,
            243-244, 250, 266-270
        related to fertility, 243, 248, 260-263
        summary, 246-251
    dead ends in the past, 202
    major research domains, 14-28
        institutional and cultural context, 25-28
        physical domain, 14-18
        psychological issues, 18-22
        social roles, 22-25
    new research agenda, 203-213
        focus on work and family linkages,
            204-205, 229-230
        life outcomes and dimension of well-
            being, 208-213, 230
        needed methodologies for, 205-208, 230
Retirement History studies, 242, 272
Rheumatism, 42, 43
Role Conflicts study, 272
Role models, 22-24

Roles of women, 19, 22-25, 38, 115-143
  changing, 130-140
    health and mentality and, 72-73, 122-124,
      209-210
    from 1950 to 1980, 116-120
    summary and conclusions, 140-144
  depression and, 19-22, 65, 122, 202
  emerging policy agenda and, 213-229,
    230-231
  in German Democratic Republic, see
    German Democratic Republic
  history's impact on, 13-14, 24, 115,
    116-120, 206, 207
  new family role system, see Family roles
  new research into, 210-212
  sex-role crossover, 128, 129-130, 135, 138,
    200-202, 212-213
    emerging policy agenda and, 213-229,
      230-231
  theories on women's life course, 118,
    120-130, 142, 215, 216, 231
    crossover theme and, 128-130
    mental health studies, 122-124
    status attainment studies, 124-128
  see also Family roles; Health; Housewife
    role; Labor force, women in;
    Psychological issues

Scandanavia, 140
Schizophrenia, 209
Seasons of a Man's Life, The (Levinson),
    4-5, 11, 128-129
SED (East German Communist Party), 157,
    162, 165, 166, 167
Self-esteem, 20, 21, 54, 64, 137
Self-expression, 95, 96
  care vs. integrity, 100-104
Separation (concept), 89, 90, 92, 94, 95,
    110, 113
  identity and, 98, 106
  see also Attachment; Relationships,
    importance of
Separation (of a marriage), 22, 115, 121, 123,
    124, 136, 139, 210
  see also Divorce; Marriage
Sex differences, see Men in adulthood,
    differences from women in adulthood
Sex-role crossover, 128, 129-130, 135, 138,
    200-202
  social policy agenda and, 213-229, 230-231
Sex Roles, Life Styles, and Childbearing, 262

Sexuality and sexual activity, 16, 17-18
Shields, Laurie, 139
Single-parent families, 25, 122, 123, 139, 184
Single women: health and mortality rates of,
    60-62, 124
  as mothers, see Single-parent families
Social change, adaptability to, 14
Social factors:
  multiple roles of women and, 22-25, 115,
    116-122
  physical health and, 15, 38, 49-69, 71-74,
    209
Social Indicators of Well-Being study, 254
Social integration, 61, 62, 63, 72
Social Networks in Adult Life, 243, 260
Social policy, 25-28, 116, 139-140, 143
  emerging agenda for, 213-229, 230-231
    community supports, 214, 217, 224-225,
      230
    economic security, 214, 225-229, 230
    equal educational opportunity, 214,
      222-224, 230
    equal employment opportunity, 214,
      217-220, 230
    supportive family policy, 214, 220-222,
      230, 231
  in German Democratic Republic, see
    German Demoratic Republic
Social Science Research Council, 3, 9
Social Security, 27, 212, 217, 222, 226,
    227-228, 231
Social Security Administration, 226
Social workers, studies of, 267, 268
Sociology, studies of women in, 267
Sommers, Tish, 139, 229
Sports, 18
Stage theories, 4-6, 8, 19, 128, 129
Staircase model of development, 4-5, 19
Statistical Pocket Book of the German
    Democratic Republic, 154
Status attainment studies, 124-128
Sterilization, 56, 57, 58
Stress, 40, 203, 210
  in life events, longitudinal study of, 274
  occupational, 65, 66
Structure of Scientific Revolutions, The
    (Kuhn), 199
Studies of Women's Attitudes, 243, 256-257
Study of Groups, 270
Study of Transitions, 273
Suicide, 39-40, 66-67, 68

Supplemental Security Insurance (SSI), 227-228
Surgery, 45-46, 47
Sweden, 131, 137, 214, 220
Symmetrical family, 130-136, 142

Taxation policy, 217, 226-227, 231
Teenage pregnancy, 220
Terman Study of Gifted Children, The, 263-264
Time Use: a Measure of Household Production of Family Goods and Services, 271-272
Time Use in Economic and Social Accounts, 255
Timing, 22, 25, 124, 125-126, 129
  see also Crossover theme; Life-span perspectives
Timing models, 4, 6-8, 125
Title IX of the Higher Education Act, 18
Truth, 95, 96, 100-104
  conflict with caring, 100-104
Tufts University, 179
Tutors, 151, 167

Unemployment, 218, 223
Unfinished Business (Scarf), 10
United Kingdom, 119, 131
University of Michigan, 23, 213
  Center for Continuing Education of Women, 224, 269
U.S. Congress Joint Economic Committee, 26, 217
U.S. Department of Labor, 4, 63, 119
U.S. Health Interview Surveys, 64, 65
U.S. House of Representatives Select Committee on Aging, 26, 217, 225
U.S. National Health Survey, 41
USSR, 132, 153, 154, 159
Uterus, prolapsed, 46

Vassar Studies, 269
Virginia Slims Women's Opinion Poll, 242, 257-258

Vocational Educational Act of 1976, 225

Welfare, 139, 140, 225
West Germany, 74, 118, 131, 153-154, 159
What is Life Like in the GDR?, 154, 163
WHO Task Force on Psychosocial Research in Family Planning, 54
Widows, 123, 124, 222
  study of, 271
Wisconsin labor force, 67, 68
Women and Equality (Chafe), 116
Women and Socialism, 163, 167, 171
Women and the Future (Giele), 10-11
Women in adulthood, see specific aspects of research on women in adulthood
Women in Midlife—Security and Fulfillment, 217, 225
Women in Modern Language Department, study of, 266-267
Women in Political Science, study of, 266
Women in the GDR: Facts and Figures, 156, 161, 165, 167, 171, 172, 189
Women Microbiologists, study of, 266
Women's centers, 224, 225
Women's Educational Equity Act, 18
Women's Equity Action League, 226
Women with Doctorates/Women in Academia, studies of, 267-268
Work, 89, 90, 93, 100, 110
  change in work roles, 22, 136-138, 143, 214
  in German Democratic Republic, see German Democratic Republic
  see also Achievement, importance of; Labor force, women in
Work and Family Life in the United States (Kanter), 205
Work histories, 204, 206, 210-211, 212, 223-224
Work History study, 242, 256
Work Incentive program, 225
Worlds of Pain (Rubin), 108

Yugoslavia, 132